Spirited Politics
Religion and Public Life in Contemporary Southeast Asia

Andrew C. Willford and Kenneth M. George, editors

Spirited Politics
Religion and Public Life in Contemporary Southeast Asia

SOUTHEAST ASIA PROGRAM PUBLICATIONS
Southeast Asia Program
Cornell University
Ithaca, New York
2005

Cornell Southeast Asia Program Publications
640 Stewart Avenue, Ithaca, NY 14850-3857

Studies on Southeast Asia No. 38

Printed in the United States of America

ISBN-13: 978-0-877277-37-8 / ISBN-10: 0-877277-37-0

Cover Design: by Robin Werner. Cover illustration: Detail from "Bulan Sabit Merah" (Red Crescent Moon), by A. D. Pirous, 1998. By permission of the artist. Digital photograph courtesy of Kenneth M. George.

TABLE OF CONTENTS

Acknowledgments   7

Introduction: Religion, the Nation, and the Predicaments of Public Life   9
in Southeast Asia
    Kenneth M. George and Andrew C. Willford

The Priestess and the Politician: Enunciating Filipino Cultural Nationalism   23
through Mt. Banahaw
    Smita Lahiri

The Modernist Vision from Below: Malaysian Hinduism and the "Way of Prayers"   45
    Andrew C. Willford

Fraudulent and Dangerous Popular Religiosity in the Public Sphere: Moral   69
Campaigns to Prohibit, Reform, and Demystify Thai Spirit Mediums
    Erick White

Islam and Gender Politics in Late New Order Indonesia   93
    Suzanne Brenner

A Sixth Religion?: Confucianism and the Negotiation of Indonesian-Chinese   119
Identity under the Pancasila State
    Andrew J. Abalahin

Relocating Reciprocity: Politics and the Transformation of Thai Funerals   143
    Thamora Fishel

Immaterial Culture: "Idolatry" in the Lowland Philippines   159
    Fenella Cannell

Picturing Aceh: Violence, Religion, and a Painter's Tale   185
    Kenneth M. George

Contributors   209

ACKNOWLEDGMENTS

As the volume's editors, we would like to thank Cornell University's Southeast Asia Program Publications Editorial Board for its unflagging support, and our contributors for their collegiality, cooperativeness, and scholarly care. Benedict Anderson's interest in this volume has been pivotal, and he offered several very helpful suggestions during the earliest stages of our work. Our thanks also go to the entire staff at SEAP Publications, and in particular, to Deborah Homsher, who has been a delightful source of editorial critique and expertise. Her steady and patient interventions in the face of our numerous delays, travels, and debates are evidenced throughout. We are extremely grateful to her for her enthusiasm, energy, and formidable editorial talents—they made this a better book.

This volume has roots in two conference panels. The first occurred at the New York Conference on Asian Studies, Association of Asian Studies, which took place at Hobart and William Smith Colleges in fall of 1999. This panel, entitled "Spirited Politics," was organized by Smita Lahiri, Thamora Fishel, and Erick White, and was chaired by Smita Lahiri. Andrew Willford served as discussant. Plans and ideas for this volume emerged at that conference. A second panel followed at the Annual Meeting of the Association for Asian Studies in Chicago, in the spring of 2001. Ken George served as discussant on this subsequent panel, which included papers by Andrew Willford, Thamora Fishel, and Andrew Abalahin. The conversations and papers launched at these two panels provided the basic blueprint for the core themes addressed in this book. Later, Suzanne Brenner and Fenella Cannell kindly accepted our invitations to contribute their respective chapters.

From Andrew Willford: I wish to thank Vasantha, Rabindra, and Anisha for their constant supply of laughter, joy, and love. Vasantha, moreover, has been more than a life partner; she has been oftentimes my harshest and most helpful critic. I also wish to thank my parents and sister for their remarkable faith and help over the years. Last, I want to thank Ken George for his insight, hard work, frank advice, and good judgment. His patience, sense of humor, and intellectual generosity have been both inspiring and delightfully stimulating.

From Ken George: I would like to thank Andrew Willford for inviting me to serve as co-editor of *Spirited Politics*. I have learned much while working with him and the other contributors. It happened that I fell gravely ill about a year after joining the project and had to bring all work to a stop for nearly six months. Andrew and the others were wonderful medicine; they waited for me to recuperate and helped reawaken my energies. They were part of the cure. To my wife, Kirin Narayan, go affectionate and unending thanks for the love and care it took to get me back on my feet, and for all the companionship before and after.

ACW & KMG

INTRODUCTION:
RELIGION, THE NATION, AND THE
PREDICAMENTS OF PUBLIC LIFE IN
SOUTHEAST ASIA

Kenneth M. George and Andrew C. Willford

The essays in this book all call attention to the salience of world religions in Southeast Asian public life. Modernization, it was once argued, should have led to the "disenchantment" of Southeast Asian social life. Specialists reckoned that nationalism and nation-building, the global rise of capitalist markets, and the broadening reach of mass media, along with the other cultural, structural, and ideological features of modernity, would so swamp religious communities, institutions, and ideas that they would become unmoored from their once-prominent place in defining and legitimating political and cultural orders. Religion, in this scenario, was to become a "private" concern, and, for this reason, largely sequestered from the central and transcendent, "secular" energies of public culture and the modern nation-state.[1] *Spirited Politics* joins a growing list of studies that see religion differently—as an enduring and increasingly significant precinct of Southeast Asian politics and public life.[2]

---

[1] See Talal Asad, *Formations of the Secular: Christianity, Islam, Modernity* (Stanford: Stanford University Press, 2003) for a critique of treating the "religious" and the "secular" as fixed and opposed categories. The "secular," for Asad, is conjunctural—a bringing together of diverse practices and knowledge—and so, "secularism" and "secularization" need to be investigated as political projects, not as the emptying of religion from social life.

[2] See, for example: John R. Bowen, *Muslims Through Discourse: Religion and Ritual in Gayo Society* (Princeton: Princeton University Press, 1993), and *Islam, Law, and Equality in Indonesia: An Anthropology of Public Reasoning* (Cambridge: Cambridge university Press, 2003); Robert W. Hefner, ed., *The Politics of Multiculturalism: Pluralism and Citizenship in Malaysia, Singapore, and Indonesia* (Honolulu: University of Hawai'i Press, 2001); Robert W. Hefner and Patricia Horvatich, eds., *Islam in an Era of Nation States: Politics and Religious Renewal in Muslim Southeast Asia* (Honolulu: University of Hawai'i Press, 1997); Charles F. Keyes, Laurel Kendall, and Helen Hardacre, *Asian Visions of Authority: Religion and the Modern States of East and Southeast Asia* (Honolulu: University of Hawai'i Press, 1994); Rita Smith Kipp and Susan Rodgers, eds., *Indonesian Religions in Transition* (Tucson: University of Arizona Press, 1987);

John Bowen observed almost a decade ago that a preponderant number of cultural analyses on Southeast Asia had shifted focus from face-to-face communities to "political public spheres defined by norms of national belonging and religious affiliation."[3] The reasons for this shift are many, but social realities in the region alone surely invited a change in focus. It appears clear to us that the spread of nationalism and the rise of nation-states in Southeast Asia have summoned forth a new zone of cultural politics: a sphere in which individuals, collectivities, and state institutions recruit and direct cultural expression toward reflexively sought social identities, political-economic goals, and ideological ends. It isn't the case that local culture doesn't matter any longer; people still lead local lives. Yet localities, local cultures, and local lives have been brought into and reconstituted through an unceasing entanglement with the nation-state, no less than with the mass media, global markets, transnational religious movements, and the myriad dilemmas of modernity. Although the rhetoric of nationalism typically has had the purpose of consolidating a people and a citizenry through idioms of belonging, such consolidation is never assured. The nation-state extends its bureaucratic and coercive presence into and across locales as a display and exercise of its own legitimacy, even as it distends the very horizons of the local. As a result, contemporary violence, conflict, and turmoil do not have a life as local phenomena alone, but reveal intricate ties to state concerns, intrigues, and interventions.[4] Indeed, the nationalistic imagination offers cultural frameworks for recasting local events as national ones, and vice versa.[5] In sum, the nation-state has become the dominant sociopolitical institution for placing collectivities and individuals "in the world"—for making them legible to each other, and for drawing them into the currents of modernity. As one group of writers has put it, "Nationhood is the social *form* that renders modernity self-conscious."[6]

Scholars have responded to this new social, cultural, and political terrain by rethinking the way they frame and prepare their cultural and historical analyses. Prior to 1980, anthropological analyses had increasingly put emphasis on the

---

Rosalind C. Morris, *In the Place of Origins: Modernity and Its Mediums in Northern Thailand* (Durham, NC: Duke University Press, 2000); and Michael G. Peletz, *Islamic Modern: Religious Courts and Cultural Politics in Malaysia* (Princeton, NJ: Princeton University Press, 2002).

[3] John Bowen, "The Forms Culture Takes: A State-of-the-Field Essay on the Anthropology of Southeast Asia," *Journal of Asian Studies* 54,4 (1995): 1050.

[4] See Kenneth M. George, "Violence, Culture, and the Indonesian Public Sphere: Reworking the Geertzian Legacy," in *Violence: Poetics, Performance, Expression*, ed. Neil L. Whitehead (Santa Fe, NM: School of American Research Press, forthcoming). See, too, James T. Siegel, *A New Criminal Type in Jakarta: Counter-Revolution Today* (Durham, NC: Duke University Press, 1998) for the story of how the Suharto regime promulgated the "nationalization of death."

[5] See Stanley J. Tambiah, *Leveling Crowds: Ethnonationalist Conflict and Collective Violence in South Asia* (Berkeley, CA: University of California Press, 1996) for a superb discussion of how complex local events may be stripped of particulars under the process of focalization and then aggregated and transvalued as an instance of a national danger or concern. The converse processes of nationalization and parochialization begin with condensed images and end by proliferating wildly across locales.

[6] Sheldon Pollock, Homi K. Bhabha, Carol Breckenridge, and Dipesh Chakrabarty, "Cosmopolitanisms," *Public Culture* 12,3 (2000): 582. (Italics in the original.) Concerning the association of the nation-state with modernity in Western social theory, see Peter van der Veer and Hartmut Lehman, "Introduction," *Nation and Religion: Perspectives on Europe and Asia*, ed. Peter van der Veer and Hartmut Lehman (Princeton, NJ: Princeton University Press, 1999).

coherence, meaningfulness, and authenticity of local cultures. The nation-state and national culture fell at or beyond the margins of analysis, and analysts did little to question their conceptualization of the local. Changing intellectual currents and the intensifying reach of the nation-state into everyday social life combined to push analysis toward a fresh appreciation for the asymmetrical and freighted play of conflicting social and cultural spheres, and for the capacity of social actors to respond—sometimes manipulatively, sometimes compulsively—to their political and cultural circumstances.[7] Although Marshall Sahlins laments that an obsession with power is "the latest incarnation of Anthropology's incurable neo-functionalism,"[8] concern over matters of domination and resistance has had the salutary effect of reopening and reorienting our ethnographic eye on Southeast Asia, especially with respect to state institutions and ideologies. Some blinding has occurred, it is true. "There is a tendency to think of states as transcendent agents," warns Mary Steedly, "guided as if by a single will . . . or by a kind of uniform animating spirit with an overwhelming power to enforce its ideological vision or to construct knowledge as it sees fit."[9] Steedly's admonition is an invitation to consider the limits, contradictions, and failures of state institutions and ideologies, and to assess how various actors and groups take advantage of, or succumb to, the nation-state's complex and often fragmentary nature, its aspirations to an elusive wholeness notwithstanding.[10]

A question that guides several of the essays in our book picks up on that invitation: In what ways do religious practices and debates provide people with room for maneuver amid the shadows and light of the nation-state? Seeking room for maneuver is not an intrinsically oppositional or resistant activity; individuals and groups can be quite calculating or complicit in using the state (and its internal contradictions) to advance their interests, religious and otherwise. All the same, seeking room for maneuver is an effort to find political footing of some kind. Debates over marriage laws and definitions of religion (contributor Andrew Abalahin on Indonesia), efforts to find Qur'anic foundations for women's rights and social justice (Suzanne Brenner on Indonesia), and televised exposés of fraudulent spirit mediums (Erick White on Thailand) reveal different groups working publicly for legal and cultural change in line with religious concerns. These debates and movements for state reform suggest a broad and deep-seated view of the state as the desired public arbiter and defender of religious values. That said, the authors' focus on the predicaments of reform also throws light on the contradictory interests, laws, and ideologies of the nation-state, especially as states come to terms with, or become proponents of, both religious pluralism and homogenizing ethno-religious discourses. Cultural nationalisms often rely on or encourage transcendent ethno-

---

[7] These currents have been adroitly summarized by Bowen, "The Forms Culture Takes," and Mary M. Steedly, "The State of Culture Theory in the Anthropology of Southeast Asia," *Annual Reviews in Anthropology* 28 (1999): 431-454.

[8] Marshall Sahlins, *Waiting for Foucault, Still* (Chicago: Prickly Paradigm Press, 2002), p. 20.

[9] Steedly, "The State of Culture Theory," p. 443.

[10] For examples of such work, see Kenneth M. George, "Designs on Indonesia's Muslim Communities," *Journal of Asian Studies* 57,3 (1998): 693-713; and Andrew C. Willford, *Cage of Freedom: The Vicissitudes of Malaysian Tamil Identity*, in preparation. Willford uses that work to argue that the nation-state's "wholeness" is illusory and a function of the nation-state's fragmentation and arbitrariness. Willford sees the ideological bid for wholeness as part of "an impossible *gemeinschaft* in capitalist modernity."

religious imaginings, sometimes appropriating religious sites and practices as national emblems (Smita Lahiri on the Philippines, and Kenneth George on Indonesia), sometimes purging or demonizing them (Andrew Willford on Malaysia). Religious discourse can also inflect the language and policy of education and rule (Fenella Cannell on the colonial Philippines) or provide the logics for conducting local politics (Thamora Fishel on Thailand).

Even a cursory acquaintance with the historical and ethnographic literature on Southeast Asia alerts readers to the long and enduring entanglement of statecraft and religion in this region.[11] It is not the goal of the essays gathered here to consider how the rise of nationalism and the nation-state changed the face of world religions in Southeast Asia, or how world religions might have shaped the emergence of the region's contemporary political forms. Our emphasis is on the predicaments that befall individuals, groups, and institutions in negotiating the transcendent discourses of religion and state in public life. Some of those predicaments ensue from the ideological conflation of nation, ethnicity, and faith, an alignment common not only to various cultural nationalisms, but also to more than a few (very troubling) culturalist analyses.[12] All of the contributors to *Spirited Politics* know very keenly how people are ideologically and materially driven to pursue communal identification with nation, religion, and ethnicity. In our view, the compulsive return to national, religious, and ethnic "foundations" arguably is a symptom of the doubt, anxiety, and contingency that haunt social life, as much as it is a capitulation to the specters of law-making and law-preserving violence that serve to shore up arbitrary foundations and origins,[13] or a gambit for social, economic, and political gain. There is no mistaking our emphasis on familiar national-religious identities: Indonesian Muslims (Brenner and George), Thai Buddhists (Fishel and White), Filipino Catholics (Cannell and Lahiri). Even our "exceptions"—Tamil Hindus in Malaysia (Willford) and Chinese Confucians in Indonesia (Abalahin)—concern the faith typically associated with the ethnic group in question.[14] *Spirited Politics* takes it energies from a

---

[11] The literature on regional statecraft and religion is vast. Two helpful and recent works with which to begin an exploration are: Tony Day, *Fluid Iron: State Formation in Southeast Asia* (Honolulu: University of Hawai'i Press, 2002); and O. W. Wolters, *History, Culture, and Region in Southeast Asian Perspectives*, revised edition (Ithaca, NY: Cornell Southeast Asia Program Publications, 1999).

[12] We particularly have in mind Samuel Huntington's, *The Clash of Civilizations and the Remaking of World Order* (New York: Touchstone, Simon and Schuster, 1996) as the most reckless if influential application of cultural determinism. For a critique of culturalist approaches in political anthropology, and a demonstration of how the Huntington thesis has been put to ideological use by the Malaysian and Singaporean governments in order to mask "economic liberalism" in their development agendas, see Aihwa Ong, "Clash of Civilizations or Asian Liberalism? An Anthropology of the State and Citizenship," in *Anthropological Theory Today*, ed. Henrietta Moore (Cambridge, MA: Polity Press, 1999), pp. 48-72

[13] See Walter Benjamin, "Critique of Violence," in *Reflections: Essays, Aphorisms, Autobiographical Writings* (New York: Harcourt Brace Jovanovich 1978), pp. 277-300; and Slavoj Zizek, "Enjoy Your Nation as Yourself!" in *Tarrying with the Negative* (Durham, NC: Duke University Press, 1993), pp. 200-237. For an application of Benjamin's conceptualization of violence by a scholar of Southeast Asia, see Henk Maier, "Telling Tales, Cutting Throats: The Guts of Putu Wijaya," in *Roots of Violence in Indonesia*, ed. Freek Colombijn and J. Thomas Lindblad (Leiden: KITLV Press, 2002).

[14] To phrase these paired identities in this manner deploys a grammar in which nationality or ethnicity serve as modifiers of a more general religious affiliation, which is itself figured as a core identification. Given the need to expose the powerful aura or spirit of the nation, and the

collective look at the ways religious, nationalist, and ethnic discourses intertwine and contribute to the making and unmaking of public culture as people and institutions assess their own aspirations, their own predicaments, and their own modernity.

* * * * *

The public-private distinction, as Susan Gal has reminded us recently, is always ideological and political; it poses unending difficulties, instabilities, and uncertainties of stance.[15] As these are relational interpretive terms, their exclusions and inclusions can be mapped onto most any precinct of social life and social experience. These mappings appear at play across a whole spectrum of social binaries and homologies, and produce powerful political effects, as in Indonesia when masculinist state discourse associates women with so-called private or domestic spheres of action (see Brenner's essay). "Public" and "private" do not describe the social world as it is, but are terms of persuasion to characterize, relative to specific political and cultural circumstances, various precincts of human activity. Religious and nationalist discourses, we would argue, are two powerful means for conjuring and authorizing public-private distinctions.

Nationalism and nationalist thought reach deeply into everyday life in Southeast Asia, and into citizens' practical understanding of public and private realms. In Craig Calhoun's formulation, nationalism accomplishes two things of special interest to us:[16] First, it potentially obscures recognition of subnational discourses and diverse counterpublics through its emphasis on the discourse of the national whole and the national common good. Second, it posits a national identity that trumps other sociopolitical and cultural identifications, and that is imagined to reside as an attribute of a modern, self-recognizing, self-constituting individual who is in no need of the mediations of gender, family, region, or class to be a member of the nation. Many precincts of modern thought and ideology treat the nation and the individual as homologous entities that are crucial to each other's workings: both are deemed whole and unfragmented. It seems inevitable that asserting that wholeness of nations and individuals requires the boundary-making repulsion or exclusion of symbolic matter and practices considered foreign to the whole. Following the Lacanian formulations offered by Peter Stallybrass and Allon White,[17] we acknowledge that the symbolic and monologic discourses of "official" identity-formation may result in the phantasms, fears, and fantasy relations that characterize the political unconscious (or the dialogic imaginary) of states and selves. The psychic and social dimensions of

---

need to acknowledge the religious pluralism of any ethnic or national group, we should also think of those who people our essays as Muslim and Confucian Indonesians, Buddhist Thais, Catholic Filipinos, and Hindu Tamils.

[15] See Susan Gal, "A Semiotics of the Public/Private Distinction," *Differences: A Journal of Feminist Cultural Studies* 13, 1 (2002): 77-95.

[16] See Craig Calhoun, *Critical Social Theory: Culture, History, and the Challenge of Difference* (Oxford: Blackwell, 1995) pp. 24-47, 231-282; and Craig Calhoun, "Nationalism and Civil Society: Democracy, Diversity, and Self-Determination," in *Social Theory and the Politics of Identity*, ed. Craig Calhoun (Oxford: Blackwell, 1994), p. 315.

[17] Peter Stallybrass and Allon White, *The Politics and Poetics of Transgression* (Ithaca, NY: Cornell University Press, 1986), pp. 191-202.

political life (and identity politics in particular) cut across public and private spheres, even as ideological constructions of "the public" and "the private" have, as a form of political work, the purpose of separating and sequestering such dimensions.

It is in the character of many such consolidating ideologies to graft a transcendent national identity to exclusionary religious, linguistic, and ethnic solidarities. As several of our essays show, nation-states rely on fictions of religious-ideological unanimity and of threatening "Others-within." As Andrew Abalahin tells us, Confucianism and citizens of Chinese descent were demonized as a threatening collective alien within Indonesia's New Order (1966-1998); the state ceased to recognize Confucianism as a religion, and outlawed "public" expressions of Chinese culture. Abalahin describes how the 1995 marriage of "Lany" and "Budi," two Indonesian "Chinese" citizens of Confucian faith, was rejected by authorities as invalid, because Confucianism did not enjoy state recognition as a religion. The long legal struggle faced by Lany and Budi proves instructive for understanding not only the position of Confucianism and the Chinese within Indonesia, but also of debates within the Chinese community regarding the need to assert or shed their Chinese identity. One response to the anti-Confucian climate came from an "integrationist" Confucian group attempting to demonstrate compatibility between Confucianism and other religions, particularly through its perceived congruence with the Javanese philosophy expressed in the state's *Pancasila* ideology. The effort to Javanize, or to be viewed as Javanized, was largely unsuccessful, however, and Confucianism failed to reclaim its status as a religion during the New Order. With the fall of Suharto, the appeal of the *reformasi* movement, and the aftermath of the vicious anti-Chinese violence in May 1998, a national mood of "atonement" led to various changes for the Chinese community. A more open climate of acceptance ensued during the Wahid presidency, and Lany and Budi ultimately secured favorable decisions from the courts.

Andrew Willford alerts us to a similar demonization in Mahathir's Malaysia: Mahathir himself depicts Hinduism as a pre-modern "psychic" threat to the modern Muslim Malay citizen (who stands in as the privileged figure of the Malaysian national whole). The figure of the Hindu "Indian" comes to signify a backward past that Malays must surmount in order to become true Muslims, and thus, true Malays. The effort to overcome the uncertainty of Malay identity thus leads to the marginalization of the country's Tamil Hindu minority. This marginalized figure, Willford argues, represents an uncanny presence within Mahathir's Islamic modernist ideology, as it unsettles—in ways that escape consciousness—the authenticity of ethno-nationalist claims to authenticity. Willford then shifts focus to the story of a Tamil Hindu medium, "Valli," who in striving to negate her social and spiritual subordination within the Tamil Hindu community and its internal hierarchies, reveals herself to be a relentlessly "doubled" figure—like Mahathir himself, who was partly of Indian descent. Both Valli and Mahathir appear to be haunted by the figure of the "Indian" as they attempt to transcend such identification. Valli seeks to surmount her low status, but in her possessed state, and in her ambivalence concerning this state, she appears be subjected to the very source of identification that her "spiritual" aspirations attempt to surmount.

In these two cases, an ideology of national purity and unanimity requires figures—the Chinese Confucian, the Tamil Hindu—that embody unacceptable histories, desires, and affiliations. The cloaking of Confucian ideas and practices as private belief in Indonesia, or of Hindu trance possessions as private exchanges and communications between supplicant-client and god-medium in Malaysia, show that the public-private distinction serves to divide the abject from the acceptable. The "private" space of the practicing Malaysian Hindu or Indonesian Confucian is a cage, not a shelter; it is a zone of confinement into which subjects have been coerced. The whole point of the legal changes sought by Chinese-Indonesian Confucians was to bring their practices into the public realm as legitimate forms of religion. Valli, by way of contrast, does not appear to have the will to challenge the boundaries of social purgatory: She declares to Willford that all of Malaysia's Hindu Tamils will be dead in ten years.

Our concern is not limited just to the uncanny figures and phantoms emanating from the political unconscious. Mediating and merging identifications pose a variety of predicaments and prospects. Smita Lahiri's chapter on the Filipino pilgrimage site of Mt. Banahaw sketches a history of cultural nationalist debate among the country's intellectual elite about how outlying and non-orthodox forms of Catholic practice should figure in a "National Symbolic" and its articulation of "authentic" national culture. The cumulative effect of that debate—authored principally by historians, anthropologists, folklorists, and writers from a relatively privileged class background—made it attractive for national politicians to seek spiritual and political capital through public visits and private audiences with Isabel Suarez, the "Suprema" who heads the principal sect at Banahaw. Politicians metaphorically drink in political and cultural capital by visiting the sacred springs of Banahaw and conversing with the Suprema. The Suprema, at the same time, reaps the benefits of national reputation and patronage as a result of such visits. To use a phrase coined by Arjun Appadurai,[18] the "production of locality" at Banahaw involves very public and symbolic exchanges between nationalist urban elites and a rural, subaltern underclass. In these exchanges, observes Lahiri, lies a reassertion of metropolitan privilege (and its attendant anxieties). This site of spiritual power has more recently been a focal point for an alliance of NGO's, community organizers quite critical of the Suprema, and an amalgam of nature-lovers and spiritual seekers.

Lahiri's chapter goes a long way in showing how a scholarly and literary elite devoted its energies to conjuring an autochthonous Catholicism that would be emblematic of the Filipino nation. Fenella Cannell's essay, meanwhile, reveals how religious ideology came to play a profound role in the colonial understanding of culture and ethnicity during the early American period in the Philippines. Cannell argues that an unacknowledged Protestant ideology inclined colonial administrators, educators, ethnologists, and others to associate lowland Filipinos with "idolatry," "mummery," and "mimicry." To the colonial agents, these suspect practices were signs that the lowland Filipinos—unlike their upland "tribal" neighbors—lacked personal authenticity and culture. Such practices impressed colonial commentators as phenomena that both defined subjugated ethnicities and accounted for the seeming cultural and religious insincerity or failure of these groups.[19] Cannell

---

[18] Arjun Appadurai, *Modernity at Large: Cultural Dimensions of Globalization* (Minneapolis, MN: University of Minnesota Press, 1996), pp. 178-200.

[19] Willford urges us to view the Protestant obsession with authentic spirituality in a Hegelian light. Willford sees in this obsession, when it is positioned against the materiality of idolatry, the subject's impossible desire for absolute spirit, or a negation of the fractured and contingent subject that aspires to transcendence, or autonomy. Under the Hegelian lens, Christianity, like the Indonesian/Melayu lingua franca that James T. Siegel analyzes in *Fetish, Recognition, Revolution* (Princeton, NJ: Princeton University Press, 1997), becomes an imitative means of

describes an American mission to cure the lowlanders of their debilitating idolatry. Ironically, the program to overturn mimicry and idolatry involved having the Filipino lowlanders *imitate* the Americans in, for example, eating corn and playing baseball. Moreover, in the campaign to coax the lowlanders to imitate Americans (as opposed to Catholic Spaniards), Cannell notes an anxious desire for subjects, who being recognizable to their new colonizers, could bestow recognition to their colonial masters. Turning the mimicry of the lowlanders to their advantage produced, on the one hand, a sense of superiority through moral uplift and an ideology of progress; but, on the other hand, a profound unease was aroused in the colonizers out of fears that this imitation of the Americans by Filipinos was less than "sincere," an outward display betraying inward duplicity. Once again doubts surrounded the true conversion of the lowlander. This, suggests Cannell, resulted in "constant uncertainty" on the part of the American colonial regime. (Comparativists and readers hungering for theoretical interventions also should note that Cannell extends her chapter to include a look at William Pietz's influential work on fetishism. She finds Pietz's insistence on the gap between the discourse of the idol and discourse of the fetish to be mistaken. In her view, Pietz's approach to modernity and to the problem of the fetish is itself a kind of thinking derived from a generalized form of Protestantism as it has worked its way into the discourses of the social sciences.)

The chapters by Lahiri and Cannell underscore how religious discourse came to inform political rule, both in colonial settings and in the "derivative" postcolonial nationalisms of the kind described by Partha Chatterjee.[20] In his chapter on painterly representations of Aceh, Kenneth George identifies a colonial discourse that associated Islam with an absence of art, an imagined absence that signified (in the minds of some) Aceh's political-cultural decline. Like the Catholic "idolatry" that troubled the American mission in the Philippines, Islam's seeming iconoclasm impressed Dutch colonial figures as a sign of Aceh's subjugation and cultural failure. Colonial misconstruals of religious visual culture functioned to mask the effects of colonial violence and dominion, and also set the stage for the predicaments of postcolonial visual culture. To explore some of those predicaments, George focuses on the political circumstances and aesthetic ideologies that shaped the career of Acehnese painter A. D. Pirous, and his effort to pioneer an art that would be emblematic of his religious, ethnic, and national heritage. Indonesian nationalism and aesthetic modernism were the first discourses to make powerful and counterposed claims on Pirous's subjectivity: The former led him to assume the role of an artist-citizen who would represent and advance the young Indonesian Republic. The latter led him to aspire to a unique and innovative artistic subjectivity. Here again we see homologies between the way the nation-state and the individual are imagined: The modern individual/artist is thought to be singular and different from all others. So too the nation-state. Pirous appears to have carried this reckoning even further, to the point where he equates the character of a nation with the character of the artist-citizen. Stunned by the neglect of Indonesian art in Western museums and galleries of the late Sixties, Pirous set about asserting an Indonesian-ness grounded in ethnicity and spirituality (two sources of aesthetic "authenticity" in

---

overhearing the other, and reveals a similarity between self and other that is menacing as it partially unmasks the colonial fantasy of mastery.

[20] Partha Chatterjee, *Nationalist Thought and the Colonial World: A Derivative Discourse* (Minneapolis, MN: University of Minnesota Press, 1986).

late-modernist ideology). He eventually came to conflate Islamic aesthetics with Acehnese aesthetics, and with Indonesia's broader cultural heritage; his private vision stands in for the common public good. But this very convergence of identifications set the stage for trauma and betrayal in the 1990s: Revelations of state-sponsored atrocities in Aceh violently split the painter's political-aesthetic vision and subjectivity, and made expression of Islamic spirituality deeply problematic vis-à-vis the political choices he needed to confront in representing Indonesia's culture of violence.

Pirous's work has been part of the Islamic resurgence that has swept across Indonesia and Malaysia since 1970, and he clearly used the nation-state and its resources to take a stance in broad debates about the public role of Islam and Islamic culture. Chapters by Suzanne Brenner and Erick White go much farther in showing how the nation-state and the public sphere become arenas for religious and social reform. Brenner notes that the Islamic resurgence did not lead Indonesian women of the 1980s and 1990s to retreat into the private or domestic sphere; to the contrary, many Muslim women became activists eager to enter into public debate about identifying and implementing Islamic values, and more broadly, about seeking social justice. These activists, as Brenner wishes to show, ranged across a broad political spectrum. They included women who wished to see the nation-state institute *shari'a* law, as well as those who sought a secular democracy that would inflect international human rights with Islamic notions of social justice. In Brenner's analysis, both conservative and liberal Islamic views about women were tethered to a blend of gender and development ideologies fostered by the New Order, to globalized discourses concerning faith and justice, and to the contradictory messages emanating from Suharto's regime. That regime was well known for the emphasis it placed on the role of women in family life. At the same time, the regime's emphasis on education, family planning, and national development beckoned women into the university and religious institute, the workplace, and the public sphere. Further still, the regime was quite active in promoting Islamic culture and values as the social ballast needed to help Indonesians negotiate capitalist development. Conservative Muslim activists were quite suspicious of the regime's programs, and acted largely to thwart what they perceived as the encroachment of Western and capitalist values into the life of Indonesian women. Liberal and feminist Muslim activists and critics of the regime countered by arguing that the Qur'anic tradition had been corrupted by centuries of patriarchal or masculinist interpretation emanating from Arab culture. Both camps argued from a theological perspective grounded in the Qur'an, the Hadith, and *fiqh* (Islamic jurisprudence), and both had much to say about the aspects of Indonesian culture and society with which they had quarrel. Interestingly, both sides depicted some of the sources of threat or corruption as extranational, one side often faulting the West, the other the Middle East (among other places).[21] Brenner takes us through various debates, writings, and interview materials, and reveals a robust debating public that seeks to include religious dimensions in addressing women's issues, in achieving justice in the home, courts, and workplace, and in preserving Muslim moral order.

---

[21] In light of arguments developed by Andrew Willford and a few other contributors to this volume, prospects for further research on Indonesia's debating Muslims might include the ways in which repulsion of "foreign" values destines their uncanny return in the political unconscious of the *ummat* (or Muslim community).

Erick White's chapter on popular religiosity and spirit mediums in Thailand gives a portrait of a different debate, this having to do with Buddhism and public culture. White begins by taking us back to 1891: Bangkok is engulfed in a great fire that happened to be prophesied by a spirit medium. King Chulalongkorn's subjects soon panic when mediums deliver prophesies of fires to come; in their panic, they engage in buying and selling of "an unusual nature." Frauds and arsonists then manipulate popular fear for their own criminal gain. It was in contrast to such popular and "irrational" religiosity—long a part of classical syncretic Theravada Buddhism—that reformist Buddhism had begun to assert its modernity, purity, and authenticity. A similar reformist sensibility motivated the ruling elite, who were eager to present themselves on domestic and global stages as progressive and modern, and who, in any case, saw prophesies of fires as public dangers. To put a check to growing disorder and economic irrationality, the Municipal Department issued a decree: No one may become possessed, under threat of arrest, investigation, and possible execution. In response, spirit mediums did not so much give up business as go underground.

A century later, spirit mediumship enjoyed a comeback from the shadows of Thai public life, when under the impact of Thailand's economic boom it became linked to the acquisition of influence and wealth. The Thai state had already for some time retreated from suppressing popular religious expression, and in the face of a new efflorescence of interest in mediums, perhaps saw little more in this phenomenon than people seeking advantage in pursuing the trappings of prosperity.[22] It did not take action. But Thailand's public sphere had changed. No longer wholly managed by the state, it now offered room for debate and maneuver by public intellectuals and citizens. In White's portrait, the reformist Buddhist monk and intellectual Phra Payom steps onto the public stage as a Habermasian figure, endeavoring to sway public opinion and mobilize the state against the moral and spiritual degeneracy he perceives in spirit mediumship.[23] White's ethnographic interest in monk-critic Phra Payom is important, for it reminds us that the public sphere is not so much a space for debate internal to a horizontal comradeship of citizens but a hierarchical arena in which elite figures attempt to speak for public interests, projects, and values and so install themselves an authoritative class of moral, political, and cultural interpreters.[24] Phra Payom's campaign also illustrates a facet of the public sphere that Jürgen Habermas left unexplored (except as a feature of private lifeworlds)—religious discourse. Key, too, to this portrait of a public figure in the public sphere is the specter of scandal, the twin shade to the sorts of "rational debate" so central to a Habermasian idea of political communication. Phra Payom's tales of how spirit mediums lured their clients into sexual license, fraud, and familial neglect are part of a rhetoric of moral outrage intended to stir the public and the state

[22] We note that the spirit medium prophesies of 1891 had to do with the destruction of property by fire; panic spread like wildfire and caused social disorder, especially in "buying and selling of 'an unusual nature.'" The prophecies of the 1990s, however, promoted capitalist investment and the accumulation of property, endeavors that were welcomed by the Thai government. But as we explain below, the monk-critic Phra Payom saw the more recent prophecies as a source of moral disorder.

[23] Phra Payom and his campaign have also been discussed by Morris, *In the Place of Origins*, p. 335.

[24] Cf., Kenneth M. George, "Designs on Indonesia's Muslim Communities." See especially discussion on page 709.

into action. The discourse of scandal, we observe, is especially suited to the mass mediation of public culture. So too is spectacle, and after Phra Payom's campaign failed to get the state to regulate spirit mediums, he resorted to assisting in the televised exposé of a well-known spirit medium. That medium divulged the secrets of the trade, demonstrating how seeming miracles are in fact easily managed deceptions; he performed them before the camera while describing them as sheer technique.

White argues that the medium of television had more reach than Phra Payom's campaign, disseminated in the print media, in terms of demystifying spirit mediumship. But in the end, televised exposés too did little to alter the cultural relationship between mediums, Buddhism, and state authority, or to undermine spirit mediumship more generally. State suppression in the 1890s, reformist efforts in 1995, and televised exposés in 1997 all conjured spirit mediumship as a public danger. In the earliest instance, neither the state nor the *sangha* sought to put a check to private interest in spirit mediumship. In the more recent campaigns, spirit mediumship is characterized as a threat to private lifeworlds; public case is made and the state is petitioned as the legitimate guardian of societal interests to intervene. Spirit mediumship is now called upon to defend itself. This is to say that even as spirit mediumship is involved in day-to-day social life of families and local communities—in short, in a lifeworld, not in civic or public affairs—it has become exposed to view and subject to public debate.

Thamora Fishel's chapter on Thai Buddhist funerals brings us explicitly to the operations of class, electoral politics, and exchange in religious practice. The chapter begins with a question: What makes funerals such a draw for Thai politicians? The appeal, suggests Fishel, lies partly in a longstanding logic of exchange that has been amplified and distended by the calculations of Thailand's emergent middle class and the adroit maneuvers of politicians seeking middle-class support. Funerals continue to feature deeply held ideas about reciprocity, ones in which merit-making, gift-giving, and patronage relations converge. Indeed, Fishel characterizes Thai Buddhism as a profoundly economic activity in which gifts are exchanged for spiritual merit. The status wishes and status anxieties of the burgeoning middle class are slaked (and manipulated) as politicians donate vast sums of money and material to the bereaved and to the community of monks, in effect becoming "hosts" for what were once family affairs. The social indebtedness of the family and neighborhood turns into a form of political capital and a likely source of votes, while the gifts to monks (from which no "worldly" return is expected) yield a perceived merit-based potency that is of use in promoting oneself in the arena of electoral politics. Contrasted with the illegal, comparatively modern, and efficient practice of vote-buying, Thai funeral exchanges imply a moral universe in which political opportunity comes in the dress of religious observance, a social advantage that emanates from fulfilling one's ritual obligations. In this light, Thai funerals look as if they form a resilient cultural canopy against the heat and rains of modernization.

But Fishel shows us otherwise. Modernization in the Thai public sphere has brought about change in the political and cultural economy of funerals, too. The expanding bourgeoisie in both the city and the province has directed a considerable part of its wealth to constructing crematoriums on temple grounds, away from charnel sites at the periphery of communities. The effect has been to shift funerals and wakes away from the home and forest edge and into the temple complexes. Fishel reports that of nearly one hundred funerals she attended, only two involved home-based wakes. The new communal crematorium is the sign of the modern Thai middle class, and home-based wakes are increasingly stigmatized by their associations with poverty and the (largely rural) "past" that the new middle class has left behind.[25] Along with this change have come new bourgeois attitudes toward the spectacle and burden of funerals. Death and the burning of the dead are, for the emerging middle class, disturbing, obscene, shocking, and disgusting; so, too, Fishel tells us, is the prospect of being too deeply indebted to local politicians. The new crematoriums and new patterns of funeral sponsorship keep such disturbing events and exchanges out of sight. They are efficient, clean, orderly, and communal. Politicians of course find such communal gatherings convenient occasions to build networks of supporters and to stay in the public eye, even while participating in the logic of reciprocity and merit-making.

In sum, Fishel suggests how a Buddhist religious observance has become an emblem of class affiliations and anxieties even as it remains grounded in longstanding ideas about reciprocity and spiritual merit. The politics of the Thai funeral are not just a matter of politicians using them to secure votes and political capital. The spatial and visual aspects of contemporary middle-class funerals are conjured in a way that produces a break with past funerary forms; emergent forms of sponsorship threaten conventional patterns of patronage. They are signs of Thai modernity and its values, and perhaps herald a more thoroughgoing reformation and rationalization of Thai Buddhism's practical economic logic.

* * * * *

The chapters that make up *Spirited Politics* were never written with the idea of showing allegiance to a uniting theoretical perspective. Nor was there common commitment on the part of contributors to a specific ethnographic or historical style of inquiry. But as a way of closing this introductory essay, we note just a few recurrent features and ideas that cut across chapters and potentially mark direction for further research. The first is the prominence of elite and middle-class discourses and interests in the ethnographic and historical investigations that make up this book. Ethnic or class subalterns are not wholly absent in our work. But the social actors who are portrayed as especially influencing public discourses on religion, politics, and culture do not come from the Southeast Asia's urban or rural underclasses. This may accord well with social realities, as well as with the call to "study up" in ethnographic work. At the very least, this suggests that elites may be using dimensions of religion and religious reform in various public arenas to articulate the hierarchies and boundaries of shifting class relations. It also invites speculation as to whether a subaltern underclass has found any effective ground for resistance, opposition, or articulation of class interests in public religious life. That elites can dominate sites of religious discourse such as courts, schools, art galleries, publications, or broadcast media means that they are able to control the ideological

---

[25] To echo a point made above in footnote 21, further research on Thai Buddhism might include consideration of how a "surmounted past" returns to haunt the political unconscious of the country's middle class.

and discursive traffic within and between nation-states, and across transnational religious communities.

The calamities and grotesques of Southeast Asian identity politics are also a central motif in much of this book. Both national and subnational communities, and the elites who seem to dominate them, have seized upon ethno-religious identities as a way of finding a place in the world and for exacting rule over others. The essays gathered here show some of the predicaments and inequities that accompany these very public and troubling processes of identification. As Stallybrass and White observed, the drive to achieve a homogenous collective identity inevitably produces a political and unconscious heterogeneity marked by the uncanny, the hybrid, or the ghostly.[26] Some of us have discovered how ethno-religious identifications have produced ironies, anxieties, and uncanny effects. Yet others of us, taking a different approach, have described opportunities, betrayals, and tragedies that come from the narrative contingency and broad play of religious and ethnic identity vis-à-vis other affiliations (e.g., gender).

Last, the formative sites for ethno-religious discourse mentioned in our book suggest that further enquiry be directed at hierarchies of location. Are galleries, television, courts, and magazines overshadowing the mosque, temple, or church as settings for the formation of ethno-religious subjectivities? What interests and what other identity positions will be served with the emergence of such sites? Are new formulations of public and private in the making? With what efficacy will the nation-state manipulate emergent sites for ethno-religious discourse? Will global and transnational forces weaken the grip of the nation-state on ethnic and religious affiliations, only to unleash new sorts of border-crossing phantasms?

Spirited Politics has brought together contributions from specialists who are concerned with the way religion has entered into the operation of state power and the nation-state's anxious articulation with identity, culture and ideas about community. In focusing on the interrelationships between religious and political transformations, this book has illuminated ways in which religious idioms and practices serve political ends, and how political resources may be mobilized for religious ends. We hope it sparks fresh questions about Southeast Asia, especially among our students, who will see things in ways we did not anticipate.

Ken George and Andrew Willford
Madison & Kuala Lumpur
July 2004

---

[26] Stallybrass and White, *The Politics and Poetics of Transgression*, p. 194.

THE PRIESTESS AND THE POLITICIAN: ENUNCIATING FILIPINO CULTURAL NATIONALISM THROUGH MT. BANAHAW[1]

Smita Lahiri

Most travelers heading to Mt. Banahaw from Manila leave the city by bus on the South Superhighway, a congested thoroughfare that passes through an industrial corridor south of the metropolis and skirts the inland lake of Laguna de Bay. If the roads are not congested, the journey to San Pablo, the provincial capital of Laguna, takes less than two hours; more often, however, travelers spend half the day on the road before transferring to a jeepney for the final twelve-kilometer run to Dolores, a rural municipality lying in Mt. Banahaw's foothills. From San Pablo onwards, the mountain dominates the landscape with its massive and mist-shrouded silhouette as well as its name, which flashes by in the painted signs of the businesses lining the roads: Banahaw Feeds, Banahaw Copra Processing, Banahaw Rest Stop, and so on. Crowded together with their heads bent over in the jeepney's low-ceilinged passenger compartment, New Age hikers, nature-lovers, and "seekers" from the metropolis glimpse these signs out of the corners of their eyes as they rub shoulders with local townsfolk and villagers (sometimes with chickens or piglets in tow), and with pilgrims from other corners of the Philippines.

Popular pilgrimage to Mt. Banahaw stands out among other translocal devotions in Filipino folk-Catholicism for its focus upon the veneration of springs, caves, waterfalls, and peaks as images or simulacra of the scenes of Christ's suffering, crucifixion, and resurrection in the Holy Lands. Although visitors headed to these *pwestos* or natural shrines trickle through Dolores and Santa Lucia all year long, the town is veritably engulfed each Holy Week just prior to Easter, when it becomes the convergence point of upwards of a hundred thousand pilgrims. Periodically kneeling on rocks to make offerings of candles and prayers in the scorching summer

[1] *Acknowledgments.* Several people read drafts of this essay and gave me invaluable advice. While assuming all responsibility for remaining errors or shortcomings, I would like to thank Ken George and Andrew Willford for their suggestions, as well as Karen Strassler, Ann Marie Leshkowitch, Jennifer Cole, Christine Walley, and Ajantha Subramanian.

sun, they ascend via a series of lesser shrines to the *pwestos* of Kalbaryo (Calvary) and Kinabuhayan (Resurrection). On every side, individuals appear to be engaging in the solemn and sometimes tearful effort of remembering, retracing, and sharing the path of the suffering Christ's journey towards the crucifixion and resurrection. Each Holy Week, Mt. Banahaw also becomes a media stomping-ground as TV, radio, and newspapers compete among themselves to capture the most compelling national images and stories symbolizing the Passion and Resurrection. (Atop Kalbaryo on Good Friday in 2000, I watched from a distance of a few feet as a TV camera crew shot footage of a group of white-clad pilgrims bearing staffs and scapulars; two days later, I relived the scene in a Manila drawing room when it was aired on an Easter Sunday newscast.)

This essay is about the power of discursive effects associated with "national culture" to reshape a particular social landscape, and about the material consequences of these transformations for the people who live there. Decades of traffic between metropolitan Manila and the locality of Dolores have undoubtedly deepened the trails crisscrossing Mt. Banahaw's *pwesto* zone and carved out new ones. As I relate below, this traffic has also worn tracks into the space of national public culture, where Mt. Banahaw has acquired a prominent image since the 1980s as an iconic site for folk-Catholic devotion. This prominence, I argue, is closely associated with the rise of cultural nationalism as a newly authoritative "discursive formation." The work of Michel Foucault has attuned scholars to the ways in which all configurations of knowledge authorize distinctive enunciative modalities. To speak from or through discourse is to lend one's statements an authority whose ultimate source lies not in oneself, but rather in the field of institutionally mediated power relations within which they are embedded.[2] This, I argue, aptly describes the situation of at least one popular-religious leader at Mt. Banahaw, who has been extensively figured as an embodiment of primordial national culture in academic scholarship and journalistic writings within the Philippines' papers of record. In situating the construction of Mt. Banahaw's image in relation to local micropolitics and forms of mediation, I hope to demonstrate how unpredictable discursive effects can be, particularly when they ripple forth out of the discursive space of metropolitan public culture and into lived places. Moreover, I will suggest that cultural nationalism's embrace of popular religiosity simultaneously subverts and reinscribes longstanding relations between social power and cultural hybridity in the Filipino context.

During my field research in 1997 and 1998, evidence of the prominence of Mt. Banahaw in Filipino public culture could be seen in academic scholarship, feature journalism, and the availability of glossy publications like *Banahaw: Conversations with a Pilgrim to the Power Mountain*, a slim volume that was first published in 1992 by the high-quality Philippine imprint Bookmark. Published under the name of Vitaliano R. Gorospe, a prominent Jesuit educator, *Banahaw* is a multi-authored work whose list of contributors, ranging from historians to theologians, anthropologists, and one nationally renowned expert on the paranormal, offers a distinguished sampling of the Filipino scholarly establishment. The main text of the book, based upon extended interviews with Father Gorospe (presumably the eponymous

---

[2] Michel Foucault, *The Archaeology of Knowledge and the Discourse on Language* (New York: Pantheon Books, 1982). See especially chapter 2, "Discursive Formations," and chapter 4, "The Formation of Enunciative Modalities," pp. 31-39, 50-55.

"pilgrim" of the book's title) simulates an interchange between an inexperienced seeker and knowledgeable guide, while also vaguely recalling the traditional format of a catechism. The text is arranged as a series of alternating questions and answers ranging in scope from the informative ("If I want to do the Banahaw pilgrimage how do I go about it?"[3]) to the didactic (What does the Catholic Church say about these beliefs and rituals?" and "What is the value of Filipino popular religion?"[4]). In perusing the text and the accompanying photographs, the reader is allegorically led on a circuit of Banahaw's most often-visited *pwestos,* and introduced to the some of the luminaries in the many religious movements headquartered here, among them Isabel Suarez, the Suprema or head of the Ciudad Mistica de Dyos (Mystical City of God).

Although the subject matter of *Banahaw* is ostensibly a localized religious tradition, the devotions and sects under discussion are repeatedly characterized as Filipino. A tone of national reverence and pride pervades the book's pages, where the Banahaw landscape and its associated folk-Catholic pilgrimage come to conjure the imagined community of the nation. The conclave of distinguished contributors who discuss Banahaw's historic and cultural significance within these same pages also creates what Laurent Berlant has called a National Symbolic, a discursive space within which images and ideas constitutive of the nation circulate.[5] It is also significant that the inside back cover of *Banahaw* depicts Fr. Gorospe in the act of receiving benediction from Pope John Paul II, an image that might be seen as dispensing supra-national authorization to Gorospe's own consecration of Mt. Banahaw as a sacred site for the Filipino nation. Within the book's covers, an orthodox Catholic sensibility pervades many of Gorospe's remarks; for instance, he cites papal authority to assuage potential visitors' fears regarding the potential spiritual danger of exposure to "fanaticism" or heterodoxy at Mt. Banahaw.[6] At the same time, Fr. Gorospe nowhere objects to the argument, made by other contributors, that *pwesto*-veneration at Mt. Banahaw reflects the persistence of pre-Christian animist beliefs and strategies for accumulating spiritual potency.[7] It is as though the authors' shared consensus regarding the Filipinoness of the Banahaw pilgrimage preempts any potential clash between their respective secular-historical and theological orientations.

The discovery and consecration of a shared patrimony, announced in the initial pages of *Banahaw,* leads directly to the assertion of the need to preserve it from corruption. Speaking as a *pator* or *pwesto*-guide (a role which, he explains, is ideally assumed by an experienced hermit or seer), Gorospe enjoins would-be visitors to cultivate a stance of respectful reverence and to avoid littering or despoiling the mountain.[8] Jaime Licuauco, the Philippines' best-known psychic, describes Mt.

---

[3] Vitaliano R. Gorospe, S.J., *Banahaw: Conversations with a Pilgrim to the Power Mountain* (Makati: Bookmark, 1992), p. 27.

[4] Gorospe, *Banahaw,* p. 60.

[5] Lauren Gail Berlant, *The Anatomy of National Fantasy: Hawthorne, Utopia, and Everyday Life* (Chicago: University of Chicago Press, 1991), p. 5.

[6] The authority cited is the encyclical of Paul VI (*Evangelii Nuntiandi*) dealing with popular religion. Gorospe, *Banahaw,* p. 60.

[7] Jose M. Cruz, S.J., "Topography of Religious Experience," in Gorospe, *Banahaw,* pp. 13-16; Jose Mario C. Francisco, S.J., "Decentering Banahaw/Deconstructing Christianity," in Gorospe, *Banahaw,* pp. 57-59.

[8] Gorospe, *Banahaw,* p. 68.

Banahaw as one of the world's foremost centers of psychic and paranormal energy, but warns that it is in danger of being debased by charlatans.[9] Even as they consecrate the Banahaw pilgrimage tradition as part of national heritage, the contributors to *Banahaw* characterize its true form as being threatened by erasure, a rhetorical move built upon an implicit claim to be able to determine authoritatively between the inauthentic and the genuine.

Despite repeatedly registering the impact of the media upon Mt. Banahaw, *Banahaw* ignores wider processes of mediation and, most importantly, its own role within them. The contributors to the volume show little self-awareness, for instance, regarding the prerogative they seem to enjoy, as elites, to define and disseminate what constitutes national-cultural patrimony. Furthermore, they do not ask what it might mean for local villagers and townsfolk to belong to a place that has become a symbolic resource for imagining the Filipino nation, while remaining in other respects a poverty-stricken and underdeveloped locality. On the surface of it, the incorporation of the long-marginalized domain of folk-Catholicism into authorized notions of national culture might seem to signal an unmitigated gesture of inclusion. Alternatively, the publication of *Banahaw* might be taken to be a moment in a process of "the invention of tradition," suggesting that the creative agency celebrated in the book belongs as much to the book's authors as to its subjects.[10] While neither perspective is wholly incorrect, both are inadequate. In this essay I acknowledge their partial merits, but move beyond them in foregrounding the historical specificity of those metropolitan discourses about Filipino national culture that have made Mt. Banahaw's incorporation both conceivable and logical. But since this is ultimately a story about the localized and material consequences of discursive effects, I shall start with an election-season anecdote set in Santa Lucia, a *barangay* (village) that serves as the gateway to Mt. Banahaw's *pwestos*.

A FLYING VISIT AND ITS REPERCUSSIONS

It was a humid afternoon in November, six months before the Presidential decision of May 1998. As I trudged uphill on the *barangay*'s only paved road towards the walled compound of the Ciudad Mistica de Dyos, I was mulling over persistent rumors predicting the appearance of a surprise guest at the celebrations for the sixty-third birthday of Isabel Suarez, the sect's leader or Suprema. Although the occasion was marked by an annual open house, my customary companions in the village had politely demurred from joining me, preferring as usual to maintain their distance from the sect. Nearing the compound's corrugated-tin gates (normally kept unwelcomingly closed), I saw a motley array of jeepneys, Toyotas, and one Mercedes parked awkwardly on the side of the steeply graded road. Passing through the gates into a large courtyard, I found rumor substantiated by the presence of a helicopter perched on a dusty adjacent field serving as an impromptu helipad. The courtyard was thronged with people peering at the exotic blue-and-yellow painted craft: straw-

---

[9] Jaime Licuauco, "Banahaw, A Reflection of Yourself," in Gorospe, *Banahaw*, pp. 71-2. In one installment of his regular newspaper column, Licuauco also warned first-time visitors to Banahaw away from Holy Week, characterizing it as a time when "mistakes" predominate over "mystics." Jaime T. Licuauco, "Mt. Banahaw Revisited." *Philippine Daily Inquirer*, April 12, 1990, p. 8

[10] Eric Hobsbawm and Terence Ranger, eds., *The Invention of Tradition* (Cambridge: Cambridge University Press, 1983).

hatted farmers dressed in their best machine-embroidered *barong tagalog*,[11] peasant women carrying umbrellas folded over their arms, and children with birthday balloons tied to their wrists.

With the identity of the mystery guest still unknown, I passed into the Suprema's abode, a two-story Spanish-style mansion with a marble portico and ornate balconies, whose first floor houses a public meeting area and large kitchen. At a long *narra* (mahogany) table in a corner of the room sat a corpulent man surrounded by an entourage of bodyguards, well-coiffed women, children, and nannies. He too was dressed in *barong tagalog*, but unlike the inexpensive polyester of the shirts worn by the farmers, the sheer and costly *piña* fabric of the visitor's handwoven confection identified it as a politician's official-nationalist trademark. I had already heard his name whispered by the small crowd watching the activity from a discreet distance, and now I recognized the visitor's face from the newspapers: it was Congressman Jose de Venecia, Speaker of the Philippine House of Legislators and a frontrunner for the presidency. Beside him and cutting nearly as recognizable a figure with her blue robes, slender figure, and dignified face, sat the Suprema, solicitously attending to her chief guest.

As I was still absorbing the fact that a busy "Presidentiable" (as the press persistently refers to candidates for the chief executive's position) had flown in to offer the Suprema his birthday greetings personally, the visit drew abruptly to a close. The Speaker rose from the table with his entourage and was escorted out to the helipad, still in conversation with the Suprema. Before ascending into the helicopter, the politician turned around to address the small crowd that had followed, straining to project his voice over the whirring of the propeller. Thanking villagers for their hospitality, he apologized for the brevity of his visit and declared himself fervently at the service of the Suprema and of all residents of the holy Mt. Banahaw (*banal na bundok Banahaw*), expressing his hope that they would not forget him come May. With this thinly veiled reference to his electoral candidacy, he climbed aboard. The helicopter took off immediately, dislodging a thick cloud of dust to settle in fine layers upon the crowd, whose constituents, taking no offence, waved gamely at the exotic craft until it was no more than a distant speck on the horizon.

A peculiar set of calculations must have prompted Congressman De Venecia's campaign managers to schedule a semi-private appearance in a village with fewer than six hundred households, a decision that seems remarkable when one considers that a national candidate can scarcely hope to visit each of the Philippines' seventy-eight provincial capitals, let alone cover even the majority of its 681 municipal seats. Later in this essay, some reasons why Santa Lucia was singled out in this way will suggest themselves.[12] For now, however, I will concentrate upon local reactions to

---

[11] *Barong tagalog* or *Barong* Pilipino is an embroidered shirt of translucent and cool fabric that is worn untucked over trousers. Worn on official or formal occasions, it serves as the national dress for men.

[12] Courting religious constituencies was apparently one of De Venecia's campaign strategies. As one work of pre-election analysis had it, "De Venecia called to the high priests of almost all religious denominations in the country . . . days before the President made public his endorsement, a national daily had the photo of De Venecia, on all fours, praying before the gods of Mt. Banahaw." Malou Mangahas, ed., *Showdown '98: The Search for the Centennial President* (Metro Manila: The Manila Times & Ateneo Center for Social Policy and Public Affairs, 1998), p. 90. The report is slightly misleading, since De Venecia was actually on his knees in the Dolores parish church; admittedly, however, he was looking up at Rosa Palau, head priestess of Camara Baja, another folk-religious movement. De Venecia's return visit to

the congressman's fleeting visit. The impression left behind by De Venecia himself was an ambivalent one. Many in Santa Lucia seemed to have already formed an opinion of him as an especially unprepossessing specimen of *trapo* ("traditional politician"), a colloquialism that handily condenses all the underhandedness, ruthlessness, and amorality associated with the realm of electoral politics in this country. On the other hand, several villagers seemed to find a certain sublimity in having received the opportunity to brush sleeves with a man who could become the country's next President.

Significantly, the exalted status of the congressman seemed to bolster the already considerable awe that was attached to the storied figure of the Suprema. Older villagers recall first meeting Isabel Suarez as the teenaged daughter of Amador Suarez, one of Mt. Banahaw's most storied *magaling na lalake* (a phrase whose meaning is strikingly similar to "man of prowess," the term used by O. W. Wolters for the precolonial Southeast Asian leader-figure endowed with soul-stuff), who established the Ciudad Mistica de Dyos in Santa Lucia.[13] Since 1962, when Isabel was supernaturally anointed as the group's Suprema by the spirit of the sect's long-deceased (and possibly mythic) foundress, Maria Bernarda Balitaan, she has gradually assumed and perfected the persona of an aloof yet charismatic holy woman. By 1997, she had become something of a household word, her spiritual gifts and authority the subject of journalistic profiles and popular legend.

Within Santa Lucia, the Suprema's national fame and apparently effortless success in attracting the attention of metropolitan notables is taken as compelling evidence of her *kapangyarihan*, a concept that connotes spiritual power as well as supernatural leadership.[14] This *kapangyarihan* is, in turn, the basis of the social authority that she exerts over a flock that numbers (by the Ciudad Mistica's own estimates, admittedly) over twenty thousand followers all over Luzon and comprises a little less than half of the residents of Santa Lucia itself. In this context, the congressman's visit to the Mistica compound came to be locally figured as one of the more memorable compliments paid in recent memory by important city people to

---

Mt. Banahaw took place a few weeks after the Suprema's birthday party. I provide a full account of the event in my dissertation. See Smita Lahiri, "Materializing the Spiritual: Christianity, Community, and History in a Philippine Landscape" (PhD dissertation, Cornell University, 2002), pp. 240-87.

[13] On "man of prowess," see Oliver W. Wolters, *History, Culture, and Region in Southeast Asian Perspectives*, rev. ed. (Ithaca, NY: Cornell Southeast Asia Program Publications/Singapore: ISEAS, 1999). For an account of the importance of *magaling na lalak* in a local Filipino context, see Brian Fegan, "Entrepreneurs in Votes and Violence: Three Generations of a Peasant Political Family," in *An Anarchy of Families: State and Family in the Philippines*, ed. Alfred W. McCoy (Madison, WI: Center for Southeast Asian Studies, 1994), pp. 33-108.

[14] John Sidel has written extensively about the place of *kapangyarihan* in Filipino politics and popular culture. See John Sidel, "The Philippines: The Languages of Legitimation," in *Political Legitimacy in Southeast Asia*, ed. Muthiah Alagappa (Stanford: Stanford University Press, 1995), pp. 136-169; "Filipino Gangsters in Film, Legend, and History: Two Biographical Case Studies From Cebu," in *Lives at the Margin: Biography of Filipinos Obscure, Ordinary, and Heroic*, ed. Alfred W. McCoy (Madison, WI: Center for Southeast Asian Studies, 2000), pp. 149-92. For a discussion of *kapangyarihan's* gendered aspect, see Mina Roces, *Women, Power, and Kinship Politics: Female Power in the Post-War Philippines* (Quezon City: Anvil, 2000), pp. 161-87. Like most analyses of Filipino political culture, the abovementioned accounts take inspiration from Benedict Anderson's famous essay on spiritual potency and leadership. See "The Idea of Power in Javanese Culture," in *Culture and Politics in Indonesia*, ed. Claire Holt (Ithaca: Cornell University Press, 1972), pp. 1-69.

the Suprema, a personage who is seen as having the power to command deference from wealthy and influential Filipinos almost as part of the natural order of things. The spectacular elements of the Speaker's visit—his campaign helicopter, the high-status food he was elaborately served, and the gunshots that were discharged into the sky to mark his departure—simultaneously served to index the Speaker's social power or *lakas* (literally "strength") as well as to render visible the Suprema's spiritually charged *kapangyarihan*.[15]

As the repercussions of the Speaker's visit registered, it became clear that the congressman's patronage was being locally cast not as an instance of a powerful politician condescending to local subjects, but instead as a demonstration of the Suprema's potency and ability to tap informally into state-derived resources. A few days after the visit, the Dolores mayor's office announced that the Speaker was joining with two congressmen from nearby districts to put together a package of funds for the upgrading of the Dolores-Santa Lucia road, the most vital element of local infrastructure and one perennially in need of repair and improvement. It was also rumored that the Speaker would arrange for Dolores to be designated a pilot site in a microcredit program to be launched by the Department of Social Welfare and Development (DSWD) with international funding. This too was interpreted by local residents as conforming to a pattern. Speaking off the record, municipal officials repeated what I had already heard from some villagers, namely that the Suprema's contacts with politicians and military brass had already yielded past patronage benefits in the form of *barangay* and municipal projects, ranging from previous rounds of road-repair to the establishment of a *barangay* health center. The Suprema, it was said, had played a crucial role in the approval of requests and the subsequent release of funds on those occasions, even though her name was never formally linked with any "pork" project. Once the promise of a certain amount of "assistance" (*tulong*) had been made by a would-be patron to the Suprema, the mayor's office could submit a request for a specific project to the relevant congressman or senator with some confidence that funds would eventually be released by a state body, such as the DSWD or the Department of Public Works and Highways (DPWH). While difficult to corroborate, villagers' and municipal officials' shared conviction that state funds flow into the area if and only if the Suprema acts as the locality's intermediary is surely significant in its own right.[16]

---

[15] By at least one account, *lakas* is viewed as an amoral form of social power which may be based on wealth or coercive force, while *kapangyarihan* is a morally charged charisma ultimately deriving from God. See Robert S. Love, "The Samahan of Papa God: Tradition and Conversion in a Tagalog Peasant Religious Movement" (PhD dissertation, Cornell University, 1977).

[16] For a sense of the varied importance of political patronage in Filipino localities, see the case studies in Benedict J. Kerkvliet and Resil Mojares, *From Marcos to Aquino: Local Perspectives on Political Transition in the Philippines* (Honolulu: University of Hawai'i Press, 1991). Readers familiar with Filipino politics will note that the Suprema plays a role that is structurally (though not culturally) analogous to the archetypically male "boss" figures seen in other places. See Sheila S. Coronel et al., *Boss: Five Case Studies of Local Politics in the Philippines* (Quezon City: Philippine Center for Investigative Journalism, 1995); Sheila S. Coronel et al., *Pork and Other Perks: Corruption and Governance in the Philippines* (Pasig: Philippine Center for Investigative Journalism, 1998); Alfred W. McCoy, ed., *An Anarchy of Families: State and Family in the Philippines* (Madison, WI: University of Wisconsin Center for Southeast Asian Studies, 1993).

It is important to note that the Suprema's preeminence in Santa Lucia does not go uncontested—a fact that I learned as I became increasingly attuned to local gossip, memory, and micropolitics during my research. Many in the village describe Isabel behind her back as *suplado* (arrogant) and *ma-arte* (affected), epithets that tarnish her reputation for spiritual potency or *kapangyarihan*, if they do not directly challenge it. Among the families with whom I stayed, each time Isabel received a mysterious visitor shielded behind the darkened windows of an upscale private car or SUV (sport-utility vehicle), malicious rumors about Isabel's "boyfriends" or secret love for imported goods would be unleashed, casting doubt on her chaste and ascetic public persona. Many residents of Santa Lucia, it turned out, held a personal grudge against Isabel because of high-handed actions committed by her family members in the past. Over the past decade or two, an influx of Mistica followers and the mushrooming of new households had increased the pressure on local land, water, and forest resources. These new settlers, I often heard it said, were denuding the mountain with new swiddens, littering and loitering in the vicinity of the *pwestos,* and even swindling unwary pilgrims. Finally, the Suprema was also widely suspected of playing power politics by attempting to fix local elections in favor of candidates close to herself. Perhaps most seriously, she was said to have made a deal with the local landowner securing low rents for her own followers, in return for a guarantee that they would not file a land claim when the government's land reform program was implemented. In short, Isabel Suarez's celebrity and her power to mediate external resources is perceived by a significant portion of the local population as an oppressive and illegitimate mode of dominance

How might we understand the relationship between the Suprema's current role as mediator of political resources in Santa Lucia, and the recent emergence of works of cultural mediation such as the book *Banahaw,* which consecrates Mt. Banahaw as a sacred site for the nation? To understand this linkage, we need to situate the rather enigmatic and (as far as I know) singular encounter between Speaker Jose de Venecia and Suprema Isabel Suarez within a distinctive history of symbolic and material exchanges between the metropolitan "center" and this rather exceptional "periphery." This exchange pattern is the outcome of the public circulation of images, representations, and claims concerning Mt. Banahaw which had, by the late 1990s, precipitated a taken-for-granted belief in the essential "Filipinoness" of the places, persons, and practices associated with it. To account for how these forms of discourse come into prominence, I start with a brief and admittedly incomplete historical sketch of the vicissitudes of Filipino cultural nationalism as a (largely) elite intellectual formation. On the basis of this account, I argue that metropolitan interest in Mt. Banahaw during the 1980s and 1990s reflected the rise in Filipino public culture of a revisionist cultural-nationalist imaginary combining both new and older aspects of nationalist thought. Subsequently, I show that in Santa Lucia this new imaginary not only reshaped the social landscape, but also fueled a micropolitics of contestation that critiqued the Suprema and, through her, the realm of national politics.

FIGURING THE NATIVE IN FILIPINO CULTURAL NATIONALISM

If political nationalism embraces legal-rational structures of organization in order to mobilize members of the nation into a polity, the project of cultural nationalism is to awaken individuals to their national identity and, as John

Hutchinson puts it, to "embed this identity in everyday life."[17] As such, cultural nationalism entails a commitment to an essentialized collective identity, materialized with reference to a common heritage of values, histories, intellectual traditions, and lifestyles. The architects of cultural nationalism tend to be scholars, artists, journalists, and writers, and their influence is often transmitted through public culture via loose or unofficial networks before undergoing formal institutionalization. In the Philippines, cultural nationalism has historically been articulated by educated and elite bearers of what I (following Vicente Rafael) will call "mestizo privilege," a term which conveys both a position at the top of the socio-economic hierarchy solidified under Spanish and US colonial rule, as well as a certain mastery over domesticated forms of foreign-derived symbolic capital.[18] As a result, one can discern an abiding but rarely acknowledged tension in Filipino nationalist thought between proponents' own historically sedimented cosmopolitan dispositions and the images of autochthonous native identity that have been privileged within efforts to imagine primordial and ancient roots for the nation.[19]

Cultural nationalism in the Philippines is generally agreed to have begun in the 1870s among the Liberal-inclined network of essayists known as the Propaganda movement.[20] While some in this circle oriented themselves towards political forms of national advocacy such as the reformist demand for the Filipino representation in the Spanish *Cortes*, others were more concerned with the project of moral regeneration through the recuperation of a distinctive Filipino civilization. Jose Rizal, for instance, re-edited and annotated a long-neglected chronicle from the dawn of the conquest, rebutting Spain's claim to have brought civilization to the archipelago and charging it with the destruction of a vibrant culture.[21] In doing so, he sounded a note of

---

[17] John Hutchinson, "Cultural Nationalism and Moral Regeneration," in *Nationalism,* ed. John Hutchinson and Anthony D. Smith (Oxford: Oxford University Press, 1994), p. 124.

[18] Vicente L. Rafael, "Taglish, or the Phantom Power of the Lingua Franca," in *White Love* (Durham, NC: Duke University Press, 2000), pp. 162-189. Mestizos of mixed native and Chinese and/or Spanish descent were prominent among the late-nineteenth-century *ilustrado* (enlightened) nationalists. Unlike during the Spanish colonial period, when mestizoness was a legally recognized social category, today it consists of a cosmopolitan and socially valued hybridity quintessentially embodied by movie stars, many of whom look Eurasian and interject English and Spanish expressions effortlessly into their Tagalog speech. As Rafael crisply puts it, "Mestizoness is the capacity, amongst other things, to speak in different registers, as if one's identity were overlaid and occupied by other possible ones." See Rafael, "Taglish," p. 167.

[19] This tension between cosmopolitanism and nativism may be seen as one manifestation of what Vicente L Rafael describes as the "predicament" shared by historical and contemporary Filipino intellectuals: "In seeking to speak for and of the nation, they find it necessary to occupy a different position by speaking on a different register: the language of an other, dominant power. In doing so, they simultaneously identify with *and* dis-identify from those at the lower, non-English-speaking rungs of the social hierarchy. Similarly, they are critical of, yet at some level complicitous with, those on top of that hierarchy." Rafael's immediate concern is the dominance of the English language in Filipino postcolonial intellectual circles, but his remarks apply with equal force to Hispanized *ilustrados* of the late nineteenth century. See Rafael, "Writing History after EDSA," in *White Love*, p. 199.

[20] See John Schumacher, S.J., *The Propaganda Movement, 1880-1895* (Manila: Solidaridad, 1972); also John Schumacher, S.J., "The 'Propagandists' Reconstruction of the Philippine Past," in *Perceptions of the Past in Southeast Asia,* ed. Anthony Reid and David Marr (Canberra: Asian Studies Association of Australia, 1979), pp. 264-280.

[21] Jose Rizal, *Sucesos de las Islas Filipinas por el Doctor Antonio de Morga, obra publicada en Mejico el ano de 1609 nuevamente sacadea a luz y anotada* (Paris: Libreria de Garnier Hermanos, 1890). See

romantic yearning for a lost Filipino golden age that has resounded in the nationalist imaginary ever since.

Yet a cultural-nationalist imaginary that was romantically fixated upon the vanished precolonial past could not readily assimilate the *contemporary* presence of internal "others" within the body politic of the imagined community. As *ilustrados*, members of an illustrious generation that had achieved unprecedented levels of education and cultivation in Europe as well as in Manila, elite nationalists were deeply invested in the ideological equation of modern civilization with Europeanization that undergirded colonialism itself. To appreciate the consequences of this stance, it is helpful to consider how nationalists regarded those sections of the archipelago's population that had rejected or eluded the colonial project of Hispanization. These included the mountain-tribes of Northern Luzon, the Moros (Muslims) of the southern island-region of Mindanao, and the "apostate" *remontados*, individuals who had withdrawn from lowland settlements and repudiated tribute, labor, and religious obligations in favor of life in outlaw communities in the hills.[22]

Some of the most inspired *ilustrado* writings artfully inverted and deployed colonial stereotypes of *remontado* superstition, Moro "fanaticism," and tribal paganism as a form of colonial critique and to gesture towards a potent but inaccessible national past. For instance, Rizal's famous novels, *Noli me Tangere* and *El Filibusterismo*, drew a morally freighted contrast between the oppression and venality of the Spanish colonial *pueblo* and the promise of its mountainous outskirts, which was repeatedly (but tragically) figured as the site of protean possibilities for moral regeneration, as well as for individual and collective liberation. It is important to note, however, that early nationalists did not advocate the rehabilitation and inclusion of actually existing internal others who fell short of the *ilustrado* model of creole cultivation which they themselves embodied. Instead, the most powerful of their cultural-nationalist writings subverted the derision of Filipino natives in Spanish colonial discourses by reframing figures of native superstition and irrationality into glyphs for a lost condition of precolonial cultural and material plenitude. This technique did less to transform the ontological status of the "native" than to construct a new kind of expertise and epistemic authority for Filipino elite nationalists themselves.[23] Foregrounding their own creole cultural sensibilities as sources of authority for constructing the imagined community, the early cultural nationalists did not repudiate mestizo privilege, but rather parlayed it into the authority to define which natives were fit to represent the nation.

This tradition of nationalist thought—a kind of nativism without natives— remained influential following the cataclysmic events of the Philippine revolution (1896) and the Filipino-American War (1896–98) that ushered in US colonial rule. While prosecuting a drawn-out campaign of "pacification" that lasted till 1901, the

---

also the commentary of Ambeth Ocampo, "Rizal's Morga and Views of Philippine History," *Philippine Studies* 46,2 (1998): 184-214.

[22] John Schumacher, "Syncretism in Philippine Catholicism: Its Historical Causes," *Philippine Studies* 32 (1984): 251-72.

[23] This was, for instance, true of the Filipino nationalist-folklorist Isabelo de los Reyes. On de los Reyes, see Benedict Anderson, "The Rooster's Egg: Pioneering World Folklore in the Philippines," *New Left Review*, March-April (2000): 47-62; W. H. Scott, "Isabelo de los Reyes, Father of Philippine Folklore," in *Cracks in the Parchment Curtain* (Quezon City: New Day, 1987), pp. 244-65; Paul Kramer, "The Pragmatic Empire: US Colonial Anthropology in the Philippines, 1901-1916" (PhD dissertation, Princeton University, 1998).

architects of the new imperial project enlisted the support of Filipino elites and permitted them to monopolize the spoils of the newly introduced system of electoral politics.[24] Even as revolutionary nationalist identifications were being kept alive by popular commemorative practices, elite and official strategies were ironically also contributing to the further saturation of Filipino society by rhetorics of cultural nationalism. Mestizo privilege was deployed in novel ways, as elites mustered nationalist imagery and pro-independence rhetoric for the benefit of voters, all the while working behind the scenes to deepen and extend their own ties with US officials and institutions.[25] At the same time, given the US rationalization of the imperial project as one that offered paternalistic tutelage in democracy, it was a logical step on the part of the colonial officials to sponsor certain public expressions of nationalism. Their decision to commemorate *ilustrado* nationalists rather than popular revolutionaries was reflected in official sponsorship of a pantheon of Filipino national heroes and a patriotic civil religion, articulated in measures that ranged from the installation of Rizal statues in public squares around the country, to the promulgation of a national history curriculum depicting the Revolution as nobly inspired, but compromised by popular ignorance, fanaticism, and irrationality.[26] In short, a complex mix of ideological factors and material interests led to the politicization and paradoxical entrenchment of a place for Filipino cultural nationalism. For Filipino elite nationalists, however, the figure of the "native" was no more accessible as an actually existing figure for positive identification than it had been during the Propagandist period. Thus, while T. H. Pardo de Tavera, the lionized intellectual of his generation, described Filipinos as conforming to a Latin "national type," with few or no indigenous characteristics, he also gloomily dismissed Latin culture as "a heritage of ignorance" that had bequeathed to Filipinos a superstitious and anti-scientific temper. Other elite nationalists exhorted Filipinos to regenerate themselves morally and materially as a nation by combining Hispanic civilization with American modernity.[27]

The Commonwealth period (1935–45) and the decades following independence in 1946 saw the institutionalization of forms of official nationalism that concretized and routinized national identity through such tools as history textbooks, town planning, the patronage of performing and fine arts, and language policy. Starting in 1936, a series of official attempts promoted the development and use of a national language based on Tagalog and known as Pilipino or Filipino, which soon established itself as the basis of national literature and as the lingua franca of the film

[24] See the studies in Ruby R. Paredes, *Philippine Colonial Democracy* (Quezon City: Ateneo de Manila University Press, 1989).

[25] Reynaldo C. Ileto, "Orators and the Crowd: Independence Politics, 1910-1914," in *Reappraising an Empire: New Perspectives on Philippine-American History*, ed. Peter W. Stanley (Cambridge, MA: Harvard University Press, 1984), pp. 85-114; Paul D. Hutchcroft, "Colonial Masters, National Politicos, and Provincial Lords: Central Authority and Local Autonomy in the Americans Philippines, 1900-1913," *Journal of Asian Studies* 59,2 (2000): 277-306.

[26] See Reynaldo Ileto, *Knowing America's Colony*, vol. 19, *Occasional Paper Series* (Manoa, HI: Institute for Philippine Studies, University of Hawai'i at Manoa, 1999).

[27] Trinidad Pardo de Tavera, "The Heritage of Ignorance," in *Thinking for Ourselves: A Collection of Representative Filipino Essays*, ed. Vicente M. Hilario and Eliseo Quirino, Filipiniana Reprint Series (Metro Manila: Cacho Hermanos, 1928), pp. 3-18.

industry and of humbler media such as radio and comics.[28] In the 1950s and 1960s, while popular cultural forms flourished as hybrid composites of Hispanic, American, and local influences, many metropolitan cultural critics scorned them as derivative manifestations of colonial consciousness. Aside from rehearsing an elegiac nativism focused upon the past rather than the present, such critiques also reflected insecurities about the Philippines' lack of monumental architecture, courtly traditions, or classical literature to match such cultural-nationalist resources as Borobodur and Angkor Wat in neighboring Indonesia and Indochina.[29] At about the same time, within national scholarship, the sketchy outlines of the primordial Filipino native began to be filled-in by disciplines like archaeology, ethnoscience, linguistics, and folklore—approaches which had an edge over written history in their ability to trace continuities of *langue duree* between precolonial native autochthons, colonial *indios*, and postcolonial Filipinos.[30]

The elusive figure of the native has also been at the center of the dynamic and often contentious field of national history scholarship. Long dominated by a focus on the exploits of elite Filipinos and colonial figures, the field was transformed from the 1960s onwards by revisionist approaches that called for history to be rewritten from Filipino perspectives.[31] This shift was inaugurated by a renewed focus upon the popular dimensions of the 1896 revolution against Spain. Retaining the epochal status assigned to it in previous accounts, a circle of scholars inspired by historian Teodoro Agoncillo expanded the definition of the event to encompass the study of "proto-revolutionary" regional and local uprisings against Spanish and US colonial authorities that occurred both before and after 1896.[32] Quick to be institutionalized, the new historiography rescued scores of local rebellions from obscurity and added new heroes to the civil-religious pantheon of the national history curriculum. In this way, historians refocused Filipino history upon figures of colonial resistance, bringing an unprecedented vividness to the previously shadowy figure of the colonized native. Whereas the *ilustrados* of an earlier generation had located the essence of nativeness in a lost golden age of precolonial plenitude, history writers in the 1970s embraced Filipinoness as a historically constituted identity smelted within the forge of colonial relations.

Partly inspired by this undertaking, another group of metropolitan scholars began to articulate a specifically *Filipino* approach to social science. "Pilipinolohiya," a collaborative project whose epicenter lay at the Diliman campus of the University of the Philippines, aimed to displace the hegemony of neocolonial discourses depicting Filipino culture and society as imitative and acculturated. According to Zeus Salazar, one of its central figures, Pilipinolohiya goes beyond a purely

---

[28] Andrew B. Gonzalez, *Language and Nationalism: The Philippine Experience thus Far* (Quezon City: Ateneo de Manila University Press, 1980).

[29] Renato Constantino, *Identity and Consciousness: The Philippine Experience* (Quezon City: Malaya Books, 1974).

[30] William Henry Scott, *Looking for the Prehispanic Filipino, and Other Essays in Philippine History* (Quezon City: New Day Publishers, 1992); Arnold Molina Azurin, *Reinventing the Filipino: Sense of Being and Becoming: Critical Analyses of the Orthodox Views in Anthropology, History, Folklore, and Letters* (Quezon City: CSSP Publications, 1993).

[31] Reynaldo Ileto, "Outline for a Non-Linear Emplotment of Philippine History," in *The Politics of Culture in the Shadow of Capital*, ed. Lisa Lowe and David Lloyd (Durham, NC: Duke University Press, 1997).

[32] Ileto, "Outline for a Non-Linear Emplotment," pp. 99-100.

intellectual approach because it demands a commitment on the part of Filipino scholars to root themselves rhetorically within the national community through the use of the inclusive "we" (indexed by the pronoun form *tayo*, or "we, including you").[33] Previous modes of nationalist thought, it was argued, suffered from a Eurocentric bias rooted in the rhetorical stances of its authors, whose adoption of the exclusive modality of *kami* ("we, not you") entailed a consistently defensive stance of "explaining" the Philippines in Western terms. The act of trading the enunciative modality of *kami* for that of *tayo* is conveyed by the deliberate adoption of strategies such as publishing in Tagalog/Filipino, building careers within the Philippines rather than abroad, and adopting an "emic" discursive vocabulary for scholarly exposition. In these and other ways, Pilipinolohiyistas like Zeus Salazar, Prospero Covar, Virgilio Almario, and others signal that they have reoriented their discourse away from the West for the sake of fostering a *pantayo* ("we, among ourselves") perspective on Filipino history, culture, and society.[34]

While social historians chose to bring the native into view by focusing on anticolonial resistance, scholars using the culturalist methods of Pilipinolohiya opened up the terrain of lowland popular religiosity to reveal autochthonous cultural logics deep in the heart of garden-variety folk-Catholicism—making it thinkable, perhaps for the first time, for elite scions of mestizo privilege to identify with their own "nativeness." Both perspectives were compellingly synthesized in Reynaldo Ileto's path-breaking work of social history, *Pasyon and Revolution*. In that book, Ileto retraced the history of nineteenth-century popular uprisings in the Tagalog provinces through songs, speeches, and pamphlets rather than standard colonial sources, brilliantly arguing that indigenous cultural logics of potency and reciprocity were crucial in mobilizing *indios* around charismatic popular leaders identified with the suffering and persecuted Christ. The wide audience gained by *Pasyon and Revolution* was partly due to the fact that it was not positioned or received exclusively as an academic study of history; in the introduction, for instance, Ileto drew direct parallels between peasant rebellions of the past and contemporary popular opposition to Ferdinand Marcos's authoritarian regime.[35] Yet the enormous impact of the book within Filipino circles might equally be seen as the result of the book's success—whether deliberate or not—in bringing together the themes of anticolonial resistance and cultural nativism, two themes which had thus far been salient but separate concerns in cultural-nationalist thought. Whereas the quotidian world of lowland Catholic religiosity had previously been assumed to be the most deeply colonized and therefore "inauthentic" domain of Filipino life, this very area was now revealed to be a rich, previously untapped source of materials for the construction of an indigenous national history and identity.[36]

---

[33] Zeus Salazar, "The Pantayo Perspective as a Discourse Towards Kabihasnan," *Southeast Asian Journal of Social Science* 28,1 (2000): 123-152.

[34] For a response to Pilipinolohiya's intellectual project, see Niels Mulder, "'We, Amongst Ourselves,'" in *Filipino Images: culture of the public world* (Quezon City, Philippines: New Day Publishers, 2000), pp. 115-45.

[35] Reynaldo Ileto, *Pasyon and Revolution: Popular Movements in the Philippines, 1840-1910* (Quezon City: Ateneo de Manila University Press, 1979), pp. 1-3.

[36] For a landmark discussion of the disappearance of the Christian lowlands as an object of legitimate cultural analysis, see Fenella Cannell, *Power and Intimacy in the Christian Philippines* (Cambridge: Cambridge University Press, 1998), pp. 241-5.

Significantly, several chapters of *Pasyon and Revolution* focused upon the Mt. Banahaw region, not only as the scene of a major uprising against the Spanish authorities in 1841, but also as a theater of persistent guerrilla resistance to occupying US forces between 1898 and 1910. Moreover, in explaining how he was able to reconstruct the "mentalities" of historical uprisings, Ileto acknowledged his debt to the ethnographic research of anthropologists Prospero Covar and Robert Love, specialists in folk-religious movements of the Mt. Banahaw area.[37] It may not be an exaggeration to say that the unnamed folk-religious practitioners consulted for these works were active, if indirect, interlocuters in the reformulations of "nativeness" undertaken by metropolitan scholars during the 1970s. At any event, the publication of *Pasyon and Revolution* also served to bring Mt. Banahaw's popular pilgrimage tradition to general attention. During the 1980s, metropolitan visitors began to visit the mountain in significant numbers, and residents of Santa Lucia also date a significant upsurge in devotions by pilgrims from all over the Philippines to this period. Not of course that this moment constituted any kind of "first contact"; as we shall soon see, the locality had already been entangled for some time in symbolic and material traffic with the metropolis. Yet up to this point, the issue of how to define and represent the figure of the Filipino native had been all but confined to the largely self-contained space of metropolitan public culture. By the 1980s, however, discursive effects associated with constructions of nativeness within cultural nationalism worked their way onto the local scene in Santa Lucia. Let us now return our attention to the locality and to those events.

ENUNCIATING THE NATION LOCALLY

If "mestizo privilege" defined metropolitan elite culture during the Spanish colonial period, in a rather different sense it shaped the social landscape of rural localities through the administrative logic of the Spanish colonial state. All over the Christian parts of the archipelago, the basic administrative unit or pueblo formally encompassed two kinds of social space—a town center or *poblacion,* whose church, convent, and municipal buildings were surrounded by the dwellings of the Hispanized *principalia* (native elite) and artisans, and a rural hinterland, where peasant producers were typically dispersed across hard-to-access *barrios* and *sitios* (villages and hamlets). Inhabitants of both spheres were subjected to socially graduated religious, labor, and tribute obligations. However, the presence of thickly forested, hilly, and only nominally administered terrain at the fringes of many pueblos allowed for the emergence of a kind of third space located beyond the moral surveillance of priests and the policing resources of the civil authorities.[38] The Mt. Banahaw region, located at the crossroads of three provinces in one of the areas where Franciscan missionary settlement was most intensive, qualified as one of many such sites of alternative or outlaw sociality. It offered the most subordinated of

---

[37] See Prospero R. Covar, "Religious Leadership in the Iglesia Watawat ng Lahi," in *Filipino Religious Psychology,* ed. L. Mercado (Tacloban: Divine Word University, 1977); "Potensiya, Bisa at Anting-Anting," *Asian Studies* (Diliman), xxviii (1980): 71-78; *Larangan: Seminal Essays on Philippine Culture* (Manila: National Commission for Culture and the Arts, 1998); Love, "The Samahan of Papa God."

[38] My discussion of this notion of a "third space" draws upon the work of Ileto, "Outline of a Non-Linear Emplotment," pp. 114-19.

the inhabitants of nearby *pueblos*—those with least access to mestizo mores—the appealing prospect of freedom from labor and tribute as well as ample means of subsistence, including hunting, swidden-clearing, and the occasional bandit sortie or cattle-rustling raid. Cut off from their parishes, most of those who become *remontados* adopted the practice of *pwesto*-veneration; indeed, in the nineteenth century, evanescent social groupings periodically coalesced here around spiritually potent hermits who lived in specific *pwestos*, a development that greatly dismayed Spanish officials in the area. Fear of the danger of subversion posed by outlaw Christian social formations ran particularly high after 1841, when Banahaw became the scene of a popular uprising that resulted in the execution of two hundred *indios*, followers of a Christ-identified former lay catechist named Apolinario de la Cruz.[39]

Following the transfer of sovereignty from one colonial power to the next, parts of the Banahaw foothills (including large tracts within the *pueblo* boundaries of Dolores) were made available to elite Filipinos seeking to develop profitable cash crops. Within a generation or two, migrants from neighboring provinces had settled in Dolores's back country, where they cleared forests, planted coconut groves, and intermarried with residents of neighboring towns, eventually establishing a new *barrio* called Santa Lucia. Meanwhile, the tradition of *pwesto*-veneration was kept alive through its adoption by new settlers, as well as by the pilgrims who were trickling in from all corners of the Tagalog region in the 1920s. Among them was a young man who would eventually bring the Ciudad Mistica movement to Mt. Banahaw; decades later, his daughter, the Suprema, would play host to Filipino national figures while becoming one herself.

Colorful accounts handed down among present-day Ciudad Mistica followers tell of how Amador Suarez first came to Mt. Banahaw on the run from authorities in his home province of Batangas, where he was sought in connection with armed robbery and cattle rustling. His sojourn at the mountain was transformed by the mystical experience of hearing a Voice speak to him in the wilderness. After directing him to the discovery of power-filled amulets (*anting*) and imparting secret knowledge in the form of Latin spells (*orasyones*), this Voice assumed the shape of a messenger bird and led Amador to several sacred *pwestos*, where he meditated and undertook ascetic rigors. Thus transformed from a petty outlaw into a spiritually potent leader, Amador left Mt. Banahaw to lead a colorful life which included marriage and fatherhood, an abortive career in local politics in his home town, and a stint of several years spent as a traveling healer dispensing amulets, working cures, and winning followers.[40] During this itinerant phase, a chance encounter with a young girl-prophet named Maria Bernarda Balitaan on the island of Mindoro led him to join her following—apparently a parent-movement of the contemporary Ciudad Mistica, now long-defunct—and set him on a path that would eventually lead back to Santa Lucia. After the girl-prophet's death, Amador became convinced that the the "mystical city" or earthly paradise repeatedly glimpsed by her in visions would come to pass atop Mt. Banahaw. Sometime in the 1950s, Amador took his followers to Santa Lucia and legally registered a religious corporation in the name of Maria Bernarda's vision. Soon he was overseeing the day-to-day affairs of a church

---

[39] See Ileto, "Light and Brotherhood," in *Pasyon and Revolution*, pp. 37-91.

[40] These details of Amador's biography are based on the account of Guellermo M. Pesigan in *Dulang-Buhay ng Bundak Banahaw: Karanasan ng Ciudad Mistica* (Quezon City: University of the Philippines [Diliman], 1992), pp. 21-8.

and residential compound built from cash and labor contributed by followers and patrons.

A time of privation when villagers rarely set foot in the parish church or *poblacion* school, the 1950s and 1960s were a period when, as an elderly resident once put it to me, Santa Lucia was "not yet civilized." This comment indicts the municipality's neglect of the village, which was not connected by road to the town center of Dolores; it also indexes villagers' internalization of the attitudes held by the *principalia* or town-dwelling elite towards themselves. The hardscrabble lives of villagers, like those of their nineteenth-century *remontado* forbears, were an anathema to the Hispanized mores of those living only a few kilometers downhill. Few things captured the contrast more starkly than villagers' apparent preference for worshipping at the mountain rather than in church. Townspeople in Dolores still recall parish priests making good on threats to withhold communion from those who even visited the *pwestos*.[41] Yet in villagers' narratives of local history, it was thanks to Amador's supernatural potency and charisma—itself strengthened by association with the Banahaw *pwestos*—that Santa Lucia's state of deprivation came to be ameliorated in the 1960s. A single landowning family held tenancy contracts with the majority of Santa Lucia's residents, including Mistica followers; Amador gained the trust of both landowners and villagers and was able to mediate between the two sides. Meanwhile, regional politicians began to seek Amador out for healing or to procure *anting* for themselves. Such accounts are in keeping with a frequently noted aspect of Filipino political culture: the need for leaders to project personal reputations for masculine prowess in warfare, virility, and leadership. Eventually, working in concert with a mayor of Dolores, Amador succeeded in directing a series of infrastructure building projects—involving the construction of roads, schools, basketball courts—into Santa Lucia as well as the town center. To this day, villagers recount the story of how the savvy Amador convinced the government to build the village a road in the same breath as they narrate tales of his *kapangyarihan*, including occasions when he healed the terminally ill with a touch or multiplied a handful of rice into a feast for a hundred.

While Filipino politicians' predilections for accumulating tokens of spiritual potency are seen by some scholars as being guided by a premodern or residual logic for legitimizing social authority, I would also link it to the rise of cultural nationalism in the Filipino public sphere. In the early 1960s, Isabel Suarez became the ceremonial leader or Suprema of the Ciudad Mistica. In subsequent decades, both father and daughter captured the attention of historians and anthropologists seeking to promote a decolonized Filipino national consciousness, and Mt. Banahaw's folk-religious sects and popular pilgrimage tradition became key sites for the elaboration of Pilipinolohiya. One of the first scholars to enlist Amador Suarez as a research informant was Prospero Covar, author of a distinguished study of the major Rizal cult in Laguna province. Covar's Geertzian symbolic accounts of key cosmological concepts in the world-view of worshipers at Mt. Banahaw inspired other

---

[41] As we have seen, official attitudes have changed enormously since the historic reforms of the Second Vatican Council. I personally know priests who have celebrated mass in the *pwestos* in order to demonstrate the Church's repudiation of previous stigmatization of popular religiosity.

researchers.[42] A steady dialogue between the Ciudad Mistica sect and the Filipino academy ensued, fostered in part by an annual summer institute in ethnographic methods, which Covar himself organized and directed for students on the premises of the Ciudad Mistica in Santa Lucia. This institute continued to yield term papers, masters' theses, and articles on the ceremonies, doctrines, prayers, and liturgical music of the Ciudad Mistica well into the 1990s. Several key monographs were also published. In addition to Reynaldo Ileto's previously noted, influential work, *Pasyon and Revolution*, one might mention Consolacion Alaras's feminist exploration of matriarchal elements within several folk-religious movements, and Guillermo Pesigan's dramaturgical exploration of the Ciudad Mistica's ceremonial forms.[43]

By the late 1980s and 1990s, a thickening swirl of symbolic representation had sedimented Mt. Banahaw as a site of personal, spiritual, and national self-realization in the metropolitan imaginary. As John Sidel has written, diverse expressions of popular national consciousness surged exuberantly into public culture after the 1986 overthrow of the authoritarian regime of Ferdinand Imelda Marcos. Articulating a distinct form of national subjectivity, movies, comics, literature, Pinoy Rock, and even e-mail-circulated jokes all brought forth images of a "new native" whose self-evident Filipinoness, lying in the realm of embodied tastes and everyday practices, seemed untroubled by scholarly concerns with authenticity.[44] It was in this context that first-person accounts of pilgrimage in the print media and depictions of *pwesto* sojourns on TV began to attest to the spread of Mt. Banahaw's fame in metropolitan circles beyond the halls of academe. As the acclaimed artist Santiago Bose produced a series of canvases inspired by experiences in Banahaw's *pwestos*, adherents of middle- and upper-class New Age movements began to repair to Mt. Banahaw's *pwestos* for astral-cleansing and *chakra*-balancing retreats.[45] A visit to Santa Lucia—preferably coupled with a private audience with the Suprema—became almost *de rigeur* for those sections of Manila's chattering classes seeking to explore their national heritage off the beaten track.[46]

---

[42] For examples, see Teresita B. Obusan, "The Mt. Banahaw Prayer: Amang Makapangyarihan," *Philippine Studies* 37 (1989): 71-80; Rene D. Somera, "Pamumuwesto of Mount Banahaw," *Philippine Studies* 34 (1986): 436-51.

[43] Consolacion R. Alaras, *Pamathalaan: Ang Pagbubukas sa Tipan ng Mahal na Ina* (Quezon City: Bahay Saliksikan ng Kasaysayan, University of the Philippines, 1988). Guillermo M. Pesigan, *Dulang-Buhay ng Bundak Banahaw: Karanasan ng Ciudad Mistica* (Quezon City: University of the Philippines, 1992). Also noteworthy are Floro C. Quibuyen, *"And Woman will Prevail over Man"*: *Symbolic Sexual Inversion and Counter-Hegemonic Discourse in Mt. Banahaw: The Case of the Ciudad Mistica de Dios* (Honolulu: University of Hawai'i at Manoa, 1991); and Vicente Marasigan, S.J., *A Banahaw Guru: Symbolic Deeds of Agapito Illustrissimo* (Quezon City: Ateneo de Manila University Press, 1985).

[44] John T. Sidel, "From Pugad Lawin to Pugad Baboy: The Making of the 'New Native,'" in *Philippine Politics and Society in the Twentieth Century: Colonial Legacies, Post-colonial Trajectories*, ed. Eva-Lotta Hedman and John T. Sidel (New York: Routledge, 1998), pp. 140-65.

[45] James A. Beckford and Araceli Suzara, "A New Religious and Healing Movement in the Philippines," *Religion* 24 (1994): 117-141.

[46] See for instance, Ben P. Banyaga, "A 'pamumuwesto' of rebirth," *NCCP Newsmag*, April-June 1995, p. 51; Jorge M. Sabino, "A mystical, magical trip through Laguna land to Banahaw," *Philippine Teachers Bulletin* 2,3 (1985): 13; Yvette S. Reyes, "Mt. Banahaw: Where Women are Priests," *Mr and Mrs*, April 18, 1995; Rita R. Villadiego, "Heeding the Call of Banahaw," *Sunday Inquirer Magazine*, March 19 1989, p. 14; Emmie G. Velarde, "Mountain of Tranquility," *Sunday Globe Leisure*, May 12, 1991 1991, p. 11.

While Amador's death in 1982 occurred before the peak of metropolitan interest in Mt. Banahaw, Isabel would prove expert at managing this attention. In contrast to her father, who embodied a kind of charisma that was essentially face-to-face or personalistic in its scope, Isabel was called upon to develop an understanding and strategic self-awareness of mediated celebrity. It is noteworthy that she has drawn heavily upon the Hispano-Christian institution of the female *santa* or holy woman in crafting her public persona, whereas her father Amador gained metropolitan attention as a seeming embodiment of premodern or precolonial cultural logics. Her reserved personal demeanor and avowed lifelong chastity, as well as the severe yet feminine robes in which she is usually attired, all identify her in the eyes of followers with a *madre* or nun. As befits her title, Isabel's charisma falls in the ceremonial or priestly mode, and is legitimized in terms of the sect's internal teachings, which depict the current pre-Apocalyptic moment as a precursor to the New Jerusalem and as an age when "women shall prevail over men."[47] Notwithstanding such heterodox teachings, the Ciudad Mistica's ceremonials and liturgy, which are officiated by female priests clad in habit and bearing miters and scapulars, attest to the sect's success in appropriating—indeed now, in these post-Vatican II times, monopolizing—the sonorous appeal of the old Latin Rite. It thus invokes a certain kind of familiarity or nostalgia in visitors above a certain age. The importance of the feel of orthodoxy to Isabel's self-projection is illustrated in the often-told account of her anointment, a story of quasi-divine election. When the previous Suprema stepped down in 1962, Maria Bernarda's spirit revealed its choice of successor to a council of elders specially convened to learn her bidding by mystical means. The tale is reminiscent of the narratives of medieval female mystics like Teresa of Avila, whose vocation was revealed to her by divine intermediaries within an event whose structure recalled the archetypical story of the Virgin Mary's Annunciation.

Yet Isabel Suarez's public persona also draws upon the authority of recent articulations of cultural nationalism. Her published remarks in a 1995 interview given to a group of teachers and students from the University of the Philippines illustrate this articulation well. When asked to clarify the teachings of her movement relative to other religions, she declared: "We in Ciudad Mistica believe that Mt. Banahaw is the altar of brave Filipino heroes like Rizal, Bonifacio, Aguinaldo, and del Pilar whose destiny it was to build the Filipino nation."[48] She went on to strike a stance that seemed to echo Pilipinolohiya's agenda of decolonizing Filipino culture and identity:

During the time of the Spaniards, Filipinos were made to venerate foreign saints. Why can't we take pains to honor our own martyrs? . . . What we do not like is the arrogance and decadence that foreign things and people bring with them. I will welcome foreigners to Ciudad Mistica, but I will talk to them only in Filipino.[49]

It is unclear whether this group of academics, her audience, recognized the imprint of discourses disseminated at their very own institution within the Suprema's

---

[47] Quibuyen, "And Woman will Prevail over Man."

[48] Mozart A.T. Pastrano, "Interview with a Suprema," *Sunday Inquirer Magazine*, October 8, 1995, p. 9.

[49] Pastrano, "Interview with a Suprema."

words—or, for that matter, whether they appreciated the Suprema's savvy deployment of images of nativeness circulating within the Filipino public sphere, which enabled her to realize "symbolic capital" from her position as a folk-religious leader within this interview.[50]

In the end, Isabel Suarez is an individual of modest rural origins who has become an icon of national culture in certain circles. Yet whether she realizes it or not, the success of her simultaneously strategic and syncretic incorporation of nativeness and Christian mysticism into her public image draws on concerns and contradictions within Filipino nationalist thought that stretch back for well over a century. Metropolitan portrayals particularly emphasize the Suprema's hybrid persona and the ability of her enigmatic demeanor to evoke foreign associations; the Filipino-American poet Luis Francia, for instance, describes Isabel's face as possessing "the aquiline features of a Maya priestess."[51] It would thus appear that Isabel has become the somewhat unlikely bearer of a form of mestizo privilege, insofar as she is able "to speak as though one's identity were overlaid with a multitude of other possible selves."[52] One might even say that Isabel has successfully enlisted the power of paradox made available by recent discourses in order to constitute herself as an "autochthonous mestiza."

Significantly, the Suprema's incorporation of cultural-nationalist idioms into her self-enunciations tends to go unrecognized by middle-class metropolitan observers. A telling illustration can be seen in Heather Claussen's recent ethnography of a Benedictine convent in Manila, many of whose middle-class postulants were associated with feminist or activist causes during their student days.[53] Because the Suprema was known to them as a compelling icon of indigenous spirituality and female power, many of these postulants regarded her as a latter-day embodiment of a precolonial female shaman or *babaylan*. On one occasion, Claussen joined her informants on an overnight spiritual retreat to the Ciudad Mistica, the highlight of which was a discussion between the postulants and the Suprema. Strengthened by this encounter, the postulants' esteem for the Suprema served as an outlet for them to express their resentment of continuing male authority and female marginalization within the Church.

Strikingly, Claussen's informants seem to have displayed little self-consciousness of the forms of privilege implicit in their own romanticization of the Suprema as an embodiment of national and spiritual authenticity. Similarly, in reading first-person narratives of Banahaw pilgrimage published in the English-language press, I have been struck by the absence of any real sense of estrangement or confrontation with the unexpected in these accounts. These examples suggest that undertaking a pilgrimage to Mt. Banahaw may work more to mirror metropolitan discourses back to urban sojourners than to expand their ways of thinking and feeling nationally. Does this blindness to the co-produced nature of Mt. Banahaw's aura of authenticity translate into yet another manifestation of mestizo privilege? At the very least, I

---

[50] On symbolic capital, see Pierre Bourdieu, *Distinction: A Social Critique of the Judgment of Taste* (Cambridge, MA: Harvard University Press, 1984), p. 291.

[51] Luis Francia, "Mount Banahaw: Mystical Mountain," *Mabuhay Magazine*, April 1992, pp. 14-19.

[52] Rafael, "Taglish," p. 167.

[53] Heather L. Claussen, *Unconventional Sisterhood: Feminist Catholic Nuns in the Philippines* (Ann Arbor, MI: University of Michigan Press, 2001), pp. 136-77.

believe that the incorporation of this particular locality into the reimagining of national culture reproduces tensions at the heart of Filipino nationalism. New constructions of nativeness within national-cultural discourse have indeed contributed to the celebrity and empowerment of "subaltern" actors like Isabel Suarez. But precisely because her successful cultivation of celebrity and external patronage depends not just upon personal charisma or peculiarities of Filipino political culture, but upon the dissemination of cultural-nationalist discourses through an elite-dominated metropolitan public culture, admiration for the Suprema may well mask the continued operation of mestizo privilege among the Filipino urban intelligentsia—a group whose members, to once again borrow Rafael's words, find themselves "critical of, yet at some level complicitous with those on top of . . . [the social] hierarchy."[54]

CONCLUSION

Like other recent writings on Filipino society, this essay has sought to understand the prominence of nationalist thinking in the Philippines following its post-authoritarian return to democracy. I have already mentioned Sidel's insightful discussion of the rise of "mirthfully irreverent" figurations of the new native in various genres of popular culture after the "People Power" movement of 1986.[55] While noting that these genres are not necessarily egalitarian in sensibility or freely accessible to all, he depicts them as a bulwark against authoritarian propaganda and official efforts to manipulate political consciousness. Such efforts are the subject of a recent book by Greg Bankoff and Kathleen Weekley on the state-sponsored celebrations that marked the 1998 centennial of Filipino independence. Bankoff and Weekley see the palpable rise of official-nationalist ideology in the Philippines as echoing recent articulations of "Asian Values" seen elsewhere in the region; more pointedly, they also critique it as a compensatory response to the erosion of state sovereignty under neoliberal policies of governance.[56] While differing in focus and argument, the works of Sidel and Weekley and Bankoff attest—as does this essay—to the lively circulation of what might loosely be called cultural-nationalist images and tropes within the communicative space created by Filipino national institutions, including but not limited to the media and the academy.

Instead of confining the scope of my discussion to the space of discourse, however, I have approached public culture by exploring how discursive effects worked their way onto the ground of everyday life in a specific locality. To understand how cultural-nationalist discourses played out at Mt. Banahaw, I have found it necessary to both historicize as well as localize them. The main developments that led to the celebrity stature and social power of Isabel Suarez, the Suprema of the Ciudad Mistica, began during the 1970s. It was at this time that efforts by metropolitan intellectuals to decolonize Filipinos' knowledge of their own society, unexpectedly (and perhaps unintentionally) began to reshape social relations in Santa Lucia. Yet, as I have shown, the privileged place of the Suprema (and indeed of Mt. Banahaw itself) in the revisionist Filipino national imaginary makes sense only

---

[54] Rafael, "Writing History after EDSA," p. 199.

[55] Sidel, "The New Native."

[56] Greg Bankoff and Kathleen Weekley, *Post-colonial National Identity in the Philippines: Celebrating the Centennial of Independence* (Burlington, VT: Ashgate, 2002), pp. 9-36.

in the context of Filipino colonial history, which has bequeathed metropolitan intellectuals a sometimes contradictory dual fixation upon both precolonial origins and colonial resistance as sources of national identity. Rather than presenting a snapshot of public culture at a given moment, I have therefore felt it important to offer an account (however sketchy) of how "nativeness" has become sedimented over well over a century's worth of discussion among Filipinos regarding their own national identity. With this historical perspective in mind, one can see how a fleeting event such as a national politician's local appearance in the course of an election campaign reflects the influence of a recent and peculiarly metropolitan construction of "national culture." In a similar fashion, we can also appreciate how the Suprema's revalorization in public culture as an icon of native and subaltern Filipinoness ironically, if unintentionally, reasserts a form of metropolitan "mestizo privilege." This discursive effect becomes particularly clear if one considers the disaffection of many residents of Santa Lucia regarding Isabel Suarez, an antipathy that has everything to do with "material" anxieties over local resources rather than "spiritual" concerns with potency and cultural authenticity. The failure of local grievances against the Ciudad Mistica and its leadership to surface in the same elite press that regularly publishes first-person accounts of mystical sojourns at Mt. Banahaw culture is a telling illustration of the forms of privilege that bring certain perspectives to prominence while marginalizing others.

Yet developments on the local scene may be changing this. In the late 1990s, I watched as local residents in Santa Lucia joined forces with community organizers and metropolitan nature-lovers to form a non-governmental association, the Green Alliance for Mt. Banahaw. The increasing prominence of NGOs and new social movements in the Philippines is an important dimension of the post-authoritarian political landscape, and is characterized by advocacy in the names of both nationalism and global civil society. The objectives of the Green Alliance—formulated explicitly in terms of the 1987 Constitution—include mobilizing opposition to unsustainable development initiatives threatening local livelihood and ecology, as well as institutionalizing local stewardship over Mt. Banahaw's environmental and cultural diversity, understood as part of the national heritage. Recently, these objectives have brought the movement into open conflict with the Ciudad Mistica, drawing attention in the national press.[57] Such developments may indicate that alliances between local and metropolitan actors, forged in part under the influence of cultural nationalism, are now reimagining Mt. Banahaw along more utopian lines. Time will tell which discursive effects will peter out and which will ripple forth.

---

[57] Juliet De Loza, "Kulto nagtayo ng mansion sa Mt. Banahaw," *Abante*, March 24, 2000, p. 1; Delfin T. Mallari, Jr., "Farmers denounce powerful cult on Mt. Banahaw," *Philippine Daily Inquirer*, April 5, 2000, p. 16.

THE MODERNIST VISION FROM BELOW: MALAYSIAN HINDUISM AND THE "WAY OF PRAYERS"

Andrew C. Willford[1]

The ideology of the Malaysian state under the stewardship of Prime Minister Mahathir Mohammad (1981-2003) underscored a need for scientific advancement, economic development, "Asian values," and, at its center, a decidedly modernist interpretation of Islam. Islam has provided an "authentic" core to an imagined Malay identity that, arguably, belies its cultural heterogeneity and dependency upon state recognition and codification. But Islam has also inspired ideologies of resistance to the Malaysian state's pro-investment and pro-capitalist development policies. In response to the increasing number of Islamic critics of the government, particularly as manifested in the growth of Partai Islam seMalaysia (PAS) during the 1970s, 80s, and 90s, the state has promoted its own Islamization agenda aimed at moralizing economic and social policies through a modernist interpretation of Islam.[2] One consequence of this moralizing Islamic discourse has been an increasing reification of ethnic and religious boundaries through their bureaucratic codification and materialization in political representation.[3] This, in turn, has also produced an ethnic

[1] I wish to thank Kenneth George, Suzanne Brenner, and Deborah Homsher for their careful readings and insightful critiques. They are not responsible, however, for the shortcomings of this chapter. Field research conducted between June 1994-December 1996 was funded by the Wenner-Gren Foundation for Anthropological Research and the Southeast Asia Council of the Association of Asian Studies.

[2] See: Michael Peletz, *Islamic Modern: Religious Courts and Cultural Politics in Malaysia* (Princeton: Princeton University Press, 2002); Shamsul A. B. , "Identity Construction, Nation Formation, and Islamic Revivalism in Malaysia," in *Islam in an Era of Nation States: Politics and Religious Renewal in Muslim Southeast Asia,* ed. Robert Hefner and Patricia Horvatich (Honolulu: University of Hawaii Press, 1997), pp. 207-27; Khoo Bhoo Teik, *Paradoxes of Mahathirism: An Intellectual Biography of Mahathir Mohammad* (Kuala Lumpur: Oxford University Press, 1995).

[3] As Peletz (*Islamic Modern*) explains, the process of Islamization has much deeper roots, and is much more complex, than my gloss here indicates. Still, since the 1980s, Islamization, as wedded to pro-*bumiputra* (Malay) policies, has led to sharpening of ethnic divides, both in terms of their bureaucratic measurement and in terms of everyday sentiments. See Chandra

"field" in which everyday interactions in Malaysia are mediated by cultural and spatial distinctions, premised upon ethnic categories and stereotypes. Within this material and discursive field, Tamil Hindus have been placed at the political and cultural margins of the nation.

In this essay, I examine the case of a Tamil spirit medium, interpreting her spiritual aspirations and ambivalences from within the politically driven field of religious ideology and ethnic representation in Malaysia. I have elsewhere described how a growing stigma attached to Hinduism within state discourses and everyday stereotypes is increasingly resisted by Tamil Hindus through participation in public rituals and in Hindu reform organizations, albeit manifested in distinct class-based forms and not without ambivalence.[4] But in considering the case of a Tamil spirit medium, who through her complex negations and affirmations of Tamil Hindu identity is already at the margins of the marginal Tamil-Hindu community, we are challenged to rethink the binary assumptions that are pervasive in theories of hegemony and resistance in relation to the subject-constituting powers of state ideology. At the same time, we see the far reach of state-sponsored ethno-nationalist ideologies through this case. In her attempted surmounting of the symbolic order, I argue, we see, in microcosm, the very conditions that may induce a person to fixate on identity, producing its uncanny hold of the psyche. That is, I argue that in order to understand the passionate zeal of subjects possessed by the nation in ethnic terms, even in its negation, we must rediscover the radical insights of the dialectic, as formulated by Hegel, but also as transposed into psychoanalytic domains by Freud and Lacan.

INDIANS AS THE UN-MODERN

Within the Malaysian ethno-religious field, the location and representation of Hinduism within the state-sponsored discourse of Malaysian modernity produces an ambivalent repression and a displacement into the past of those elements within Malay culture deemed both pre-modern and un-Islamic. Malay cultural practices suspected of deriving from an Indian-Hindu source have been targets for reform or purging altogether. Mahathir himself wrote: *"Hinduism and animism . . . had shaped and controlled the Malay psyche before the coming of Islam . . . If the Malays were to become Muslims, these old beliefs must be erased and replaced with a strong and clear Islamic faith."*[5] This urgency was echoed by an interlocutor of mine, a Malaysian Chinese professional, who suggested to me that Hinduism resonates in much of Malay culture and in the unconscious beliefs of many Malays. He said that the government must suppress Hinduism, as it exists very "near the surface" of Malay consciousness.

Muzaffar, "Political Marginalization in Malaysia," in *Indian Communities in Southeast Asia*, ed. K. S. Sandhu and A. Mani (Singapore: Institute for Southeast Asian Studies, 1993), pp. 211-236.

[4] Andrew Willford, "'Weapons of the Meek': Ecstatic Ritualism and Strategic Ecumenism among Tamil Hindus in Malaysia," *Identities* 9 (2002): 247-280; "Possession and Displacement in Kuala Lumpur," *International Social Science Journal*, n. 175 (2003): 99-109

[5] Mahathir Mohammad, quoted in Khoo, *Paradoxes of Mahathirism*, p. 52. (Emphasis added.) While not isomorphic with a general Malay sentiment or subjectivity, Mahathir, being the principal architect of Malay-Islamic modernism, has had a profound influence upon everything, ranging from the semiotics of the capital city's skyline (and more recently, the design of Putrajaya, the new administrative capital), to the media campaigns to represent the utopian vision of a culturally authentic, yet totally modern, Malaysia.

This nearness, this recognition of Malayness within Hinduism, and vice versa, I argue, is a source of an ethnic uncanny, and drives (and reflects) a compulsion for (and of) ethnic categorization—that is, as fetishes. This displacement effect produces a fetish or metonymic desire, following Lacan, to freeze identity, and hence, magically masking its contingency and emptiness through the maintenance of stereotypical boundaries that are institutionally realized. Again, to quote Mahathir, regarding the need to reinforce core rituals, faith, and belief (*ibadah* and *aqidah*), he writes, "There is evidence that if these areas in the teaching of Islam were neglected, the old animistic beliefs *would again take control of the Malay mind.*"[6] The compulsion to repeat, in other words, masks the recognition of identity's fragile hold.

Under Mahathir's leadership, Islamic reform was a chief concern. The "identity" I have suggested above with regards to Malay-Islamic modernism has institutional referents which "reinforce" an aspired-to identity. While most would argue that the apparent naturalization of ethnicity in Malaysia deters multiethnic class alliances, this persistence of ethnic identification does not, therefore, represent the resilience of primordial ethnic ties. Rather, the actual fluidity of ethnic and religious boundaries—and the challenge to cultural and political legitimacy that it produces, particularly as experienced by those cultural elites who benefit from ethnic politics yet fear the violent upheavals that have swept neighboring countries—produces a fixation with codifying hierarchies of ethnic and religious difference. The magical effect, or fetish-quality, of ethnicity, as many scholars of Malaysia have noted, has masked the *Real* of class privilege and its arbitrary cultural justifications.[7] The rigid ethnic field that has emerged in Malaysia—itself a product of a colonial legacy of ethnic, class, and spatial segregation—suggests, or even belies, a more syncretic possible imagining; but such an alternative would, I argue, undercut the aspirations of postcolonial elites who have ruled Malaysia through ethnic politics while simultaneously exposing to the same elites (and their followers) a repressed cultural logic of ethnic fluidity that has been masked by the edifice of ethnic and status difference. The everyday representation and material experience of an ethnic Other, in other words, elides the relational and mutually transformative workings of identity as understood in Hegel's master/slave dialectic. As Freud has also shown, symbolizing the Other within, under certain pathological conditions, requires externalizing that uncanny presence most threatening to identity—that is, in its fixated-upon form. But the cultural imaginary that fixes identity does not make social reality outside of power and history, though the dialectical threads of the latter are produced in tandem with elements of the former. Therefore the stigmas that are attached to Hinduism cannot be interpreted outside of the material conditions facing Malaysian Hindus today, which, indeed, owe much of their existence to a history of indentured labor, colonialism, and ethnic policies productive of the "plural society."[8] Similarly, a class-differentiated resurgence of Hinduism in Malaysia must be

---

[6] Mahathir Mohammad, *The Challenge* (Petaling Jaya: Pelanduk Publications, 1986), p. 19. (Emphasis added.)

[7] This integration of Hegelian, Lacanian, and Marxian understandings of the dialectic, and the nature of ideology within the social, draws upon Slavoj Zizek's, *The Sublime Object of Ideology* (London: Verso, 1989).

[8] See Michael Stenson, *Class, Race, and Colonialism in West Malaysia: The Indian Case* (St. Lucia, Queensland: University of Queensland Press, 1980); and K. S. Sandhu, *Indians in Malaya* (Cambridge: Cambridge University Press, 1969) for the history of Indian indentured and wage labor within colonial and postcolonial Malaya.

understood in the context of material realities plaguing many Indians, in addition to the stigmas attached to the poor and the working class. That is, as Pierre Bourdieu has often argued, symbolic and material capital are convertible, and thus various distinctions produce and are produced within fields of material power. But when Bourdieu or Louis Althusser grant great subject-making capacity to state ideologies and habitus, respectively, others, perhaps most influentially, James Scott,[9] assume perhaps too much potential for disorder and subversion through everyday and/or ritual acts of resistance. While the latter implicitly invokes a rational subject, who, though clearly dominated, is not hegemonically constituted, the former often seem to locate subject-making powers beyond the grasp of human agency and resistance. Both approaches, as a result, lose sight of the relational and unstable nature of identity. And while both produce important social insights, we cannot gain access to the inner and contradictory compulsions of identity-fixation through the structural models of domination, and/or the rational subject who cleverly circumvents ostensible sociopolitical constraints upon himself or herself.

The story of the Indian diasporic community in Malaysia, I contend, must be anchored within the negative and dissonant ethnic politics of the Malaysian nation-state. In particular, the disavowal of the Indic or Hindu past, as noted above, in the crafting of the modern Malay Muslim subject, as witnessed above in Mahathir's words and policies, has had an impact upon the sentiments of Indians who are sensitive to this veiled temporalizing discourse surrounding Hinduism.[10] But rather than representing the latter in detail, here, I will focus upon the case study of a Tamil spirit medium and in that way follow the analytic progression from macro-perspective to micro-. The medium's story, I hope to convince you, serves as an instructive window into the ambivalent politics of identity within the Tamil Hindu community—which, in turn, offers us a critical vantage point from which to assess the modernist nation-building project, albeit, and necessarily, through the looking-glass, or from below. While acknowledging the idiosyncratic nature of my encounter with the medium, I maintain that one method of gaining access to state ideology is through attention to individual subjectivity, ethnographic transference and countertransference notwithstanding.

"A LOT OF EVIL GOES ON DOWN THERE."

The distance between high- and low-status Tamils was exacerbated by colonial labor discourses and recent political and economic changes, and is reproduced through contemporary social and cultural practices.[11] The marks of an elite are partially ascribed, but also cultivated and enhanced, through education, occupation,

---

[9] See James Scott's *Domination and the Arts of Resistance* (New Haven: Yale University Press, 1991), or *Weapons of the Weak* (New Haven: Yale University Press, 1986). See Pierre Bourdieu, *Outline of a Theory of Practice* (Cambridge: Cambridge University Press, 1977); and Louis Althusser, "Ideology, and Ideological State Apparatuses," in *Mapping Ideology*, ed. Slavov Zizek (London: Verso, 1994), pp. 100–140.

[10] This is a theme I take up in greater detail elsewhere. I have argued that in Mahathir's negations of the past, elite Indians come to recognize themselves as the anterior future of Malay authenticity.

[11] Andrew Willford, "Cage of Freedom: The Politics of Tamil and Hindu Identity in Malaysia and Bangalore, South India" (PhD dissertation, University of California, San Diego, 1998).

material possession, fashion, and taste. To the elite, community space is a less salient component in identity formation (both as a self-definition and as ascripted). In contrast, the "Indians," as an ethnic category within the discourse of a multiethnic nation, are identified, and themselves identify with, specific Indian spaces. The Indian working class and poor patronize such places in order to obtain desired products within a narrow proximity; but they also congregate in order to feel part of the in-group in a society in which they, as, in their minds, the least admired of all Malaysians, often perceive themselves to be second-class citizens. Their social interactions and consumption of popular culture through mass media produce a somewhat recognizable Tamil identity. This phenomenological construct, however, is not only a set of dispositions, tastes, fashions, and idioms,[12] but also becomes internalized as part of the individual's self-identity through repetition. Class position is obviously a highly determinant factor in the reproduction of social and cultural identity. That is because identity is not only a self-construct; rather, a person's identity is partially shaped by far-reaching discourses ascribed by more dominant groups. That is, "Indian space" and identity are also perceived to be stigmas by both Indians and non-Indians. It is in the "little India" where the stereotypes of Tamils are produced and/or perceived to exist. Indeed, the title to this section comes from a warning I received from an Indian university student about conducting research in Brickfields, an Indian enclave.

A number of tangible social problems exist in many urban Indian enclaves. There are many urban poor, including squatters and the homeless. Like any urban area with substantial poverty, there are the associated problems of depression, suicide, crime, prostitution, alcoholism, and violence (both domestic and criminal). While not wanting to legitimize the racializing discourses that are already oppressive, I am suggesting that these stereotypes, as unfair as they often are, also reflect deep anxieties that permeate the working-class Tamil enclave.[13]

There is also a perception that the competitive urge to conform and keep pace with others is another reason why working-class Tamils are unable to raise their standard of living. All of this suggests that their marginalization, both economically and socially, contributes to a profound sense of insecurity, which in turn generates the conforming and competitive behavior which further stigmatizes the community. Moreover, this discourse motivates the elite Indians to distance themselves through various cultural and spatial distinctions (i.e., living outside the enclave). The stigma

---

[12] In George H. Mead's formulation, one might call this the "generalized Other" that becomes, ultimately, part of the socially mediated self. The generalized Other is the internalized image of oneself as seen through the eyes of others—that is, the interpretation of what other social actors expect of oneself. This self-image, which forms a portion of the personality, is constructed socially through symbolic interactions. George Herbert Mead, *Mind, Self, and Society*, vol. 1 (Chicago: University of Chicago Press, 1934). Bourdieu's notion of habitus could be similarly defined, though the self-reflexivity suggested by Mead is not addressed by Bourdieu, though, importantly, power and class are. Lacan's phenomenological "mirror" of the Other, while certainly similar to Mead's constructs in theorizing a socially mediated self, departs radically in its dialectical, and hence conflictual, model of the social self. In that sense, too, Lacan, as he himself claims many times, is closer to a Freudian position, whereas the ego-psychologists, drawing upon symbolic interactionism and Mead, have departed from Freud's position regarding the doubling of the self and the theory of the unconscious being the "discourse of the Other . . . in which desire is bound up with the desire for recognition." Jacques Lacan, *Ecrits: A Selection* (New York: Norton, 1977), p. 172.

[13] A more detailed account of these stereotypes appears in Willford, "Cage of Freedom."

or "evil" associated with "Indian" space is also reflected in unorthodox religious behavior. Spirit mediums are able to utilize this environment while also exhibiting symptomatic markers of it. We can see how mediums are able to gain symbolic empowerment; and, at the same time, we see how an "illegitimate" form of Hinduism concerns and, perhaps, hauntingly taunts those professing the "highest" exegetical understandings in the religion. This reveals the ambivalence and uncanny nature of identification on both ends of the orthodox-unorthodox, higher-status and lower-status continuum. I suggest that the lack of ideological closure or certainty concerning one's status contributes to the social distancing that plagues and divides the Indian community.

The financial and social insecurities felt by many Tamils in working-class areas are believed by critics to result in a culture of competitiveness and conformity. Debts are all too common, and a certain amount of despair pervades the lives of many. A so-called "culture of poverty,"[14] with its concomitant lack of self-esteem, is witnessed through inward-directed criticism the Tamils themselves offer about their community. Higher-status Indians are themselves very conscious about the stigmas associated with being "Indian." One college-educated Tamil-Malayalee mixed woman put it rather bluntly to me:

> The Tamils are the worst race . . . *I mean the Klings.* You have chosen the *worst of all people* to study. When I was studying at UM [University of Malaya] the Tamil students used to make fun of me because I wanted to be different. I joined drama class and had lots of Chinese friends, and for that they made me feel weird.

While she went on to further condemn "the Tamils," it is clear that she is referring to the conforming behavior of working-class Tamils ("Klings") as opposed to behaviors of the elite, more Westernized Indians. Working-class Tamils also critique their own community in varying degrees. I often heard complaints from Tamils about the status of their community. One shopkeeper would ask me why his people were "so superstitious" (visiting astrologers, mediums, and gurus) and "foolish" with their finances (buying unnecessary luxury items such as cars, gold, and cell-phones). Another young man complained bitterly about the Tamil love affair with films as well as their embrace of "gangsterism" and "corrupt MIC leaders."[15] Yet another, possessing a college degree, spoke to me of Tamil "cultural defects" and their apparent lack of "intellectual capacity." One encounter was as memorable as it was depressing for me. An elderly Tamil woman approached me on the street in Brickfields and asked me to come to her flat to see her daughter. She explained to me that her daughter was "very pretty" and *"just like your wife"* (she had seen me with my wife before); but, she claimed, "there are *no good Indian men left* . . . They are all very naughty."

Working-class Tamils are not only affected by this collective low self-esteem, but are also witnessing the slow death of their neighborhoods. The "Malayanization"

---

[14] See D. Jeyakumar, "The Indian Poor in Malaysia: Problems and Solutions," in *Indian Communities in Southeast Asia*, ed. K. S. Sandhu and A. Mani (Singapore: Institute for Southeast Asian Studies, 1993), pp. 405–437.

[15] Indians are often blamed for being disproportionately involved in organized crime. The MIC, or Malaysian Indian Congress, is the principal political party representing Indians within the ruling Barisan National coalition.

and Islamization of urban space had significantly reduced the Indian flavor of sections within Kuala Lumpur.[16] Economically, the rising cost of rent and real estate in Kuala Lumpur has made it difficult for ethnic enclaves to survive the pressures of capitalist development. Brickfields is being transformed into a business corridor adjacent to downtown. Luxury apartments have sprung up in the neighborhood for the last ten years. The massive "KL Sentral" rapid transit and railway station, which was being constructed in Brickfields during the mid-1990s, promised to be the main transportation artery for the metropolis and nation.[17] Accordingly, luxury hotels, apartments, and shops were slated for construction nearby, and many have since been built. Old shophouses, housing quarters, and hundred-year old terrace houses have been slated (or rumored to be marked) for demolition. The hundreds of Indian squatters have been or are being displaced as new projects continually tear away at the fabric of the old community.[18]

Spirit mediums are gaining popularity in Malaysia's urban working-class areas. While this tradition originated in the villages of Tamil Nadu and was commonly seen in the estates, the urban areas are now witnessing more such activity. This is probably due to two main reasons: the arrival of mediums looking for work in urban areas after the closures of many plantations left them without clients; and the insecurities associated with marriage, financial, and other worries discussed above have led many to search for supernatural assistance.

There are a number of spirit mediums in Brickfields. Most give advice on personal problems including, but not limited to, health, marital abuse, and infidelity, missing persons, and mental illness. Still others help people who were possessed by evil spirits. Those who become spirit mediums are usually of low social status, with little or no formal education, and generally are poor. Through their spiritual activity they are able to gain some livelihood, and, perhaps, respect from others. Mediums receive payment through gifts received or, in some cases, through nominal fees charged for their services. Those locally reputed to be "powerful" are able to survive through their practice. Higher-status Indians often speak disparagingly about

---

[16] An "Indian" revivification of Brickfields is occurring today, as compared to the mid-1990s, when I observed a decline. New and ornate temples have been built, or modified, and more Indian restaurants have been established. The presence of hundreds of Indian nationals, who work primarily in the IT (computer technologies) sector, has added new business to the Indian enclave, as many have chosen to live in Brickfields because of the ambience and availability of food, temples, music, video stores, and so forth. While this change has been taking place, the gentrification process continues, with more high-rise apartments replacing low-cost flats and squatter areas. The new Brickfields, while retaining an Indian flavor, is not the same as the old Brickfields, in many instances.

[17] KL Sentral was completed more recently and now serves as the main railway and Light-Rail Transit station.

[18] Evidence of social and psychological strain among Tamils is perhaps indicated by an alarming suicide rate. Between 1990 and 1993, 1,700 Indians were reported to have committed suicide. In comparison, suicides among Malays and Chinese were only 343 and 568 respectively during the same period. Selvi Gopal, "Subculture of Poverty," *The Sun Megazine* [sic], July 16, 1995, pp. 7-8. While this is not to say that Malaysian Indians are a community with a deathwish, there is a clear sense of crisis and fear among the working class and poor. This statistic is all the more frightening when one considers that the total Indian population is significantly lower than that of the Malays and Chinese. Perhaps it should be noted, however, that suicide is a common passive-aggressive theme in Tamil cinema when other avenues for vengeance have been exhausted. I do not mean to imply, however, that it is culturally condoned.

mediums, calling some frauds and criticizing others as demonic. Still, many with whom I spoke believed that the mediums were indeed "powerful" even if they themselves would be unlikely to turn to one for assistance. Occasionally higher-status Indians sought the services of mediums, but for the most part their clientele came from the working class. There is an analogous relationship between the growing popularity of spirit mediums and the increasing incidence of vow-taking witnessed at Thaipusam, the most popular ritual and collective pilgrimage among Hindus in Malaysia.[19] They are similar in that both primarily involve the working class; and perhaps most importantly, both the penitents and the clients of spirit mediums are seeking some tangible empowerment through divine intervention. They differ in that Thaipusam is clearly a collective as well as a private expression of this search for empowerment, whereas spirit mediums attend to private needs. The collective assertion is also readable as an assertion against, or negation of, the ethno-symbolic order. That is, the political dimension of spiritual ecstasy or transcendence may be considered. In contrast, the instrumental nature of the "spiritual power" is more pronounced in the medium-client transaction. Nevertheless, the connection between ethno-symbolic power—that is, Malay Islamic nationalism—and class/status hierarchies suggest too a relationship between mediumship and the political. One can, for example, see the politics of consciousness itself being dramatized through the ambivalent actions and thoughts being enacted by a spirit medium, as well as among those who patronize and/or recoil from them. The following case study of a spirit medium in Brickfields illuminates this idea.

"THE WAY OF PRAYERS"

I entered Valli's world through the recommendation of an employee at a Tamil bookstore who told me that she knew a "woman who was a god." Naturally intrigued, I agreed to follow her to the woman's flat after work one evening. Valli lived in a three-bedroom flat above the main road in Brickfields. Entering her place, I was immediately struck by the size of the shrine in her living room. One whole wall had been converted into an altar with color pictures of the Hindu deities. While Shiva and Sakti were prominent, there were also shrines for other gods, and surprisingly, for Guru Nanak, the founder of Sikhism.

Valli greeted me warmly and promptly served tea and snacks. She told me that it was no accident that I had visited that night, explaining that she would be performing "special" *puja* (worship) that evening. Sharing her flat with her was a close disciple, together with her fourteen-year-old son and a twenty-seven-year-old niece. Valli described herself as thirty-five years old, but still a "beautiful lady." She said that she had inherited a "power" from her mother, adding that all the women in her family "had the Amman" (were possessed by the Mother Goddess, or Sakti). To me, however, she seemed quite normal, articulate, and talkative. Her disciple, whom she simply called "Akkah" (older sister), warned me that I would witness a complete transformation of Valli's personality when she became possessed by Kaliamman (the Goddess as Kali).

---

[19] See Raymond Lee, "Taipucam in Malaysia: Ecstasy and Identity in a Tamil Hindu Festival," *Contributions to Indian Sociology* 23,2 (New Delhi) (1989): 317-337, and Willford, "Weapons of the Meek."

That night was *Ikyam*—the festival of the full moon, when it is believed by Tamils, so I was told, that the *nagas* (snakes) mate. According to Valli, it is considered auspicious to perform *pujas* to Kaliamman at this time; and in particular, it is believed to be a good time for unmarried women to ask Amman for a husband. That night the woman from the bookshop and her friend, Valli's niece, were to perform the *Ikyam* ritual. Prior to the ritual, two small banana trees inside clay pots were purchased. The two women, together with Valli and her disciple-friend, bathed. Valli seemed concerned that rules of purity in the living-room shrine were strictly observed. In addition to bathing, the two women put on yellow *sarees*, the color used during festivals by pilgrims performing a vow. They also untied their hair and removed all bodily adornments. Valli put on a black or dark blue *saree* with gold trim and a yellow-gold blouse underneath. Prior to this, margossa leaves were draped from the altar in order to keep "evil spirits away." Various Indian sweet dishes were also prepared and placed before the shrine together with apples, oranges, and starfruits.

Prior to the ritual, Valli went into her room for about ten minutes of quiet prayer. She emerged and asked her niece to bring the cassette stereo with the "Amman songs." The niece joked and said that she was "Amman's DJ." This title seemed appropriate, as the niece played a cassette of Amman and Sakti songs derived from Tamil films.[20] Valli was deep in concentration for about ten minutes. Suddenly, she began to breathe in and exhale deep and slow breaths. The breaths became slightly faster and more audible. She was in deep trance. "Akkah" nudged me, smiled and said, "that is not Valli."

Valli (or Kaliamman?) rose, rocked her head back, laughed, and took a cup of milk that had been offered at the altar and poured it over her head (*pal abhishekham*). She then took the remainder and drank it, spilling it from the sides of her mouth. In a deliberate manner, she wiped her lips with her arm and laughed eerily. In this act she (as the goddess) was indicating acceptance of the milk offering—otherwise anointing oneself and consuming the deity's food would be sacrilege. "Kaliamman" spoke in Tamil only, in contrast with Valli, who mixed Tamil with English. She directed the bookstore clerk and her niece to prostrate before her. Then she instructed the two young women to each tie a *tali*[21] string around the banana tree. After tying the *tali*, both were told to take the *parang* (machete) and cut the tree. Both in turn forcefully hacked their respective banana trees in half with the sharp blade. After completing this, they prostrated again before Valli and received the blessings of the Goddess. Valli placed her right hand upon their downward-facing heads and held it steady for about thirty seconds as she imparted the blessing.

Another ritual was then performed. This one was an *Agni Homa* (fire sacrifice to Agni, Lord of Fire) for "Akkah," Valli's disciple. "Akkah" had explained to me

---

[20] In Tamil films, Amman or Sakti songs are often utilized when a female or group of females is about to be empowered or possessed by the goddess. The songs build in rhythmic intensity and climax as the deity is manifested in the person or persons.

[21] A *tali* is a golden string with a gold pendant which is used in the Hindu marriage ceremony to denote literally the "tying of the knot." At the exact moment of marriage, the groom ties the string around his bride's neck. Three knots must be tied for the marriage to be completed. The wife is expected to wear the *tali* for the remainder of her life. After a certain time has elapsed, the string may be replaced with a permanent gold chain. A Hindu priest must conduct the transfer of the *tali* pendant's power to the gold chain. After completing the ritual transfer, the yellow string is usually thrown into the sea.

earlier that evening that she had accepted Valli as her Guru after suffering much in her life. She told me how she came from a wealthy Punjabi family and had been married to a doctor. About ten years earlier, her husband had fallen ill and eventually died. She lost her house and much of her savings trying to raise her son. After her son was a bit older, she had resumed her career as a school teacher. After suffering much, she eventually came to meet Valli. She explained to me that all her suffering had begun after an incident in her shrine room. While praying, a snake had entered the room, terrifying her. A snake catcher was called, and the snake was disposed of. Shortly thereafter her husband had fallen ill and died. Later, after telling her sad story to Valli, she was told that she suffered because she, "Akkah," had rejected her, Valli. Valli explained that the snake had actually been her, as the goddess, in the form of a serpent. "Akkah" claimed not to have believed the medium's proclamation at first, but later she came to realize that Valli knew much about her life, especially during her possession trances. "Akkah" also told me that her life had vastly improved since accepting Valli as her Guru. She added that she knows it sounds "unbelievable," but insisted that she spoke the truth.

The *Agni Homa*, "Akkah" explained, "was rarely done and quite dangerous if done improperly." Valli had constructed a small, cross-shaped brick fire-pit in her living room. This was positioned before the living room altar. Upon it, Valli drew sandalwood *Saivite* markings (the *tripendi*, or three horizontal lines). A number of camphor cubes were placed into the pit and lit. Valli carefully added camphor cubes to maintain the flame. Once the fire was regulated, she began to ladle ghee (clarified butter) into the flames. Speaking little, the entranced Valli instructed her disciple to pour seven handfuls of grain into the fire. She then blessed "Akkah" in the same manner described earlier. After completing this ritual for her, Valli invited all of us present in the room (the niece, her friend, "Akkah"'s son), myself included, to throw seven handfuls of grain into the flame. When it came to be my turn, my seventh handful produced a loud popping sound in the fire. Upon hearing the sound, Valli cried out and fell back on the floor behind her. As she lay there on the floor, tears appeared in her eyes. "Akkah" and the others looked concerned. After a few minutes, Valli was lovingly "revived" by her disciple. Once she had regained normal consciousness, Valli explained that the Amman had left her body at that exact moment.

Valli and "Akkah" told me that I was very "lucky" to have come that particular evening because they had waited several years to agree to do this "dangerous" ritual. I was slightly surprised myself to see a spirit medium perform a ritual usually associated with priestly orthodoxy. This orthodox discursive positioning by Valli, along with her earlier attention to details of purity and authority, suggested to me that this was an individual who had a ambiguous relationship with orthodox Hinduism.

A few days later I again visited Valli. I found her then, and in subsequent visits during the next six months, to be more than willing to tell me stories from her childhood and adult life. I could scarcely stop her from pouring out her life history, punctuated by certain "supernatural" events inflected by Tamil Hindu mythology and folklore.

In addition to the main altar described above, Valli had a smaller and "fiercer" looking altar devoted exclusively to Kali. This Kali is bathed in a red light and flanked on the right by a sharp brass trident; it is given meat offerings, as opposed to the milk and fruit offered before the main altar. Valli's niece dutifully played the devotional songs as her aunt gradually became more entranced. Valli once again fell into trance with a slight rocking motion, in time to the music, and deliberate breathing. This time, however, she held her foot in the camphor flame for what seemed to be a long time (perhaps twenty seconds). She then grasped the trident and placed it in the flame. After it became blackened by smoke, she inserted the trident into a plate of mutton curry and rice. She then sat down and devoured the food offering with both hands.[22] After taking the meal, the possessed Valli distributed a handful of rice to each of us which we were to accept as *prasadam* (sanctified food). She then cut some limes and covered the open sides with *kunkumum* (red ochre powder). Finally, she called each one of us to accept Kali's blessings. Again, she summoned me last and had me stand before her for many minutes. She placed her hand upon my forehead as if she were going to place the *kunkumum* (the mark of Kali's blessing) on my brow. But in contrast to the way she blessed the others, she held her hand for a long time in silence. While still in trance, Valli told "Akkah" that I possessed "Krishna's power." She did not address me directly, speaking to her disciple who in turn told me that I should come the following day for more "prayers." I was instructed to bring twenty-five limes with me the following day.

I came prepared with the limes, and after Valli had submerged herself in the same ritual-invoked trance, my *puja* began. Valli began cutting limes, covering them with *kunkumum,* and then proceeding to throw them into the camphor flame. Twice she had me lean forward while she circled my head with a lime three times in a clockwise direction. She then said that I could now ask anything from the goddess. To her surprise, I answered that there was nothing that I wanted to ask of Kaliamman. To my surprise, she then prophesized that I would *"go the prayers way"* without the Amman's help. She added that "Krishna's power" was very strong in me and would eventually lead me to turn back from my worldly commitments unless she, as "Amman," intervened.

Valli suggested that I purge Krishna's hold on me through another *puja*. She instructed me to collect the following items for the ritual: a framed "photo" (picture) of Krishna; three fruits (she suggested grapes, oranges, and apples); a jasmine flower garland; eleven limes; one packet of incense; ten cubes of camphor; one packet of *kunkumum*; three *manjals* (turmeric roots); and six glass bangles. The exactness of her instructions inflected orthodoxy and priestly knowledge. She assured me that Krishna's *puja* was very "powerful and dangerous" and warned that only "Amman's power" was strong enough to "fight the god." Other markers of orthodoxy included the adherence to vegetarian food offerings and her announcement that she would not eat meat on the day of my ritual. Also, she informed me that I would have to be shirtless and wear a *veshti* (white sarong) during this ritual—a practice usually reserved for the strictest of *Agamic* or orthodox temples.

The ritual itself lasted about an hour. After her trance had commenced, Valli began to cut the limes and placed them before the image of Krishna. She arranged the jasmine garland (*mala*) around the picture and offered the fruit and incense together with a silver cup of milk. Following this, she placed a sandlewood and *kunkumum pottu* ("third eye") upon the deity's face.

Even before these common acts of worship, Valli had burned the camphor cubes in her brick fire-pit. She had then asked me to remove my shirt and pants and to tie the *veshti* around my waist. In another orthodox convention, she asked me to

---

[22] Indians usually eat only with the right hand.

perform the *arati* before the Krishna image, after which she tied a yellow string (which she had prepared with turmeric powder) around my neck (*tali*) and instructed me not to remove it for three days. I was told to walk around the fire and makeshift Krishna shrine nine times while holding a small flickering clay lamp filled with ghee. After I had completed this, Valli had me sit before her. She sprinkled holy water on my head, placed a *mala* around my neck, smeared *kunkumum* on my forehead, and, lastly, handed me a blossomed lotus flower together with some fruits, a packet of *kunkumum*, and assorted flower buds. She instructed me to take the Krishna "photo" home and place the flowers and fruits before it.

Valli fell out of trance after completing the ritual. She stood up, her body stiffened, and she fell backwards into the arms of "Akkah," who was prepared to catch her. After returning to "normal consciousness," she warned me that I must faithfully perform *puja* to the Krishna "photo" now that the god's "power" inhabited the image after this ritual. By propitiating the deity, she explained, I could keep him happy and use his power to protect my household; however, if I failed to perform the *puja* regularly, Krishna would bring ruin to my domestic life. She also added that I should never let anyone pray to this "photo" except for myself. For her part, Valli appeared to be exhausted, claiming that the battle between Amman and Krishna had been intense, but that Amman had prevailed in convincing Krishna to let me live my life.

If we unravel my apparent Faustian tryst with Krishna as directed by the medium, the ritual suggests an ambiguous and contested relationship between Valli and Hindu orthodoxy, while also positioning the Indological orientation of the anthropologist. The following interpretation cannot be separated from the asymmetrical, yet dialectical, nature of our interaction. Still, I would argue that we can learn about Valli's marginal relationship with orthodox Hinduism through her manipulation of symbols in the ritual involving me, though her symptoms are partially and temporarily displaced. But at the same time, she is aware that her authority with me (as eager anthropologist searching for "authentic" mediums) is different than it would be with an orthodox Hindu.

Valli's "battle" with Krishna reveals her ambivalence regarding this deity. While Valli did possess a portrait of the infant Krishna on her wall, it was not part of her prayer shrine. Yet after encountering my alleged "Krishna power," she embarked on a theological interpretation that brought the god into her cosmological realm, and eventually onto her prayer shrine, as we will soon see.

Krishna is worshiped primarily by Vaishnavites,[23] and in Malaysia, this would be limited to higher-status groups such as Malayalees and Tamil Brahmins. It is not surprising, however, that Valli associates me with Krishna after our first couple of meetings (no arrogance implied!). Prior to her rituals, Valli and I had spent a few hours getting to know one another. I had explained my interest in Hinduism and imagine that I must have seemed to her to possess a considerable amount of "book-learned" Hinduism. Though she was literate in Tamil and understood spoken English, she had not read many of the canonical texts in Hinduism. Making this into

---

[23] These are worshipers of Vishnu and his incarnations. Krishna is considered an avatar (incarnation) of Vishnu. Krishna is often honored in household shrines and in some temples, but in comparison with Murugan, Mariamman, or Ganesha, his popularity is less visible. Ashrams and other neo-Hindu organizations will usually teach Krishna's gospel, the Baghavad Gita, through lectures and classes. Thus, on the whole, Krishna worship is associated with middle-class devotees who are English educated.

a virtue, she would tell me that she was never taught how to perform effective rituals, but somehow, "miraculously," she knew exactly what to do and when to do it. Also, she "knew how to help the people" through a divine intuition. While asserting the superiority of the "divine gift" over "book-learned" religion and the orthodox proprieties suggested by it, she was intrigued to find a *"velaikaran"* (white man) who took "her" religion seriously enough to make personal sacrifices[24] in order to study it first-hand. I believed that her response to me not only revealed that she was impressed to some degree by my interest, but also illuminated her own reverence for Hindu propriety, even while it simultaneously generated the "battle" within her, a battle marked by her effort to assert her superior spiritual "power," as granted by the goddess. This ambiguity, in turn, is born out of the social marginality of her life experiences in modern Malaysia. But first, back to the imagery of Krishna in Valli's world.

When attributing Krishna-power to me, Valli locates me within the Brahminical or orthodox tradition. But her disdain for orthodoxy, born out of her low position in the Hindu social hierarchy, was more ambivalent than either of us anticipated. Rather, my position as foreigner (and therefore a person less likely to share orthodox disdain for the practitioners of "lower forms" of the Hindu religion) provided for a dialogic ethnographic space. That is, Valli was to discover a new "reverence" (although partial and ambivalent) for Hindu orthodoxy through the opportunities her association with me provided. Had I actually been an Indian Brahmin or other high-status Hindu, such interactions would have been unlikely.

Valli, although often ridiculing Brahmins, swamis, and vegetarians, expressed an interest in visiting temples and ashrams, as well as in attending cultural functions usually associated with the higher-status groups. Clearly, Valli wished to appear "legitimate" in her knowledge of Tamil and Hinduism as my interlocutor, while also wishing to attend such functions with my assistance, relying on my legitimacy as foreign researcher. In this negation of social (and spiritual) marginality, the desire for recognition—both mine and from clients/disciples—reveals a doubling of self and desire for singularity, or a fixing of self and other that transcends (in fantasy, but actually suspends) their dialectical tension. This is what Lacan refers to when he writes that "desire is a metonymy."[25] In this struggle or desire to overcome duality, as Hegel argued, prefiguring both Lacan and Heidegger, *"any victory is defeat,* since what the one consciousness gains it loses in its opposites . . . since it is a consciousness of the opposite as its essence, a consciousness of one's own nothingness." (emphasis added)[26] The moment of negation and self-certainty cannot surmount, and indeed provokes, the uncanny effect of recognition, in which the source of one's being is revealed as both transcendent, yet contingent. Valli cannot

---

[24] Valli had noted that my interests and related actions were incompatible with what a "normal" woman would want from a good husband. By this she meant that financial security and children were the first priorities in a marriage. Indicative of Krishna's "destructive power" in my life was my temporary move to Malaysia. She also thought me "ascetic" in my mainly vegetarian diet, which in her mind is associated with Brahmins and orthodoxy. She would make fun of me, calling me *"samiyar,"* which can mean anything from a shamanic medium to an orthodox Hindu swami; perhaps this indicated a deliberate blurring of spiritual hierarchies on her part.

[25] J. Lacan, *Ecrits: A Selection*, p. 175.

[26] Georg Wilhem Friedrich Hegel, *Phenomenology of Self-Consciousness: Text and Commentary,* commentary by Leo Rauch and David Sherman (Albany: SUNY Press, 1999), p. 36.

surmount this paradox. That is, the act of surmounting the other, the source of her own recognition, is simultaneously a form of self-annihilation in the mimetic appropriation of orthodox forms. Moreover, in that desire for an impossible transcendence, a transgressive, indeed, *corporeal reality* drives the fantasy behind the fetish-point of fixation, as we will see below.

At times Valli would ridicule "Brahmin"[27] men as "womanish." "Men should act like men," she would tell me, perhaps also commenting upon the androgynous appearance of Krishna in popular art. She leveled her most angry comments at Brahmin priests in the temples, telling me that when she "saw their greedy faces" she "wanted to kill them." But killing them was not enough, she would joke with a crazed expression, she wanted to "cook their balls and eat them." Here she was assuming (in parody, I think) the angry and blood-lustful aspect of Kali against the vanities of "proud" men, and, perhaps, too, revealing the transgressive erotic desires that are provoked in and by her negation of "womanish" men.

The hostile challenge to orthodox authority also extended, at other times, to men in general. She would sometimes suggest that Amman longed for the crushing defeat of "Indian men." On more than one occasion she said that she tried not to walk the streets in Brickfields because when she saw an Indian man's face, she would become angry and feel the "Amman-power" coming into her. She told me that in her own life she had experienced rather unsatisfactory relationships with Tamil men. First, in her family, her brothers were "weak," succumbing to alcoholism, debt, and letting their wives "tell them what to do"; and in her own romantic relationships, she had come to prefer dating Chinese men because they treated her "as a lady."

Still, through, and perhaps in spite of, our conversations, she harbored an incomplete reverence for "book-learned" Hinduism. In particular, she seemed drawn to the ideas of neo-Hindu ascetics such as Ramakrishna, Vivekananda, and Sivanananda. Their ascetic "purity," and especially their *bhakti* (devotion) impressed her, she claimed. While certainly not learned in their writings, she would spend the afternoons reading their condensed works in the local Hindu magazines that I regularly purchased and often left for her perusal. She told me that I had awakened in her an interest in the *samiyar* (ascetic) way. The "battle with Krishna" had decisively moved her towards a serious, yet skeptical, interest in more prestigious forms of Hinduism. Looking beyond the face value of this newly awakened curiosity, however, I find that her desire to appear "authentic" and recognizable to me—the countertransference of my desire—must also be considered.

Valli sometimes accompanied me on visits to ashrams, temples, and religious societies. Within *Agamic* (orthodox) temples, she would perform the *archenai* (songs of praise) in the "proper" manner, buying a ticket like everyone else, and accepting the *prasadam* (sanctified offerings) from the *pusari* (priest). These actions were meant to demonstrate to me her "legitimate" knowledge, but they were also something more; this was an opportunity for her to explore her religion as it is practiced by those she most resents. It was as if she were re-evaluating her ambivalence to orthodox religion by temporarily separating the act of worship from her resentment of "Brahmins." She also visited The Divine Life Society, an ashram run by a swami

---

[27] Since there are actually very few Brahmins in Malaysia, I took her comments to be directed at the high-status Hindus who attended neo-Hindu organizations and participated in the fine arts, especially classical dancers and musicians, as well as orthodox priests (some of whom actually were Brahmins).

and *brahmacharis* (renouncer-monks training to be swamis). The Swami-in-charge was overseas at the time, but a young *brahmachari* granted us an interview. While I sought information on the organization, Valli spoke bravely of her "praying way" to the young monk. He listened patiently as she told of the many who seek her help, both financially and spiritually. She pleaded with him, explaining that she could not support so many people as she was only "a praying lady" of limited financial resources, and finally asked him if she could refer people to the welfare and medical services offered by the ashram. The monk gently smiled and assured her that she could always tell people to come to the ashram for assistance. After leaving the ashram, Valli repeatedly praised the young monk for his "gentleness" and "humbleness." At that time, it did not bother her that the ashram was patronized almost exclusively by high-status Indians.

In another ashram, Valli was given the opportunity to perform the *abhisheckham* (anointing of the god) at their *puja* for Krishna. She seemed thrilled and appeared to take the act very seriously. Later, however, she confessed to me that she was very nervous, and with hands shaking, almost dropped the ladle of sacred water standing in front of *"those kind of Indians"* (i.e., higher status). Valli, at one point, even said that she had not had opportunities to visit "places like these" before.

After these events, Valli began to discuss performing another *puja* to Krishna in her house. She told me that I needed to do so in order to receive his full blessings; but, more importantly, she explained that since I had taken the picture of Krishna from her house after the first ritual, a kind of spiritual void upon her shrine was created. That is, the god would be unhappy to have been invoked in a shrine-room and never thereafter honored and worshiped at that same shrine. In a ritual similar to the one described earlier, Krishna was reinstalled upon her altar (I had purchased another portrait of the god). Valli loved the picture and seemed to have changed her attitude somewhat to one less confrontational with the deity.

I began to wonder about my influence upon Valli after these events. While this had not been my conscious intention, it was obvious that my research had both sparked her interest in and given her an opportunity to see how the other side prays. It was also hard to know how much of her efforts were intended to impress me,[28] rather than reflecting a spiritual longing on her part—or how the contradictory desires fueled one another in dialectical tension. Aside from her attending temples and ashrams, we discussed Hindu theology. She also read neo-Hindu apologists in religious magazines. She agreed in principal with their non-dualistic philosophy and claimed to share in that knowledge directly. That is the reason, she explained, why she feeds crumbs to the ants, birds, and rats—for they are all part of God. On the other hand, she counseled her clients utilizing an animated cosmos in which very real spirits, gods, and demons played havoc with human lives. The inner "battle" between these contradictory theologies is consistent with the interpretive tension between the transcendent and immanent nature of God, which is common to the Tamil devotional tradition.[29] In Malaysia, this theological tension is inflected by class and status divisions, or a compulsion to differentiate and inscribe hierarchy. Only in Valli this tension was more profound, reflecting not only alternative interpretations,

---

[28] My wife certainly thought this was the case after meeting Valli and witnessing her prayers.

[29] See George Hart, "The Nature of Tamil Devotion," in *Aryan and Non-Aryan in India*, ed. Madhav Deshpande and Peter E. Hook (Ann Arbor, MI: University of Michigan Press, 1979), pp. 11–33.

but the stark contrasts between her social marginality and her insights drawn from the rich ambiguities of Hinduism—as well as a desire to "locate" and be "located" within the discourses of the ethnographer. When I asked her directly how she explained her contradictory beliefs, she told me that the "gods are real, and must be respected." She warned me not to mock the Hindu gods and goddesses. "Akkah" also confirmed that as a Sikh she had entertained earlier doubts, but now saw that the "Indian way" (e.g., Tamil-Hindu) of praying brought the "best results." Valli added, however, that there is "only one God."

The apparent ease with which she accepts the ambiguities of her theological positions belies a deeper anxiety within Valli. She would often mention her fears of being swept away in the "*samiyar* way" (living monastically).[30] Valli flatly stated that she "didn't want to meditate," preferring to enjoy her life. She poked fun at vegetarians and swamis, and added that she was young still and wanted to enjoy "meat and sex." But as mentioned earlier, she also felt compelled to observe "rules of purity" during rituals. Also, she was increasingly busy with a steady stream of new clients "with so many problems" that demanded her attention and unique "powers." Thus she was often required by her own beliefs to act "clean." She told me that she "can't go sleeping with men because I am a praying lady." Yet she resented the goddess's hold on her, often despairing over her lack of freedom to "enjoy life" as a young and somewhat free-spirited (from an orthodox Hindu perspective) woman. Indeed, she transgressed her lifestyle as a "praying lady" in her ongoing affair with a married Chinese man. So while resisting brahminical models, she finds herself entrapped within discourses of "purity," and suffers from the guilty conscience it generates. The inner tensions mounting from this ambivalent religious identity were evidenced in her public persona, which oftentimes posited the superiority of "Amman's power" over orthodox religiosity.

Aside from her many comments, one incident, perhaps best of all, clearly demonstrated her disdain for orthodoxy. Valli liked hearing devotional singing (*bhajans*) within temples, but she also easily slipped into trance or wept openly upon hearing the emotionally charged, lyrical, and intense rhythms. One temple that attracted a particularly large group of devotees for *bhajans* was a Lakshmi-Narayan (*Vaishnava*) temple in Kuala Lumpur. Every evening at six, *bhajans* and *puja* were performed for Lord Krishna. The devotees who attended this devotional service were generally middle-class. Malayalees, North Indians, and some Tamil Brahmins would attend. Very few working-class Indians felt comfortable in this temple. Nevertheless, Valli enjoyed hearing the songs and viewing what, in her words, was the "most beautiful Krishna" she had ever seen.

Upon entering the sanctum, the devotees were separated by gender with males on the right and females on the left. After a half-hour of meditation, followed by an *arati puja*, a tabla player began to play and was soon joined by a harmonium player who led the congregation into the first *bhajan*. Valli, deeply moved by song, swayed as she joined the chorus. On one occasion she quickly left the hall after ten minutes of singing. She later told me that she felt the "Amman entering her" and did not want to lose control in front of so many people. On another day, she did in fact lose herself completely during the singing. She fell into trance, stood up, and danced around the temple, much to the surprise of the other devotees. It is not uncommon to see this

---

[30] Recall, too, that *samiyar* is used to describe spirit mediums. Therefore, this could also be interpreted as a statement of ambivalence about her occupation.

behavior during a festival, or even during a *puja* in a low-status temple, but extremely rare to witness such a performance in a high-status temple, particularly during a Krishna *puja*.

While engaged in this dramatic display for the temple audience, she began to imitate classical dance steps. Her actual movements, of course, were not skilled or in any way "classical," but later Valli would claim otherwise and insist that she had, in fact, danced flawlessly in a manner only a trained dancer could manage. She reiterated to me that she, under normal consciousness, could not have performed like a "master" dancer.

Valli's trance had attracted much concerned attention from other devotees. She seemed to bask in the glow of their attention. An elderly gentleman tried to calm her down, and Valli seemed to slouch into his arms. Others rushed to observe as he lay her down on her back. The man, who seemed genuinely concerned for her welfare, asked others to make space around her. To my surprise, a few of the onlookers touched her feet, a gesture that would usually be unthinkable, considering her low status. Yet some of the high-status devotees were apparently uncertain about the authenticity of this possession, but sufficiently convinced to be moved to pay her respect usually reserved for a swami, parents, or icon of a deity. As was the case with her dancing, she later claimed with a boast that "all were frightened of her" because she clearly manifested "Amman's power."

As in her battle with Krishna, her possession in the temple revealed her ambivalent relationship with Hindu orthodoxy. When she tried to sing the devotional songs in the company of high-status Hindus in a manner consistent with an orthodox worship ceremony, her emotions had gripped her. What was it she was expressing through her trance? Was it anger? Resentment? Her spiritual power? Probably all of the above. What is significant, however, is that for all her ambivalence, she ultimately believed that her "power" was freely given from the goddess to her. There is thus no need for orthodox conventions regarding status and purity when approaching the sacred. Valli was asserting her spiritual authority over those who, in her mind, considered themselves to be among the more advanced spiritual aspirants in Hinduism. Furthermore, the fact that some, though clearly not all, considered the possibility that her possession was "authentic," and not staged, or worse, "demonic," clearly demonstrated how ambiguous the *bhakti* tradition is concerning the immanent and transcendent aspects of god. Valli was able to utilize this ambiguity to achieve brief moments of status-empowerment through the anxious recognition she received from normally higher-status Hindus. At the same time, this enactment was simultaneously transgressive of proper decorum and marked her as low status. Moreover, that she is possessed by the very thing she negates, the presumed spiritual ascendancy of higher-status Hindus, suggests a submission, on Valli's part, to a symbolic order that fuels her desperate strategy of "mastery"—a surmounting of hierarchy that ultimately subjects Valli to the reason of hierarchy. Her moment of empowerment, however brief and subversive, is also a moment of mimicry (of orthodoxy) and an evacuation of self in the act of possession.[31] But such a strategy would only be utilized by someone in a position of

---

[31] For excellent analyses of self-evacuation through possession outside of Malaysia, see Rosalind Morris's, *In the Place of Origins* (Durham: Duke University Press, 2000); Fenella Cannell's, *Power and Intimacy in the Christian Philippines* (Cambridge: Cambridge University Press, 1999); and Isabelle Nabokov's *Religion Against the Self: An Ethnography of Tamil Rituals* (New York: Oxford University Press, 2000).

extreme social marginalization. Valli's childhood and adult life sheds further light upon her less-than-harmonious relationship with Hindu orthodoxy.

Valli grew up in the Tamil estate town of Selim River, today about two hours' drive north of Kuala Lumpur. This area is known for the poverty of its predominantly Tamil residents, poverty resulting from estate closures and the buying out and consolidating of lands by multinationals. Automation and a greater emphasis on oil palm, as opposed to rubber, extraction has sent many rubber-tappers searching for work in towns and cities. Valli's brother, a security guard in Penang, confirmed her description of Selim River as a place where the Tamils "are left with a very bad circumstance and no proper water and electricity—only the temples are left untouched." Still, Valli spoke with a nostalgia for the rural lifestyle of the estate, with its surrounding jungle, often contrasting it to the "busy" life in the city. Though poor, her childhood had been full of enchantment and mystery. She told me that the "power" runs in her family. As a child she would see her mother get possessed by "Amman," and eventually her mother earned a reputation as a powerful medium throughout their estate. Her mother, she said, would drink chicken blood after performing animal sacrifices during *pujas* for her clients, a practice which Valli no longer approved of.

Valli explained that at an early age she knew she differed from others. While her friends loved to gossip in the village, she preferred to roam the jungle, climbing trees and catching small animals. She claimed that, on one occasion, she had caught, dismembered, and cooked a small bird while playing in the forest near her home. This sort of behavior, very unbecoming of a Tamil girl, distanced her from other children. Valli said that she grew weary of the world and knew early on that she desired a life "in the forest, with the birds and monkeys." Her social alienation reached its pinnacle at the age of nine when she was being chased by some other children. When she ran into the thick forest to hide, her foot got caught in a hole, and as her fright intensified, the "power" came to her for the first time. With the "Amman" inside of her, she was able to free herself from entrapment.[32] From that time onward, she began to see manifestations of her powers. Aside from feeling the goddess's presence, her dreams "always came true"; and she possessed an elaborate knowledge of rituals which came to her without training. Like her mother, she had inherited the powers.[33]

Valli's belief that powers ran in the family was further confirmed by tales of her grandparents, which she related to me. Valli's grandparents were from India. One day they were traveling by foot to another village in search of employment. They stopped to pray under a tree because there was no temple there. While praying, her grandfather had a vision instructing him to go to Madras. Upon arrival in Madras, he was offered employment in Malaya as a rubber-tapper by the British. Through prayer, Valli maintained, a desperate situation had been averted by the Lord. After arriving in Malaya, her grandparents were employed on an estate in Selim River,

---

[32] It is (too) easy to interpret this event in Freudian terms, with the act of being "caught" in the "hole" a repressed symbolization of a traumatizing sexual encounter. This, however, did not occur to me at the time, and thus I did not question Valli further concerning this event. That her "power" emerged in the rage of this event does, however, suggest that there is more to this story than meets the eye.

[33] Her sisters also believe they have "special powers," but they say that Valli has the "highest" powers of all in the family, except for the now-deceased mother. While I was doing research, Valli's niece, whom she was raising, also began to experience possession trances.

where her parents were also born. Her grandfather, she also claimed, knew exactly when he was to die. The day before, he asked his wife to "cook nicely and wear a nice *saree*" because he would die the next day. Similarly, he asked his children to sing and dance for him, after which he enjoyed a fine meal and said good-bye to his family. While they did not believe him, in obedience they complied with his wishes. To their shock, after completing his farewells, he lay down "and closed his eyes for good."

As mentioned, Valli's mother was unusual. Her blood sacrifices had earned fear and some respect from other Tamil laborers. But as a priestess of this variety, she was also avoided by others. Valli, her daughter, must have been somewhat isolated from other children as a result. Her father, on the other hand, did not have special powers, but he was a strict man who "never let anyone come to visit us in the house." He also only allowed the children to play outside with others for a short while every day. One can only imagine what impact this had on Valli's ability to make lasting friends.

Following the relative freedom of early childhood, Valli's responsibilities mounted after her father passed away when she was a teen. She was forced to leave school, which she greatly enjoyed, and work to help support the family. Her brothers, she said, were "weak" and did little to help the family or themselves. One brother became an alcoholic, while another drifted from job to job. It was up to her, the unmarried daughter (her two elder sisters had started families of their own), to support the family.

Valli worked as an office assistant in the Malaysian army. While this was a good job, she faced racial jokes and sexual innuendo. From these experiences, she concluded, the "Indians will all be dead" in Malaysia in a matter of ten years! She also grew wary of men. After leaving the army, she moved to Kuala Lumpur, where she found a clerical job within an American company. For many years she worked in the company, making friends with American workers, Malays, and a few Chinese. Indians, she claimed, were jealous of her popularity and success within the company. On the whole, however, she enjoyed these years.

Her social marginality within the Tamil community increased as she remained unmarried. A Tamil woman who is unmarried after the age of twenty-five is unlikely ever to wed. Moreover, being unmarried is a stigma, especially among working-class Tamils. She also found herself increasingly consumed with other people's problems (other family members and clients seeking her advice). As her "practice" picked up, she no longer had the time or energy to work full-time. Indeed, she bitterly complained that her powers were almost a curse now, forcing her always to open her house to clients and people seeking a place to rest for the night.

Perhaps her childhood, spent in relative poverty and social isolation, had made her empathic towards others. While I knew her, Valli's house was always occupied by people with serious problems. She would let them sleep over, eat, and drink her tea without charge. There were four elderly widows who frequented her flat, sometimes at the same time. These women had no place to turn for help, and Valli would offer them her hospitality. Valli complained from time to time about her lack of freedom, but said she felt pity for the widows, all of whom had suffered from family neglect and financial ruin. Valli also realized that she had no choice but to help the poor who turned to her. After all, she reasoned, her reputation as a "holy woman" depended upon her good reputation.

Sometimes Valli would host other mediums who visited in search of her guidance or simply for a place to rest. Valli always made it a point to evaluate their spiritual powers, while at the same time pitying them. She would tell me stories about their lives that explained their predicament, suggesting that their search for spiritual powers was related to their suffering in life—an observation she never directly made of herself. Though sometimes she apparently resented her obligation to help such troubled people,[34] she also enjoyed being the more masterful of the marginal, for clearly she had talents for communication and insights into human psychology that separated her from some of the others. Still, Valli was a somewhat marginal figure in Brickfields. As a Kali medium, an unmarried woman, and a Hindu from a low-caste background, she was stigmatized, even among the working class. I was told by one man who saw me talking to Valli that I should avoid her because she was possessed by "a devil" which made her an "evil" woman.

Valli's clients came to her with a variety of difficulties. Some had marital problems, while others were haunted by demonic beings. I witnessed how effective Valli was in treating her clients. She was a very attentive listener with a keen intuition for people's problems. While in trance, she would utilize the information given to her by the client, adding what she read "between the lines." She also possessed some knowledge of Hindu mythology and folklore (much of it derived from Tamil films), which she used to animate her interpretations. Once a teenage boy came to her after being repeatedly attacked by a *jinn* (demon, or "genie") while sleeping. The boy even had mysterious cuts and scratches on his back as "evidence" of the malevolent force. He said that he had been to numerous temples and consulted with many priests and other mediums to no avail. Valli, whom he called "a very powerful lady," was able to cure the boy through a combination of counseling and ritual. She did perform a *puja* for him, receiving Amman's power and blessings, after which she gave the boy instructions for keeping the demon at bay. Perhaps equally importantly, she counseled him on facing his fears. Valli, unlike the priests and other mediums, was able to discover that the boy had been abused by his father, who had since died. The *jinn* had only started to attack him after the father's death. By suggesting a connection between these events, she helped him to face feelings of rage, guilt, and fear. But by also enabling the boy to externalize his fears, she gave him a means to tame the *jinn* with help from the protective and nurturing "Amman." Furthermore, the talismans she gave him, which included certain prayers and simple rituals, instilled in him a confidence and courage. As far as I know, he was free from the demon for many months thereafter. From time to time, he returned to ask advice concerning other areas in his life.

Another client was a very poor young woman whose husband had disappeared, leaving her to raise a baby girl. The woman was taken in by Valli for a couple of weeks, during which a set of *pujas* were held. This particular woman was very nervous and talked almost non-stop. She asked me to look at her husband's picture, hoping I had seen him somewhere. Fearing the worst (that he had met with an accident), she implored Valli's help. Valli listened to the woman's incoherent story for a few days before suggesting a ritual. Once again, after performing the possession

---

[34] I had a chance to observe and talk with many local mediums who came to seek Valli's hospitality and instruction. Some seemed much less in control of their emotions and thoughts than Valli was. I surmised from this that some mediums would be comparatively less able to offer insights into other people's needs or problems.

trance, Valli offered Amman's assurance to the woman that everything would turn out fine. She also counseled her on her marriage. Valli had concluded, with the goddess's help, that the young woman had frightened her husband away by "talking too much." A good wife, she maintained, must let the husband have some peace in the home. I asked Valli how she would help the woman when her husband was nowhere to be seen. She confidently stated that Amman would take care of things. Sure enough, the man returned to the young woman after two weeks.

Other clients came with financial problems, alcohol-related problems, and concerns over infidelity. The point I want to make here is that Valli was perceptive in understanding the insecurities faced by working-class and poor Tamils. She, who lived at the margins of Tamil society, among people who are in turn living at the margins of Malaysian society, knew the fears faced by people in similar circumstances. Utilizing cultural resources at her disposal—that is, Hindu folklore and a belief in powers manifested through individuals capable of controlling these powers—she was able to provide narratives that made sense to some, and ultimately gave them a feeling of power or mastery in a situation of utmost desperation. In a place like Brickfields, with its many insecurities, the medium functions to embody "dangerous powers" for the benefit of those most needing divine intervention. As Gananath Obeyesekere[35] argues, this representative performance is one mechanism that enables the most oppressed to enhance their status by communicating with the divine, while simultaneously allowing the individual medium to cope with her or his own intrapsychic needs. Utilizing cultural resources allows such individuals to offer therapeutic services, as Sudhir Kakar[36] has argued, to others sharing the same sociocultural milieu. But given my present concern with locating Valli within an ethnic and national frame, what makes her story significant?

CONCLUSION

The story of the medium underscores the ambiguous distinctions that Tamils in Malaysia are compelled to make. On the one hand, Valli is challenging brahminical authority by making claims of spiritual power. Her challenges are seen in her erratic public behavior and commentary. At the same time, she also appropriates orthodox ideas and presents them as authenticating devices for her own clients and disciples. Though considered unorthodox within a Hindu hierarchy, Valli is quite concerned about matters of purity when conducting rituals. At times, she appears to appreciate conventional Hindu practice, only to reject it when it threatens her self-recognition, that is, the Real of her mirrored or doubled self. The important point is that she, and many others of low status, do not fully accept their marginality. They resist through a direct experience of power, which is provided by the trance. While Valli may have orthodox inclinations from time to time, she prefers to follow the "way of prayers" and seek the experience of an immanent God who does not care about one's class and status. Mediums can either be seen as true devotees, "mad" with devotion, or,

---

[35] See Gananath Obeyesekere, *Medusa's Hair* (Chicago: University of Chicago Press, 1981).

[36] See Sudhir Kakar, *Shamans, Mystics, and Doctors* (Delhi: Oxford University Press, 1984), and his *The Analyst and the Mystic* (Chicago: University of Chicago Press, 1991). Kakar elaborates on the notion that, as I have suggested here, the mystic or medium exemplifies in their intensified performance of conflictual discourses a symptom that is more widely shared by a community, though with lesser intensity.

among the orthodox, as unsophisticated Hindus still stuck in spiritual "kindergarten."[37] It is the ambiguity within the system that allows for some maneuvering. Valli, in other words, is not the "docile" Tamil, interpellated by a state and/or elite Indian discourse, as produced in reaction to a Malay Islamic state discourse; rather, she also is capable of distancing herself from elites, and occasionally even garnering their attention. At the same time, we must see her profound desire to challenge orthodoxy in light of the status obsessions within the Tamil community, which, in turn, speaks to the stigma of being "Indian" in Malaysia. I have argued that status insecurities are intimately related to the production and assertion of spiritual distinctions. As the spiritual negates or transcends the stigma of the social order, it, too, succumbs to a fetishistic understanding of itself that is manifested in the compulsion to intra-ethnic class and status difference. Valli, among others, negates, albeit with necessary ambivalence, the identity that simultaneously possesses her. Valli's paranoia regarding the demise of Indians in "ten years" correlates to a socio-symbolic order that she desperately seeks to surmount. Yet, as Freud suggests, the surmounting, too, produces the uncanny of "secret" familiarity.

I have argued that underlying the processes whereby symbolic capital is reproduced are economic factors that greatly determine the accessibility of status-enhancing practices and attributes. Moreover, the prevalent negative stereotypes attached to working-class Tamils are reproduced within or attributed to the space of the ethnic enclave, which also is a function of class. Middle-class and wealthy Indians go to great lengths to distance themselves culturally and spatially from these sites of marginality. But religious practices, particularly within the *bhakti* or devotional tradition, contain within them a certain ambiguity between so-called "high" and "low" forms of Hinduism, thus perhaps exacerbating the need in the minds of elites to distance the "orthodox" from the "non-orthodox."[38] While this apparently further widens social cleavages within the Tamil community, it also provides opportunities for mediums and other low-status devotees to challenge the spiritual supremacy of more orthodox practitioners. Yet, in the case of Valli, we see, even in her dramatic reversals or negations of hierarchy, an identity that possesses her that is ambivalently, yet resolutely, "Indian." Moreover, Valli's identity crisis, as manifested in her moments of transcendental fantasy, cannot be understood outside of the context of nationalist ideology and the position of Malay Muslims and Hindu Tamils within its symbolic order. In this sense, Valli's case serves to illustrate and theorize the modernist nationalist vision from below. While she is not simply a product of her habitus, or a rational actor producing a "hidden transcript" of critique, Valli as exemplar helps us understand the phenomenal powers of identity-fixation and negation, born out of the ambivalent crucible of social stigma.

On the other hand, such "resistance," involving what James Scott would call the "hidden transcript"—an ironic appropriation of symbols as an incipient form of social critique necessarily prior to social mobilization—emerges from the specific

---

[37] Orthodox Hindu apologists often describe the status of the devotee in these evolutionary terms. I was often told, for example, that while those who worship demigods, or practice mediumship, are not outside the Hindu tradition, they are still at the "kindergarten" stage of spiritual evolution.

[38] This notion is discussed in Hart, "The Nature of Tamil Devotion," and David Mearns's, *Shiva's Other Children: Religion and Social Identity Amongst Overseas Indians* (Delhi: Sage Publications, 1995).

constraints imposed by a very tangible material and discursive topography in Malaysia. Interpreting the practice of spirit mediumship within a marginalized ethnic enclave stigmatized by its class and ethnic representation cannot be undertaken without consideration of the ambivalence felt by "Indians" as they are made subjects within an intrusive state-sponsored system of representational politics premised upon fixed ethnic categories. As suggested here, an authoritarian and relentless drive towards the modernist vision necessitates the fixing of ethnic categories. In Malaysia, this has been accomplished, in part, through the institution of purely instrumental ethnic-based parties utilized to further bourgeois and elite interests. The process has been particularly challenging for Malays, who must repress a great deal of their own emotional and spiritual life as they are instructed to purge the irrational Hinduized elements from their culture. The disavowal of Hinduism belies the depth of contact and interface between South and Southeast Asia, a rich heritage and complex cultural formation that now haunts the present political leadership as it attempts to silence the uncanny of ethnic fluidity.

Returning to Valli, we can now ask: is this a case of resistance from below? While Valli's story illuminates obvious continuities and parallels between Tamil mediumship in South Asia and in Malaysia, the relevance of her complex response for our purposes is its vantage upon the structural and ideological marginality from which she makes sense of her world. She was herself a product of the estate system that brought Tamil labor into Malaysia, and her migration to Kuala Lumpur was necessitated by the restructuring and disposal of cheap labor. Her experiences working in the Army, and later in an urban company, exposed Valli directly to the stigmas attached to her ethnicity. While she lamented the plight of Indians in Malaysia with foreboding, she also expressed ambivalence towards other Indians. Her own marginality within the Tamil community placed her at odds with those of higher status; but at the same time, she clearly incorporates the stereotypical stigma attached to her ethnicity when she criticizes other working-class Tamils who are even less fortunate than her. Finally, her location within an enclave under economic siege, while certainly providing her with many clients who face significant problems, probably also informs her fears for the future of Indians in Malaysia.

While her vision may be from below, we should not assume she has been interpellated as a subject by the state without resistance. Clearly, she is capable of critique and reflexivity. But at the same time, we must also ask what is produced by her critique. She, in assuming her role as medium, though clearly able to express a challenge to one unitary logic through a "hidden transcript," is simultaneously identifying herself within the ethno-religious discourse of the state. While the terms interpellation or habitus, as used by Althusser and Bourdieu, respectively, may write out human agency too quickly, there is also no denying that the ambivalence experienced by Valli, or by elite Hindus for that matter, belies a dialogic and dialectical construction of self-identity. However, the future is as unpredictable as it is potentially volatile. That is why Freud's insights into the uncanny as a process that escapes the closure of symbols (i.e., putting the "past" into the "past") are so thought provoking. As signification is never complete or stable, and is always resisted, attempts to freeze ethnic types within a national discourse always involve repressions and potentially violent repercussions. While I do not believe all the Indians "will be dead in ten years," as Valli suggests, it is not clear yet what the future holds for the Indian working class in Malaysia.[39] One thing is fairly certain, however, the ethno-religious field in Malaysia is unlikely to dissolve.

---

[39] Indeed, Malay-Indian clashes in a squatter area of Kuala Lumpur in 2000 left six Indians dead and many more injured. The injuries and deaths occurred almost exclusively on the Indian side, suggesting a more orchestrated attack, rather than a spontaneous riot.

FRAUDULENT AND DANGEROUS POPULAR RELIGIOSITY IN THE PUBLIC SPHERE: MORAL CAMPAIGNS TO PROHIBIT, REFORM, AND DEMYSTIFY THAI SPIRIT MEDIUMS

Erick White

A "Proclamation Prohibiting Thai and Chinese Spirit Mediums" was introduced as law in Siam in 1891.[1] As written, the law contains a relatively brief and limited set of specific legal instructions. It is, however, preceded by a much longer explanation of the circumstances leading up to its creation. In the same month as the law was issued, the proclamation begins, a great fire arose in Bangkok. The fire spread widely, "destroying property and taking many lives." King Chulalongkorn requested an investigation of the fire's cause and discovered that prior to the fire, a spirit medium had predicted just such a tragedy. When the fire arose, furthermore, there were reports of spirit mediums in various sub-districts in the city who were prophesizing the occurrence of more fires. As a result, the populace became very worried, and gathered together to protect their homes. Much buying and selling of an "unusual nature" occurred. It was in response to these dramatic events, the law explains, that the Municipal Department decided to issue a decree ordering local administrators and the constabulary police to prohibit spirit possession.

Yet while local incidences of possession at shrines died down, the law goes on to explain, mediums continued to become possessed "stealthily under cover" (*laup lak*) in other sub-districts. Furthermore, they continued to predict future fires as well as illnesses. In turn, the general population continued to be carried along in turmoil, passing along fearful predictions by word-of-mouth. Additional fires were reported, and evidence that someone was setting them was obtained by the royal government.

---

[1] My discussion of the proclamation is based on a copy of the law printed in "Spirit Mediums: Saints in the Human Body or Deceivers of the World?" *Manager Weekly*, September 23-29, 1996, p. 42 (in Thai). The title of the law in Thai is: *Prakaat Haam Mai Hai Thai Lae Ciin Song Cao Nai Thii Tang Tang*. In this article, I transliterate Thai according to a simplified and slightly modified version of the ALA-Library of Congress system designed to indicate vowel length without diacritical markers.

Bands of spirit mediums and their followers, the law explains, were known to devise plans designed to make the populace believe in their sacred powers and provide them with offerings. Consequently, "other hooligans" (*khon phaan*) saw this as an opportunity to intimidate and threaten the populace and provoke fear, all in order to pursue their own interests and seek material benefits. Acting in collusion, spirit mediums "lied" (*kohok*) about deities descending and possessing mediums. After the prophecies were spread widely and the populace was driven into bouts of fear, these hooligans "devised their fraudulent plans" (*khitaan kaanthucarit*) and engaged in arson.

After recounting the dangerous breakdown in public order that instigated the creation of the new law, the 1891 proclamation proceeds to explain what exactly the new law entails. Absolutely no person, Thai or Chinese, should become possessed. If someone does become possessed, regardless of the sub-district within which he or she is located, the constabulary police will seize him or her and investigate the matter, even if it is known that those possessed did not intend to defraud anyone. In addition, since the lighting of fires is very dangerous to all life and property, the municipal department, district administrators, and village headmen should investigate any fires and arrest any criminals who set them. Any reliable eye-witnesses to the event should provide information to the municipal department for investigation. If the report turns out to be true, the Royal Treasury will grant a reward to the witness. Criminals found guilty, the proclamation concludes, will be executed.

Neither classical syncretic nor modern rationalist Theravada Buddhism have ever ascribed any central or significant religious value to the experience of spirit possession. The tradition of classical syncretic Theravada Buddhism, which was hegemonically dominant in the pre-modern era, however, also never denied the reality of spirit possession or the authenticity of spirit mediums. Instead, it merely treated spirit possession and spirit mediums as both irrelevant to the ultimate soteriological goal of liberation from *samsara* and subordinate to the more ethical and virtuous non-soteriological goals of making Buddhist merit and improving one's karmic heritage in this life. Spirit mediums, from the perspective of classical syncretic Theravada Buddhism, trafficked with either capriciously malevolent or ambiguously benevolent supramundane entities, referenced in the Thai language by the semantic markers *phii* or *cao*, respectively. Spirit possession was restricted in its social relevance to matters of either treating personal illness by supplicating or exorcising offending *phii* or ensuring the collective prosperity of local communities by propitiating those tutelary *cao* that could guarantee agricultural fecundity and social harmony. At a fundamental level, such matters, while an inevitable and legitimate concern of the laity, were not considered matters of much concern to either the Buddhist Sangha or individual Buddhist monks.[2]

---

[2] A few of the clearest and most comprehensive discussions of spirit possession within the context of Thai religious complexity and syncretism are: A. Thomas Kirsch, "Phu Thai Religious Syncretism: A Case Study of Thai Religion and Society" (PhD dissertation, Harvard University, 1967); S. J. Tambiah, *Buddhism and the Spirit Cults in North-east Thailand* (Cambridge: Cambridge University Press, 1970); Robert Textor, *Roster of the Gods: An Ethnography of the Supernatural in a Thai Village* (New Haven: Human Relations Area Files, 1973). A useful discussion of spirit possession in the context of Northern Thai Buddhism and society can be found in Walter Irvine, "The Thai-Yuan 'Madman' and the 'Modernising, Developing Thai Nation' as Bounded Entities Under Threat: A Study in the Replication of a

This general attitude of benign indifference, however, was challenged by the emergence of modernist Theravada Buddhist religious reform in the nineteenth century. Taking its cue, in part, from the rationalist, scripturalist bias of Christian theological hermeneutics and apologetics that was dominant among educated European elites in the era of high colonialism, modernist reform Buddhism in Siam constituted a revisionist effort to "revive" a pure Buddhism, shorn of what were now perceived as its supernaturalist and non-Buddhist accretions. Part of this dynamic of reformation, in fact, was explicitly concerned with reforming popular religiosity and suppressing or eradicating those undesirable syncretic innovations that had taken root in the Siamese cosmological worldview, as Buddhism had slowly adapted itself over centuries to those animistic and Brahmanical modes of religiosity also present within Siamese society and culture.[3]

As a result of this reform mentality, many previously tolerated popular beliefs and practices, now perceived as resolutely non-Buddhist in origin and character, were increasingly likely to be conceptualized as irrational and primitive remnants of an earlier stage of civilizational evolution that was infused with the magical and the superstitious. In this dynamic of ideological and praxeological revisionism, *saiyasaat*—an amorphous term designating esoteric knowledge, Brahmanical instruction, and magically potent incantations—became a diffuse intellectual category that was opposed to rationality and which defined all those beliefs, practices, and traditions of supramundane power that were not perceived as fundamentally governed by a (reformist) Buddhist logic. Fortune telling and astrology, amulets and love potions, divination and spirit possession—all of these could potentially be designated as *saiyasaat*. Moreover, among those endorsing modernist reform Buddhism, these syncretic practices were perceived as irrational, ineffective, and ultimately illusory, while the practitioners and clients involved with these practices were regarded as presumably either deceptive or deluded.[4]

It is important to recognize, however, that, in late-nineteenth-century Siam, the extent of modernist reform Buddhism's social appeal and public support was limited primarily to that minority of Buddhist monks, royal elites, state bureaucrats, and public intellectuals who were both familiar with the unique intellectual challenge of Christian and Western thought and strongly affiliated with and committed to the Chakri dynasty's modernizing project of nation-state building. Prince Mongkut, prior to his accession to the Siamese kingdom's throne as Rama IV in 1851, was

---

Single Image" (PhD dissertation, School of Oriental and African Studies, 1982), and Gehan Wijeyewardene, *Place and Emotion in Northern Thai Ritual Behavior* (Bangkok: Pandora, 1986).

[3] The classic analyses of modernist reform Buddhism that address the question of its critical relationship to popular religiosity include: Craig Reynolds, "Buddhist Cosmography in Thai History, with Special Reference to Nineteenth-Century Culture Change," *Journal of Asian Studies* 35,2 (1976): 203-220; S. J. Tambiah, *World Conqueror and World Renouncer: A Study of Religion and Polity in Thailand Against a Historical Background* (Cambridge: Cambridge University Press, 1976); Yoneo Ishii, *Sangha, State and Society: Thai Buddhism in History* (Honolulu: University of Hawaii Press, 1986); and Peter Jackson, *Buddhism, Legitimation and Conflict: The Political Functions of Urban Thai Buddhism* (Singapore: ISEAS, 1989).

[4] In many ways, in fact, these forms of popular religiosity and syncretism, of supernaturalism and superstition constitute an almost necessary ideological and psychological "other" against which reformist claims of religious authenticity, doctrinal orthodoxy, and moral progress can be asserted and celebrated. One wonders, consequently, whether they can ever be overcome or eradicated in any final sense without also simultaneously and paradoxically undermining modernist reform Buddhism's legitimating justification for its own purifying existence.

central to modernist reform Buddhism's development and propagation within Siam as both an authoritative interpretation of traditional Siamese religious belief and practice and as an institutional force within the Siamese Buddhist Sangha. The new monastic lineage Mongkut founded, the Thammayut, carried on this new modernist tradition after his accession and throughout the reign of subsequent rulers, including Mongkut's son, King Chulalongkorn, who ruled Siam from 1868 until 1910. The Thammayut's claim to ecclesiastical independence, authority, and even prominence within Siamese Buddhism was endorsed and supported, in turn, by key figures in and around the ruling Chakri royal family. These individuals gained cultural and political legitimacy from a vision and standard of Buddhist belief and practice that could be presented as both rational, progressive, and modern to those European powers that threatened Siam with colonialism, and superior, pure, and authentic to those regional Siamese political authorities who resisted Chakri-dominated nation-building.[5]

It is this modern reformist sensibility, endorsed primarily by a relatively narrow segment of the country's political, social, and intellectual elites, which clearly animates King Chulalongkorn's 1891 proclamation to suppress spirit possession. As the proclamation indicates, spirit mediumship in Bangkok at the end of the nineteenth century was perceived by the ruling monarch as deeply and inevitably embroiled in intellectual confusion, moral degeneracy, and social chaos. While the 1891 proclamation implicitly justifies itself by arguing that it seeks the long-term goal of greater economic and political stability, its more immediate concern and justification is to save the Siamese populace from criminal abuse and victimization. Framed as an effort to protect the Thai public from those deprivations of fraud, deceit, and larceny that it can no longer benignly neglect, the law ideologically mobilizes the institutions, personnel, and resources of a modernizing state in the service of policing, exposing, and suppressing a form of irrational popular religiosity, now seen as fundamentally dangerous in its public social consequences. In the eyes of an absolute monarch, who sees himself and the elite-staffed state apparatus he governs as fundamentally rational, moral, progressive, modern, and Buddhist, spirit mediumship is no longer simply a matter of personal health and local well-being, no longer just a private, idiosyncratic, or individual belief and practice that deserves indifference. It has become, instead, a clear example of those public, moral, social, and criminal dangers that arise when the irrationality and fraudulency of popular religiosity threatens to turn citizen-subjects into victims. As such, it is also an example of those previously private vices that turn into public dangers when the welfare of citizen-subjects is now, more than ever, the concern of a monarch who strives to be perceived as benevolently and proactively protective of his national population in the interest of both civilizational enlightenment and law and order.

The response of King Chulalongkorn at the end of the nineteenth century to the perceived threat of spirit mediums raises a set of complicated political issues, questions, and dilemmas that perennially appear and reappear, even more than a century later, whenever Thai political, ecclesiastical, and cultural elites seek, from the

---

[5] The definitive study of Mongkut and the Thammayut order remains Craig J. Reynolds, "The Buddhist Monkhood in Nineteenth Century Thailand" (PhD dissertation, Cornell University, 1972). The best study of the social and political context of modernist reform Buddhism as an intellectual movement can be found in Jackson, *Buddhism, Legitimation and Conflict*.

perspective of modernist reform Buddhism and its concerns about irrationality and fraud, to police, scrutinize, and critically reform or suppress popular religiosity. First, there is the frequent dilemma of how to justify, much less carry out, the paradoxical task of reforming or suppressing, in the public's interest, a set of beliefs, practices, and practitioners that are popular not only in the sense of being unofficial or non-elite, but also in the sense of being widespread among the masses. Second, there is the question of who should police, scrutinize, reform, or suppress popular religiosity. Should the responsibility fall primarily upon agents of the modern state—such as local bureaucrats, the police, public prosecutors, and judges—or are those agents in the institutions of civil society who are affiliated with or sympathetic to the modernist agenda of state-dominated reform Buddhism and public welfare—like Buddhist monks, public intellectuals, and mass media journalists—also necessarily or even primarily important as well? Third, what mixture of persuasive techniques and strategies should elite-led reforms of popular religiosity rely upon—coercive repression, legal regulation, social eradication, cultural marginalization, ideological co-option—and what vision of the greater public good motivates their intervention? And finally, just how successful are these efforts at reforming popular religiosity and restoring public order, and what explains, in any given historical era, the limitations that these efforts inevitably encounter?

In the remainder of this essay, I will explore these questions by examining two brief, but very public, debates about popular religiosity that occurred in Thailand in the mid-1990s and which centered on charges of irrationality, fraud, deceit, and larceny in the practice of spirit mediumship. Both of these debates were animated by a desire on the part of elite critics to portray spirit mediumship as a public scandal and a social danger, and both of these temporary demonizations of spirit mediumship relied heavily upon the technology of the mass media to shape the contours of the debate. Both of these debates reveal the complexities involved when contemporary Thai elites seek to define and expose forms of popular religiosity as irrational and fraudulent within the lived social experience of actors, rather than assert merely publicly that they are irrational and fraudulent. Both of these debates also illuminate how a set of elite concerns and fears broadly similar in tone and substance to those held by King Chulalongkorn at the end of the nineteenth century have had to adapt to a markedly different political, social, and cultural environment one hundred years later, as well as the particular constraints this new environment imposes on campaigns for the reform of popular religiosity.

PHRA PAYOM, STATE REGULATION, AND THE LEGAL CHALLENGE OF SPIRIT MEDIUMS AT THE END OF THE TWENTIETH CENTURY

During the 1980s, spirit mediums were generally satisfied with occupying an established—if subordinate, marginalized, and generally publicly unacknowledged—role within that loosely defined realm of syncretic, popular Buddhist religiosity perceived as unorthodox by the official Buddhist ecclesiastical establishment.[6] This was true despite the fact that the number of spirit mediums

---

[6] As one informant explained it to me, the widespread reluctance among spirit mediums at that time to strive assertively for a more public and legitimate status within mainstream Thai society and religiosity was, in part, a response to the very public and official suppression by the Thai state in the early 1970s of a famous spirit medium, Suchaat Kosonkittiwong, and the

continued to grow throughout the decade. As the 1990s progressed, however, a range of broadly unorthodox religious practices and beliefs that were previously marginal began to take on a more prominent public presence in the Thai social imagination. These loosely organized assemblages of techniques and ideologies, all profoundly devotional in ethos and attentive to desires for the acquisition of wealth and influence, resonated widely with a Thai populace heady from the optimism that had accompanied a sustained decade-long economic boom that began in the mid-1980s. Whether focused on magic monks, Chinese gods, or royal spirits, these distinct movements, organizations, cults, and charismatic leaders cohered into a broader popular religious sensibility focused on the attainment and justification of worldly success by means of supernatural sacral power of a non-traditional Buddhist nature. Carried along in the wake of these developments, spirit mediums and the practice of possession emerged from the margins of popular religiosity, proliferated even more rapidly, and gained a heightened public prominence during the 1990s.[7]

By the mid-1980s, however, the Thai state was retreating from its historic, self-appointed role to monitor, constrain, and, if necessary, suppress those unorthodox, non-establishment forms of popular religiosity that conflicted with the modernist reform Buddhism deeply embedded in the nationalized and centralized Buddhist ecclesiastical establishment. This retreat was the result of a variety of long-term historical changes: the declining institutional power of the Thai state in general, the weakening institutional authority of national Sangha ecclesiastical officials in particular, and the fact that the Thai state's political legitimacy was increasingly more dependent upon delivering economic growth and deepening democratization than upon serving as the protector and benefactor of Theravada Buddhism and the Sangha.[8] This sharp retreat from Chulalongkorn's assumption that Thai rulers and the Thai state had a responsibility to police and reform popular religion and morality in order to preserve general public well-being, however, had profound consequences for both spirit mediums and their critics.

Due to this increasingly laissez faire attitude by the Thai state towards all forms of religious expression, both within the bounds of the state-regulated Sangha and beyond it in the amorphous realm of popular culture, spirit mediums in the 1990s were, for the most part, benignly neglected by state institutions. Unless they stepped over very clear legal boundaries prosecutable under existing civil law—those issues of harm, fraud, and loss of property initially raised in the 1891 proclamation—spirit mediums typically were free to pursue their own religious goals in whatever innovative manner they saw fit. Yet while organized and official legal suppression by the state was a relic of the past, public criticism was not. Various intellectual

---

large religious movement that had formed around him. For analyses of this spirit medium, the religious movement he created and led, and the Thai state's eventual repression of both him and the movement, see Shusuke Yagi, "*Samnak Puu Sawan*: Rise and Oppression of a New Religious Movement in Thailand" (PhD dissertation, University of Washington, 1988), and Peter Jackson, "The Hupphaasawan Movement: Millenarian Buddhism among the Thai Political Elite," *Sojourn* 3,2 (1988): 134-170.

[7] For a more complete discussion of the emergence and flowering of these "religions of prosperity," see Peter Jackson, "Royal Spirits, Chinese Gods and Magic Monks: Thailand's Boom-Time Religions of Prosperity," *South East Asia Research* 7,3 (2000): 245-320.

[8] Peter Jackson, "Withering Centre, Flourishing Margins: Buddhism's Changing Political Roles," in *Political Change in Thailand: Democracy and Participation*, ed. Kevin Hewison (London and New York: Routledge, 1997), pp. 75-93.

elites—monks, academics, and journalists, most prominently—would occasionally direct a public, critical gaze on the practices, motivations, and/or beliefs of spirit mediums. It was rare, though, when this criticism would become too pointed or would try to reach beyond the rhetoric of moral edification in presenting itself as the best solution to the problem. But moments of heightened social criticism and calls for more than just edification did occur, as the following example reveals.

From mid-September until early October in 1996, the ever-controversial topic of spirit mediumship reemerged from the shadowy corners of Thai public awareness and briefly occupied the crowded stage of national concerns. While the contemporary Thai print and electronic national media frequently, if sporadically, cast a critical spotlight on the apparently self-evident irrationalities, dangers, and deceptions of spirit mediumship, during these few weeks in the Fall of 1996, the coverage was more widespread and sustained than usual. In part, this was because it was instigated by Phra Payom, an outspoken Buddhist monk and public intellectual who is well-known for successfully using the media simultaneously to both further his own modernist reform-oriented religious projects and advance his reputation as a virtuous monk. The sustained attention, however, also reflected the fact that this time there was more to the story than the usual anguished assertions that spirit mediums were a sign of Thailand's increasing moral chaos, intellectual bankruptcy, or spiritual degeneration. The novel addition to this almost stereotypic set of criticisms was that Phra Payom, in conjunction with other interested parties, was calling for a legal crackdown on spirit mediums and pushing for the revival and/or rewriting of Chulalongkorn's 1891 law designed to prohibit spirit mediumship. Newspaper reports indicated that suggested amendments were under study by a parliamentary senate committee, as a first step designed to aid legislators in the drafting of new regulations. Those involved explained to the media that further developments were expected within the month. As weeks passed, however, nothing further was heard about these legal reforms. No crackdown followed, no legal laws were revised, and the proposed legislation presumably died in committee, never to be heard of again.[9]

Clearly in retrospect, Phra Payom's initiative was as much an exercise in moral instruction on the public stage of the mass media as it was an effort to advance a particular legislative agenda. The former, in fact, was no doubt designed to strengthen the success of the latter. As a media-savvy modernist reformer, Phra Payom is well-versed in the strategies and rhetoric of using contemporary communications technology, including mass print and electronic mediums, to reinforce an elite, reformist vision of Buddhist authenticity and propriety. The gist of Phra Payom's message, despite later addendums and modifications, was clear: spirit mediums are frauds and cheats, and their customers are better off returning to a reliance on foundational Buddhist principles of self-reliance, self-discipline, and self-development. According to Phra Payom, the principles of Buddhism are quite clear on the matter—possession is "incorrect" (*mai thuuktaung*), a matter for "the irreligious" (*phuak nauk sasana*), and something in pursuit of which true Buddhists shouldn't "lose their way" (*long thaang*).[10] The fundamental problem, Phra Payom

---

[9] "Panel ponders checks on black magic practice," *Nation*, September 26, 1996, p. A2; "Spirit Mediums: Saints in the Human Body or Deceivers of the World?"; "Spirit Mediums, the social indicator: you might not believe, but don't insult them!" *Nation Weekly*, September 27, 1996, pp. 28-30 (in Thai).

[10] "Spirit Mediums: Saints in the Human Body or Deceivers of the World?"

claimed, is that so many Thais are religiously uneducated and don't understand the true principles of Buddhism. Instead of believing in karma and relying on the benefits of their own actions, most are gullible and weak. They fruitlessly beseech supernatural gods with offerings, hoping for miraculous interventions in innumerable ways, including via spirit mediums who claim to be the temporary, worldly hosts of the gods. Moreover, some wayward monks are embroiled in the deceptive activities of spirit mediums, thus misleading the laity into thinking spirit possession is useful and valid. Rather than relying on the temporary soothing effect of dependency on the supernatural, Phra Payom declared, Thais would be better off rigorously applying themselves in the practice of the Buddha's Four Noble Truths. Here is a scripturally endorsed true medicine, he asserted, for permanently removing the poisons of the mind, developing a stable mental condition, and fostering right thinking, all of which will really assist in the eradication of anyone's problems.[11]

In this message of spirit possession as anti-Buddhist and spirit mediums as purveyors of misguided magic and superstition, Phra Payom echoes ideas long ingrained in the hegemonic, rationalist discourse of reformist and elite modern Thai Buddhism. Phra Payom, therefore, implicitly appealed to a venerable intellectual lineage of reformist doctrine in his public denunciations. In addition, Phra Payom also strongly and repeatedly criticized the mediums as thieves and swindlers. Here again was yet another long-established elite stance from which to criticize spirit mediums as practitioners of a dubious popular religiosity. Fraud was the reason, the reformist monk claimed, he could no longer sit idly by in silence. Practically every time Phra Payom was interviewed by the media, in fact, he recounted one or two anecdotal tales of deception, thievery, and immorality by spirit mediums. A woman, for example, was lured to a cave by a medium for a special fate-altering ceremony, and once there she was induced to smoke laced cigarettes and sleep with the medium. Or in another case, a wife stole millions of baht from her husband in order to donate it to a greedy medium, instead of using the money to support her family, raise her children, or take care of her parents. Due to the deleterious influence of spirit mediums, Phra Payom implied, husbands were incited to lethal rages, families were split asunder, and sexual impropriety ran rampant.[12] In denouncing these practices in a rhetoric that mirrors contemporaneous critical commentary on the financial and sexual scandals of famous charismatic monks, Phra Payom described greed and lust running unconstrained throughout the community of spirit mediums, wreaking havoc wherever it took root. In Phra Payom's eyes, fallen monks and deviant mediums become ideologically equivalent as proper objects of condemnation by morally outraged, virtuous monks.

Faced with this criminal immorality, Phra Payom proposed a legislative initiative designed to buck historical trends and prod the Thai state into legally controlling and regulating spirit mediums. To this end, Phra Payom forwarded a petition to several governmental oversight committees. The petition called for the review and potential revision of the 1891 law designed to control spirit mediums. This law, Phra Payom had realized, was still on the books but had not been enforced in recent memory. Phra Payom admitted that little was known about the actual historical enforcement of the law, but he asserted that, in fact, those who broke the

---

[11] "Phra Phisalathammaphathi [Payom] opposes mediums—beware black magic," *Master: Beyond the Superficial Lifestyle,* 1,16 (October 1996): 78-81 (in Thai).

[12] "Spirit Mediums: Saints in the Human Body or Deceivers of the World?"

law—both the spirit medium and the person seeking out the medium—had been whipped as punishment in the past. Acknowledging that for a modern sensibility this punishment is relatively harsh, Phra Payom stated that his petition was intended instead merely to prod the relevant authorities into determining if this law had been repealed or not, and if not, whether it should be enforced or revised. His central purpose, he claimed, was only to protect future victims from any predation by spirit mediums. In this manner, the reformist monk avoided any specific discussion of appropriate punishments for perceived infractions of the law. Instead, he suggested in several media interviews that bureaucratic regulation was perhaps an additional avenue of legal control that the government should pursue. Phra Payom proposed that the state administer and regulate spirit medium shrines, thus suggesting that the shrines be managed in a manner resembling the way Buddhist temples are overseen by the Religious Affairs Department. These shrines should have to be formally registered with the appropriate governmental officials, he suggested. The government should also determine and enforce a clear set of stages by which a spirit medium shrine is established. Additionally, the responsible authorities should oversee their establishment and limit the number that are opened in any given province.[13]

While the details of Phra Payom's overall proposal were sketchy,[14] a clear three-pronged policy for dealing with the danger of spirit mediums can be distilled from his various specific criticisms that were published in different venues within the national print media. First, those mediums who steal or harm others should be fully punished under whatever laws, civil or otherwise, are applicable. Second, the regulatory power of the state should be utilized to administer and regulate the creation of spirit medium shrines. Third, the government should pursue educational campaigns designed to inform Thai citizens about the dangers that spirit mediums present. Conducting a one-man public relations campaign designed to raise the Thai people's consciousness, Phra Payom explicitly compared such an exercise to ongoing governmental efforts to alleviate the problems of alcohol, drug addiction, and child prostitution.[15]

Whether Phra Payom was advocating state-led legal regulation or eradication is, in fact, somewhat unclear. His rhetoric and suggestions slide ambiguously back and forth between these two policy options. Several times during his interviews, for instance, Phra Payom states that he isn't opposed to all forms of spirit possession. He explicitly states, in fact, that he has no problem with the occasional acts of possession performed by those he labels customary spirit mediums. Rather, his deepest concern is directed solely at mercenary spirit mediums who engage in possession daily and receive money in return for their efforts. It is the excessive greed and insolence these latter mediums display that causes him to worry about the future of Buddhism and Thai society.[16] Regardless of the specific focus of his moral outrage or the particular

---

[13] "Spirit Mediums, the social indicator: you might not believe, but don't insult them!," p. 30.

[14] Most journalistic reports selectively quoted from Phra Payom and other commentators, integrating their quotations into the overarching narrative of the articles. The most sustained popular press reporting of Phra Payom's thoughts are contained in one long question-and-answer interview with him. See "Phra Phisalathammaphathi [Payom] opposes mediums—beware black magic."

[15] Ibid.

[16] See, for instance, "Spirit Mediums, the social indicator: you might not believe, but don't insult them!," p. 30. While Phra Payom doesn't clearly distinguish between these two types of

policy he wishes to see the state pursue, however, the significance of Phra Payom's petition lies in his uniquely robust vision of the role of law and the state in addressing the apparent dangers of spirit mediumship. Unlike most other contemporary critical commentators who bemoan the irrationality and chicanery of spirit mediums, Phra Payom refused to accept the current civil code and the passive attitude of the state as the best solution. Instead, he envisioned an expanded and activist state bureaucracy and a revised legal code as the keys to solving the numerous and troubling problems that, in his opinion, spirit mediums pose to Thai society.

But none of these legal revisions or policy innovations came to fruition. One of the main lessons from Phra Payom's failed initiative then is that—in contrast with the political situation one hundred years previously—in the 1990s, the many officials of the Thai state's bureaucracy—administrative bureaucrats, police, politicians, lawyers, judges, etc.—remain extremely reluctant to intervene legally within the field of popular religion, at least as far as it concerns spirit mediums. This remains the case even when they are prodded by complaints from intellectual, religious, and cultural elites who seek to foster an atmosphere of public scandal, moral panic, and social disorder. And this reluctance persists, even though the state already is in possession of a law that would seemingly justify the punishment, and even suppression, of spirit mediums in the interest of preserving public order. In this sense, the Thai state seems determined firmly to resist not only initiating, but even pursuing, any general legal policy of intervention or regulation that would place it at the forefront of a movement to control or reform the current culture of popular religiosity. The Thai state doesn't even appear to be interested in pursuing a policy of inciting or supporting campaigns of moral condemnation and religious edification designed to reduce the appeal of what, from the perspective of establishment Buddhism, are clearly undesirable forms of popular religion. What are the reasons, however, for this unyielding refusal to proactively address public criticisms about the irrationality, fraud, and chicanery of contemporary spirit mediums?

THE THAI STATE AND SPIRIT MEDIUMS: LIMITATIONS TO THE LEGAL REGULATION OF POPULAR RELIGION

The manner in which contemporary public scandals involving Buddhist monks are discussed and addressed is, in many ways, reminiscent of Phra Payom's critical approach to spirit mediumship—both his diagnosis of the dangers it poses and his proposed solution of legal deterrence, moral re-education, and administrative regulation by the Thai state. While the specific details of each scandal are obviously unique, a consistent pattern of similar themes dominates the commentaries surrounding monastic scandals—a violation of Buddhist principles, the danger of

---

mediums, his statements have strong overtones that suggest he is drawing a contrast between "customary" or "traditional" spirit mediums and "professional" or "modern" spirit mediums. For instance, he describes the former as only becoming possessed occasionally, perhaps just once a year, and acting according to custom. The latter, however, sneak off and act in secret, deceiving and victimizing the public. Much of the distinction, therefore, relies in the final instance on a judgment of moral intentionality inflected through a vision of changing historical temporality. Those mediums with "traditional" good intentions are no problem, while those "modern" mediums seeking to take advantage of others are a problem.

unorthodox practices and/or beliefs, sexual misconduct with followers, financial impropriety or chicanery with donated funds, and sad tales of the laity being victimized.[17] In these cases as well, public critics call upon the Religious Affairs Department and the Sangha Supreme Council, the secular and ecclesiastical institutional arms of the Thai state that oversee all Buddhist monks, to restore the moral legitimacy and public authority of Buddhism by punishing the guilty and improving the training of monks. As in any large national bureaucracy, however, neither of these two institutional authorities typically are quick to intervene, if they ever intervene at all. And if they finally do authoritatively act to resolve a scandal, the process of bureaucratic adjudication and resolution is often long and convoluted and the final decision ambivalent and unsatisfying. Moreover, in the current political era dominated by the state's laissez faire ethos vis-à-vis religion, officials are frequently reluctant to intervene definitively and curb perceived excesses. And in those cases when either the Department or the Council has eventually responded to public criticism, all in the name of state authorities empowered and obligated to uphold national law, their response has consistently been slow, ambivalent, and frequently ineffective.[18]

When it comes to contemporary scandals involving spirit mediums, however, the Thai state currently declines to take any such direct punitive or administrative action in the interest of upholding religious propriety and public morality. Moreover, even after Phra Payom's effort to clarify and pass legislation that would have legally empowered agents of the Thai state actively to pursue the matter, the state continues to follow a passive, reactive, and piecemeal strategy of response. Despite Phra Payom's complaints and suggestions, the Thai state declined to coordinate any campaigns of legal suppression or moral education directed at spirit mediums or their followers. Instead, what followed was only more of the same—continuing episodes of general public criticism fueled by exposé journalists and critical monks.

Yet despite the general retreat of the Thai state since the mid-1980s from its previously robust policy of policing and repressing non-establishment Buddhist religiosity, civil and ecclesiastical authorities do, nonetheless, occasionally intercede in scandals involving certain Buddhist monks. But why then was Phra Payom's call for a mixture of state prohibition and regulation regarding spirit mediums so easily ignored? Even more importantly, what does this refusal tell us about how the Thai state at the end of the twentieth century envisions its relationship to popular religiosity in general and spirit mediums in particular, as well as the role of law in this relationship? Why can't spirit mediums, for instance, be treated like Buddhist monks from the perspective of the Thai state?

The most general explanation for the failure of Phra Payom's attempt to provoke the Thai state bureaucracy into disciplining spirit mediums is that his rhetoric ignored several contemporary ideological and institutional characteristics of both the Thai state and the subculture of contemporary professional spirit mediums, characteristics that make his legal and administrative solutions highly unlikely to

---

[17] For a detailed discussion of some of the more notable recent scandals and an analysis of their wider significance, see Charles Keyes, "Moral Authority of the Sangha and Modernity in Thailand: Sexual Scandals, Sectarian Dissent, and Political Resistance," in *Socially Engaged Buddhism for the New Millennium* (Bangkok: Sathirakoses-Nagapradipa Foundation and Foundation for Children, 1999), pp. 121-147.

[18] Some of the most famous cases of the past decade include the investigations of Phra Nikorn, Phra Yantra, Phra Prajak, and Phra Dhammachayo.

succeed. First, from the perspective of the Thai state's dominant political and religious elites, spirit mediumship is too ideologically suspect and religiously dubious to be granted the legitimacy that state-guided administration and regulation would inevitably entail. While spirit mediums, in fact, widely share and endorse most mainstream Thai Theravada Buddhist beliefs and values, a stigma of "superstition" and impropriety still clings to them among the general public. If Phra Payom's condemnation of them as morally equivalent to drugs and prostitution is, in fact, an accurate measure of elite attitudes, then spirit mediums—like drugs and prostitution—are, from a policy perspective, a private vice that cannot be eradicated and should, instead, be controlled through legal means in only the most egregious of cases. Moreover, any legal intervention should be limited and punitive in character, not comprehensive and regulatory. Few public intellectuals and critics, after all, call for the bureaucratic recognition and regulation of drugs or prostitution by the Thai state. In this sense, just like drug and prostitutes, spirit mediums are not perceived to be a potential public virtue appropriate for guidance and moral uplift through the benevolent leadership of the royal government.

Second, even if the Thai state decided to pursue bureaucratic administration and regulation as a policy, it would find it very difficult to implement this policy successfully. The beliefs and practices that circulate within the subculture of spirit mediums are highly informal and non-standardized. There is no canonical or centralized authority within this subculture that can definitively distinguish between authentic and inauthentic beliefs, legitimate and illegitimate rituals, proper and improper conduct. While general normative expectations are shared throughout the subculture, innovations and exceptions are just as frequently cultivated by mediums and sought after by followers and clients. It is, therefore, unclear just what principles internal to the subculture any state bureaucracy would or could appeal to in order to determine what defines a properly established shrine or the proper conduct of a medium. And there certainly are not any relevant principles on these points within the canonical Buddhist scripture or monastic regulations. In this sense then, the ideological organization of the subculture of spirit mediums is fundamentally unlike the subculture of the Thai Sangha under establishment Buddhism, in which the legitimacy and authority of central beliefs and practices have become formalized, standardized, and bureaucratized. Lacking these institutional foundations supportive of homogenization and standardization, the Thai state would find it incredibly difficult to intervene in any coordinated fashion in order to rationalize and systematize either the beliefs and practices or the behavior and teachings of spirit mediums.

Third, the Thai state lacks the institutional capacity to enforce any principles, rules, or beliefs it might decide to endorse and promulgate among spirit mediums. The subculture of spirit mediums is profoundly non-institutionalized as a social collectivity, with no formal association representing their aggregate identity or interests, and no institutionalized hierarchy establishing what is and isn't appropriate behavior. Charisma, as a result, is fundamental to any medium's personal claim to religious legitimacy and authenticity. As a result, the subculture is loosely organized around interlocking social networks, is hierarchically unstable, and lacks any centralized elite with the authority to demand generalized conformity or allegiance. In this sense, again, the subculture fundamentally differs at the organizational level from the modern Buddhist Sangha, which possesses a complicated, but functionally clear, administrative and hierarchical structure that mirrors in many ways the organizational design of the national government. As a result, it is very unclear how the Thai state could convince spirit mediums to assist in their own administrative regulation according to formal procedures.

Fourth, and finally, as a tool of discrimination and adjudication in matters of religious authority and spirituality, civil law is too imprecise and coarse grained. How will the government legally distinguish between "professional" and "customary" mediumship? How will the law determine when someone is really possessed and when someone is merely engaged in fraud? How will the legal system discriminate between legitimate and illegitimate ritual services while still protecting the Thai citizen's constitutional right to freedom of religious belief? The 1891 law on spirit mediums avoided these complicated questions by pursuing a simple and straightforward strategy of prohibition and suppression. A policy of regulation and moral education, however, would demand that these questions be answered, at least provisionally. These very same legal ambiguities, in fact, were commented on by numerous police officers, lawyers, and doctors when asked by reporters what their reaction was to Phra Payom's initiative. As a deputy permanent secretary in the Education Ministry himself clearly explained: "This matter is delicate and concerns an individual's belief, a right to a belief. We can't force anyone to believe or not believe something."[19]

Given the improbability of a state-led policy of administrative regulation and the high profile of concerns about freedom of religious belief, it is not surprising that the Thai state's public reaction to spirit mediums remains passive and sporadic, centering primarily on minimizing individual abuses and excesses while avoiding any general public policy of suppression. Hemmed in by groups who are concerned to protect each citizen's civil rights and freedoms and a general public increasingly sympathetic to forms of popular religiosity considered marginal or unorthodox by establishment Buddhism, the Thai state prefers the status quo over a more aggressively repressive or regulatory approach. Consequently, from the perspective of state institutions, there is little need to review or revise the existing century-old law on spirit mediums as it stands. That law's goal was suppression of spirit mediums as a collective category of religious actors. Since the contemporary Thai state would rather pursue a strategy of correcting and punishing individual abuses by individual spirit mediums, the existing civil laws regarding theft, fraud, and sexual crimes would seem to be an appropriate enough legal tool. And that is, in fact,

---

[19] See "Panel ponders checks on black magic practice." In my own interview with this same deputy permanent secretary, he reiterated the identical concerns that critics of Phra Payom had previously raised: that the constitutional guarantee of freedom of religion makes this kind of legislation difficult to create and enforce, that civil laws already exist to deal with larceny and deception, so new ones are not needed just for spirit mediums, and that one could not easily legally distinguish between cases of real and false possession. Before explaining all these points, however, he first stressed a more important point to me—spirit mediums were not a matter over which the Education Ministry had any direct oversight or responsibility. The Education Ministry only dealt with "principal religions" (*sasana lak*) like Buddhism, Christianity, Islam, and Sikhism. Spirit mediums, as a matter of mere "belief" (*khwaamchua*) that involved capriciously malevolent spirits (*phii*), was not a topic with which the Ministry needed to be concerned. He suggested in an aside, however, that perhaps the Interior Ministry was the appropriate responsible administrative body. As these comments indicate, it is not very surprising, in the end, that the Education Ministry declined to take up enthusiastically Phra Payom's suggestions that the Thai state involve itself in the administrative regulation and moral education of spirit mediums.

the stance taken by most lawyers, police officers, civil servants, and intellectuals interviewed by journalists during Phra Payom's media campaign.[20] Consequently, even as Phra Payom sought through the mass media to advance his reform campaign, legal experts hinted that the status quo was both preferable and perfectly reasonable.

TELEVISED EXPOSÉS AND THE MOMENTARY NATIONAL DEMONIZATION OF PROFESSIONAL SPIRIT MEDIUMS (AGAIN)

As Phra Payom's failed effort to rouse the Thai state against spirit mediums clearly reveals, in the 1990s, the responsibility for initiating, organizing, and executing public campaigns aimed at controlling, suppressing, or eradicating the "excesses" of popular religiosity clearly falls primarily on the shoulders of non-state actors in the realm of civil society. Concerned monks, critical public intellectuals, and crusading investigative journalists, consequently, have come to occupy center stage as the principal and most vocal critics of what they perceive to be improper forms of popular religious belief and practice. And it is these self-appointed protectors of the public's well-being, and not the royal Thai state or its bureaucratic representatives, who are currently the main instigators behind those occasional public demands that action be taken against the supposed impropriety and dangerous behavior of spirit mediums.

The demands of these critics are usually a mixed bag of proposals, ranging from those that recommend an intensified policing and civil prosecution of spirit mediums to those that favor educational campaigns aimed at the general Thai public. These criticisms and demands are usually framed rhetorically by the urgency of public scandal, with some high-profile case of deception, impropriety, or illegality involving a spirit medium fueling the strident call for public action this time, finally. Substantively, these critics are rarely willing to rely solely on the institutions of civil society to correct the problems and dangers posed by spirit mediums. Rather, they almost inevitably, like Phra Payom, also call upon various Thai state authorities to intervene definitively in the field of popular religion and solve the problems at hand. In these pleas, one can hear a clear nostalgia for earlier eras when the state acted as a definitive and authoritative moral arbiter of religious propriety and authenticity in the interest of the Thai public. And yet such demands are almost quixotic, because the contemporary Thai state is, as previously explained, consistently reluctant, for very clear ideological and institutional reasons, to treat private scandals involving spirit mediums as a public religious controversy requiring special state attention.

Public scandals, criminal abuse, and moral exhortation in the Thai mass media, however, have a limited, and perhaps even declining, capacity to persuade and influence the Thai public. There is, after all, a relatively constant stream of scandals involving politicians, bureaucrats, businessmen, celebrities, and other public figures

---

[20] For example, one police officer interviewed by journalists explained: "The actions are of a mad person, but you can't use laws since mediums are widely accepted in society. Public relations and education are better." In a similar vein, a lawyer asserts: "No law says you have to ask for permission to open an abode or that you have to register one, as is the case with a foundation. It is all up to the individual. But if there is swindling or physical harm resulting from their actions, civil laws are relevant." See "Spirit Mediums, the social indicator: you might not believe, but don't insult them!"

circulating across the front pages of newspapers and the opening segments of television news reports. True revelations and novel scandals are actually much rarer commodities than might be expected, especially when it comes to the excesses of popular religiosity and the irrationality, fraud, and larceny often ascribed to it. Occasionally, however, a truly novel angle on an old staple of scandals emerges, and such was the case with spirit mediums a year after Phra Payom's failed public campaign to reform and discipline spirit mediums legally.

On September 1, 1997, ITV, an independent cable channel in Thailand, broadcast on its weekly investigative show "Exposed" (*Thaut Rahat* in Thai), the first segment of a three-week, multi-part exposé on the secret techniques of Thai spirit mediums. The initial, most dramatic segment, however, centered on the confession of Chuchaat GnaamKaan, a well-known spirit medium who had been serving his Chinese deity (*cao*) and assisting suffering and anxious Thais for twenty-six years in Chantaburi. As the segment unrolled, Chuchaat proceeded to reveal in explicit and dramatic terms the naturalistic techniques he had used over the years to perform unusual feats, which observers, including his own disciples and clients, had interpreted as miracles proving that a divine being—in his case, the Chinese god Cii Kong—was indeed possessing his body. Two additional segments on the topic of spirit mediums were broadcast over the following weeks. These segments chronicled the further investigations of numerous "Exposed" investigative reporters as they interviewed many other spirit mediums and reported on the suspicious activities and assertions they had discovered during their investigations. Each segment conveyed the strong hint that deception, impropriety, and chicanery were in the air, even if such accusations were never directly asserted as such by the reporters. This general message was not surprising to the show's audience, however, since deception, impropriety, and corruption were, after all, what the cable television show was famous for revealing to a viewing public eager for that exceptionally visceral and immediate sense of revelation that only the visual medium of television can provide. As the weeks passed, newspapers and magazines subsequently picked up on the scandalous buzz floating around spirit mediums, and especially Chuchaat's revelation of secret techniques, by publishing articles either about or inspired by these documentary segments. Even Phra Payom joined in on the exposé, inviting Chuchaat to his temple so that he could disclose yet again these secret techniques in a repeat performance that was also videotaped for subsequent distribution and sale to interested parties.

What was so provocative about this scandalous revelation of fraud and deception was that never before had an "insider" stepped forward to disclose those "secrets" of the profession that usually remained "backstage" as the privileged knowledge only of practitioners. Moreover, the revelations were compelling and dramatic because, rather than simply publishing in print his revelations of artifice, Chuchaat literally performed them for a national media audience, while also explaining them through his own simultaneous spoken commentary. This performance of artifice and deceit and its accompanying simultaneous demystification were, appropriately enough, filmed at Chuchaat's shrine with Chuchaat dressed in the full regalia of mediumship. And, as if to reinforce indelibly in the viewer's mind the many senses of inversion that characterized the moment, Chuchaat's videotaped demonstration of these techniques for a national viewing audience was performed in front of an immediate on-screen audience, one composed of his own assistants, disciples, and clients. At the same time, however, this intimate audience of followers was supplemented by a large gathering of anonymous strangers who came to view the occasion and participate in its combined ceremonial and carnival-like atmosphere. The televised media event was defined, consequently, by an excess of overlapping and disjunctive messages and audiences.[21]

As a result of his relaxed, jovial, and talkative manner, Chuchaat's presence dominates the first "Exposed" episode, as he proceeds systematically through an exposition of technique after technique involved in the creation of "miracles" (*pathihaan*) and supernatural feats. After a mere twenty minutes or so into the television show, he has already performed many of the most popular acts of self-mortification practiced by Chinese spirit mediums in Thailand: driving a lance through one's cheeks; thrusting a sharpened trident into one's stomach; walking across a long pit of burning hot coals; cutting one's tongue repeatedly with a sword until bloody; extinguishing the roaring flame of a pack of candles in one's mouth; sitting effortlessly on a chair of long nails. Throughout many of these acts of self-mortification, Chuchaat acts out the stereotypic dramatic behavior and reactions any informed audience would expect of a possessed spirit medium, only to then step back out of this role, now revealed as pure artifice, in order to explain patiently the tricks of the trade, so to speak. With a lance already through one cheek, he discusses the need to choose one that is not too wide. With his tongue dripping blood, he explains the medical value of the alcohol blown on the sword blade prior to cutting himself. While bouncing up and down gently on a throne seat full of spikes, he points out that both the distance between the spikes and the thickness of the costume's fabric is crucial to success. And throughout all these displays of purported miracles, now "revealed" as simple acts of bodily self-mortification that anyone can master, Chuchaat as Chuchaat remains present and engaged with his audience—an implicit rebuke to the fundamental claim made by spirit mediums that when possessed by the gods they enter into a dissociative trance in which their consciousness and personality are temporarily effaced.

In many ways, the three-week ITV exposé shared a fundamental set of underlying assumptions and explicit messages with Phra Payom's public campaign in 1996. Spirit mediums are a social problem in need of a solution. Belief in spirit possession flourishes due to weaknesses in the character, education, or rationality of those who seek it out or indulge in it. Its authenticity is dubious at best, and more appropriately, it should be viewed as performance, as artifice, as chicanery. Yet the ITV-televised exposé and its subsequent follow-up episodes produced a much more sustained and powerful critical atmosphere toward spirit mediums among the general public than did Phra Payom's legislative and media campaign the previous year. This was due, in part, to the fact that the exposé simply intensified and expanded the critical, skeptical message of this common, modernist elite discourse about spirit mediums. The exposé clearly went beyond a more typical stance of

---

[21] My focus in this particular discussion is the ideological message within, and reception of, the ITV program as a mass media and televised representation of spirit possession. Consequently, I do not address the print media accounts about Chuchaat during this and subsequent events, nor do I analyze the event itself as a performative experience for the immediate audience watching it. Since I was not in Thailand when this scandal broke, the latter analysis would, in any case, be very difficult for me. My analysis, therefore, is based on a careful viewing of a copy of the ITV documentary segments. For a first-hand description and quite different analysis of this media event, see Rosalind Morris, *In the Place of Origins: Modernity and its Mediums in Northern Thailand* (Durham: Duke University Press, 2000), pp. 332-349.

respectful, restrained skepticism and instead presented an assertive, demanding perspective that sought to reveal and demystify, rather than merely just question, and which sought to convey that revelation and demystification directly to the viewer so she could judge the evidence for herself.

The extraordinary persuasive power of ITV's investigative reporting, however, was not just due to the fact that it delivered a more extreme and insistent version of modernist, elite skepticism vis-à-vis popular religiosity. Rather, the power of ITV's critique had much to do with the medium of television through which it was delivered, especially when compared with the print mass media that was, more typically, the prime media venue for other previous public campaigns against spirit mediums, as in the case of Phra Payom's failed 1996 effort. In this sense, the unusual impact of ITV's televised exposé was rooted in crucial differences in the way that television could disseminate and rhetorically construct this critical elite discourse about spirit mediums in a manner that the print mass media could never match.

To begin with, the ITV exposé was much more accessible to the general public than the reporting by any print publication could ever be. In part, this results from the fact that a greater number of Thais watch television than read newspapers or magazines. Television sets are a crucial consumer good for any household, and so even the poorest households typically own one. Even though cable television is more restricted in its distribution than the free public channels, its viewing audience is still quite large, even when compared to national publications, and that doesn't even take into consideration the spill-over effect as public television channels report on news and topics that originally aired on private television channels. This greater accessibility also results from the fact that as a communication medium, television is not dependent upon the formal literacy of its audience. Instead, because it relies on more basic visual and verbal skills, the number of potential television viewers is much greater than any news, editorial, or journalistic investigation that is dependent upon a print medium for its dissemination.

In addition, the technology and production format of television facilitates more easily the reproduction and elaboration of any particular discursive message or ideology. Visual images and clips from the ITV exposé could be reproduced and disseminated much more easily and quickly than any similar effort that had to rely on the daily, weekly, or monthly printing cycle of the print media. This timeliness, in fact, helped to facilitate the elaboration of a single message across many media and many days. "Exposed" incorporated this element of elaboration into its very programming by running consecutive television episodes on the same topic, returning to the same issues over and over again in a repeated act of elaboration and clarification. The consequences for the general public were more pronounced, accordingly, because the material was no longer just a single moment of criticism lost and forgotten in the perpetual blur of other media reporting.

The ITV exposé also garnered more public attention and had a broader and more significant effect precisely because it was packaged in a rhetoric of scandal and exposé. Certainly many newspapers and magazines also exploit this rhetorical framing strategy when reporting news. It is, in fact, very common with regards to political and economic affairs among both "quality" and sensationalistic newspapers. Some sensationalist newspapers like *Khao Sot* also regularly engage in this presentational strategy when reporting on religious scandals such as corrupt or disgraced monks. "Exposed," on the other hand, was the rare television show whose wide appeal was predicated explicitly on its repeated ability to reveal the hidden, to uncover corruption, and to foster scandals, and to do so with an air of respectability and reliability. The show was seen as accurate and not simply as an effort in sensationalism for the sake of profit. That is why interested people regularly tuned into it. As a result, the very rhetorical format of "Exposed" was almost guaranteed to foster more interest and attention by the public.

Most importantly, however, the ITV exposé was so powerfully disruptive as a public critique because of the rhetorical structure and formal aesthetics used to deliver its criticisms and revelations. On formal grounds, Chuchaat's declarations were so impressive and attention getting precisely because they weren't simply a verbal or written argument by an expert. Journalists and public intellectuals have spilled much ink in criticism of spirit mediums, but to little comparable effect. In the ITV exposé, however, one heard such criticisms from a respected insider, from one who clearly had privileged knowledge of what went on "backstage" among spirit mediums themselves. Moreover, these criticisms were not simply logical arguments that had to rely on the spoken or written word for their persuasive power. Rather, armed with the authority and authenticity of a recent defector, Chuchaat offered up a performance buttressed with all the sensory richness and illusion of a face-to-face interaction that television can muster. Given his particular message about performative deception, the medium of televised communication was crucial to the effectiveness of Chuchaat's demystifying message. Aesthetically, Chuchaat offered up a parody and comedic inversion of spirit medium behavior and beliefs, as both practiced and imagined. After establishing through his attire, words, and actions the conventional subcultural frame of reference and interpretation appropriate for understanding the self-mortification practices, Chuchaat repeatedly proceeded to break that frame in order to reposition those practices as deception and human artifice. The dominant message of skepticism and denial he was trying to convey, consequently, became almost unassailably final and authoritative as the dominant meaning of the event for those in the viewing audience predisposed to such a message.

THE THAI MASS MEDIA AND SPIRIT MEDIUMS: LIMITATIONS TO THE ELITE DEMYSTIFICATION OF SPIRIT MEDIUMS

ITV's exposé on spirit mediums, like Chulalongkorn's 1891 proclamation and Phra Payom's 1996 legislative and media campaign, was an exercise in the moral critique of religious irrationality and fraud by a modernist reform elite in the interest of the general public. All of these critical efforts were, in some sense, exercises designed to educate the Thai public about the dubiousness and danger of spirit mediums, as well as to protect the well-being of the Thai public. ITV's goal, however, was neither the legal suppression of a pernicious form of popular religiosity nor the administrative reform of popular religiosity in order to make it more rational and less dangerous. ITV's exposé, instead, pursued moral critique in a starker, more foundational vein: it sought, quite simply, to educate and reform both popular religiosity and the Thai public through demystification. Moreover, ITV sought to do this by providing definitive evidence that spirit mediums were what modernist critics had always charged they were: frauds, charlatans, and—by extension—deceptive thieves. For ITV, the definitive power of their demystifying critique lay in the fact that their televised revelations about the mundane truth of supposedly supernatural and miraculous feats were advanced by a long-standing, well-known spirit medium himself, a spirit medium who through his own public confession now perfectly represented that passage from irrationality and fraud to enlightenment and critique that they hoped the Thai public as a whole would replicate.

There is no denying that ITV's televised disclosures were provocative, compelling, and influential. Moreover, Thepchai Yong, the senior ITV director for "Exposed," had little doubt about their broader social impact. With an air of great satisfaction during an interview almost a year after the exposé was broadcast, he explained to me that for all those Thais who formerly sat on the fence, believing in spirit mediums "50/50," as they say in Thai, the episodes had helped finally and definitively to convince them that spirit possession simply wasn't real. Thepchai added that people even came up to him after seeing the episode to tell him that they no longer believed in mediums or that their mother no longer sought out mediums for any kind of assistance. As for the followers of mediums, Thepchai asserted with certainty that "Exposed" had helped to foster the beginning of real questioning and skepticism. Thepchai also admitted, however, that broadcasting the episodes had provoked strong denunciations from many mediums who had seen the show. They claimed that while Chuchaat may be a charlatan, they certainly were not, and they challenged ITV to come and test them. Elaborating further upon the impact of the exposé's revelations, Thepchai explained to me that one month after the ITV segments had aired in 1997, attendance had declined significantly at the annual Chinese Vegetarian Festival in Phuket, a popular ten-day religious festival in which the participation of hundreds of spirit mediums in various states of miraculous self-mortification is crucial if the festival's numerous ceremonies of public procession are to be considered a success. Even Phuket governmental officials blamed his TV show for the province's notable drop in tourist revenues during the month of the festival, Thepchai added. Demystification had seemingly succeeded beyond even the hopes of the ITV investigative reporters and producers.

When I returned to Thailand for the summer of 1998, spirit mediums were somewhat reluctant to talk in detail about the ITV exposé, but many confirmed Thepchai's assertion that it had made life difficult for them, particularly in the immediate aftermath of its broadcast. They felt roundly denounced and stigmatized; strangers openly expressed disdain or hostility towards them; some followers abandoned their mediums and entourages; and the number of clients seeking assistance dried up to some degree for several months. In response, many mediums took on a lower public profile and cut back on the scale and excess usually associated with their important annual public ceremonies, inviting fewer people to them, while generally displaying more discretion and reserve in their execution as well.

But the world of spirit mediums after ITV's exposé wasn't turned entirely upside down, as Thepchai himself would likely have conceded. Much of the impact, in fact, seemed relatively short lived. Nearly a year after the exposé, spirit mediums still had plenty of followers. New clients continued to seek them out for supramundane assistance. They still carried on their private and public activities much as before, even if in their public appearances they were perhaps more reserved and cautious than had previously been the case. While their assertions of supernatural authenticity and authority had been bruised and battered somewhat, they had not been, in the end, either definitively discredited nor fundamentally undermined as a source of spiritual refuge and miraculous assistance among a relatively wide spectrum of the Thai public. As the Thai economy continued to decline into recession and stagnation at the end of the 1990s, moreover, some public commentators even noted that there seemed to be an increasing interest on the part of the Thai public in the miraculous kinds of supernatural advice and assistance that spirit mediums, among others, regularly provided to their clients.

To understand why ITV's campaign of demystification against spirit mediums ultimately had such a limited impact, it is necessary, as was the case in understanding the limitations of Phra Payom's campaign of moral censure and reform, to look more closely at the subculture of spirit mediums itself. In particular, I argue that three characteristics of this subculture help to explain why modernist elite demystification, even demystification as dramatic and compelling as that provided by Chuchaat in the ITV exposé, is ultimately limited in its persuasive ability to redefine spirit mediumship as fraudulent popular religiosity. All of these characteristics, moreover, are rooted in the specific social and cultural dynamics that define the relationships existing both between spirit mediums and between spirit mediums and their followers and clients.

First, there already exists within the subculture of spirit mediums a robust and explicit discourse about fraud, chicanery, and inauthenticity. Spirit mediums and their followers frequently accuse other spirit mediums of not really being possessed, of putting on a show and pretending to be possessed when they really aren't. Similarly, many clients approach spirit mediums already armed with skepticism and suspicion, only believing in them, as Thepchai put it, "50-50." They already are perfectly willing to believe that some spirit mediums are frauds and faking possession. As a result, they critically visit a variety of spirit mediums, seeking to determine which ones are real and which are not, which ones truly reveal a miraculous insight into their current condition and past history and which, instead, get facts wrong or only provide vague answers. In other words, Chuchaat's revelation that he had been faking possession for more than twenty years hardly constituted, on its own, a startlingly revelation to spirit mediums, their followers, or their clients. They already knew that some mediums weren't authentic, which is precisely why many mediums challenged ITV to test them instead. Besides, revealing that one spirit medium is a fraud hardly proves, from their perspective, that all spirit mediums are a fraud, much less that the very idea of spirit mediumship and spirit possession is false.

Second, within the subculture of spirit mediums, belief in the supernatural power and efficacy of spirit possession is not founded solely on the authenticity of miraculous acts of self-mortification. While some mediums engage in dramatic acts of self-mortification to prove the authenticity of their possession, not all spirit mediums do. Moreover, even those spirit mediums who do engage in self-mortification only tend to do so during special public events. No spirit medium I am aware of, after all, performs acts of self-mortification every time a client, either new or established, seeks him or her out for help and advice. Instead, when judging the authenticity of spirit possession and the efficacy of a spirit medium's supernatural assistance, clients and followers rely on a more diverse set of behavioral cues and ritual practices. Various signs of dissociation, as well as transformations in speech, personality, and temperament, usually serve as indications of authentic possession, while spirit mediums serve clients through a variety of practices such as divination, sacralization, blessing, and healing that are not dependent upon self-mortification as the authenticating ground of their supramundane efficacy. In fact, the vast majority of any spirit medium's thaumaturgical services consist of ritual practices that other religious actors in Thai society, such as Buddhist monks, regularly perform as well. ITV, of course, never claimed that these other commonly shared ritual practices were fraudulent or deceptive. Thus, the central thrust of ITV's claim to demystification—naturalistic explanations for supposedly miraculous feats of self-mortification—failed to undermine or delegitimize significantly those general claims to religious authority and authenticity made by spirit mediums.

Finally, and most importantly, the elite critics at ITV also fundamentally misunderstood the foundations of authority and authenticity within the subculture of spirit mediums. Reflecting a modernist reform perspective, the investigative reporters and producers at ITV assumed that a spirit medium's authority and authenticity is simply the result of reasoned beliefs grounded in cognitive claims of truth and falsity. Consequently, proving that their acts of self-mortification are not supernatural miracles would seem to constitute definitive proof that the authority and authenticity of spirit possession and spirit mediums is false. In fact, however, the abiding authority and authenticity of any spirit medium in the eyes of his followers and clients is rooted, instead, in a more complex mixture of culturally meaningful cognitive, affective, and social experience. In particular, the religious authority and authenticity—and thus by extension, the legitimacy—of spirit mediums is a product of their effectiveness, first, in constituting themselves as persuasive, charismatic presences in the lives of their followers and clients and, second, in fostering over time psychologically intense and intimate forms of mutual identification, recognition, and need between themselves and their followers and clients.

This complex social and performative foundation of authenticity and authority is exactly what is missing for most of the ITV audience watching Chuchaat's televised confession. It is, in fact, rendered nearly impossible by the large-scale and televised nature of the performative event itself. Its centrality to the social and cultural dynamics of the subculture of spirit mediums, however, is ironically revealed during a brief, televised moment after Chuchaat's confessional performance is over. Several loyal followers of Chuchaat are interviewed on camera and asked what they think of Chuchaat's confession and revelations. Many respond by indicating that they aren't really sure what to make of his assertions. A few, however, also proceed to confess rather sheepishly that they still believe in the reality of spirit mediums, and, moreover, they even still believe that Chuchaat is really an authentic spirit medium. Paradoxically then, the charismatic intimacy and identification underlying Chuchaat's authority and authenticity as a spirit medium has survived, at least initially, even his own explicit attempt to deny and disavow it. It is not surprising, therefore, that Thepchai, in all honesty, had to admit that ITV, in the end, could only provoke the beginning of skepticism among the followers of spirit mediums, since even Chuchaat could do no better.

CONCLUSION

Spirit mediums, and the subcultural world they inhabit, typically exist in the shadowy margins of Thai collective consciousness, appearing only briefly and sporadically on the blurry edge of either the national media's critical and demystifying gaze or the political and cultural elite's agenda of cultural reform. As a set of actors with stigmatized beliefs, values, and practices, the members of the subculture, for the most part, often seem to prefer those shadows. They are quite aware of the fact that at the best of times they evoke ambivalent feelings of skepticism and respect, while at the worst of times they provoke associations with moral decline, social chaos, religious fraud, financial corruption, and violent chicanery. These associations have been a perennial feature of the Thai elite's attitude toward popular religiosity in general ever since the rise of modernist reform Buddhism in the nineteenth century. As such, they have helped to fuel numerous elite-initiated campaigns of prohibition, reform, and demystification designed to solve the problem of popular religiosity by rendering it invisible, inoffensive, or inconceivable.

Spirit mediumship has found itself subject to such projects of moral and religious improvement in the interest of the public's welfare for more than one hundred years. A century ago, Thai monarchical rulers, confident of not only their own moral propriety and religious progressiveness but also the benevolent, patrimonial authority of the modern state they led, relied on the coercive and rationalized power of the law to control spirit mediums through suppression. A policy of policing, prohibition, and judicial punishment lay at the heart of their efforts to guarantee social order and public well-being by eradicating the irrationality and fraudulence of spirit possession from the public sphere. These same general fears, updated in their specifics for a new historical era, continue to animate the sporadic public attacks on spirit mediums in the 1990s. In the contemporary era, however, the Thai state—partly because of its own institutional weakness and partly because of the influence of a competing, modernist ideology of religious freedom and tolerance—has retreated from its earlier willingness to use law and the coercive power of state authority to suppress and prohibit spirit mediums, as well as most other forms of popular religion perceived as unorthodox or deviant.

With the Thai state less certain of its own moral propriety and benevolent authoritarianism, the responsibility for protecting the public from the dangers of spirit mediumship has devolved instead onto a different set of self-appointed guardians and arbiters of the collective good—virtuous monks, public intellectuals, and zealous reporters. Bereft themselves of any significant and coercive institutional power and unable to coax the Thai state into flexing some of its administrative or legal authority in the service of their projects, these public guardians are frequently left with only the power of moral persuasion and media performances at their disposal. Evoking shocking images of either social decline and chaos or personal disrepute and deception, consequently, these crusaders must struggle on their own to educate and inoculate the Thai public against the supposed moral and social dangers of spirit mediums.

While occasionally these public advocates achieve momentary success in demonizing, ostracizing, and marginalizing spirit mediums, they can never actually eradicate the source of their anxieties. Misunderstanding in many ways the fundamental social relations within the subculture of spirit mediums as well as the psychological appeal of spirit mediumship to followers, clients, and the public at large, these guardians of the public sphere frequently stumble and fail when pursuing their efforts of reform and demystification. And yet, while neither prohibition, reform, nor demystification as strategies of social control seem capable of ever achieving definitive or even significant success, there is every indication that they will return over and over as rhetorical tropes within future campaigns that demand, yet again, a resolution to the problem of spirit mediums and which demand this goal with that same passionate intensity and breathless urgency that has characterized all previous campaigns.

ISLAM AND GENDER POLITICS IN LATE NEW ORDER INDONESIA[1]

Suzanne Brenner

The expanding influence of the Islamic movement in Indonesia, as in other parts of the Muslim world, has often been viewed as a sign of a growing social conservatism, particularly where women are concerned. When significant numbers of young women on and around university campuses took to wearing Islamic dress in the late 1970s and early 1980s, for example, many Western observers, as well as some Indonesians, saw this as a step backward for Indonesian women, an indication that the "veiled" women and those who encouraged their new style of dress had subscribed to a view of gender relations that placed them in a clearly subordinate position to men. For those who were most dismayed by the sight of covered young women, the turn to Islamic dress seemed to foreshadow a creeping fundamentalism and the inevitable retreat of Indonesian women, college educated or not, to the home.

Yet as the 1980s wore on and gave way to the 1990s, it became clearer that the impact of the Islamic movement on women and gender relations in Indonesia was more complex than might have initially been assumed. The widespread retreat to the domestic sphere that some had feared did not occur, as many women (veiled or not) who were involved in the movement completed their education and became employed in the public or private sectors. While there were pockets of true fundamentalism in which women were encouraged to devote themselves primarily to domestic roles after marriage, and in which a strict gender segregation was observed, these groups constituted a minority of those who were active in the Islamic movement. Most Islamist women maintained an active presence in public domains, even if they avoided mixing too closely with men.

One could argue, in fact, that the Islamic movement itself gave some women the motivation and the opportunity to take up public roles as activists who were committed to bringing about change in Indonesian society. As one author has

[1] I would like to express my sincere thanks to Farha Ciciek, a sociologist and gender activist who assisted me in arranging and conducting the interviews on which this essay is partly based, and who has been sharing her insights on women and the Islamic movement in Indonesia with me for more than fifteen years. I wish to state, however, that she bears no responsibility for the conclusions reached here.

written about women's involvement in the global Islamic movement, "Contemporary Islamist women are not only the subjects of controversy but also very active participants in the process of public debate."[2] Given the limited opportunities for political expression or social activism that were open to students and others under the repressive Suharto regime, the Islamic movement provided important channels for those who were disaffected with the conditions of New Order Indonesia to become involved in grassroots efforts to transform their society. Women were as eager as men to participate in these efforts. Even some women whose views of gender had been shaped by the more conservative elements of the movement often felt it their duty to work towards change through *dakwah* (proselytizing) activities, if only among other women or through involvement in Muslim student organizations.

Activist women ranged the entire political spectrum, from those who hoped eventually to see an Islamic state and strict application of *shari'a* (Islamic law) as the basis of the Indonesian political and legal systems, to those who envisioned a secular democracy based on international standards of human rights, where Islam's role in society would be primarily spiritual and moral rather than political. What these women shared was a commitment to change and to the implementation of values that can loosely be called "Islamic," however those are defined, within Indonesian society. What divided them were often fundamentally divergent views about the place of religion in state and society, the proper roles of women in relation to men, and whether the words of the Qur'an and hadiths should be interpreted literally or liberally.[3]

In this essay, I will look at Islam and gender politics in the 1980s and especially 1990s. Against the background of the Suharto regime's policies toward women, I will examine some of the controversies and forms of activism that arose in Islamic circles around gender issues. Although I will discuss conservative (a term that I generally prefer to fundamentalist) Muslim views on gender, which had a clear impact on Indonesian society during this period, I will focus more on forms of gender activism in Indonesia that are self-consciously Islamic in character, but which run counter to the conservative forces that are stereotypically associated with Islamization. I am primarily interested here in the gender politics of some of the most liberal Muslim activists, those who have chosen to struggle for women's rights by combining elements of global feminism with ideas about political democratization and social justice that they see as fundamentally compatible with, or even deeply rooted in, the essential spirit of Islam. What distinguishes Islamic gender activists from secular feminists (who may themselves be Muslim) is that the former interpret and convey ideas about women's rights through a specifically Islamic medium, paying particular attention to the ways in which religion has adversely affected women as well as to its

---

[2] Nilüfer Göle, "Snapshots of Islamic Modernities," *Dædalus* 129,1 (Winter 2000): 91-117. Both Göle and Maha Azzam have suggested that in the Muslim world Islamist movements have actually provided opportunities and ideological legitimacy for women's public activities in some contexts, rather than preventing those activities. See Göle, "Snapshops of Islamic Modernities," p. 99, and Maha Azzam, "Gender and the Politics of Religion in the Middle East," in *Feminism and Islam: Legal and Literary Perspectives,* ed. Mai Yamani (New York: New York University Press, 1996), pp. 217-230.

[3] Hadiths are the traditional accounts of sayings and deeds attributed to the Prophet Muhammad and his companions.

potential for fostering social justice and the improvement of women's situation in society.

During the late Suharto era, there emerged a number of nongovernmental organizations as well as individual activists and scholars who were dedicated to promoting women's rights and improving the conditions under which women lived and worked in Indonesia.[4] Their efforts were part of a larger agenda to bring about social and political change, a goal that was shared by many other Indonesians and that ultimately contributed to the downfall of the long-entrenched Suharto regime. Some of these groups approached the issue of women's rights from an Islamic perspective, even as they focused on matters that are generally seen as secular rather than religious in nature, such as workers' rights, violence against women, or reproductive health. While I would not claim that these organizations and individuals or their views on gender are broadly representative of the Islamic resurgence in Indonesia—a remarkably diverse movement that defies broad generalizations in any case—I do believe that their work needs to be examined as a significant but largely overlooked part of the attempt within some sectors of contemporary Indonesian Islam to foster social justice and a vital civil society in Indonesia.

I will suggest, moreover, that both conservative and liberal Islamic views on women were tied in important ways to the gender ideologies and development-oriented, pro-capitalist policies of the Suharto regime, as well as to the wide-ranging influences of globalization. This was an era of social flux in Indonesia, in which the cultures of Western and East Asian capitalism, global Islamism, and transnational discourses on human rights and feminism regularly bumped up against each other as well as against the particular forms of authoritarian government and crony capitalism that characterized the regime. The debates that emerged over women during this period reflected this intermixing of global and domestic ideologies. In exploring both conservative and liberal Islamic perspectives on gender issues, I will try to show that, despite their contradictions, both can be seen as products of the peculiar blend of ideologies that infused Indonesian society during this period and of the contradictory messages that emanated from the New Order regime itself.

CONTRADICTION AND CHANGE: WOMEN UNDER THE SUHARTO REGIME

The so-called New Order period, which began amid the political turmoil and violence of 1965-66 and ended with President Suharto's resignation in 1998, was an era in which the regime attempted to depoliticize women and gender issues—just as it worked to depoliticize other domains of Indonesian society—and to promote a new and (it hoped) stabilizing domesticity for Indonesian women. By encouraging women to concentrate on domestic life, the regime clearly aimed to make women the pillars of secure families that could serve as the building blocks of social and political stability and national development. The political women's organizations of earlier

---

[4] I am using the term "nongovernmental organization" (or NGO) to refer to organizations that in Indonesia during the New Order period were commonly called LSM (*lembaga swadaya masyarakat*, or self-help organization). The term NGO itself was discouraged after 1983 because of its presumed anti-government connotations, though it has been more widely used since the downfall of the Suharto regime. See Gerard Clarke, *The Politics of NGOs in South-East Asia: Participation and Protest in the Philippines* (New York: Routledge, 1998), esp. p. 38.

decades, which included the nationalist organizations of the 1930s and '40s as well as the mass leftist organization GERWANI in the 1950s and '60s, among others, were replaced in the Suharto years by bureaucratic, state-sponsored organizations like Dharma Wanita (Women's Duty) and PKK (Pembinaan Kesejahteraan Keluarga, or Family Welfare Guidance), which fostered the idea that a woman's service to her family should be closely identified with her (and her husband's) service to the nation.[5] The emphasis on women's domestic functions was also formalized in the Marriage Law of 1974, which clearly stated that the husband is the head of the family *(kepala keluarga)*, while the wife's role is that of housewife (or mother of the household, *ibu rumah tangga).*[6]

As I have argued elsewhere, and as others have also observed, the authoritarian Suharto regime treated the family as one of the most important keys to maintaining its own political control; ideological control over women and the family was vital to maintaining control over the nation. I have suggested, too, that the regime attempted to deflect attention from the real social, political, and economic problems that plagued Indonesia during this period by refocusing public scrutiny on the moral behavior of women. The well-behaved New Order wife and mother thus served as an ideological linchpin of the stable, prosperous family as well as the stable, prosperous nation.[7]

Yet the New Order period was not all bad for women. Although many people who have written about the gender politics of the Suharto government, including

---

[5] For a history of GERWANI and other Indonesian women's organizations, see Saskia Wieringa, "Aborted Feminism in Indonesia: A History of Indonesian Socialist Feminism," in *Women's Struggles and Strategies,* ed. Saskia Wieringa (Aldershot: Gower, 1988), pp. 69-89. Another short history of women's organizations can be found in Sukanti Suryochondro, "Timbulnya dan Perkembangan Gerakan Wanita di Indonesia," in *Kajian Wanita dalam Pembangunan,* ed. T. O. Ihromi (Jakarta: Yayasan Obor Indonesia, 1995), pp. 30-68. For two brief retrospectives on Indonesian women's organizations from a post-New Order perspective, see Krishna Sen, "Women on the Move," *Inside Indonesia* 58 (April-June 1999) (online edition; no page numbers available) and Susan Blackburn, "Women and the Nation," *Inside Indonesia* 66 (April–June 2001) (online edition; no page numbers available), at http://www.insideindonesia.org.

[6] Law No. 1 of 1974, Article 31(3). The Marriage Law did offer some protections for women, however—for instance, by stipulating that both the prospective husband and wife had to consent to a marriage before it could take place, and in giving husbands and wives equal rights to divorce—in response to the long-standing demands of Indonesian women's rights organizations for marriage law reform. See Kathryn Robinson, "Images of Femininity: Difference and Diversity," in *Muslim Feminism and Feminist Movement: Southeast Asia,* ed. Abida Samiuddin and R. Khanam (Delhi: Global Vision Publishing House, 2002), pp. 215-251. Robinson also offers a profile of Dharma Wanita and PKK in that article, which examines the New Order regime's policies toward women and the resulting changes in women's lives over the course of the New Order period.

[7] Suzanne Brenner, "On the Public Intimacy of the New Order: Images of Women in the Popular Indonesian Print Media," *Indonesia* 67 (April 1999): 13-38. Julia Suryakusuma coined the term "State Ibuism" (roughly, State Mother-/Wife-ism) to describe the regime's ideological approach to women; she defines this as "the domestication of Indonesian women as dependent wives who exist for their husbands, their families, and the state." (p. 98) She, too, sees this ideology as "part and parcel of the bureaucratic state's effort to exercise control over Indonesian society." (p. 102) In the same article, she discusses the important role of state-run organizations like Dharma Wanita and PKK in promoting State Ibuism. Julia Suryakusuma, "The State and Sexuality in New Order Indonesia," in *Fantasizing the Feminine in Indonesia,* ed. Laurie J. Sears (Durham, NC: Duke University Press, 1996), pp. 92-119.

myself, have been justifiably critical of the government's efforts to domesticate and depoliticize women and to coopt them into the vast machinery of a repressive regime, the decades of the 1970s, 1980s, and 1990s did see a number of improvements for Indonesian women as well. These included higher levels of education and literacy rates for females (as well as for males);[8] the expansion of the middle classes; and generally higher standards of living in Indonesian society.[9] Because the government encouraged both males and females to delay the age of marriage, which was reinforced by changing societal attitudes about what ages were proper and desirable for starting a family, it became possible for more young women to complete secondary and higher education before marrying and having children.[10] The Suharto government's controversial but effective family planning program, which strongly urged (and sometimes coerced) couples to limit themselves to two children, dramatically reduced the birthrate, thereby enabling women to devote more time to themselves, their smaller families, and in some cases, their careers.[11] Finally, at the same time that it promoted the idea that a woman's duties to her family were paramount, the regime also encouraged women to become educated and to participate actively in national development. Many Indonesian women successfully pursued careers as civil servants or in the private sector.[12] To be sure,

---

[8] According to one source, for example, in 1971 only 57.5 percent of Indonesian girls between the ages of ten and fourteen were attending school. By 1990 that number had risen to 82.5 percent. Source: Iwu Dwisetyani Utomo, "Adolescent and Youth Reproductive Health in Indonesia: Status, Issues, Policies, and Programs." Policy paper available online at http://www.policyproject.com/pubs/countryreports/ARH_Indonesia.pdf.

[9] One indicator of this higher standard of living is life expectancy. In 1960, the average life expectancy in Indonesia was only forty-two years; by 2000, it had reached nearly sixty-six years. Source: Canadian International Development Agency web site (http://www.acdi-cida.gc.ca). The average life expectancy in 1999 was 67.4 years for Indonesian females and 63.5 years for males. Source: UNESCO Country Profile on Indonesia (http://www.unesco.or.id/apgest/pdf/indonesia/indonesia.pdf).

[10] The Marriage Law of 1974 officially set the minimum age of marriage at sixteen for females and nineteen for males. Although some marriages were still contracted before that age, particularly in rural areas, the median age at marriage did gradually increase. One source reports that the mean age at marriage in 1971 was 18.8 years in rural areas and 21.1 years in urban areas. By 1990, the mean age at marriage in rural areas had risen to 20.5 and in urban areas to 23.5 years. Source: Iwu Dwisetyani Utomo, "Adolescent and Youth Reproductive Health in Indonesia," p. 7.

[11] According to government statistics, Indonesia's fertility rate was 5.6 children per woman in the late 1960s; by 1992, it had declined by nearly 50 percent to about 2.9 children per woman. The most rapid decline in fertility rates occurred in the 1980s, when the national Family Planning Program expanded to include the entire nation. Infant and child mortality rates also declined substantially during this period. These changes can be attributed in part to the effectiveness of the government's family planning strategies, along with improvements in healthcare, the reduction of the poverty rate, and the urbanization of the population, among other factors. Source: Web site for Department of Foreign Affairs, Republic of Indonesia (http://www.deplu.id.). See also Anders Weidemann, "The Indonesian Family Planning Program and the International Conference on Development and Population: A Comparative Follow-Up Field Study" (Lund, Sweden: Lund University Programme on Population and Development Report No. 26), 1999.

[12] In the early 1990s, approximately one-third of all jobs in the massive Indonesian civil service were reportedly held by women. Although there were relatively few women at the highest echelons, many middle-level positions, including those in public education and public health, were staffed by women. *Indikator Sosial Wanita* (Jakarta: Central Bureau of Statistics, 1991), cited in Robinson, "Images of Femininity," p. 218.

middle- and upper-class women gained the most from all of these changes, but even women of the lower classes obtained some benefits from the reduced birthrates and longer life expectancy, increased access to education, and the expansion of the Indonesian economy.

Changes in women's lives and lifestyles, which were elements of the larger social transformations that occurred during the Suharto years, inevitably contributed to controversies and debates regarding women's roles in the home, in the workplace, and in the wider society. The fact is that the regime's goals of rapid modernization, capitalist development, and ideological as well as bureaucratic control over the population depended heavily on women's participation in the work force, their higher levels of education, as well as on their "voluntary" participation in government-sponsored organizations and activities from the national level down to the neighborhood level. The expansion of the economy also hinged in part on women's willingness to become eager consumers of the new commodities that were flooding the market. While many people welcomed the higher standards of living in Indonesian society, the rapid shift in values and lifestyles that accompanied urbanization, industrialization, modernization, and the rise of the culture of capitalism also created social disjunctions, tensions, and anxieties that were not easily resolved. Women's behavior became a symbolic focus of these tensions, as is often the case in societies undergoing rapid transformation. Changes in women's behavior were scrutinized and sometimes decried, especially when those changes involved greater freedoms, power, or autonomy for women than they had experienced in earlier times.

It is not surprising, then, that when criticisms of the Suharto regime and its policies issued forth from Islamist quarters, becoming more vocal as the Islamic movement gained in strength, there seemed to be a disproportionate emphasis among Muslim conservatives on how women had been led astray by the nation's embracing of capitalism and Western (or "un-Islamic") values—a point to which I will return in the next section. It is also interesting to note that when the Islamic movement began to pick up momentum on and around college campuses in the early 1980s and after, many of those who were attracted to the movement were young women who had clearly benefited from the improvements in educational opportunities and economic development of recent decades. A significant number of both females and males who joined Islamic student organizations came from small-town families that had managed to climb their way into the middle classes during the New Order period. Many of the women represented the first generation of females in their families to complete high school and go to college. In previous generations, few such women would have had the opportunity to go to the cities, removed from the immediate supervision of their parents and the expectation of early marriage and motherhood for females, to attend universities or other institutions of higher education.

For these young women, being able to go to college was a welcome opportunity, but it also brought them into new situations for which their upbringing had not prepared them. A substantial number of the women had been educated in *pesantren* (traditional Islamic boarding schools), where they had lived and studied under strict codes of behavior that prevented them from mixing with males and that had rarely allowed them to experience the world outside school grounds on their own.[13] Even those who had gone to public schools had usually lived fairly circumscribed lives. While I do not want to oversimplify their motivations for joining Islamic student organizations, which are complex, it is probably safe to say that the organizations provided them with an immediate group of peers, many of whom had come from similar backgrounds.[14] Besides giving them a sense of belonging to a community of people with shared experiences and values, the Islamic organizations also offered them codes of behavior, morality, and often dress that may have alleviated their sense of confusion or discomfort at being on their own in the city for the first time. For those who had been raised in devout households or sent to *pesantren* for their education, belonging to an Islamic organization reinforced the religious upbringing that had been an integral part of their lives before coming to the city. However, not all of those who joined Islamic organizations were from devout backgrounds; some of those who were attracted to the movement became considerably more religious than their own families, sometimes to the consternation of their parents, who feared that their children had become "fanatical" Muslims.

Young Islamist women, then, seemed to embody some of the contradictions of the New Order period. Having benefited directly or indirectly from the development-oriented policies of the regime, they nevertheless chose to participate in a movement that was often quite critical of that regime and its political, economic, and moral corruption. Taking full advantage of the opportunity to leave their small-town backgrounds in order to pursue higher education and, many hoped, solidly middle-class lives, they also willingly took up the disciplines and self-restrictions of the Islamic resurgence, which were especially rigorous for women.[15] Yet becoming involved in the Islamic movement did not necessarily mean accepting subordinate status to men. Some of these women even took up leadership roles in Islamic organizations. In 1996, for instance, I interviewed a student at IAIN (Institut Agama Islam Negeri, or National Islamic Institute), the highly regarded, state-run Islamic

---

[13] Many *pesantren* provide secular as well as religious education to their students. This makes it possible for *pesantren* students to attend secular or Islamic universities after graduation. For a broad study of the institution of *pesantren*, see Zamakhsyari Dhofier, *The Pesantren Tradition: The Role of the Kyai in the Maintenance of Traditional Islam in Java* (Tempe, AZ: Program for Southeast Asian Studies, Arizona State University, 1999).

[14] For more on Indonesian women's motivations for joining the Islamic movement and taking up Islamic dress, see Suzanne Brenner, "Reconstructing Self and Society: Javanese Muslim Women and 'the Veil,'" *American Ethnologist* 23,4 (November 1996): 673-97.

[15] Scholars who have written about women's involvement in the Islamic movement in other countries have similarly observed that the social changes that have resulted in increased levels of education, employment opportunities, and mobility for women have also led, in an apparent paradox, to their voluntary participation in a movement that seems to restrict them. In an insightful article about the women's mosque movement in Egypt, for example, Saba Mahmood notes that the ability of large numbers of women, for the first time in Egyptian history, to hold public meetings in mosques to teach and study Islamic doctrine has been "facilitated by the mobility and sense of entitlement engendered by women's greater access to education and employment outside of the home in postcolonial Egypt. In the last forty years, women have entered new social domains and acquired new public roles from which they were previously excluded. A paradoxical effect of these developments is the proliferation of forms of piety that seem incongruous with the trajectory of the transformations that enabled them in the first place." Saba Mahmood, "Feminist Theory, Embodiment, and the Docile Agent: Some Reflections on the Egyptian Islamic Revival," *Cultural Anthropology* 16,2 (May 2001): 203-4.

university that has campuses in a number of Indonesian cities. This young woman was the first female head of the Yogyakarta chapter of PMII (Pergerakan Mahasiswa Islam Indonesia), a large Islamic student association with close ties to the mass Islamic organization Nahdlatul Ulama. She and many others in PMII had originally come from small towns and a traditional Islamic *pesantren* education, but the open atmosphere in Yogyakarta (where, as she put it, "the influence of feminism is spreading,") had led some of them to question the notion that women were not well suited to being leaders, as well as other ideas about women that had been passed down to them as part of their traditionalist upbringing. Many of her male friends had urged her to assume a leadership role in the organization, and she claimed that she had encountered no resistance from either males or females to becoming the head of the local PMII. She ultimately hoped to use her education in Islamic philosophy and theology to become an interpreter of hadiths, with the hope that she could reinterpret these Islamic texts from a perspective that was more sympathetic to women than the traditional interpretations.

The New Order period, in short, brought about extensive changes for Indonesian women—changes that sometimes seemed to give rise to their own contradictions. As the Suharto regime celebrated modern Indonesian women and the progress they had made as emblems of *pembangunan,* national development, it simultaneously called on them to maintain the proper moral order and "Eastern" or "traditional" values of Indonesian society by exercising self-restraint and self-sacrifice. They were urged to keep the needs of their husbands, their children, and the nation foremost in their minds.[16] Alternative discourses on women and gender also emerged from outside the regime during this period, such as those that were generated by conservative Islamists as well as by liberal and feminist critics of the Suharto government. Conservative Islamic discourses reinforced and even surpassed the regime's efforts to control women and to focus their lives on the home. Liberal feminists, on the other hand, criticized the regime's conservative gender policies as well as other forces in Indonesian society, including capitalism and conservative Islam, which they saw as perpetuating the inequalities and hardships that women suffered, despite the gains that they had made in some areas.

In the sections that follow, I will give examples of some of these conflicting discourses on gender from the late Suharto era, focusing on those of Muslim conservatives at one end of the spectrum and Muslim feminists at the other. Critics of the regime's policies at both ends of the Islamic spectrum were clearly responding to the transformations that had occurred in Indonesian society, especially in women's social roles and relationships with men, over the course of the New Order period. At the same time, these critics drew on global discussions and debates regarding women and gender issues that sometimes became intermeshed in Indonesia in unusual ways. I will concentrate in particular on the perspectives of Islamic feminists, whose approaches to gender issues were among the more unexpected products of these interpenetrating global discussions, and who saw both the Suharto regime and many of its conservative Muslim critics as fostering

---

[16] Kathryn Robinson also points out the inconsistency between the New Order regime's gender ideologies and the effect of its development-minded policies on actual gender roles and relations. As she puts it, " . . . in broadcasting an essentialised image of the ideal Indonesian woman as loyal wife and dutiful mother, the regime denied the transformation and diversification of women's roles that its own relentless campaign for material expansion had helped to bring about." Robinson, "Images of Femininity," p. 215.

ideologies and policies that led to the continued subordination and abuse of Indonesian women.[17]

CONSERVATIVE MUSLIM VIEWS ON WOMEN

The late 1970s and the 1980s witnessed a worldwide Islamic resurgence, spurred on by the 1979 Islamic revolution in Iran and by other political and social developments with widespread significance for Muslim societies. In Indonesia, the country with the largest Muslim population in the world, this period marked the beginning of a revitalization of Islamic belief and practice that had a deep impact on many aspects of social and political life—a movement that at present shows no sign of diminishing. The impact of the global Islamic movement in Indonesia was heightened by national developments. The Suharto regime promoted what is often referred to as "cultural Islam," and advocated the practice of religion in general, as a way of maintaining social stability and ostensibly to prevent the revival of communism (which had been eradicated by the anticommunist massacres and arrests of 1965–66). While insisting that the government remain secular (at the same time that it officially mandated the belief in one God) and fostering the concepts of religious pluralism and tolerance in Indonesia, over time the regime increasingly demonstrated its support for Islam, the religion of nearly 90 percent of Indonesia's population. Measures taken by the government included, among many others, coordinating the annual *haj* for thousands of Indonesian pilgrims; sponsoring the building of mosques and prayer halls; backing the establishment of Islamic banks; making it more difficult for Muslims to marry non-Muslims; and courting Muslim intellectuals through its establishment in 1990 of ICMI (Ikatan Cendekiawan Muslim Indonesia, Association of Indonesian Muslim Intellectuals). Each of these measures was carefully calculated to work to the regime's political benefit. However, the regime also strove to ensure that religion would not get in the way of capitalist development or political stability, carefully monitoring Muslim associations and individuals for any signs of political Islam, and quickly moving to suppress any Islamists who were seen as a potential threat to the regime's own control over the nation.

---

[17] Not all Islamic gender activists choose to refer to themselves as feminists, and I include in the category "Islamic feminist" people who might not necessarily use this label themselves. I take a broad approach to the term "feminism" here, using it to encompass, as Paidar puts it, "any type of activism by women focusing on their gender interests within any political or ideological framework." (p. 64) An Islamic feminist, by this definition, is someone who engages in "gender activism within an Islamic framework." (p. 57) Parvin Paidar, "Feminism and Islam in Iran," in *Gendering the Middle East*, ed. Denise Kandiyoti (Syracuse, NY: Syracuse University Press, 1996), pp. 51-67. It should be noted that there are precedents for using the term "Islamic feminism" in the Indonesian context. For example, Lily Zakiyah Munir writes about the "Islamic feminism movement" (*gerakan feminisme Islam*), which "makes the teachings of Islam the foundation for examining the position and role of women." Lily Zakiyah Munir, "Pengantar Penerbit," in *Memposisikan Kodrat: Perempuan dan Perubahan dalam Perspektif Islam*, ed. Lily Zakiyah Munir (Bandung: Mizan, 1999), p. 5. Similarly, Budhy Munawar-Rachman writes, "What is distinctive about Islamic feminism (*feminisme Islam*) is an intensive dialogue between the principles of justice and equality that are found in religious texts—for example, the Qur'an, Hadiths and religious traditions—and the reality of how women are treated in Muslim society." Budhy Munawar-Rachman, "Islam dan Feminisme: Dari Sentralisme Kepada Kesetaraan," in *Membincang Feminisme, Diskurses Gender Perspektif Islam*, ed. Mansour Fakih et al. (Surabaya: Risalah Gusti, 1996), p. 202.

With the growth of the Islamic movement, the Suharto regime was forced to come to terms with a popular movement that it was not able to control completely from the outset. Despite the fact that the regime dealt harshly with those it accused of advocating an Islamic state in Indonesia, the Islamic movement nevertheless became a channel for expressing discontent with the regime and with the social and political status quo, among both Muslim conservatives and liberals. Although the regime successfully coopted many Muslim leaders, and many members of the middle and upper classes themselves became more devout even as they continued to support the political status quo (including high-ranking officials of Suharto's government), there were still Muslim critics of the regime who would not allow themselves to be coopted or to be placated by its concessions to Islamic interests, which increased over the course of the 1980s and 90s.[18]

During the New Order period and beyond, Muslim conservatives who felt that Western values had become too pervasive in Indonesian society waged a relentless campaign to convince the public that Muslim families and the society at large were in grave danger as a result of improper behavior that reflected "foreign" rather than "Islamic" moral standards. While both men and women were entreated to behave in accordance with Islamic codes of conduct, women in particular were targeted for having strayed from Islam by exposing their bodies, selfishly pursuing their own careers and personal pleasures instead of focusing on their families, and otherwise behaving inappropriately or even immorally. These messages were conveyed to women through popular Islamic books and magazines; through sermons at *pengajian*, group recitations of the Qur'an that take place in mosques, homes, or other locations; and at meetings of Islamic organizations, which flourished during this period.

Women were enjoined by proponents of conservative Islam to wear modest Islamic dress, covering their entire body, hair, and neck.[19] They were instructed that their highest purpose and duty in life was to be good wives and mothers who would faithfully serve their husbands and raise the next generation of observant Muslims. While all Muslims are equal in the eyes of God, they were told, there is a clear separation of male and female functions and obligations that is based on the innate, God-given differences *(kodrat)* between the sexes. Women are responsible for taking care of children and the home, while men are expected to deal with the world outside the home and to support the family financially. A woman's greatest glory is to fulfill her domestic obligations as well as she possibly can, rather than to seek personal satisfaction in the working world. Women were warned that abandonment of their familial duties on a large scale would result in the unavoidable decline of the

---

[18] On the cooptation of Muslim leaders by the Suharto regime, as well as resistance to that cooptation, see, e.g., Robert W. Hefner, *Civil Islam: Muslims and Democratization in Indonesia* (Princeton: Princeton University Press, 2000), esp. chapter six; and Mohammad Fajrul Falaakh, "Islam and the Current Transition to Democracy in Indonesia," in *Reformasi: Crisis and Change in Indonesia*, ed. Arief Budiman, Barbara Hatley, and Damien Kingsbury (Clayton, Australia: Monash Asia Institute, 1999), pp. 201-211.

[19] Some fundamentalist groups encouraged women to cover their faces, hands, and feet as well, though the number of Islamist women who covered their faces was small. A further point that should be raised is that not all women who wear Islamic dress subscribe to conservative Islamist views. Many liberal Muslim women, even those who work for women's rights, also wear some form of Islamic dress; they see no inherent contradiction between their clothing style and their political views, and often find that wearing modest dress makes other Muslims more receptive to their ideas.

institution of the family, with children being neglected and divorce becoming rampant. Without strong families, society would soon break down and people would forget their religious duties. The consequences of ignoring one's obligations as a Muslim woman, in short, would be dire.

Books and magazines containing messages like these, which aim to capture a large Muslim audience, have a wide circulation in Indonesia. One typical book of this type that was published in the early 1990s, consisting of just under one hundred pages of commentary and advice, is entitled *Emancipation, Career, and Women*.[20] Here the author argues that Western-style "emancipation" (*emansipasi*) for women is a trap that leads them out of the home and away from the teachings of Islam, ultimately bringing about great harm to the women themselves, their families, and society. Physically and emotionally women are of different character from men, he suggests, based on his reading of Islamic texts; women are more delicate, pliant, and soft, while men are stronger, more agile, and better able to struggle and compete to overcome hardship and adversity. (p. 86) Women's "nature and function" (*kodrat dan fungsi wanita*, p. 15) make them best suited to childbearing, childrearing, and caring for the home, while men are inherently better equipped to deal with the harsh demands of the working world. As the head of the household, a man has the right to supervise and control the behavior of his wife and family. According to Islamic principles, men should properly be in charge of women; first, because men are better suited by nature to working outside the home, and second, because men have a duty to support their families. (p. 86)

Career women, the author proposes, should actually be seen as "creatures of a third gender" (*makhluk jenis ke tiga*); they would rather push their way into the working world of men, trying to act like males, than to follow their naturally feminine character (*fitrah kewanitaannya*). (p 16) Furthermore, men's divinely ordained leadership over women becomes meaningless when women and men are placed in the same sphere of employment with the same status or rank. (p. 89) The text on the back cover states that the book is aimed especially at the "younger generation of intellectual Muslim women" and that it is intended as a criticism of people's negligence concerning the teachings of religion and as a warning about "the danger that threatens us" (*bahaya yang mengancam kita*) and "the terrible wave of 'emancipation and careerization of women' [*gelombang dahsyat 'emansipasi dan karirisasi wanita'*] that is increasingly sweeping over us these days."

In an interview that I conducted at his home in Yogyakarta in 1997, Mohammad Thalib, the author of this book and a former lecturer at several Islamic universities, underscored his deep commitment to the kinds of views expressed in his book. He denied that Islam treats women as inferior to men, but he also claimed that God gave men superiority (*kelebihan*) to women in certain areas, which entitles them to be the leaders of women within the family. He stated without hesitation that women's primary place is in the home, and that there are great perils in store for civilization

---

[20] M. Thalib, *Emansipasi, Karir dan Wanita* (Solo: Ramadhani, 1991). The author of this book, a prolific writer of short, popular books on Islam and family matters, told me in 1997 that he had already published twenty-eight such books; he was planning to write 180 in all. To save time, he would dictate the books into a tape recorder and someone else would type them into a computer. He claimed that ten thousand copies of his books could be sold in six months. I purchased this book in Gramedia, a major Indonesian bookstore chain, which had a large selection of similar books on Islam, women, and the family. At the time of purchase, the book had already gone into its fourth printing.

when women insist on behaving like men and vice versa. Feminism and "the culture of free sex" (which he saw as being closely linked to each other) would inevitably lead women to refuse to marry and have children altogether. Indeed, this process had already begun in the United States, he argued; he predicted, moreover, that the United States would collapse *(ambruk)* within fifty years because of its loose moral standards. "America doesn't think logically" *(Amerika tidak berfikir logis)*, he remarked. "People don't realize that things like free sex and homosexuality are dangerous." He felt that there was a great need for books like his, which would serve as a warning to Indonesians about the risks they faced if they followed in the footsteps of the West. "I'm making a contribution towards solving civilization's problems" *(Saya memberikan kontribusi untuk menyelesaikan masalah peradaban)*, he declared, explaining what drove him to write so many books on the subject of Islam, women, and the family.

Views like Thalib's were commonly expressed in conservative Muslim circles. The influence of these views was growing in some sectors of Indonesian society—a society that has a very long history of women working outside the home, and where Islamic laws and prescriptions affecting women and their relationships with men have often been softened or circumvented in practice as they have encountered local cultures.[21] The fact that women throughout the Indonesian archipelago had traditionally engaged in farming, trade, and other extradomestic activities to contribute to the family's livelihood, and that public space had never been symbolically demarcated as a male domain, did not prevent Muslim conservatives from attempting to impose codes of behavior on women that were associated more with Middle Eastern cultural conventions than Southeast Asian ones. The real targets of conservative discourse on women were not long-standing local practices, however, but the new "freedoms" for women that were associated with images of the West—images that were constantly bombarding the Indonesian public through television, film, and other forms of mass media. *Emansipasi* for women implied licentiousness, neglect or abandonment of the family, and choosing a life of self-gratification over one of religious and moral obligation.

In the eyes of many people who shared Thalib's views, the New Order regime had been far too lax in allowing Western values to flood Indonesian society along with Western goods and Western investments. Many felt that the regime had done little to stem this tide of Western permissiveness and immorality and that a stricter application of Islamic laws and values was needed to prevent Indonesia from going

---

[21] One example of this can be found in the patterns of inheritance among various Indonesian ethnic groups whose members are mostly or exclusively Muslim. Although Islamic rules of inheritance prescribe that daughters should receive only half the inheritance that their brothers receive, in practice many Indonesian Muslims evade this requirement by providing equal shares of the inheritance to sons and daughters (a fairly common practice in Java, for instance, where it is considered the inheritance pattern traditionally preferred by Javanese), or even giving larger shares to daughters than to sons. Among the matrilineal Minangkabau, who consider themselves devout Muslims, highly valued ancestral property, including land and houses, is passed down from mother to daughter, bypassing sons altogether. See Evelyn Blackwood, *Webs of Power: Women, Kin, and Community in a Sumatran Village* (Lanham, MD: Rowman and Littlefield, 2000), esp. p. 55. Robinson also briefly discusses the complicated relationships between local cultural practices and Islamic conventions, particularly with regard to gender issues (including inheritance), among three Indonesian ethnic groups. Kathryn Robinson, "Gender, Islam and Culture in Indonesia," in *Love, Sex and Power: Women in Southeast Asia,* ed. Susan Blackburn (Clayton: Monash Asia Institute, 2001), pp. 17-30.

the way of the morally bankrupt nations of the West. The government's unwillingness to implement *shari'a* was also a sore point for some Muslim conservatives, who believed that a legal system based primarily on Western jurisprudence did not properly serve the needs of a largely Muslim nation.[22]

Staunch Muslim fundamentalists also went considerably farther than the regime in trying to convince people that women's place was, above all, in the home. Although the Suharto government urged women to dedicate themselves first and foremost to the welfare of their families, it did not really try to stop them from entering the working world. On the contrary, women's labor—whether in factories, offices, rice fields, or schools—was crucial to the New Order's development plans and the growth of the economy. Cheap female labor was essential to producing such commodities as Nike shoes and bluejeans for the competitive global market.[23] In addition, the regime sometimes came into conflict with Islamist factions over other policies concerning females, as seen in its initial unwillingness to allow girls and young women to wear the Islamic headscarf in public schools and universities—a policy that was eventually overturned in 1991 under the pressure of lawsuits and the vocal demands of Muslim leaders and citizens.[24] Thus, while there were certain

---

[22] Since Independence in 1945, the Indonesian state has been a secular one. In the early years of the Republic of Indonesia, there were sharp political battles over whether the Indonesian Constitution should require all Muslims to follow the rules of *shari'a*. Muslim leaders argued that the Constitution should include a phrase obliging all Muslim citizens to carry out their religious duties, and an original draft of the preamble to the 1945 Constitution (which later became known as the "Jakarta Charter") included a vaguely worded clause to this effect. Some devout Muslims went so far as to insist that the Indonesian state itself and its legal codes should be based on Islam. However, there was stiff resistance to these proposals from those who advocated a secular state and civil legal code, and the secularists prevailed. The seven words requiring the state to carry out the requirements of *shari'a* for all Muslims were dropped. This did not silence Islamist factions, who have continued to call for the implementation of *shari'a* in Indonesia, with some recent successes in the post-Suharto era. Indonesia does have Islamic courts which have been used primarily in matters of family law such as divorce and inheritance disputes, but their scope of authority has remained somewhat limited. On the debates over the implementation of *shari'a* from the early period of the Republic through the post-New Order era, see the Introduction and subsequent essays in *Shari'a and Politics in Modern Indonesia*, ed. Arskal Salim and Azyumardi Azra (Singapore: Institute of Southeast Asian Studies, 2003). For a broader discussion of the relationship between the Indonesian state, civil law, and Islamic legal traditions and practices, see John R. Bowen, *Islam, Law, and Equality in Indonesia* (Cambridge, UK: Cambridge University Press, 2003).

[23] On the exploitation of female labor as an integral part of the New Order regime's industrial development policies, and for an in-depth look at the effects of these policies on young, rural women and their families, see Diane Wolf, *Factory Daughters: Gender, Household Dynamics, and Rural Industrialization in Java* (Berkeley: University of California Press, 1992).

[24] In January 1991, approximately five hundred young women wearing *jilbab* (Islamic dress that includes the headscarf) gathered at Al Azhar Mosque in Jakarta to celebrate the Ministry of Education's declaration that it would permit students to wear the Islamic headdress to school. The decision was made following a meeting between Ministry officials and representatives from the government-sponsored Council of Indonesian *Ulama* (Majelis Ulama Indonesia, or MUI), a body of prominent Muslim leaders and officials from the Ministry of Religious Affairs that advises the government and issues statements (*fatwa*) on religious and social issues. Prior to that time, some female students had been forbidden to wear the headscarf in public schools or even expelled for doing so by school principals who said that it did not meet the code for school uniforms. In the late 1980s, some female students, represented by the well-known female lawyer Nursjahbani Katjasungkana of the Indonesian Legal Aid Institute (Lembaga Bantuan Hukum), sued their principals for banning the headscarf or

similarities between the regime's views on women and those of conservative Muslims, notably in that both saw control over women and the family as central to establishing and maintaining social order, Muslim conservatives tended to see the government's policies as encouraging permissiveness and moral corruption, while the regime often considered Muslim conservatives' views (especially those of true fundamentalists) to be extreme.

I would like to point out that in spite of the uncompromising pronouncements made by conservative Muslims—frequently men—about women's nature and proper roles, even those women and men who belonged to relatively conservative Muslim student groups did not always agree with the idea that women should devote themselves exclusively to the home after marriage. Many women who were studying for their degrees were reluctant to shut the doors that a university education had opened for them. For instance, when I asked the head of the women's section of a conservative student group in Yogyakarta, Jama'ah Shalahuddin, whether she hoped to work after marrying and having a family, she told me that she did, though there would have to be a "process of negotiation" *(proses perundingan)* with her husband first. Dewi was studying psychology and wanted to go on for her masters degree, ultimately hoping to pursue a career in counseling. "It would be a pity if all my knowledge were to go to waste," she smiled. In other words, ideology did not always translate to practice, and even those who could reasonably be placed on the conservative end of the Islamist spectrum did not necessarily adopt conservative dogma wholeheartedly.

Alternative Muslim Perspectives: *Gender* and Islamic Feminism

While conservative Islamic discourse on women did have an influence on the Indonesian public, not all Muslims were swayed by the conservatives' arguments. Many moderate Muslims (as well as non-Muslims) found such views on gender to be out of step with the trajectory of modern Indonesian society, labeling them as regressive rather than progressive. Liberal Muslims, especially those who supported the notion of gender equality, regarded the conservatives' pronouncements with alarm, fearing that widespread adoption of such opinions would result in dramatic setbacks for Indonesian women and women's rights. They also realized, however, that in the increasingly religious climate of Indonesia in the 1990s, Muslim conservatives' strident condemnation of women's "Westernized" behavior, their insistence on men's God-given right to be leaders of women, and their efforts to restrict women's activities could not be effectively opposed by secular responses alone. They thus developed a religious counter-discourse that attempted to answer conservative Islamic views on women and gender with alternative interpretations of Islamic texts–interpretations that were far more compatible with the principle of gender equality than those offered by the conservatives.

---

expelling them. The decree allowing the headscarf in public schools was issued while the lawsuits were still pending. *Jakarta Post,* January 21, 1991 (page numbers not available). Even after this decision, however, there were still some restrictions on wearing the headscarf in certain situations that were regulated by the government. For example, in the early 1990s several students told me of their indignation at being required to remove their headscarves for the official photographs needed to secure their high school diplomas or drivers' licenses. See Brenner, "Reconstructing Self and Society," p. 679.

These alternative readings were, they insisted, in keeping with the underlying spirit of the Qur'an and the teachings of the Prophet Muhammad. The original intent of the Qur'an and the Prophet had been to protect women and to uphold their basic equality with men in the eyes of God, they maintained. But that intent had been corrupted by centuries of Qur'anic exegesis that was profoundly biased by the patriarchal tendencies of Arab cultures. The liberal interpreters claimed that by looking beyond this male-biased exegetical tradition to the essential spirit of Islam, Muslim women would take their place beside men as equals rather than as subordinates, with women given their due rights within the family and society.

This alternative religious discourse on women did not arise in a vacuum. During the late 1980s and especially the 1990s, the movement to promote women's rights had been gaining momentum in Indonesia, even as Islamic conservatives were condemning the evils of Western feminism and attracting greater numbers of followers. There was particular interest in gender issues in NGO circles, which were broadly concerned with fostering human rights, of which women's rights were seen as a part. NGO activists in Indonesia were attuned to the efforts of international organizations that were working to raise global awareness of gender issues. They were also influenced by the high-profile, UN-sponsored international conferences on women and on population and reproduction issues in Nairobi (1985), Cairo (1994), and Beijing (1995). Some local organizations that received grants from international agencies like Oxfam or NOVIB (Netherlands Organization for International Development Cooperation) were told that if they wanted their funding to continue, they would need to devote greater attention to gender issues. These granting agencies conducted training sessions among the leaders of local NGOs to promote an awareness of gender concerns and to help them to institute gender-focused workshops and programs. While some local organizations took this more seriously than others, by the early to mid-1990s a substantial number of Indonesian NGOs had some focus on gender, whether serious or superficial, as part of their overall program.[25]

The emphasis on gender issues within NGOs apparently influenced public views as well. By the mid-1990s, talk of *gender* (which usually implied the notion of gender equality) had become commonplace, not only in NGOs but also in universities, in public forums, and in the mass media.[26] Although people with a conservative bent were suspicious of the concept, the word *gender* appears to have been somewhat more palatable to the Indonesian public than *feminisme*, a term that smacked of Western hedonism and loose moral values for many Indonesians, including some who were actively working to promote women's rights.[27] While there were ongoing

---

[25] Interview with Mansour Fakih, Indonesian representative for Oxfam UK, Yogyakarta, July 31, 1997.

[26] The meaning of the Indonesian word *gender* (pronounced like and sometimes spelled *jender*) in casual usage was often somewhat different from its English equivalent, as I discovered after some initial confusion at hearing remarks like "That's a really *gender* ad" *(Iklan itu sangat gender)* or "My father was *gender* ahead of his time" *(Bapak saya sudah gender duluan).* In colloquial Indonesian, the term *gender* had come to mean something like "equality between the sexes." To say that an advertisement or one's father was very *gender* meant that they seemed to advocate equality between males and females.

[27] I was told that the wide acceptance of the term *gender* resulted partly from its adoption by the Ministry of Women's Affairs, which gave it an aura of public legitimacy (Farha Ciciek, personal communication). In 1993, the New Order government asserted its commitment to equality between males and females, which "was to be achieved by subjecting government

debates about what "gender equality" *(kesetaraan gender)* should mean in practice, the issue of women's rights had become a more legitimate topic for public discussion—a topic which, however, continued to provoke controversy and emotional responses from various segments of the population.

The recognition that gender issues gained in the 1990s came somewhat belatedly. Among the general population and even among the ranks of NGO activists and intellectuals, the struggle for women's rights had been eyed with some skepticism during the earlier years of the New Order. Feminism was by no means unknown, particularly among educated urbanites, but many Indonesians who associated the women's rights movement with the more extreme versions of Western-style feminism considered it an imported movement that reflected "foreign" values, and which was therefore inappropriate to the Indonesian cultural context. Until the late 1980s, even those NGO activists who might otherwise have been sympathetic to the goals of feminism (whether or not they actually accepted the term *feminisme*) tended to see gender issues as less pressing than other problems that plagued New Order Indonesia. These problems included a government that was rife with corruption from top to bottom; lack of democratic social, political, and legal institutions and a robust civil society; continued widespread poverty; extensive human rights abuses; and a sharply inequitable distribution of wealth. Inequality between the sexes was seen as a matter that was relatively minor in comparison to these issues. Furthermore, there was a good deal of confusion about what exactly "equality" would, or should, entail. Did it mean that women would have to behave like men and abandon all aspects of their femininity? That men would lose their status and respect as the head of the family? The idea of equality was threatening to those who saw it as undermining local religious and cultural traditions. The small number of Indonesians who did embrace a Western-style feminism, such as those who founded the pioneering Indonesian women's rights organization Kalyanamitra in 1984, were often criticized for trying to push a radical agenda that was incompatible with Indonesian culture and out of sync with the most urgent needs of Indonesian society.

By the mid-1990s, some of the resistance to the notion of gender equality and women's rights had been eroded by the efforts of local and international NGOs, which tried to make people understand that terms like "gender equality" or "women's rights" did not mean that women would have to behave like men, or that women who embraced these concepts would come to think of themselves as superior to men, or that they would have to abandon the ideals of marriage and motherhood and dedicate themselves to a self-indulgent life of free sex as a result—all of which were common stereotypes associated with feminism. NGOs tended to focus on what they saw as the most concrete and pressing problems faced by Indonesian women, such as poverty, exploitation and sexual harassment in the workplace, rape and domestic violence, and reproductive health issues. At the same time, they worked to educate the public—and themselves—on the broader social, political, economic, and religious factors that contributed to these problems for women.

Those who chose to take a religious approach to these issues in addition to, or in place of, secular approaches, believed that the dominant "patriarchal" interpretations

---

policy to 'gender analysis' *(analisa jender)*, as if to acknowledge the need to address inequalities of power between women and men." Robinson, "Images of Femininity," p. 216. In 1997, women's issues were debated for the first time in the campaign leading up to the national elections. Ibid., p. 248.

of Islamic texts and the conservative approaches of religious leaders were fundamental obstacles to women's rights and gender equality in Indonesia. There was a growing recognition among Muslim gender activists that in order to overcome these obstacles, they would need to address directly, rather than ignore or attempt to circumvent, the influence of Islam. Some international funding agencies, such as the Ford Foundation, also came to recognize the value of incorporating religion into the effort to advance women's rights and provided grants to local NGOs that were engaged in these activities.

Muslim gender activists in Indonesia were aware of, and sometimes in contact with, Muslim feminists from other countries. The writings of Muslim feminist scholars like Fatima Mernissi and Riffat Hasan were translated into Indonesian and read and discussed by many people who were sympathetic to their arguments. Muslim women's rights organizations both in and outside Indonesia shared information and ideas with each other and sometimes participated in each others' seminars and publications. One organization whose members were in contact with Muslim feminists in Indonesia was Sisters in Islam, based in Malaysia.[28] Aihwa Ong writes about Sisters in Islam, which has been working to promote gender equality within an Islamic framework and to fight the increasing power of conservative *ulama* (Islamic theologians and leaders whose religious pronouncements often have the force of law) in Malaysian society.[29] As in Indonesia, Muslim feminists in Malaysia have argued that women should be well educated in both secular and religious matters, and that they should engage in *ijtihad*, the use of independent reasoning, to interpret the Qur'an and other Islamic texts for themselves, instead of relying solely

---

[28] For example, articles by Indonesian gender activists were included in a book entitled *Islam, Reproductive Health and Women's Rights,* which was based on a regional workshop organized by Sisters in Islam in 1998. The four-day workshop included participants from Indonesia, Malaysia, the Philippines, Singapore, Thailand, Egypt, Pakistan, and the U.S. (from Sisters in Islam's web site: http://www.sistersinislam.org.my/publications/health.htm). *Islam, Reproductive Health, and Women's Rights,* ed. Zainah Anwar and Rashida Abdullah (Petaling Jaya: Sisters in Islam, 2000).

[29] Aihwa Ong, "Muslim Feminism: Citizenship in the Shelter of Corporatist Islam." *Citizenship Studies* 3,3 (1999): 355-371. See also Aihwa Ong, "State Versus Islam: Malay Families, Women's Bodies, and the Body Politic in Malaysia," in *Bewitching Women, Pious Men: Gender and Body Politics in Southeast Asia,* ed. Aihwa Ong and Michael Peletz (Berkeley: University of California Press, 1995), pp. 159-194. Ong suggests that with the tacit support of the Malaysian government, which also seeks to contain the power of the *ulama* so as to maintain an environment that is hospitable to capitalist development and modernization, the Sisters use newspapers and other public forums to debate *ulama* proposals that they see as oppressive to or discriminatory against women, such as proposals to make the wearing of Islamic dress *(hijab)* compulsory or to support men's right to beat their wives or to commit polygamy. Ong, "Muslim Feminism," pp. 362-3. In its mission statement, Sisters in Islam declares, "Our efforts to promote the rights of Muslim women are based on the principles of equality, justice and freedom enjoined by the Qur'an as made evident during our study of the holy text." The statement continues: "We uphold the revolutionary spirit of Islam, a religion which uplifted the status of women when it was revealed 1400 years ago. We believe that Islam does not endorse the oppression of women and denial of their basic rights of equality and human dignity. We are deeply saddened that religion has been used to justify cultural practices and values that regard women as inferior and subordinate to men, and we believe that this has been made possible because men have had exclusive control over the interpretation of the text of the Qur'an." Source: Sisters in Islam's web site (http://www.sistersinislam.org.my/home_mission.htm).

on the interpretations of others (usually men).[30] This enables Muslim women to participate fully in public debates over religious matters that affect them and the future of their society. The emphasis on careful reading of the Qur'an and other key Islamic writings in order to seek out new interpretations that allow for the possibility of gender equality lies at the heart of the Islamic feminist movement in various parts of the Muslim world.[31]

Muslim feminists in Indonesia, then, took part in dialogues that crossed national and regional boundaries and that concerned the global community of Muslims. As Ong remarks, "Muslim feminists from around the world have formed links to compare experiences and strategies on combating patriarchal rule in the name of Islam."[32] Even with support from both international funding agencies and a transnational network of Muslim gender activists, however, the challenges of using a religious approach to promote women's rights were still considerable. First, gender activists had to contend with the deepening impact of conservative Islam in Indonesian society. They often found themselves at odds with conservative factions over such issues as domestic violence, reproductive rights, and women's right to enjoy equal status with men in the home, the workplace, and in the sphere of religion. Second, they knew that if they wanted their messages to reach the large population of Indonesian Muslims, they would need to gain a degree of acceptance by Muslim leaders and teachers both in the cities and the countryside, as these teachers have a great deal of influence over how local people understand Islamic texts and codes of behavior. Most Indonesians do not have a sufficient command of Arabic language or Islamic theology to interpret the texts on their own, relying on those more knowledgeable than themselves for religious guidance. In order to speak to these Muslim leaders on their own terms—that is, through a religious discourse rather than, or in addition to, a secular discourse—it was necessary for at least some gender activists to have sufficient knowledge of Islamic theology, history, and hermeneutics to be able to debate with religious leaders about the interpretations and legitimacy of particular passages in the Qur'an and hadiths.[33] Arguing for

---

[30] Ong, "Muslim Feminism," p. 361.

[31] See Budhy Munawar-Rahman, "Islam dan Feminisme," esp. p. 202. For discussions of similar efforts made by Muslim feminists in Iran, see Afsaneh Najmabadi, "Feminism in an Islamic Republic: 'Years of Hardship, Years of Growth,'" in *Islam, Gender, and Social Change*, ed. Yvonne Yazbeck Haddad and John L. Esposito (New York: Oxford University Press, 1998), pp. 59-84; and Valentine M. Moghadam, "Islamic Feminism and Its Discontents: Toward a Resolution of the Debate," in *Gender, Politics, and Islam*, ed. Therese Saliba, Carolyn Allen, and Judith A. Howard (Chicago: University of Chicago Press, 2002), pp. 15-51.

[32] Ong, "Muslim Feminism," p. 361.

[33] The legitimacy of the Qur'an itself could not be questioned—though apparent inconsistencies in the text and the meanings underlying specific passages could be debated—but the hadiths and other commentaries on the Qur'an that had been passed down over the generations were still subject to scrutiny. Those who had an intimate knowledge of the technical details of Islamic history and theology were able to argue that certain commentaries might not be valid because they had been composed by someone whose legitimacy as a Qur'anic interpreter was questionable or because they contained ideas that were not in keeping with the fundamental spirit of the Qur'an. Another argument for the reinterpretation of Islamic texts was that the social and cultural contexts in which Muslims now live are very different from those that were present at the time of the revelation of the Qur'an, and that these changes have to be taken into consideration in applying Islamic principles to contemporary life. For a useful discussion of the arguments given for and against textual reinterpretation, and the complexities of engaging in such reinterpretation, see Bowen,

women's rights from a religious perspective meant being able to demonstrate convincingly that those rights did not conflict with the basic tenets of Islam.

While most Muslim gender activists did not have this kind of in-depth knowledge of the religion, they relied on those who did have sufficient knowledge to make the theological arguments to support their cause. A thorough understanding of Islamic doctrine was needed in order to arrive at new interpretations of Islamic texts that were held to be the source of many problems for women in Muslim societies, such as the widely cited verse of the Qur'an, Surah An-Nisa, Verse 34, which is often understood (some say misunderstood) as supporting the idea that men are essentially superior to women and that a man is permitted to beat his wife if she disobeys him. In addition, a fair number of both male and female activists had studied in *pesantren* prior to attending college, and some had obtained degrees from Islamic universities, including the well-respected National Islamic Institute (IAIN). This background gave them enough familiarity with Islamic doctrine to allow them to engage in debates on some of the religious aspects of women's issues, even if they did not regard themselves as experts.

A small number of intellectuals with expertise in Islamic studies joined formally or informally with NGO activists to promote their cause in Islamic schools, public conferences, informal workshops, university campuses, and the mass media. Although they faced an uphill battle, they did enjoy the moral and to some extent institutional support of Abdurrahman Wahid, the General Chair of Indonesia's largest Islamic organization, Nahdlatul Ulama (commonly known as NU), as well as some other liberal-minded Islamic leaders.[34] As the prominent leader of NU, Wahid worked to transform the organization, which had a mostly rural base and which until that point had generally been known for its traditionalism. In the 1980s, Wahid and others who shared his views proposed that this mass organization had the potential to help bring about fundamental changes in Indonesian society. Their agendas for reform focused on the development of civil society and the empowerment of rural Indonesians, who constituted a significant majority of the population but who generally lacked wealth and political power. They saw Islamic leaders *(ulama)* as the potential agents of this social transformation who should be urged to participate actively in the movement to bring about change.[35] While not all

---

Islam, Law, and Equality in Indonesia, esp. chapter 7 ("Historicizing Scripture, Justifying Equality"), pp. 147-169.

[34] Abdurrahman Wahid, known informally as Gus Dur, eventually became President of the Republic of Indonesia in October 1999 (his tumultuous tenure as President ended in July 2001 when he was removed from office by the Indonesian legislature [MPR, or People's Consultative Assembly]). The organization that he headed before becoming President, Nahdlatul Ulama–reportedly the largest Muslim organization in the world with at least 30 million members–was founded in East Java in 1926. NU is widely influential in Indonesia, particularly in rural areas of Java and Madura. Many of the *pesantren* in this region—roughly seven thousand by some counts—are affiliated with NU, and the organization draws much of its popular support from former students and leaders of these Islamic schools. See Rosalia Sciortino, Lies Marcoes Natsir, and Masdar Mas'udi, "Learning from Islam: Advocacy of Reproductive Rights in Indonesian Pesantren," *Reproductive Health Matters* 8,11 (November 1996): 86-96.

[35] Deep tensions developed in the organization between those who supported Wahid's position and more conservative *ulama* who felt that he was trying to secularize the organization and its goals. See Suzaina Kadir, "Contested Visions of State and Society in Indonesian Islam: The Nahdlatul Ulama in Perspective," in *Indonesia in Transition,* ed. Chris

of NU's leadership agreed with Wahid, his support did make it possible for some liberal Muslim activists to promote their causes either directly or indirectly through NU and some of its affiliated organizations and schools. Wahid was also a supporter of women's rights, which made it possible for gender activists to get a foot in the door, sometimes quite literally, at some *pesantren* and other organizations with ties to NU that might otherwise have been suspicious of their programs.[36]

One of the NGOs that benefited directly from these developments was an organization called Society for *Pesantren* and Community Development (Perhimpunan Pengembangan Pesantren dan Masyarakat, otherwise known as P3M). P3M was founded in Jakarta in 1983 by a group of individuals, some of them members of NU, who envisioned a program of *pesantren*-based community development. From the outset it had dedicated itself to promoting social justice and change by using a liberal Islamic approach. Its members worked against what they perceived as the wrongful use of Islam to legitimate the interests of the dominant political and economic groups in Indonesia.[37] The organization focused its energies on raising critical awareness of how Islam in contemporary Indonesia might be made more responsive to the many social problems that the country faced. P3M sponsored discussions among Islamic leaders and teachers, especially those affiliated with *pesantren,* to encourage them to reexamine classical religious texts (especially those known as *kitab kuning*) in a new light and to reinterpret them in ways that were more open to modern visions of social equality and social justice.[38] Recognizing the influence that *pesantren* leaders *(kyai)* held in Indonesian society, P3M's activists believed that convincing these leaders to consider alternative interpretations of Islamic texts could be a step towards addressing the nation's problems. This was in keeping with Wahid's ideas about encouraging change by promoting critical dialogue about Islam in contemporary society.

While women's issues were not a central focus of P3M in its earlier years, by 1994 the organization had started an outreach program to promote the study and discussion of Islamic laws pertaining to women *(fiqh an-nisa),* with the goal of raising public awareness about the problems facing Indonesian women and the role of religion in either contributing to or potentially alleviating those problems. P3M's program on women focused in particular on women's reproductive health and rights. The organization published books and other publications, including a monthly newsletter that was sent out to *pesantren* and also made available online through P3M's website. Under the guidance of a well-known women's rights activist named Lies Marcoes Natsir, P3M conducted intensive workshops at *pesantren* and

---

Manning and Peter van Diermen (Singapore: Institute of Southeast Asian Studies, 2000), pp. 319-335.

[36] Wahid's wife, Nuriyah Rahman, holds an advanced degree in Women's Studies from the University of Indonesia (received in 1999) and is herself a gender activist. She is particularly involved in the effort to combat violence against women and was active in promoting women's rights during her brief tenure as First Lady.

[37] Sciortino et al., "Learning from Islam," p. 89.

[38] *Kitab kuning* (literally, "yellow books") are works in Arabic that are considered core texts to be studied in *pesantren.* They cover the subjects of jurisprudence *(fikih),* the traditions of the Prophet (hadith), mystical practice *(tasawuf),* and Arabic language, among others. Howard Federspiel, *A Dictionary of Indonesian Islam,* Monographs in International Studies, Southeast Asia Series Number 94 (Athens, Ohio: Ohio University Center for International Studies, 1995), p. 133.

other sites to promote open discussion in the Muslim community, especially among Islamic teachers and leaders, on issues concerning female sexuality, reproductive rights and health, and Islam. Among the issues discussed were women's sexual rights and needs; the high maternal mortality rate and other health problems related to pregnancy, childbirth, and illegal abortions in Indonesia; prevention of unwanted pregnancies and the spread of sexually transmitted diseases; rape and domestic violence; the continuing problems of early marriage and marriages arranged against young women's will; and the lack of knowledge among Indonesian girls and women about matters concerning their reproductive health and rights. The workshops combined practical and straightforward discussion of sexual and reproductive matters with a critical reexamination of religious texts and attitudes that were deemed relevant to these issues. The goal was to advance women's knowledge, rights, and health by educating them and by promoting a progressive approach to Islam. Arguing that the interpretations of the Qur'an that had been passed down over the centuries were full of cultural biases and distortions that deviated from the genuine essence of Islam, P3M's activists encouraged the workshops' participants to consider alternative interpretations that were more sympathetic to women's rights and to the climate of contemporary Indonesian society. A basic premise was that the underlying spirit of Islam aimed to protect and uplift women, not to make them suffer, and that women and men are equal in the eyes of God.[39]

Lies Marcoes Natsir related to me in an interview that she had begun to think of herself as a feminist when she had attended a course on feminism in India in 1990, led by the prominent Indian feminist Kamla Bhasin. When asked why she had come to the course, Lies Marcoes Natsir had replied, by her own account, "I've come here because I'm a Muslim, and I have the fundamental belief as a Muslim that actually in Islam there is no discrimination towards women." But others had challenged her, asking if it were not true that Islam supports polygamy, unequal inheritance by women and men, and other practices that are discriminatory towards women. She was startled by their challenge, but also felt emboldened to declare herself a feminist at that time, because she suddenly realized that although there were aspects of Islam that were problematic, there was also something in the religion that was more sympathetic to women and to the ideals of feminism. She had long been involved in women's issues, but this was the first time that she had been willing to call herself a feminist, a term that she had previously feared. "I realized, 'Yes, because I'm a Muslim, I'm a feminist.' I held the belief that surely within Islam there must be a place to which one can return . . . that in Islam there are the values of justice, but also that in Islam, in the reality of Islam, there is in fact the basis for injustice as well." If one studied the Islamic texts by themselves, she had eventually concluded, one would never find anything like a feminist perspective in them unless one were willing to approach them "methodologically" (*dengan metodologi*, i.e., through contextual reinterpretation). "Because the texts are indeed discriminatory! What puts men and women on an equal footing are the spiritual aspects of the religion. But if you look at the sociology [of Islam], you'll still find that the one [i.e., the man] is higher than the other [the woman]."

Lies Marcoes Natsir and others at P3M had experienced a remarkable willingness among Islamic teachers and others in *pesantren* circles to engage in discussion on issues concerning women's reproductive rights and Islam, as long as

---

[39] Sciortino et al., "Learning from Islam."

they approached these topics by means of established methods of Islamic textual analysis and debate. This openness to new ideas among *pesantren* people frequently exceeded that of Muslims who had no *pesantren* affiliation, including those in universities, she had found. Muslims who were less knowledgeable about Islam often seemed to be more easily threatened by the challenges that she and others were posing to established interpretations of Islamic texts. Regardless of the degree of immersion in Islamic scholarship, however, she had discovered that Indonesian Muslims were generally more open to dialogue about women's reproductive and sexual rights when the ideas were presented through a religious rather than a secular medium.

One of P3M's publications, apparently inspired by the organization's success in promoting discussion of these issues in religious schools, was a book written by its director, Masdar Mas'udi, entitled *Islam and Women's Reproductive Rights: A Dialogue of the* Fiqh [Islamic jurisprudence] *of Empowerment.*[40] The book is written as a fictional dialogue between a female student at a *pesantren* and the *nyai*, the wife of the school's head who oversees the girls' section of the school. The student asks the *nyai* a wide range of questions concerning Islam, reproduction, sexuality, marital issues, and women's roles in the family and wider society. In turn, she receives the older woman's careful answers, with fairly detailed religious explanations. A few of the many questions posed are: According to Islamic law, does a woman have the right to refuse to have sex with her husband? (Yes, at least under certain circumstances.) And does a husband have the right to demand that his wife have sex with him? (No, not if it means that the woman will suffer as a result.) Does a woman have the right to demand sexual satisfaction? (Yes, to the extent that her husband is physically capable of complying.) Is it permissible to use birth control? (Yes—at least Islamic law is interpreted that way by most Islamic leaders in Indonesia, although there is some controversy over it.) Is a woman allowed to have an abortion? (Yes, provided that certain requirements are met.)[41]

The author cites verses from the Qur'an and hadiths to lend support for his liberal views on women's rights; he also questions the religious legitimacy of certain hadiths that appear discriminatory towards women. Masdar engages in a process of textual reinterpretation that leads him to some highly controversial conclusions about Islam and women's rights. By putting his words into the mouth of the fictional *nyai*, he attempts to make these ideas more acceptable to the average reader. As one

---

[40] Masdar F. Mas'udi, *Islam dan Hak-Hak Reproduksi Perempuan: Dialog Fiqih Pemberdayaan* (Bandung: Mizan, 1997).

[41] With abortion being illegal in Indonesia, the idea that having an abortion could be considered acceptable constituted a challenge to the state as well as to the views of conservative Muslims. The use of contraception, however, has been strongly encouraged by the state since early in the Suharto regime and is accepted by many, though not all, Indonesian Muslim leaders. This has not always been the case, though. In the 1950s, when the Indonesian government took a pro-natalist stance, the leadership of major Islamic organizations and councils (including Nahdlatul Ulama, Muhammadiyah, and the Council of Indonesian Ulama [MUI]) rejected the provision of contraceptive services, arguing that Islam sees reproduction as a central purpose of marriage. Later, however, when the government reversed the pro-natalist policies of earlier years as it sought to control population growth in Indonesia, these organizations also changed their positions. In the 1970s, the Council of Indonesian *Ulama* and Islamic leaders at the Ministry of Religious Affairs gave full endorsement to the government's launching of a national family planning program. Sciortino et al., "Learning from Islam," pp. 87–88.

might expect, Masdar's book was praised in liberal and feminist circles and sharply criticized by hard-line Muslim conservatives, who perceived it as a tract that smuggled in dangerous ideas from the West in an Islamic guise. Mohammad Thalib, for example, mentioned to me that Masdar had been irresponsible in his writing and "had clearly gone outside the lines" of basic Islamic principles. The book, which uses relatively accessible language, seems to have been intended as an alternative to the short, popular, and mostly quite conservative books on women and Islam that have attracted a mass market audience in Indonesia—books like Thalib's *Emancipation, Career, and Women*. Although it is doubtful that it reached as wide an audience as those books generally do, it did receive a good deal of attention in the print media, undoubtedly increasing the visibility of P3M and its programs.

Masdar, who received a traditional *pesantren* education through secondary school and subsequently studied Islamic Law at IAIN in Yogyakarta, had the formal credentials to be taken seriously as an interpreter of Islamic texts, but more conservative Muslims felt that he had strayed from the Islamic mainstream and that some of his ideas were at best simply questionable, and at worst were a threat to Islam and society. When I interviewed him about six months after the first printing of the book, he mentioned that some people were worried by its discussion of gender relations, fearing that if many women were to read the book it would lead to behavior that was "turned around" (*terbalik*, reversing the proper order of things) or that "went too far." Masdar himself, a former journalist, was convinced of the need to break open the "rules" of religion that were generally assumed to be set in stone, not open to further questioning. "We have to undertake a process of deconstruction towards some religious discourse that until now has been taken as given by the Muslim community [*Harus dilakukan semacam proses dekonstruksi terhadap sebagian wacana keagamaan yang selama ini justru sudah dipandang sebagai given oleh umat.*] In truth, this isn't easy to do," he commented. He found matters of gender to be particularly challenging because they were so frequently considered to be immutable; the very fact that they were seen as closed to discussion was what made them so interesting to him. Masdar considered women's rights to be an integral element of human rights, arguing that the democratization (*demokratisasi*) of Indonesian society meant guaranteeing equal rights for all people, including the right of all women to have control over their own bodies and lives.

As a somewhat ironic coda to P3M's relative success, if only on a limited scale, in promoting women's rights in the 1990s, it should be mentioned that the organization underwent an upheaval a few years after the publication of the book *Islam and Women's Reproductive Rights* when it was discovered that Masdar Mas'udi, the director, had taken a second wife. Although Indonesian law, following Islamic law, permits Muslim men to have up to four legal wives at the same time, the state discourages multiple marriages, and many women—even religious ones—find polygamy repugnant. That someone known as an outspoken advocate for women's rights had himself quietly indulged in this practice sent shock waves through the Islamic feminist community and especially through P3M. A number of its staff members resigned in protest, some joining or participating in the creation of other organizations, such as the Islamic feminist organization Rahima, to carry on the activities in the area of women's rights for which P3M had been known. This event served as a painful reminder of the considerable obstacles, both practical and ideological, faced by the proponents of Islamic feminism in Indonesia.

CONCLUSIONS

The Islamic movement that arose in Indonesia during the Suharto era generated intensive debates about women's behavior, rights, social roles, and essential, God-given nature *(kodrat)*—debates that show no sign of subsiding at the present time. In this essay I have contrasted the perspectives of conservative Muslims with those of liberal Islamic gender activists, both of whom see their own approaches to gender issues as representing the true spirit of Islam. While the former tend to emphasize male control of women and their sexuality, along with the need for women to be self-disciplined and accepting of men's leadership in the home and in the wider society, the latter have worked to promote women's autonomy and empowerment, including their right to exercise control over their own bodies and to enjoy equal rights with men in all spheres of society.

Although there is a sharp difference between the approaches to gender issues taken by Muslim conservatives and Muslim liberal feminists in Indonesia, I have also tried to show that both perspectives should be seen not only as products of the Islamic movement itself, or of its intersection with other transnational discourses (such as those of global feminism), but also as stemming in part from the gender ideologies and policies of the Suharto regime, which embodied fundamental contradictions. The regime sought to bring women under control by emphasizing their duty to be self-sacrificing and self-restrained for the sake of family and nation, underscoring the idea that a woman should support her husband's role as the unchallenged head of the family.[42] However, the state also depended on women's labor, consumer power, increasing levels of education, and participation in public life to meet its goals of national development. At the same time that the national Department of Religion sponsored Islamic prayer meetings for women in the villages and urban neighborhoods of Indonesia, with sermons that repeatedly stressed their religious and national duty to be good Muslims, devoted mothers and wives, and model citizens, the regime also directly or indirectly encouraged women to pursue the privileges and choices that were available to members of the growing middle classes. This included following careers and lifestyles that sometimes ran counter to idealized images of Indonesian or Muslim womanhood.

Such contradictions are, it seems, endemic to the process of nation building, particularly in countries that are seeking an ideological basis for a seamless national identity while simultaneously undergoing the difficult process of trying to unify a citizenry that is deeply fragmented on the basis of class, region, ethnic group, and religion. Women almost invariably play a crucial emblematic role as the bearers of national identity and as the moral foundations of a strong nation, symbolically representing and protecting the nation's integrity.[43] Yet the requirements and successes of "modernization" or "development" themselves depend on, or result in, the active social, economic, and political participation of women in ways that often bring them into conflict with their glorified symbolic images, and which may in fact

---

[42] For further discussion of the state's efforts to convince women of the need to be self-restrained, and how this ideological program reconfigured older Javanese ideas about the value of exercising self-control and the roles of women in the family, see Suzanne Brenner, *The Domestication of Desire: Women, Wealth, and Modernity in Java* (Princeton: Princeton University Press, 1998).

[43] For a thoughtful and detailed discussion of this point in the context of modern India, see Purnima Mankekar, *Screening Culture, Viewing Politics: An Ethnography of Television, Womanhood, and Nation in Postcolonial India* (Durham, NC: Duke University Press, 1999).

undermine the political legitimacy and stability that the ruling regime so badly needs.

Looking back, it should hardly have been unanticipated that some women who were able to avail themselves of the opportunity to receive a higher education, for example, would also use that education to challenge the practices of an authoritarian regime, or that some of those women who were exposed to the concepts of global feminism and human rights through the proliferation of NGOs in Indonesia during the New Order period would then turn a critical eye toward the situation of women in their own country. Nor should we be too surprised that some of the women who chose the path of higher education and a middle-class lifestyle also accepted the disciplines of the Islamic movement, which in its own ways echoed the New Order regime's insistent call to women to be self-disciplined and willing to make sacrifices for the greater moral and social good. By supporting Islamic institutions and encouraging the practice of religion in daily life, however, the regime unwittingly furthered the growth of a religious movement whose members were often highly critical of the regime itself, and who ultimately helped to bring about its demise.

The transformations that took place in Indonesia during the Suharto era awakened persistent questions and anxieties about women's and men's proper relationships to each other and their roles in the family and broader society. These questions were accentuated by the impact of the global Islamic movement, which has generated deep divisions over gender issues not only in Indonesia, of course, but wherever it has taken hold.[44] Complicating these changes in Indonesia was the fact that the Islamic resurgence overlapped in time with the rise of NGOs that sought to promote democratization, a strong civil society, and women's rights. While these organizations were restricted in the scope of their activities by the repressive tactics of the regime, they exerted their own influence on public life, eventually contributing to the events that led to Suharto's resignation in 1998 in the wake of a severe economic crisis.

Although some aspects of the Islamic movement and these other social movements have worked at odds with each other, particularly where women's rights are concerned, there has been some meaningful cross-fertilization between them as well. One example of this can be found in the activities of NGOs, intellectuals, and others who have worked to promote women's rights within an Islamic framework. These Muslim activists have argued that the advancement of women's rights is central to the processes of democratization and social reform in Indonesia. At the same time, they have been trying to counteract what they see as the potentially dangerous effects of conservative Islam on women.

Significantly, both Islamism and feminism tend to be preoccupied with the roles of women in the family and the society at large. But while conservative Muslims typically argue for the primacy of women's domestic roles, warning against the

---

[44] For examples from other countries, see Afsaneh Najmabadi, "Hazards of Modernity and Morality: Women, State and Ideology in Contemporary Iran," in *Women, Islam and the State*, ed. Deniz Kandiyoti (Philadelphia: Temple University Press, 1991), pp. 48-76; Nilüfer Göle, *The Forbidden Modern: Civilization and Veiling* (Ann Arbor: University of Michigan Press, 1996); Nayereh Tohidi, "Gender and Islamic Fundamentalism: Feminist Politics in Iran," in *Third World Women and the Politics of Feminism*, ed. Chandra Mohanty (Bloomington: Indiana University Press, 1991), pp. 251-267; Valentine Moghadam, "Revolution, Religion, and Gender Politics: Iran and Afghanistan Compared," *Journal of Women's History* 10,4 (Winter 1999): 172-195; and Ong, "State versus Islam."

dangers of Westernization for the God-given moral order that guarantees men the right to be leaders of women, feminists insist that women must be granted full access to the public sphere, as well as equality with men in the family. For both conservative and feminist Muslims, women's sexuality is another critical point of concern, but while conservatives focus on the control of female sexuality as a way of protecting the Muslim moral order, feminists are more concerned with the protection of women from sexual exploitation, harassment, and violence, as well as with women's fundamental rights to enjoy full sexual and reproductive health, knowledge, and autonomy.

The downfall of the Suharto regime did not bring about an end to the debates about women and gender issues in Indonesia—far from it. As conservative Islam has continued to make headway among the Indonesian population, Muslim feminists have carried on their campaign for gender reforms in government, in the legal system, and in the broader society. The implementation of elements of *shari'a* in Aceh and other regions of Indonesia has raised concerns that women will lose rather than gain rights in post-New Order Indonesia.[45] Although Megawati Sukarnoputri became the first female President of the Republic of Indonesia following the impeachment of President Abdurrahman Wahid in July 2001—over the loud protests of some Muslim conservatives who insisted that a female head of state is not acceptable under Islam—this did not guarantee that gender issues would be pushed to the forefront of the state's agenda, since Megawati is not known as someone who is especially concerned with addressing the specific problems of women.

There are only two certainties at this point in time: first, that as long as conservative Islam continues to influence public discourse on gender in Indonesia, and until the state implements genuine reforms guaranteeing women adequate protection against domestic abuse, sexual violence and harassment, and exploitation, there will continue to be voices agitating for gender equality in Indonesian society. Second, there can be no doubt that for as long as Indonesia continues to search for its national identity—in what will surely be a long and painful process—images of women will continue to be invoked as symbols of national, ethnic, and religious identity, inevitably catching real women in the crossfire of competing visions for the future of the nation.

---

[45] See, for example, the collection of articles under the heading "Kontroversi Posisi Perempuan Dalam Syari'at Islam" (Controversies on the position of women in Islamic law) that appeared in the periodical *Swara Rahima* 2,1 (August 2001). *Swara Rahima* is published by the Islamic women's rights organization Rahima in cooperation with the Ford Foundation.

A SIXTH RELIGION?: CONFUCIANISM AND THE NEGOTIATION OF INDONESIAN-CHINESE IDENTITY UNDER THE PANCASILA STATE[1]

Andrew J. Abalahin

On July 23, 1995, Budi Wijaya Po Bing Bo and Lany Guito, two Indonesians of Chinese ancestry, were wed according to Confucian ritual at the Boen Bio temple in Surabaya. Two weeks later, on August 7, Budi applied to have the marriage registered with the local Civil Records Office (Kantor Catatan Sipil, KCS). Four months later, the KCS responded: it would not register Budi and Lany's marriage because their ceremony was invalid, since Confucianism was not recognized as a religion by the Indonesian government.

Budi did not accept the KCS's decision. On the one hand, he declared, "I cannot deny the religion I believe in." On the other, he scoffed, "Are they kidding? They want me to get married twice?" (*Masak, saya harus menikah dua kali?*) He filed suit against the Surabaya Civil Records Office at the Surabaya State Administrative Court (Pengadilan Tata Usaha Negara, PTUN). On September 3, 1996, the PTUN affirmed the KCS decision. Budi persisted, appealing the case to the next higher court in Surabaya, the State Administrative High Court (Pengadilan Tinggi Tata Usaha Negara, PTTUN). The appeal too was in vain: on March 17, 1997, the PTTUN backed up the rulings of both the KCS and the PTUN. Meanwhile, the plaintiff and his wife had already brought a child, Fuji Yaohana, into the world. Thanks to its parents' convictions and to those of the Indonesian state, the child (a "cute baby" [*bayi yang mungil*]," according to press reports) remained an *anak haram*, a "forbidden child," the fruit of *kumpul kebo*, cohabitation (literally, "congress of carabao").

A third rejection of his petition did not defeat Budi's resolve. Eventually reaching the Supreme Court, the case would take three and a half years in all to

[1] This essay began as a term paper written in January 1994. For its updating, I am indebted to the generous help of Ben Abel and Antonius Made Supriatma for sharing their encyclopedic knowledge of contemporary Indonesian affairs.

resolve. On March 30, 2000, almost two years after the "fall" of the New Order, the Supreme Court voided the rulings of all lower authorities and declared Budy and Lany's marriage valid.[2]

Why did state authorities persist for so long in denying recognition to the plaintiffs' marriage? Why was the couple so determined in demanding that recognition when they might have conformed to state requirements by holding a Buddhist ceremony? Why did the Supreme Court finally grant recognition to their Confucian ceremony? What was at stake for the parties involved in this controversial case?

In answering these questions, we are compelled to consider a further series of more basic ones: Why have members of Indonesia's Chinese minority sought to present Confucianism as a religion? Why has the Indonesian state refused to recognize it as such? What does the de-recognition of Confucianism under Suharto's New Order tell us about the vagaries in the relationship between the Indonesian state and the Chinese minority? Why should the Indonesian state concern itself with defining what is and what is not a "religion" (as opposed to either simply approving of some religions and not others or refusing to take up taxonomy altogether)?

Let us start with the last question. With over 88 percent of its population subscribing to Islam, Indonesia possesses the largest national community of Muslims in the world. At the same time, Indonesia is usually described as a "secular" state. This characterization is not strictly accurate, since the state ideology, the Pancasila, identifies "Belief in The One Supreme God" as the first of its five principles, the one that is said to animate the rest.[3] For a citizen to profess such a belief, however, is not enough: he must confirm it by declaring his adherence to one of the "monotheistic" religions recognized as such by the state. As Budi and Lany's case shows, this is not a demand in the abstract: no document issued by the state, including the obligatory identification card (*kartu tanda penduduk* or KTP[4]), is complete without the applicant filling in his or her *agama*.

As is well known, in the wake of the abortive coup of September 30, 1965, the suppression by the new Suharto regime and its allies of the world's largest communist party outside the socialist bloc entailed the slaughter of half a million to a million Indonesians. To brand someone a "communist" became tantamount to a death sentence. Despite the fact that Indonesian communists on the whole did not regard subscribing to atheism as the *sine qua non* of being a communist,[5] the New

---

[2] PBS, RK, and Lutfi Yusniar, "Hadiah Mahkamah Agung untuk Perkawinan Konghucu," *Forum Keadilan* 44 (February 11, 2001), p. 72; Zed Abidien and Rachmat Cahyono, "Iman, Hak Asasi, Undang-Undang," *D&R* (*Detektip dan Romantika*), August 9, 1997, p. 24. The entire case history, with summaries of all the rulings, is contained in "Masalah Hukum Pencatatan Perkawinan Khong Hu Cu," *Varia Pengadilan* 179 (August 2000): 49-76.

[3] Rita Smith Kipp and Susan Rodgers, "Introduction: Indonesian Religions in Society," in Rita Smith Kipp and Susan Rodgers, *Indonesian Religions in Transition* (Tucson: University of Arizona Press, 1987), p. 17. The other four are: 2) "Just and civilized humanitarianism"; 3) "the Unity of Indonesia"; 4) "Democracy guided by the principles of consensus and representation"; and 5) "Social justice for the whole Indonesian people."

[4] The KTP also records Chinese ethnicity and association with the banned Communist Party (one-time membership in it or family relation to one of its members).

[5] This is reflected in the Islamist party Masyumi's need to declare that their faith forbad Muslims to join the PKI(see M.C. Ricklefs, *A History of Modern Indonesia, c.1300 to the Present* [London: MacMillan, 1981], p. 249) and in the comment of a bicycle-tire repairman to a former Islamic activist student, "The Communists are like everyone else—those who want to pray,

Order regime employed belief in The One Supreme God (*Tuhan Yang Mahaesa*) as an ideological shibboleth to exclude communists from full membership in the national community.

If the Pancasila state cannot properly be called "secular," nor would it be sufficiently precise to designate it generically "theist." It relies on a rather specific notion of what "theism," as a concept, comprehends. *Agama*, conventionally translated as "religion," is used in Indonesian official discourse more narrowly than the English term is commonly used in English discourse (indeed, to cover the semantic range of the latter, Indonesian has imported from Dutch the word *religi*). An *agama* is a religious system that fulfills the following criteria: 1) it must "constitute a way of life for its adherents"' 2) it must "teach belief in the existence of The One Supreme God"; 3) it must "have a holy book [*kitab suci*]"; and it must "be led by a prophet [*nabi*]."[6] Currently, the Indonesian state recognizes five *agama*: Islam; Protestantism; Catholicism; Hinduism; and Buddhism. For all religious systems that the government does not consider *agama*, official jargon insists on the term *kepercayaan*, "belief."[7] These include tribal animisms, mystical movements, and "deviant" sects, such as the Jehovah's Witnesses.

Far from detaching itself from organized religion as a secular state would, the Indonesian state attaches organized religion to itself without subordinating itself to any single manifestation of it. Indeed, it can be argued that through the four directorates general[8] under the Department of Religion, the state subordinates the religions.

However, it can be just as cogently argued that, in practice, the principle of "Belief in One God" imposes an Islamic framework on the state. The monotheism *Sila* (principle) ensures the minimum Islamic requirement that the state authority over Muslims not be a heathen, *kafir* one. In its definition of an *agama*, the state adopts the Islamic notion of tolerating "Peoples of the Book" (*ahl al-kitab*) and "invites" religious communities to define *themselves* as "Peoples of the Book" or risk falling outside the protections of the Pancasila's version of the *dhimma*, the "indefinitely renewed contract through which the Muslim community accords hospitality and protection to members of other revealed religions, on condition of their acknowledging the domination of Islam."[9] This is *only a partial* restoration of the *dhimma*, as the Pancasila state accords *theoretical* equality to all the religions it

---

pray; those that don't, don't. It's up to them." Pipit Rochijat, "Am I PKI or Non-PKI?," *Indonesia* 40 (October 1985): 50.

[6] Hasbullah Bakry's phrasing cited in Seno Harbangan Siagian, *Agama-agama di Indonesia* (Semarang: Penerbit "Satya Wacana," 1989), p. 21.

[7] The sharp distinction that certain authorities seek to draw between *agama* and *kepercayaan* extends even to the terms covering their adherents: an *agama* has *penganut* ("those who submit [to it]") or *pemeluk* ("those who embrace [it]"), while a *kepercayaan* has *penghayat* ("those who comprehend or who practice [it]"). The further distinction reinforces the notion that an *agama* is transcendent, coming from some higher source outside the individual, outside humanity, while a *kepercayaan* is subjective, arising from within the individual, within humanity.

[8] One directorate general manages both Hinduism and Buddhism—at the expense of the latter, since the Director General has always been a Hindu. This can be interpreted as discrimination against Chinese in favor of *pribumi* (in this case, Balinese). See Titi A. S., Multa Fidrus, and Nezar Patria, "Kesedihan Umat Buddha," *D&R*, November 8-14, 1999, pp. 36-37.

[9] See definition of "Ahl al-Kitab," *Encyclopedia of Islam* (Leiden: Brill, 1999), I, p. 264 [CD-ROM edition], and definition of "Dhimma," ibid., II, p. 227.

recognizes. Thus, depending on one's stake in the issues, Indonesia can be regarded as a semi-, quasi-, or pseudo-Islamic republic.

While many indigenous Indonesian ethnic groups have succeeded in winning *agama* status for their religious traditions, the Confucianism followed by many of Indonesia's Chinese, having once enjoyed recognition under the Old Order, *lost* that status under the New Order. This paper will explore the reasons why, among religions practiced in Indonesia, Confucianism has suffered this anomalous fate.

THE SIXTH RELIGION: CONFUCIANISM UNDER THE OLD ORDER

The *"agama*-nization" of Confucianism under the Pancasila state traces its origins to the identity politics of the Chinese[10] within the plural society of the eighteenth and nineteenth century Netherlands Indies. This project of religious reinvention embodied contradictory impulses. It set out to fight assimilation into the Muslim majority culture, yet at the same time reflected a deeper, unconscious acculturation to it; considered from another angle, it sought a type of "modernization" that characterized the civilization of the Dutch colonial masters.[11]

The very concept of *"the* Chinese" as a bounded and guarded community with an exclusive ethno-racial identity began as a European colonial fantasy. When Europeans arrived in the port cities of Java in the sixteenth century, they found a Muslim mercantile elite of diverse origins, Chinese, Indian, Persian, and Arab, as well as Javanese and Malay. By the end of the seventeenth century, officials of the Dutch East Indies Company (VOC, Vereenigde Oost-Indische Compagnie) looked at the descendants of the same elite and in many cases insisted on seeing "Chinese" where the Javanese only saw Javanese aristocrats. The fantasy served the interests of the Dutch, who considered it essential to their domination to arrest and reverse the traditional process of foreigners assimilating into the Javanese elite.[12] This policy was formalized in the mid-nineteenth century when the colonial administration slotted

---

[10] For convenience's sake, I will use the term "Chinese" to denote the ethnic group living within Indonesia, just as one would use terms such as "Javanese," "Makassarese," or "Minangkabau" without adding "-Indonesians." When I wish to refer to members of the indigenous ethnic groups considered as a category, I will call them *"asli* Indonesians" rather than use the *"pribumi"* of current officialese.

[11] Charles A. Coppel, "Is Confucianism a Religion?: A 1923 Debate in Java," *Archipel* 38 (1989): 125.

[12] On the sixteenth century, see Armando Cortesão, trans., *The Suma Oriental of Tomé Pires* (London: The Hakluyt Society, 1941). On the late seventeenth century, see Benedict Anderson, *Imagined Communities* (London: Verso, 1991), pp. 167-68; and Mason Hoadley, "Javanese, Peranakan, and Chinese Elites in Cirebon: Changing Ethnic Boundaries," *Journal of Asian Studies* 47,3 (August 1988): 513-16; on the key mediating role of "Sino-Southeast Asian" traders and diplomats in precolonial and extracolonial contexts, see Anthony Reid's "Flows and Seepages in the Long-term Chinese Interaction with Southeast Asia," in *Sojourners and Settlers: Histories of Southeast Asia and the Chinese,* ed. Anthony Reid (St. Leonards, Australia: Allen and Unwin, 1996); on the hybrid Sino-indigenous cultures, separate from both the "pure" Chinese and the indigenous, whose development European colonial policies encouraged, see G. William Skinner's "Creolized Chinese Societies in Southeast Asia," also in *Sojourners and Settlers*. On the Chinese in late eighteenth- and early nineteenth-century Java, see Peter Carey, "Changing Javanese Perceptions of the Chinese Communities in Central Java, 1755-1825," *Indonesia* 37 (April 1984). On an example of "Chinese" as a category of tax obligation rather than a strictly ethnic-racial label, see Kasian Tejapira, "Pigtail: A Pre-History of Chinese in Siam," *Sojourn* 7,1 (February 1992).

this conjured community of "*the* Chinese" into the small class of "Foreign Orientals" (*Vreemde Oosterlingen*) between the far less numerous "Europeans" at the top and the far more numerous "Natives" (*Inlanders*) at the bottom, completing a hierarchy of three race-based legal classes.[13]

Despite generations of Dutch manipulations, indigenous religion and culture continued to exert a powerful attraction on Indies Chinese as late as the 1860s, something that vexed members of the *peranakan* elite who had themselves become invested in building up the Indies Chinese community as a "nation" (*bangsa*) of its own. A "revival" of the Confucian "religion" was part of a general reorientation towards China and Chinese-ness. There was much to "revive."[14] According to one scandalized commentator writing in the postscript to the rules for an ancestral hall founded in 1864 in Surabaya, Indies Chinese (those literate in Chinese script in any case) paid lip service to the teachings of Confucius and Mencius, while following more avidly those of Laozi and the Buddha. Moreover, they followed such "depraved" Javanese customs as giving *slametan* feasts and making pilgrimages to *kramat*, the graves of Muslim holy men.[15] In his 1955 study of the Semarang Chinese, Donald Willmott records that traditional *peranakan* households, in addition to worshiping many lesser but more accessible gods, honored an omniscient and omnipotent *Tuhan Allah*, supreme ruler of heaven and earth who had no image but to whom they made monthly ritual offerings and burned incense. "Scholarly persons" equated this *Tuhan Allah* with the *Thian* (*Tian*) and *Siang Tee* (*Shangdi*) of the Confucian classics.[16]

The mid-nineteenth-century proliferation of ancestral halls like Surabaya's Hokkien Kong Tik Soe prepared the ground for the founding in 1900 of the Tiong Hoa Hwee Koan (THHK, Chinese Meeting Hall, hence Chinese Association) the first Chinese nationalist movement in the Indies. The THHK designed its reforms of

---

[13] This meaning of "Foreign Oriental" dates only to the nineteenth century. In VOC Batavia, the administration regarded the Chinese as the "Natives" of the place and called Makassarese, Balinese, and other people from the archipelago to the east of Java "Foreign Orientals." See Sumit Mandal, "Finding Their Place: A History of the Arabs in Java Under Dutch Rule, 1880-1924" (PhD dissertation, Columbia University, 1994), p. 55. On the late-colonial meaning of "Foreign Oriental" and the legal status of those placed in this category (consisting mostly of Chinese, but including also Arabs and Indians), see C. Fasseur, "Cornerstone and Stumbling Block: Racial Classification and the Late Colonial State in Indonesia," in *The Late Colonial State in Indonesia: Political and Economic Foundations of the Netherlands Indies, 1880-1942,* ed. Robert Cribb (Leiden: KITLV, 1994), pp. 31-56; and Charles A. Coppel, *Indonesian Chinese in Crisis* (Kuala Lumpur: Oxford University Press, 1983), pp. 3, 6, 11, 13-15.

[14] The religion that the ancestors of the Indies Chinese brought to and maintained in their new home was a folk polytheism syncretized with religious Taoism and Mahayana Buddhism, its myriad deities pictured as occupying posts in labyrinthine celestial and infernal bureaucracies. Confucian figures did come to be incorporated into popular religion, as were other historical figures, and the familistic values to which the Indies Chinese subscribed did bear a Confucian stamp even in the absence of the "moral priesthood" of scholars and officials that was so powerful back in China. See Lloyd E. Eastman, *Family, Fields, and Ancestors: Constancy and Change in China's Social and Economic History, 1550-1949* (New York: Oxford UP, 1988), pp. 42, 57, 59.

[15] Claudine Salmon, "Ancestral Halls, Funeral Associations, and Attempts at Resinicization in Nineteenth-Century Netherlands India," in *Sojourners and Settlers: Histories of Southeast Asia and the Chinese,* ed. Anthony Reid (St. Leonards, Australia: Allen and Unwin, 1996), pp. 197-98.

[16] Donald Earl Willmott, *The Chinese of Semarang: A Changing Minority Community in Indonesia* (Ithaca: Cornell University Press, 1960), p. 207.

peranakan culture (i.e., the de-indigenizing and re-Sinifying of their customs) in accordance with "the teachings of the Prophet Confucius,"[17] and the Chinese-language schools for whose founding the THHK is best remembered took as their principal aim the promotion of those teachings.[18]

In the early 1910s, as the THHK shifted its emphasis to expanding its educational program, those especially committed to the religious program formed local Confucian religious societies, Khong Kauw Hwee (in Mandarin, *Kongjiao Hui*) in various Javanese cities.[19] From 1923 to 1926 and again from 1938 until the Japanese invasion in 1942, these local organizations were united in an all-Indies federation, the Khong Kauw Tjong Hwee (*Kongjiao Zonghui*), the previous incarnation of today's Majelis Tinggi Agama Konghucu Indonesia (Matakin).

The repackaging of Confucianism as a religion with a "prophet," "scriptures," and even "sermons" was vehemently challenged from the start. Dutch Protestant missionaries, on the one hand, dismissed traditional Chinese religion as mere superstition and, on the other, denied that Confucius's teaching constituted a religion at all. The THHK responded that Confucianism purified of Buddhist and Taoist accretions was *the* true religion of the Chinese and that, moreover, Confucianism was a religion of the "knowable" and as such more rational and "up-to-date" than Christianity.[20] For their pains, other Chinese often accused the THHK leaders, many of whom had indeed been educated in missionary schools, of being

---

[17] Kwee Tek Hoay, *The Origins of the Modern Chinese Movement in Indonesia*, trans. by Lea E. Williams (Ithaca: Southeast Asia Program, Cornell University, 1969), p. 13. Kwee Tek Hoay was a *peranakan* writer and an advocate of *Sam Kauw/Tridharma* (Three Teachings/Ways, i.e., Confucianism-Taoism-Buddhism).

[18] Charles A. Coppel, "The Origins of Confucianism as an Organized Religion in Java, 1900-1923," *Journal of Southeast Asian Studies* 12,1 (March 1981): 184. Cf. the major THHK figure Lie Kim Hok's words in a 1903 article: " . . . Many Chinese in China believe in all three religions [Confucianism, Taoism, and Buddhism], while the Chinese in the Indies also believe in Islam . . . " Quoted in Leo Suryadinata, "Chinese Minority Religions Before World War II," *The Culture of the Chinese Minority in Indonesia* (Singapore: Times Books International, 1997), p. 132.

[19] Coppel, "The Origins of Confucianism," p. 185. The English term "Confucianism" conflates two entities that the Chinese terms keep distinct: *Rujia* and *Kongjiao*. *Rujia* refers to the philosophical system that profoundly influenced most aspects of social life in China through its impact on the values of the family and the ideology of the state; *ru* means "scholars," and *jia* means a school of philosophical thought (as in *Daojia*, "Taoist philosophy"). The expression *Rujia* emphasizes not a founding Prophet, but a tradition of sages extending long before and long after Confucius himself. *Kongjiao*, on the other hand, translates as "the teachings [*jiao*] of Confucius," and is modeled on terms designating institutionalized doctrinal religions, e.g. *Fuojiao* ("teachings of Buddha," Buddhism), *Huijiao* ("teachings of the Uyghurs," Islam), *Tianzhujiao* ("teachings of the Lord of Heaven," Catholic Christianity), *Jidujiao* ("teachings of Jesus," Protestant Christianity). The formal concept of *Sanjiao* (*Sam Kauw*), which acknowledges the complementary truths of the teachings of the Sages Confucius, Laozi, and Buddha, dates only to Ming times. In 1895, the intellectual Kang Youwei unsuccessfully advocated that Confucianism be made the state religion of the Qing Empire to the exclusion of Buddhism and Taoism. A US-educated disciple of his later attempted to establish a "Confucian church" (*Kongjiaohui*). Kang Youwei established a Confucian society in Singapore, and in 1903 visited Java to propagate his ideas of a "Confucian revival." It was apparently to follow a suggestion of his that the Boen Bio (*Wenmiao*, the "Temple of Literature)" in Surabaya was converted from a *xuetang*, a traditional school for teaching Confucian classics, into a *lithang*, a proper Confucian temple. Suryadinata, "Chinese Minority Religions," pp. 128, 130-31.

[20] Coppel, "The Origins of Confucianism," pp. 126, 179.

under Christian influence and propagating Christian customs. In the 1920s, it was the turn of Indies Chinese secular nationalists to attack the Confucian "church." In his sarcastic newspaper polemics, Kwee Hing Tjiat did not bother to dispute Confucianism's status as a religion, but rather recommended that the Chinese subscribe to no religion at all, for it made people "hypocritical and foolish." The journalist blamed Confucianism in particular for making China backward and encouraging slavishness and cowardice in the Chinese. He even praised Qin Shihuang's burning of Confucian classics and burying of Confucian scholars, asking if the Khong Kauw Hwee leaders would not deserve the same fate if they had lived in the Han dynasty (for all his reading of Hu Shih and Western Sinologists, he got the dynasty wrong, as critics were quick to point out).[21]

The last decades of colonial rule saw accelerating political mobilization among all populations in the Indies, both "Native" and "Foreign Oriental." Unfortunately for the position of the Chinese after Indonesian independence, this mobilization pulled the two groups even farther apart, as the Chinese agitated for the privileges enjoyed by nationals of a foreign country (casting an envious eye on the Japanese and on Taiwanese subjects of Japan, who had been "promoted" to "European" status in 1899), and *Inlanders* found their first mass political organization, Sarekat Islam, initially to agitate against Chinese merchants. The alienation of the Chinese from emerging Indonesian nationalism led the majority of them to remain neutral during the 1945-49 independence struggle. In a few places, Indonesian irregulars, perceiving the Chinese as pro-Dutch, attacked them, provoking Chinese to organize self-defense units; such clashes made a deeper impression than the limited Chinese participation in the revolution. When Indonesia received its independence, *Inlanders* became citizens of the new republic automatically, but the great majority of Chinese lacked birth certificates to confer *ius soli* privileges and had to submit to naturalization procedures. Naturalization as "Indonesian citizens," however, did not guarantee acceptance as "Indonesians" by *asli* Indonesians; indeed, the fact of naturalization marks Chinese as separate from the "natives" as surely as the colonial legal system did.[22]

Two distinct strategies have been formulated for incorporating the Chinese into the Indonesian nation in a more profound way than the mere extension of formal citizenship: "integration" and "assimilation." "Integration" signifies a process whereby the Chinese *as an ethnic group* would be accepted as one of the ethnic groups (*suku*) constituting the Indonesian nation. "Integration" would allow the Chinese like the other *suku* to preserve the cultural marks of their distinctive communal identity. "Assimilation," on the other hand, denotes a process whereby *individual* Chinese would sincerely and genuinely join the Indonesian nation by abandoning just such

---

[21] Leo Suryadinata, "Confucianism in Indonesia: Past and Present," *The Chinese Community in Indonesia: Seven Papers* (Singapore: Chopmen Enterprises, 1977), pp. 48-49, 52-53.

[22] On political development of the Chinese community during the late-colonial, revolutionary, and early independence periods, see Mary Frances Ann Somers's dissertation, "Peranakan Chinese Politics in Indonesia" (Cornell University, 1975), pp. 119-23, 145-60, and 187; and from Coppel, *Indonesian Chinese in Crisis*, pp. 16, 44-46. On the debates on naturalization, see M. Tabrani, *Soal Minoriteit dalam Indonesia Merdeka* (Jakarta: Sin Po, 1950), pp. 22-23. For details of the 1958 citizenship treaty between Indonesia and the People's Republic of China, see C. S. T. Tansil, *Hukum Kewarganegaraan Republik Indonesia* (Jakarta: Sinar Grafika, 1992), pp. 15-22. For a summary of the controversies over citizenship for the Chinese, see Yoe-Sioe Liem, *Überseechinesen–eine Minderheit: Zur Erforschung interethnischer Vorurteile in Indonesien* (Aachen: Rader, 1986), p. 409.

distinctiveness. Conflict between two opposing national ideological streams carried into the Chinese community, as Chinese divided themselves into two camps, "integrationists" and "assimilationsists": the former established the Badan Permusjarawatan Kewarganegaraan Indonesia (Baperki, the Consultative Body for Indonesian Citizenship) in 1954, a mass organization that increasingly aligned itself with Sukarno and the Indonesian Communist Party (PKI, Partai Komunis Indonesia), while the latter formed the Lembaga Pembina Kesatuan Bangsa (LPKB, Institute for the Promoters of National Unity) in 1963 (following up on a 1960 manifesto) and received army patronage from the start. Confucianism as an organized religion was one of the institutions embodying Chinese distinctiveness that became an issue in the integration-versus-assimilation debate.

Evidence from an official appointment book-cum-desk reference for 1951-52 produced by the Ministry of Religion implies that Confucianism was officially recognized as early as 1950.[23] In this climate of apparent official recognition, local Confucian associations took the opportunity to reestablish a pan-Indonesian organization such as had existed before the Japanese occupation. The three conferences in Solo (December 1954, April 1955, and July 1956) gathered representatives of the individual Khong Kauw Hwees of Surabaya, Solo, Semarang, Bogor, Cirebon, Ciampea, and Banjaran and culminated in the first congress of the Perserikatan K'ung Chiao Hui Indonesia (Federation of Confucian Religion Societies of Indonesia).[24]

Within this same period, the Gabungan Sam Kauw Indonesia (The Three Religions Federation of Indonesia) also developed rapidly, aiming to "unify, propagate, and practice" the three religions that were the ingredients of traditional Chinese syncretism: Confucianism, Buddhism, and Taoism. Willmott records that there were thirty or more Sam Kauw Hwee in this federation in 1955, most of which were of only recent foundation. The membership of the Sam Kauw and Confucian (as well as the Theosophical) societies tended to overlap to a certain degree (according to Willmott, the Semarang Sam Kauw Hwee also included a few *asli* Indonesians). Moreover, in addition to new translations of the Confucian classics being published in the late 1950s, two translations of the Taoist *Daodejing* appeared at the beginning of the 1960s. The multiple religious affiliations of many Chinese are probably reflected in 1957 government statistics that count 729,400 persons (0.75 percent of the total Indonesian population of 83.1 million) as belonging to a sectarian category called "Agama Buddha/Kong Fu-tse."[25]

During Guided Democracy, Confucianism benefited from Sukarno's patronage of Baperki and the integrationist stream in the Chinese community. In 1965, Sukarno,

---

[23] Kementerian Agama, *Agenda Kementerian Agama: 1951-1952* (Jakarta: Kementerian Agama, Bagian Publikasi dan Redaksi, Djawatan Penerangan Agama, [1951?]). This handbook lists the birth and death of Confucius as well as the Lunar New Year and Tsing Bing (*Qing Ming*) as official holidays.

[24] *Di-4 Samudra Semuanja Saudara* (Semarang: Konggres VIII MATAKIN, 23 December 1971), pp. 72-73. Note the shifts in terminology (e.g. Khong Kauw > K'ung Chiao > Agama Konghutju) from Indies transliterations of Hokkien expressions to Wade-Giles (i.e., international) Mandarin versions to Indonesian terms and renderings.

[25] Willmott, *The Chinese in Semarang*, p. 251; Claudine Salmon and Denys Lombard, *Les chinois de Jakarta: Temples et vie collective* (Paris: Editions de la Maison des Sciences de l'Homme, 1977), p. 89; Kamil Kartapradja, *Aliran Kebatinan dan Kepercayaan di Indonesia* (Jakarta: Yayasan Masagung, 1985), p. 55.

perhaps, as Suryadinata speculates, under pressure from religious leaders fearing the prospect of a PKI-dominated "godless state," issued a presidential decree "On the Prevention of the Abuse and/or Besmirching of Religion" that named six officially recognized *agama*: Islam; Protestantism; Catholicism; Bali-Hinduism; Buddhism; and Confucianism; but *not kebatinan* mysticism.[26] As Clifford Geertz notes, intensive Balinese "agitation" and Sukarno's support prevailed over the Ministry of Religion's original position that the Balinese religion was not a "genuine" religion.[27] The legitimation of Bali-Hinduism assured the Balinese of their place within the Indonesian nation and set a precedent that was to be followed by animist ethnic groups. The concurrent legitimation of Buddhism and Confucianism might similarly have been expected to promote the integration of the Chinese as a *sukubangsa*, a constituent ethnic group of the nation.

BUDDHIST SECT OR RENEGADE CULT?: CONFUCIANISM UNDER THE NEW ORDER

The victory of integrationism, however, did not come to pass. Baperki's patrons fell from power during the suppression of the left after the abortive September 30, 1965 coup, and the new regime dissolved Baperki in December. The ascendant assimilationists in the LPKB wasted little time in assaulting the position of Confucianism. In an August 1966 address to the Army Officers' College Sindhunatha, the head of the LPKB blamed Confucianism for diverting *peranakan* loyalties to China and praised Chinese conversions to Christianity.[28] The following February, M. F. Liem Hok Liong (alias M. F. Basuki Soedjatmiko), the head of the LPKB in East Java and deputy editor of the Surabaya weekly *Liberty*, in a series of articles in that publication first urged abandoning the veneration of ancestral ashes on the grounds that this practice was a cultural, rather than a religious, duty, and then refuted claims that Confucianism was a religion. Liem's diatribes proved so noxious that the central LPKB leadership warned Liem never again to broadcast his personal opinions in articles that the public might mistake for expositions of official LPKB views; the leaders were prompted to take this stand by Oen Tjhing Tiauw, both a major assimilationist and a Confucianist, who reminded them that Sukarno's Presidential Decree No. 1 of 1965 had formally recognized both Confucianism and Buddhism as religions and protected them from attacks like Liem's.[29] Clearly, the

---

[26] In 1961, the Ministry of Religion promulgated a definition of religion whose criteria included "a holy scripture, a prophet, the absolute overlordship of *Tuhan Yang Maha Esa*, and a system of law for its followers." Niels Mulder sees this formulation as specifically designed to "deny mysticism [Javanese *kebatinan*] its place under the Indonesian sun." In 1957, Sukarno himself had hesitated to accede to *kebatinan* petitions for recognition as a religion. See Niels Mulder, *Mysticism and Everyday Life in Contemporary Java: Cultural Persistence and Change* (Singapore: Singapore UP, 1978), pp. 5-6. See also Leo Suryadinata, "Khonghucuisme di Indonesia: Dahulu dan Sekarang," *Kebudayaan Minoritas Tionghoa di Indonesia*, trans. Dede Oetomo (Jakarta: Penerbit PT Gramedia, 1988), p. 69 and note 87.

[27] Clifford Geertz, "Religious Change and Social Order in Suharto's Order," *Asia* (1972): 27-84.

[28] Siauw Giok Tjhan, *Siauw Giok Tjhan Remembers: A Peranakan Chinese and the Quest for Indonesian Nation-hood*, Book II, ed. Bob Hering (Townsville, Queensland: James Cook University, 1976), p. 72.

[29] M. F., "Masalah Abu Leluhur dan Sintji," *Liberty* 701 (February 11, 1967): 2, 26; and "Kepertjajaan Tjina & Kuil-2 di Indonesia," *Liberty* 702 (February 18, 1967): 32. See also Coppel, *Indonesian Chinese in Crisis*, p. 107.

portion of the Chinese community who clung to "alien" traditions was a constituency neither as small nor as inarticulate as Liem was claiming.

Liem's writings appeared soon after Soemitro, the East Java provincial commander, had instituted a range of anti-Chinese measures including banning the celebration of the Imlek (Lunar New Year) and Cap Go Meh (Lantern) festivals.[30] On December 6, 1967, Suharto did issue a Presidential Instruction that actually imposed formal restrictions on the practice of Chinese religions. Chinese devotional practices were now to be performed only within the family circle or individually. Similarly, celebrations of Chinese religious and customary festivals were now to be conducted within the family circle and not "glaringly" in public. The Presidential Instruction empowered the Ministry of Religion (in cooperation with the Attorney General) to determine the categories of Chinese religion, beliefs, and devotional and customary practices, and charged the Minister of Home Affairs and the Attorney General to see to the safe and orderly enforcement of the policy.[31]

Suharto's Instruction did not quite yet amount to a formal derecognition. Indeed, in 1969 the Dewan Perwakilan Rakyat (DPR, the national legislative assembly) passed a law reaffirming Sukarno's 1965 law that clearly defined Confucianism as an officially sanctioned religion. In 1971, just as he, Nasution, and other military officials had done before, Suharto himself attended the Matakin congress, announcing that, "The Confucian religion [*agama*] has obtained a proper place in this country that is based on the Pancasila." Less than ten years after the Presidential Instruction, local authorities seem to have enforced it less and less stringently: in August 1977, a traditional grand procession, "glaringly" complete with dragon and lion dances, traveled the four kilometers from the Tay Kak Sie temple to the Sam Po Kong temple in Semarang.[32]

The Perserikatan K'ung Chiao Hui Indonesia moved swiftly to show itself deserving of that "proper place." At its Sixth Congress in August 1967, it desinified its name to Madjelis Tinggi Agama Konghutju Indonesia (Matakin, Council of the Confucian Religion in Indonesia); the Sam Kauw organization similarly changed its name to Tri Dharma (Three Paths). Matakin designated a canon of nine holy books, the Su Si (*Si Shu*, "The Four Books") and the Ngo King (*Wu Jing*, "The Five Classics"),

---

[30] Decreed on December 31, 1966, these included restrictions on where WNA (*warga negara asing*, "foreign citizens," i.e. resident Chinese with non-Indonesian passports, usually either Republic of China or People's Republic of China citizens, as opposed to WNI, *warga negara Indonesia*, "Indonesian citizens," i.e. resident Chinese with Indonesian nationality) could do business and take residence in East Java, the imposition of a head tax on WNA, and a ban of the use of the Chinese language or script in economy, finance, administration, and telecommunications. Inferring from this prohibition, Chinese began removing signs in Chinese characters on the outer walls of temples or covering them up with signs in Indonesian; after all, Soemitro remarked, "We can no longer see the existence of those Chinese temples. So too with the sacred relics which are decorated with pictures that smell of China. We will restore them to the indigenous." Coppel, *Indonesian Chinese in Crisis*, pp. 99-103, 200 n. 30.

[31] Complete Indonesian text of the instruction in Lie Tek Tjheng, *Masalah WNI dan Masalah Huakiau di Indonesia*, Jakarta: Lembaga Research Kebudayaan Nasional, LIPI, 1969, pp. 54-55.

[32] Suryadinata, "Khonghucuisme," p. 69, 69 n. 87; Hidayat Z. M., *Masalah Cina di Indonesia* (Bandung: Lembaga Kebudayaan Universitas Padjadjaran, 1976), p. 26; Seno Joko Suyono, "Menunggu Pangakuan," *D&R*, February 15-20, 1999, p. 22; Josephus Primus, "Angin Segar Khonghucu," *D&R*, November 8-14, 1999, p. 37; Coppel, *Indonesian Chinese in Crisis*, p. 164. Siauw (*Siauw Giok Tjhan Remembers*, p. 80) reports that a *Cap Go Meh* procession was reported in *Kompas* in February 1976.

and authorized Indonesian translations of these Confucian "Old" and "New Testaments," as a *Tempo* writer dubbed them. Furthermore, the council set down Eight Principles of the Faith (*Rukun Iman*), a kind of *"fiqh,"* a system of ritual obligations, and prescribed ceremonial procedures for worship in *lithang*, Confucian temples.[33] The souvenir book of the Eight Confucian Congress (December 1971) comprises a collection of essays that reveal Matakin's "marketing strategy": to argue for the religious character of Confucianism (including Confucius's status as a prophet) and for its compatibility with other religions, with Javanese philosophy, and with the Pancasila, but most of all to propose Confucianism as an "infrastructure of mentality training" (*prasarana pendidikan mental*) for the realization of the state's development plans, one that inculcated sacrifice for the good of the nation and submission to authority figures in an entrepreneurial class excluded from political power.[34]

Despite Matakin's efforts, the government progressively stripped Confucianism of its *agama* status. In 1973, a memo from the State Intelligence Coordinating Agency (Bakin, Badan Koordinasi Intelijen Nasional), denied Confucianism was a religion because among other things it "did not recognize an afterlife." Two years later, in a circular to all the provincial governors, the Minister of the Interior stipulated that Confucianism was not among the choices for the "Religion" blank in state documents (however, in a 1978 attachment to that circular, the Minister permitted couples registering for marriage to fill in the blank themselves if they were not adherents of the recognized *agama*).

A Presidential Instruction issued out of a January 27, 1979 cabinet session clearly stated that Confucianism was *not* a religion. The ninth Matakin congress, to be held in February, was abruptly cancelled, and no more such conferences were to be permitted under the New Order. On April 5, the Minister of Religion Alamsyah Ratu Perwiranegara informed the Matakin leaders that the Directorate General for Hinduism and Buddhism would now oversee Confucianism as well.[35]

On October 15, 1980, the Ministry of Religion, the Attorney General, and the Ministry of Home Affairs issued a joint decree that reiterated and elaborated on Presidential Instruction No. 14 of 1967.[36] The new decree defined forms of worship that were culturally affiliated with China as any forms of activity originating in and expressing the experience of "beliefs, spirituality, or spiritism" (*"kepercayaan, kerokhanian, kejiwaan,"* but not *"agama"*) that contained characteristics or motifs of Chinese-ness. Examples were specified: "processions, celebrations of religious feasts, dragon performances, lion dances, etc." Furthermore, the vague 1967 phrasing, forbidding Chinese religious and customary celebrations in public, was clarified; these were "not to be turned into public spectacles nor take place in public streets or buildings or in other areas open to the public," and were only allowed "within the limits of the grounds of a household or of a place of worship already designated for [the purpose]."

---

[33] Suryadinata, "Confucianism," p. 57; "Khong Hu Tju S.O.S," *Tempo*, March 27, 1971, pp. 35-36.

[34] *Di-4 Samudra Semuanja Saudara*. pp. vii, 99-102.

[35] Suyono, "Menunggu Pengakuan," p. 22; P.BS, RK, and Lutfi Yusniar, "Hadiah Mahkamah," p. 73; *Apa dan Siapa sejumlah orang Indonesia 1985-1986* (compiled by *Tempo*) (Jakarta: Pustaka Grafitipers, 1986), p. 325; Leo Suryadinata, "Chinese Minority Religions After World War II," in his *Culture of the Chinese Minority*, p. 165.

[36] Complete text in *Pembauran* 25 (Jan-March 1981), p. 15.

We can get a glimpse into what it was to like to grow up as a Confucian believer in New Order Indonesia from the accounts of Budi Wijaya and Lany Guito, the couple with whose struggle to have their Confucian marriage registered we began this paper.[37]

Budi was born in 1963, the son of a Chinese immigrant who had immigrated in the 1940's, settling in Surabaya. He stresses that he did not grow up immersed in a Chinese environment. He lived in a neighborhood that was overwhelmingly *asli* Indonesian, and he was educated through junior high in local schools managed by an army foundation. During this phase of his education, which would have been in the 1970s, his Confucianism presented no problem—he was excused from the mandatory religion classes because there were no Confucian teachers available to teach him his religion.

This changed when he entered an *"SMA yang bertendensi/bermisi agama,"* a sectarian or missionary, i.e. Christian, senior high school, whose student body was evenly divided between non-Chinese and Chinese (or as he puts it, *"warga asli"* and *"warga non-asli"*). There he was required to take religion class (teaching the religion of the school). There he found himself debating with a teacher about whether Confucianism was a religion—the teacher rolled out the "classic" charges that it had no prophet, no scripture, no houses of worship, no belief in God, nor in hell, nor in a day of judgment. At the same time, he grew close to the religion teacher who fed his growing curiosity about Confucianism, passing on to him knowledge the teacher had received from his own father while all the while no one suspected that the teacher, a native of North Sulawesi, was of Chinese descent. Budi served as the head editor of the Confucian *Tripusaka* bulletin. He went on to attend a college that was 90 percent Chinese, a campus that, in his words, could have been in Singapore or Taiwan by the look of the student body. However, in that environment too he was pressured to abandon Confucianism; a friend of his, now an assistant dean of the literature department at a Surabaya university, told him he prayed for his conversion every day.

Lany was born in the 1970s. In elementary school, she took classes in the Confucian religion as her parents had registered her as a Confucian. When she was in junior high school in 1984, she was forced to embrace Buddhism as a replacement for Confucianism or pick another religion altogether. Upon hearing that the school was no longer permitted to teach Confucianism as a religion, some students met at the Pak Kik Bio *lithang* and resolved there to meet the principal, to inquire about the changes, and to ask that Confucianism continue to be taught. The only reply they got was "This is a regulation from the Department of Education and Culture." Lany ended up taking the class on Buddhism, but only to add to her "knowledge" since she found it "impossible to believe in it." After the curriculum change, many other students converted from Confucianism to other religions, some indeed out of pure conviction.

Entering a Christian senior high school gave Lany a number of shocks. Though not daring to mention Confucianism by name, teachers there denigrated its rituals. Instructors in religion and Pancasila moral formation often gave incorrect information about Confucianism and ridiculed Lany when she tried to disabuse

[37] Budi Wijaya [and Lany Guito], "Dinamika Minoritas Konfusiani: Sebuah Catatan," in Anly Cenggana at al., *Hak Asasi Beragama dan Perkawinan Khonghucu: Perspektif Sosial, Legal, dan Teologi* (Jakarta: Gramedia, 1998), pp. 1-26.

them and her classmates. At one point, she recounts, a student who had lost at gambling killed himself by taking poison. One of the teachers explained to the class that the student did not fear hell because he was a member of the school Prayer Alliance (Persekutuan Doa).[38] The teacher asked students in the front row to give their opinion about hell. When her turn came, Lany declared, "My religion does not teach about hell but puts stress on how to lead life correctly in this world." The teacher was not satisfied with the answer and later mocked her as the "kid who doesn't understand about hell."

These experiences and activities organized by older students, such as a Confucian "bazaar" at the Pak Kik Bio, inspired Lany to learn more about Confucianism and how to apply its teachings to everyday life. She helped out at children's worship at the Pak Kik Bio temple, eventually becoming the Coordinator of Children's Worship in 1989. She also worked on the *Tripusaka* bulletin of which her future husband had been the editor when he was a teenager.

Budi and Lany's school experiences are representative of Confucianists (1,365,000, or 0.7 percent of Indonesia's population[39]) who found themselves under pressure to convert to Christianity and Buddhism from the late 1970s onward. The abolition of the last remnant of the exclusive Chinese education system with the closing of the Baperki WNI schools after 1965 forced Chinese to turn to Christian, particularly Catholic, schools; these enjoyed a reputation superior to that of state schools[40] and offered the bonus of an environment where Chinese were less of a minority. Exposure to Christians led to a flood of conversions. Educational advantages did not attract Chinese converts alone: Christianity offered a level of emotional support and congregational solidarity that uninstitutionalized, individual- and family-oriented traditional Chinese religion never provided[41] (note the importance of novel Confucian youth organizations in sustaining Budi and Lany in their beliefs).[42]

---

[38] Students had a choice between joining the Prayer Alliance or, if they weren't Christian, taking a test on religious ritual. Most opted for the Prayer Alliance and ultimately were drawn or drifted into Christianity.

[39] This statistic—0.7 percent—cited by Budi Wijaya is the same figure given in a 1976 survey—the same is given for Buddhists. See Suryadinata, *Culture of the Chinese Minority*, p. 125. Cf. the 1971 census that counts Confucianists at a little under 100,000 or 1.2 percent of the population at that time (ibid., p. 69) and the 1980 statistics that calculate the number of persons in the category of "Other" (outside the five *agama*) to equal 1.0 percent; this category would have consisted mostly of Confucianists after the Dayak were reclassified as "Hindus." See Biro Pusat Statistik, *Beberapa Ciri Pemeluk Agama di Indonesia, 1980* (Jakarta: Biro Pusat Statistik, 1984), pp. 4, 6. It is clear that different sources determine religious affiliation differently: Suryo Hutomo, the Matakin head, placed Confucianists at 3,000,000 in 1971, which would have to mean he counted all Chinese as his coreligionists. It is likely that more than half of Indonesia's four to six million Chinese are now Christian, and the rest are divided between Buddhists and Confucianists.

[40] "Catholicism seems to breed success in Indonesia, whether with Chinese or with Javanese," remarked a Semarang Chinese in a 1988 study. See Stuart William Greif, *Indonesians of Chinese Origin: Assimilation and the Goal of One Nation—One People* (New York: Professors World Peace Academy, 1988), p. 22. "Islam," commented a Yogya Chinese man, "is not associated in the popular mind with rational or practical education." Ibid., p. 39.

[41] Willmott, *The Chinese of Semarang*, pp. 244-45.

[42] Conversions to Islam have been on a far smaller scale—the Muslim component of Indonesia's Chinese population remains less than 1.0 percent—but have included some well-publicized cases involving prominent figures, such as Junus Jahja (Lauw Chuan Tho), an ex-

The other alternative for Confucianists (and more generally for practitioners of traditional Chinese religion) has been Buddhism. Although the majority of Buddhists in Indonesia are Chinese, the religion has not only universalist credentials refuting any charge of its being an "ethno-religion," but also has *nationalist* ones, inasmuch as Borobudur has become an icon of Indonesia's glorious precolonial past. Nonetheless, just as Confucianism had to reinvent itself, Buddhism too had to repackage itself (though not to the same extent) for the consumption of the New Order state. Though it clearly has a founder and a canon of scripture, strictly speaking it does not recognize any god, much less The One Supreme God (the Lord Buddha is not a deity). Indonesian Buddhist leaders have made up for this deficiency by combing scriptures and identifying Buddhist equivalents such as *Sanghyang Adi Buddha* and *Atti Tjatam Abhutam Akatam Asamkhattam* ("Someone who is not born, not formed, not created but Absolute")—but Buddhists are content to use the general expression "Tuhan Yang Maha Esa" or "Yang Maha Esa."[43]

Buddhism too has had to "desinify." Not merely were temple inscriptions and signboards in Chinese characters covered over or hidden away, but the names of temples were changed to Sanskritic, Buddhist ones, as mentioned above. The clangingly Chinese cacophony of *klenteng* was replaced by the sussurant Indo-Javanese euphony of *wihara* (with some loss of accuracy, as *wihara* literally means a functionally quite different institution, a monastery). A further adaptation and attempt at desinification has been the promotion via non-Chinese (mostly Balinese) monks of closer ties to international Theravada Buddhism. In the mid-1980s, the Ministry of Religion moved more directly against "Chinese-ness" by issuing an instruction discouraging the use of the Chinese language in the Buddhist community; this has meant that the Chinese translations of the *Tripitaka* and other Buddhist scriptures used by the various Chinese Mahayana Buddhist sects have not

---

Protestant and a signer of the 1960 assimilationist charter. He proclaims conversion to Islam is a means to achieve "total assimilation" with the Indonesian nation (proponents of conversion also advocate intermarriage with *asli* Indonesians); since 90 percent of the Indonesian population is Muslim, he believes, so too should 90 percent of the Chinese population be Muslim. See Coppel, *Indonesian Chinese in Crisis*, pp. 164-65, and Leo Suryadinata, "The Dakwah Movement Among the Indonesian Chinese," in his *Culture of the Chinese Minority*, pp. 189-194. For its part, the New Order regime expressed approval of such conversions, but never explicitly pressured Chinese to convert to Islam, which in any case would mean to apostasize Christianity or Buddhism, which are recognized *agama*. In any case, the Indonesian public may perceive present Chinese conversions to Islam to be as opportunistic as Chinese conversions to Christianity allegedly were under the Dutch; at the same time, they may see present conversions to Christianity as a sign that the converts are maintaining an exclusivist stance, merely exchanging one minority status (Chinese with no automatic *asli* allies) for another, safer one (Christian with many, prominent *asli* coreligionist allies). In many parts of western Indonesia, notably Padang, home of the avidly entrepreneurial and devoutly Muslim Minangkabau, Chinese constitute the majority of the Christian minority, which further inclines the people of western Indonesia to equate "Chinese" with "Christian."

[43] See Leo Suryadinata's discussion in "Chinese Minority Religions After World War II," in *Culture of the Chinese Minority*, pp. 177-79. The controversial Bhikkhu Ashin (The Boan An) apparently inserted the word Adi ("Superior") before "Buddha" in his Indonesian translation of a passage from a tenth century Javanese Buddhist text. "Adi Buddha" would seem to be distinct from and superior to the historical Buddha.

been generally available in Indonesia and Buddhists have had to travel to Hong Kong, Taiwan, or China to study their religion.[44]

The failure of a Confucian *agama* to gain recognition as such under the New Order is all the more striking when one considers the success of *asli* Indonesian ethnic groups in getting their traditional religious systems classified as *agama*. As mentioned before, the pioneers in this effort were the Balinese. An unprecedented central administration, the Parisada Hindu Dharma, imposed an "ecclesiastical hierarchy" on their myriads of local temples, translated and distributed the Vedas and other Hindu scriptures, organized sermons and collective prayers, and raised up altars to *Sang Hyang Widhi Wasa*, the One Supreme God represented by three empty thrones; all around this busy activity, polytheistic business as usual proceeded even more busily, *odalan* festival after *odalan* festival. Other ethnic groups who were liable to persecution as pagans—highlanders or interior peoples under threat of domination by Muslim lowland or coastal peoples—lobbied for recognition of their traditional belief systems as sects of Hinduism; most notable in this regard were the Toraja with their *Aluk To Dolo* and the Dayak with their *Kaharingan*. (For such groups, just to separate out "religion" from the total complex of cultural practices was a novelty, never mind giving a name to the "religion" and then grafting this abstraction on to the even more distant abstraction of a "world religion" hardly ever previously encountered.)

One group, at least, struggled to avoid "capture" by Hinduism. On Bali's neighboring island, Lombok, the Boda, a small community of non-Islamized Sasak and some heterodox Muslim *wetu telu* (Three Times [Islam], syncretistic Islam on Lombok) adherents opted to embrace *Buddhism*, wishing neither to join their orthodox Muslim *wetu lima* (Five Times [Islam], orthodox Islam on Lombok, referring to the five daily prayers) neighbors nor accept association with the Hinduism of the Balinese. Since the only Buddhists in the provincial capital of Mataram were inappropriately Chinese, the only people the Parisada Hindu Dharma (as the local representative of the Directorate General for Hinduism and Buddhism) could send to the new Buddhist community's inauguration ceremony were Hindu Balinese. If the arrival of these Hindu Balinese as the deputies of Buddhism did not cause the new Buddhists enough consternation, the arrival in 1973 of Buddhist monks with shaven heads and saffron robes dispatched from Jakarta to stimulate the movement disturbed the Boda even further: this Buddhism which they had invited into their community was something altogether different from the *adat* they were really concerned in preserving.[45]

Confucianism was in a position no better than, and perhaps worse than, these new "Hindu" and "Buddhist" sects. From the point of view of the state, either Confucianism was a mere "belief system," only a "manifestation of culture," or it was a sect of Buddhism: along with "several Buddhist religions [*sic*, *"beberapa agama Budha,"* probably meaning a number of Chinese Mahayana schools], Taoism and

---

[44] H. Fachrudin Ilyas, ed., *Buku Laporan Hasil Musyawarah Umat Beragama Kristen, Katolik, Hindu, dan Buddha: 1984-1985* (Jakarta: Departemen Agama, 1986), p. 265; Titi A. S., Multa Fidrius, and Nezar Patria, "Kesedihan Umat Buddha," *D&R*, November 8-14, 1999, p. 36.

[45] Geertz,"Religious Change"; Jane Monnig Atkinson, "Religions in Dialogue: The Construction of an Indonesian Minority Religion," in Kipp and Rogers, p. 270 (note 5); Joseph A. Weinstock, "Kaharingan: Life and Death in Southern Borneo," in Kipp and Rogers, pp. 71-73; Sven Cederroth, "From Ancestor Worship to Monotheism: Politics of Religion in Lombok," *Temenos* 32 (1996): 7-36.

Confucianism were grouped "under the shade" of the Majelis Tri Dharma Indonesia (Council of the Three Ways [i.e. Three Teachings, *Sam Kauw/Sanjiao*]).[46] Thus, Confucianism was a marginal presence within a Buddhist Depag bureaucracy that had no directorate general of its own and so was itself a marginal bureaucratic unit within the Hindu-dominated Directorate General for Hinduism and Buddhism that in turn was marginal within the Muslim-controlled Department of Religion.[47]

Strangely, the case that most closely parallels that of Confucianism is that of *kebatinan* (literally, "inwardness"), mystical sects that deviate from Islamic orthodoxy or reject an Islamic affiliation altogether. These sects (47 at the 1955 congress, 245 currently registered with the government) formed an umbrella organization in 1955 and have been holding congresses since that time, and they have been actively lobbying for the recognition of *kebatinan* as an *agama*. However, the Department of Religion has blocked any moves towards recognition, preferring to treat their members as heterodox, heretical, or apostate Muslims and setting up a special section for the Supervision of Belief Movements in Society (Pakem, Pengawasan Aliran Kepercayaan Masyarakat) in 1954. This section, transferred to the Department of Justice in 1960, went on after 1965 to collaborate with the police in liquidating *kebatinan* sects that had allegedly been "infiltrated" by leftists. From 1978 to 1985, the Department of Education and Culture "managed" the sects through a Forming Directorate for Practitioners of Belief Systems Focused on The One Supreme God (Direktorat Pembinaan Penghayat Kepercayaan terhadap Tuhan Yang Mahaesa). After 1985, Education and Culture split these responsibilities with Interior.[48]

In addition to purely religious and security concerns, an ethnic issue has also been raised by the *kebatinan* sects' efforts to gain recognition from the state. *Kebatinan* has been traditionally associated with Javanism, with the syncretistic proclivities that alienate other ethnic groups more committed to Muslim orthodoxy (as well as more orthodox Javanese Muslims) from the nominally Muslim Javanese. The military government, though dominated by Javanese "statistical" Muslims (and for a time even by Javanese Catholics), could no more grant so huge a concession to *"echt"* Javanese culture, by recognizing *kebatinan,* than it could "indulge" the Confucianism of the Chinese. After all, the Javanese for their numerical and other strengths, the Chinese for their commercial power, and both for their perceived "superiority complexes" have been perceived by other groups as the new "colonial masters" ruling Indonesia.

---

[46] "Masalah Hukum Pencatatan Perkawinan Khong Hu Cu," p. 72.

[47] Titi A. S., Multa Fidrus, and Nezar Patria, "Kesedihan Umat Buddha," *D&R*, November 8-14, 1999, pp. 36-37.

[48] Mulder, *Mysticism*, pp. 4-6.The umbrella organization of the sects changed its name no less three times: from Badan Kongres Kebatinan Indonesia (Body of the Indonesian Spiritualist Congress) to Badan Koordinasi Karyawan Kebatinan, Kerohanian, Kejiwaan Indonesia (Functionaries' Coordinating Body for Spiritualism, Spirituality, and Spiritual Power) to Sekretariat Kerja Sama Kepercayaan (Secretariat for Cooperation among Belief Systems) to Himpunan Penghayat Kepercayaan terhadap Tuhan Yang Mahaesa (Association of Practitioners of Belief Systems Focused on The One Supreme God). See Eko Y.A.F., Josephus Primus, and Titi A. S., "Aliran Kebatinan, Sabdopalon, 500 Tahun Kemudian," *D&R*, August 9, 1997, pp. 18-19.

CONFUCIANISM IN THE NEW DISORDER: FIVE IS NOT ENOUGH

In the 1990s, Budi and Lany's struggle to obtain state validation for their marriage was not an isolated one. On December 30, 1996, the Civil Records Office (Kantor Catatan Sipil, KCS) of East Jakarta refused to register the marriage of Gumirat Barna Alam and Susilawati, practitioners of the *kepercayaan* ADS (Agama Djawa Sunda, Sundanese-Javanese Religion), arguing that the marriage was invalid because it had only been conducted according to Sundanese customary law and not according to any religious law, as required by the 1974 marriage law. As Budi and Lany had done the previous year, the couple appealed the decision to the State Administrative Court (Pengadilan Tata Usaha Negara, PTUN) of Jakarta. Unlike Budi and Lany, they received satisfaction much more swiftly: little over half a year later, on July 14, 1997, Marina Sidabatur, chief judge at the State Administrative Court of Jakarta ruled in favor of the couple's suit against the KCS and ordered the office to register their marriage. The judge maintained that the KCS's decision was an arbitrary exercise of power that did not take into account the psychological effect of the decision on the plaintiffs and especially on any children born of the union. She stressed that marriages according to customary law were permitted, citing a subsequent clarification of the marriage law and invoking a 1978 statement by President Suharto. Though it was not material to her argument, she added that *kepercayaan* as such were not forbidden in Indonesia.[49]

The PTUN's ruling in favor of Gugum and Susi provoked a denunciation from KISDI (Komite Indonesia untuk Solidaritas Dunia Islam, the Indonesian Committee for Islamic Global Solidarity), which asserted it undermined the faith of the Islamic community and destabilized inter-faith harmony. KISDI backed up its written pronouncement with public protest, holding a *tablig besar* (large public preaching session) on July 26, 1997. Another group, the Forum Komunikasi Generasi Muda Islam (Islam's New Generation Communication Forum), had demonstrated in front of the Supreme Court two days earlier. A poster unfurled at one of these protests read:

> Followers of marriage according to mere belief systems do not include the *ijab kabul* [consent from the bride's *wali*, the senior male in her family, as required by Islamic law]. It is the same as living in sin [*kumpul kebo*]. Various high officials such as the Minister of Religion himself, Tarmizi Taher, insisted that *kepercayaan* were manifestations of culture and not of religion and could therefore not provide the basis for a valid marriage.

Penghayat themselves expressed little reaction openly, but, when contacted by a *D&R* reporter, Tulus Kusumo Budoyo, member of the Presidium of the Federation of Practioners of Belief Systems (Himpunan Penghayat Kepercayaan), they countered that it was inhumane to charge people with cohabitation: "How does one decide what is cohabitation? Weddings of practitioners according to customary ceremonies have a religious quality and are civilized. . . . Love your fellow man, just as you love

---

[49] "Dari Masaran sampai Nyeureuhan," *D&R*, August 9, 1997, p. 21; Titi A.S., "Kepercayaan di Mata Hakim," *D&R*, August 9, 1997, p. 17. Another case was that of Prialin and Endang, a couple from Pati, Central Java, practitioners of the Sapta Dharma teaching. See Tomi Lebang, Irawan S., and Ahmad Solikhan, "Gelombang Protes Perkawinan," *D&R*, August 9, 1997, p. 17.

yourself. Don't play power games, for there is a higher power." In a letter to the editor of *D&R*, Darmaningtyas, a freelance researcher, wrote, "[Those who meddle in these marriages] seem to have too much time on their hands. On what basis do they reject [these marriages]? Who can know about a person's happiness? Only those involved and the Creator. If it's like that, is this not domination of (or arrogance towards) others?" Another letter to the editor pointed out that the belief movements had existed "since the times of ancestors, long before the five religions recognized by the government entered this country, they are as old as the Motherland Archipelago [*pertiwi Nusantara*]."[50]

Ultimately, the controversy boiled down to rival interpretations of the phrasing of the 1974 marriage law, whose ambiguities derived in turn from the phrasing of Article 29 of the 1945 Constitution:

> The state guarantees the freedom of each resident to embrace his or her respective religion and to worship according to his or her religion and his or her belief system. [*Negara menjamin kemerdekaan tiap-tiap penduduk untuk memeluk agamanya masing-masing dan untuk beribadat menurut agamanya dan kepercayaannya itu*]

Secular nationalists such as Sukarno maintained that this wording distinguished "religions" from "belief systems" and recognized the legitimacy of both, while less religiously neutral nationalists, like Hatta, argued that the expression "belief system" merely qualified the word "religion" and that the constitution was only recognizing "religions."[51] Therefore, weddings had to be conducted according to religious law first, and customary ceremonies were optional and had to be performed after the religious ceremony. In a 1975 *Kompas* article, Hasbullah Bakry argued that the wording was designed to accommodate the weddings of those who did not yet have a religion, who did not know of religion at all, or who were continuing the customs of their ancestors. Busthanul Arifin rejected this interpretation, saying that it only applied to weddings among the people of isolated tribes (*suku terasing*) who were "still primitive," people "who are indifferent as well . . . [If] there is no legal agreement—no problem. [It doesn't matter to them] if their parents are married or not."[52] It is ironic that, while Islamists had in general gone to great pains to draw a sharp and unequivocal dividing line between religions (*agama*) and belief systems (*kepercayaan*), when debating the interpretation of marriage law they did not hesitate to conflate the two terms into a "single substantive" (*satu substansi*). Equally ironic is the *penghayat* arguing for "two substantives" (*dua substansi*) "side by side," religions and belief systems, when it came to the marriage law, since their usual goal was to persuade the government to upgrade their *kepercayaan* to *agama* status.

Let us now return to Budi and Lany's case. The KCS offered them two alternatives. One was to wed again, but this time according to the rites of one of the

---

[50] Ulfa Rono, "Perkawinan Gugum-Susi Sah" (letter), *D&R*, August 23, 1997, p. 7.

[51] To hammer in his point, Busthanul Arifin claimed that translating the phrase *"agamanya dan kepercayaannya itu"* (those, their religions and their belief systems) into English would clarify the correct interpretation: *"Bila dibahasa-Inggriskan baru jelas*, religious believes [*sic*]. *Keliru bila itu dianggap dua substansi yang terpisah."* (It's only clear once it's put into English, *"religious believes."* It's mistaken to regard it as two separate substantives)

[52] "Gelombang Protes Perkawinan," pp. 16-17.

recognized religions. The other was to produce another Boen Bio marriage certificate, but one where the word *"agama"* was dropped from the name of the issuing organization, Makin (Majelis Agama Khonghucu Indonesia, Indonesian Council for the Confucian Religion), from the stamp, and from the heading. Budi refused to do either, later articulating his stance thus:

> Not all the various actions against Chinese need be met with protest, particularly given the character of Chinese people, which prefers compromise. Yet, there are also certain things that must be upheld. One rightly must struggle to preserve the performance of religious worship and the associated attributes because they bear on one's personal relationship to one's Creator and at the same time do so as a form of building up oneself [*pembinaan*] within the framework of *nation and character building* [*sic*, in English].

Beginning on August 7 and almost every week thereafter, Budi sent a letter to the KCS asking them to explain their decision. He was surprised at their refusal because he knew of others who had successfully had their Confucian marriages registered. The couple was even willing to pay a bribe (*menyediakan dana lebih*, prepare an extra donation) as some of these others had done. But no reply to their appeals was forthcoming.[53]

In its September 3, 1996 ruling on Budi and Lan's appeal, the Surabaya PTUN, citing a 1981 circular from the Head of the Supreme Court, stipulated that if the couple insisted on registering their "non-religious" marriage, they would have to apply *first* for a special dispensation in the form of a letter of decree from the Head of the State Court saying that they *would* be carrying out a wedding not based on religious prescriptions.[54] In effect, Budi would still have to marry a second time after all.

Budi and Lany were encouraged in their struggle by the support of prominent Islamic leaders. Most important among them were Nurcholish Madjid, a member of the national human rights committee and of ICMI (Ikatan Cendekiawan Muslim Indonesia, the Association of Indonesian Muslim Intellectuals) and Abdurrahman Wahid, the head of NU (Nahdlatul Ulama, the Association of Muslim Scholars), and president of the WCRP (World Conference on Religion and Peace). In September 1996, after the failure of the first appeal before the Surabaya PTUN, the Minister of Justice announced to a parliamentary commission that the government was studying three alternative solutions for Budi and Lany's problem: 1) declare Confucianism a religion; 2) make a regulation whereby the marriage would be registered, but only in the form of an administrative report stating that the marriage had already taken place; and 3) authorize a special registration for those who do not marry according to the rites of a recognized religion.[55] It was not likely solution #1 would be in the offing. On September 15, the Surabaya police authorities issued a circular denying the existence of a Confucian religion in Indonesia and "suggesting" that no activities

---

[53] Budi Wijaya [and Lany Guito], "Dinamika," pp. 17-18. Cases entailing bribery were perhaps the more recent ones, since the KCS had been refusing to register Confucian marriages since 1992 on the grounds that Confucianism was not a religion. See Zed Abidien and Rachmat H. Cahyono, "Iman," p. 24.

[54] "Masalah Hukum Pencatatan Perkawinan Khong Hu Cu," p. 50.

[55] Budi Wijaya [and Lany Guito], "Dinamika," p. 23.

be conducted under its name; this nearly caused the Boen Bio Makin to cancel the customary distribution of alms to the poor at the King Hoo Ping ("All Souls") festival.

That was the state of affairs through 1998. Budi and Lany's lawyer, Trimoelja D. Soerjadi, had argued that the rulings of the KCS and the PTUN refusing to recognize their marriage were in conflict with several laws and with the General Principles of Good Government (Asas Umum Pemirintahan yang Baik).[56] Indonesia changed presidents twice before the case advanced to its last appeal. Trimoelja's arguments would only be heard in the era of *reformasi*, after one of those Islamic leaders sympathetic to the plight of Budi, Lany, and Fuji Yaohana rose to leadership of the nation: that is Abdurrahman Wahid—Gus Dur.

On August 22-23, 1998, Matakin held its first congress in more than a quarter century. This was a year after the collapse of the Thai *baht* opened the curtain on the Asian economic crisis. This was three months after the riots that pushed President Suharto into handing the government over to his Vice President Habibie. Unfortunately, those riots were only part of the wave of violence that swept the country and that included widespread attacks on the Chinese, most notoriously on Chinese women, many of whom suffered public rape. The small steps made to reverse discriminatory New Order policies towards the Chinese and Confucianism were not only expressions of *reformasi,* but also acts of atonement.

The August congress was remarkable because its dozens of participants were meeting on the grounds of a Muslim boarding school, the Asrama Haji Pondokgede. Even more striking was the fact that Malik Fajar, Habibie's Minister of Education and Culture, gave his permission to Matakin to hold the congress and in so doing "in his personal capacity took notice of the existence of Confucianism" (*pribadi memberi perhatian kepada eksistensi Kong Hu Chu*) even when there remained no formal government decision to restore it to *agama* status. The new atmosphere was reflected in the bluntness of Chandra Setiawan's words to *D&R*: "It is very strange that the intelligence agency takes it upon itself to take care of religion. To dare to say that the *Su Si* [*Sishu*, the Four Books] and the *Ngo King* [*Wujing*, the Five Classics] are not holy books is blasphemy."[57] At the same time, having drafted and sent a letter to the Minister of Religion, the Minister of the Interior, and President Habibie asking that the legality of Confucianism be recognized, the congress delegates still waited patiently for their reply, keeping in mind Confucius's dictum from the *Su Si*: "Mankind's destruction lies in losing hope."

Slowly, Chinese *and* non-Chinese were bidding farewell to the New Order by reviving long banned public expressions of Chinese culture, most spectacularly the *barongsai*, the lion dance integral to many Chinese festivities. At sunset on November 7, a crowd of two thousand people, including both Chinese and *asli* Indonesians, gathered at Semarang's Pantai Marina to watch the dancers "unfurl" the *barongsai* to perform a *tolak bala* (misfortune-dispelling) ritual, this time specifically to tame restless seas, with a motherly Guanyin to calm *la Niña*.

On November 19, the *barongsai* took to the streets for the first time since Suharto's 1967 decree concerning Chinese customs forbad such public displays. This was in Solo (Surakarta), which had been the site of especially severe anti-Chinese rioting that past May. The Solo public had an unlikely party to thank for the

---

[56] "Masalah Hukum Pencatatan Perkawinan Khong Hu Cu," p. 49.

[57] Suyono, "Menunggu Pangakuan," p. 22.

initiative to bring out the lions and dragons (*liong-liong*) back again;[58] the Muhammadiyah-derived Partai Amanat Nasional (PAN, National Mandate Party) had commissioned the *barongsai* troupe to celebrate the establishment of a local branch of the party. PAN also sponsored similar spectacles in nearby Boyolali and Karanganyar (and tried to do the same in Yogyakarta, but there could not obtain official permission). In the garden behind Salatiga's Hok Tek Bio temple, every Thursday and Sunday afternoon, seventy people, old and young, Chinese and non-Chinese, practiced *barongsai* moves, having formed a troupe named Naga Mas. Activists from PAN, PDI-P (Partai Demokrasi Indonesia–Perjuangan, The Indonesian Democratic Party of Struggle), and the Yayasan Geni (a human-rights NGO), and students from the local IAIN (Institut Agama Islam Negeri, State Institute for the Islamic Religion) were joining in the challenging job of reviving this performing art.

The real test of the new tolerance would come with the first Imlek (Lunar New Year) celebrations after the end of the New Order. It was feared that in 1999 the Chinese festival would fall on the same day as Lebaran, the end of Ramadan, creating a situation that could well be conducive to violence. Despite such anxieties, the Chinese community in their many temples (twenty-four in Semarang alone) proceeded to prepare for elaborate celebrations, perhaps to show its spirit had not been crushed by the atrocities of the past year and to avail itself of the goodwill of non-Chinese authorities and organizations, such as the mayor of Semarang, who had attended the beachside *tolak bala* ceremony, and the PAN, whose members were ready to thwart provocateurs plotting to spark anti-Chinese riots. Particularly impressive were the projected festivities in Solo for Cap Go Meh (the Lantern Festival on the fifteenth day of the lunar new year). Performers from *wu shu* (martial arts) schools in Semarang would come to animate six pairs of auspicious animals (*barongsai*, frogs, and *samsu*); the troupes would parade through the city, each departing initially from one of four points, three Buddhist *klenteng* and the main Confucian *lithang*. The processions were intended to launch the Cap Go Meh celebrations and to exorcise (*meruat*) from Solo the spirit of savagery that had consumed it the previous May.[59]

By the time the next Imlek came around, the position of Confucianism would be greatly strengthened in Indonesia. At the October 1, 1999 inauguration of the first general session of the parliament drawn from the first general election after the end of the New Order—the first free election since 1955—Amien Rais included Confucianism among the religions he mentioned in the opening prayer. Early the following year, Abdurrahman Wahid, the candidate who had won the presidency in those elections, issued a presidential decision (Keppres No. 6 Tahun 2000) that withdrew Suharto's 1974 instruction outlawing public expressions of Chinese culture. The new president attended the Imlek celebrations on January 28, giving a speech where he "acknowledge[d] and honor[ed] the existence of Confucianism and the equality of civil rights for the Confucian community [*umat agama Konghucu*] in Indonesia."[60]

---

[58] The *barongsai* began its progress through the city at the Avalokitesvara (i.e. Guanyin, thus Buddhist) temple at Pasargede, where a Confucian clergyman blessed it and sent it on its way.

[59] Seno Joko Suryono et al., "Barongsai, Kera Sakti, dan Cap Go Meh," *D&R*, February 15-20, 1999, p. 21; Irawan Saprapto et al., "Dag-Dig-Dug Menjelang Imlek," *D&R*, February 15-20, 1999, p. 15.

[60] Primus, "Angin Segar Khonghucu," p. 36; PBS, RK, and Lutfi Yasniar, "Hadiah Mahkamah," p. 72.

It was now that the Supreme Court took its cue from the president and ruled on Budi's third appeal of his suit against the Surabaya KCS. In support of its decision to recognize Budi and Lany's marriage, the court cited the following: 1) the guarantees for freedom of religion in the 1945 constitution; 2) the phrasing of 1974 marriage law as interpreted to recognize the validity of weddings that satisfied the stipulations of belief systems, as well as of religions; 3) the inconsistency between Sukarno's 1965 decree including Confucianism among the religions of Indonesia and the 1983 circular of the Coordinating Minister classifying Confucianism as a "philosophy of living" (the court did not take it upon itself to resolve this debate); and 4) the 1978 circular of the Minister of the Interior that permitted the registration of marriages of those who did not belong to one of the five religions, leaving it to the newlyweds themselves to fill in the "religion" column on the documents. And finally, the Supreme Court argued that the KCS's decision to refuse to recognize Budi and Lany's Confucian marriage was not based on the law and that it so violated the General Principles of Good Governance (Asas-Asas Umum Pemerintahan yang Baik), specifically the principle of legal assurance and the principle prohibiting discriminatory action, that it had to be nullified. The Supreme Court ordered the Surabaya KCS to register Budi and Lany's wedding and to pay the costs of the case during every stage of the suit (as much as Rp.150,000).

It remains to be seen how much of "a new breakthrough in the era of *reformasi*," as lawyer Frabs Hendra Winarta had dubbed it, the Supreme Court's decision will prove to be. Chandra Setiawan, the head of Matakin, pointed out that although the decision had heartened Confucianists, there still remained many Confucian couples who had not yet succeeded in gaining KCS recognition for their marriages. Many offices still refused to register Confucian marriages, maintaining that the Supreme Court's decision applied only to the specific case of Budi Wijaya and Lany Guito and did not necessarily establish a precedent for handling analogous cases. In Surabaya itself, another Confucian couple, Charles Tee and Suryawan, were encountering the same obstacles Budi and Lany had faced in trying to register their marriage. When questioned by a journalist, the official concerned said he had decided to apply the old regulations, since the Minister of the Interior had yet to answer his query regarding whether the Supreme Court decision was applicable, by extension, to other Confucian unions. Even the Jakarta KCS, otherwise quite up-to-date regarding legal reforms, persisted in insisting that Confucianism was a belief system, not a religion, and that Confucian couples had to conduct their ceremony according to the rituals of one of the five recognized religions in order to have their unions registered. In the face of such resistance from low-level officialdom, Chandra Setiawan hoped for an explicit order that instructed every KCS to register Confucian marriages.[61]

Still, it cannot be denied that the Supreme Court handed down a landmark ruling, as Frans Hendra Winarta claimed, when it recognized Budi and Lany's right to have their marriage registered regardless of the current state classification of their religious beliefs. At the very least, the decision opened up a space for commentators such as Winarta to voice certain ideas in Indonesia's "post-authoritarian" environment. The state, he declared, was guilty of violating human rights by

---

[61] "Masalah Hukum Pencatatan Perkawinan Khong Hu Cu," pp. 51-53, 76; Frans Hendra Winarta, "Perkawinan Konghucu," *Forum Keadilan* 44 (February 11, 2001), p. 68; Zed Abidien and Rachmat H. Cahyono, "Iman, Hak Asasi, Undang-Undang," *D&R*, August 9, 1997, p. 24; PBS, RK, and Lutfi Yasniar, "Hadiah Mahkamah," p. 73.

pursuing policies that discriminated on the basis of culture, race, and religion. Indonesia was a state based on the rule of law (a *rechtstaat*) rather than on the rule of force (a *machtstaat*), and as such should treat all citizens equally, including in matters of religion. Religion was a private matter, not to be subject to state meddling; the conscience must be truly free, as asserted in the UN's International Covenant on Civil and Political Rights (it has been rare to see Indonesians, especially state representatives, appealing to universal legal norms and not merely to the Pancasila and the 1945 Constitution). The principle that religion be separated from the state—which was taught by Mohammad Hatta, Sukarno's partner in founding the nation, as Winarta points out—should be upheld. Making this argument, Winarta invokes the phrase in European languages, "*scheiding van kerk en staat/separation of truth* [sic] *and state*"—a felicitous mistranslation into English from Dutch—or from Indonesian?![62]

What then might the career of Confucianism under Indonesia's Pancasila state suggest about the nature of the relationship between religion and the nation-state? What might it reflect of the nature of nationalism itself? While Confucianism's status has come under such debate because it touches upon the status of the Chinese and thus upon the nationalist state's heritage of assumptions derived from the colonial regime, this debate has aroused even more passion because it concerns the role of religion under the Pancasila and thus also concerns the place of Islam, the specific religion that drove a great part of the nationalist struggle and that informs the Pancasila itself, even as the latter circumscribes and evades Islam's claims. In the ways it has structured the negotiation of religious identity, the Pancasila state makes in its language an overall concession to Islamists, but leaves loopholes for other constituencies. Perhaps, the Pancasila state after all is structured more along the lines of traditional, historical Islamic states than of that sort of Islamic state projected by the radical Islamists. The Pancasila state displays the unequal pluralism of such polities as the Ottoman and Mughal empires. Perhaps radical Islamists, by contrast, are thinking, dreaming of a nation more closely resembling the classic nineteenth-century, Western nation-state model, which projects the "fullest alignment of habitus, culture, attachment, and exclusive political participation."[63] For them, however, "nation" notionally emerges out of "faith community," as it does in the modern evolution of the Arabic and Turkish equivalents for "nation," *milla* and *millet*.

If Confucianism does finally win re-recognition as an *agama*, it will be a sign that the state has begun to transcend the colonial reflex to separate out the Chinese. If the state no longer imposes conditions that drive Confucianists to seek to win such re-recognition, it will indicate that a genuine secularism has succeeded in making the state over in its own image, rather than in that of Islam's fabular "society of Medina." However, even if these changes come to pass, those who prefer to see Chinese persons as "Foreign Orientals" might still continue to insist on seeing them in this guise without recourse to the lenses of five—or fifty—*agama*.

The solidarity demanded by the nation-state of its citizenry seems to rely upon a "fiction of unanimity." That obligatory unanimity—in the Indonesian case, a

---

[62] As the lawyer Frans Hendra Winarta dubbed it in his article "Perkawinan Konghucu," p. 68.

[63] Benedict Anderson, "Long-Distance Nationalism," in his *Spectre of Comparisons: Nationalism, Southeast Asia, and the World* (London: Verso, 1998), p. 70.

unanimous belief in The One Supreme God and in the American case a unanimous . . . well, increasingly again, belief in The One Supreme God[64]—helps undergird the foundational fiction of nationalism: the idea that all members of the national community agree on "the essentials," that they are all fundamentally "alike," and thus are deserving of the legal equality that is one of the key blessings of citizenship in a modern nation-state. In seeming contradiction to the conventional understanding of democratization, it appears that the guiding principle of the modern-state is *exclusion* rather than inclusion. Unlike in the pre-modern non-nation-states, difference cannot merely be "tolerated." It must be "accepted," "embraced," even "celebrated," but first it must be refigured via fictions of unanimity as ultimately "no difference at all." The construction of an extra-national Other, the "traitor among us," the un-believer and the non-national (combined in the Chinese-Indonesian Confucianist), appears indispensable to conjuring up solidarity.

Ideological shibboleths become all the more essential when other solidarizing fictions, such as myths of common origin, race, or culture, are less easily invoked. In this respect, Indonesia resembles the United States more than it does the Philippines, another ex-colony where an ethnically diverse assemblage of "Natives" re-envisioned itself as "Nation." The cultural engineering of three and a half centuries of Spanish colonialism created a supra-ethnic majority in the Philippines that came to share far more than a common religion. Dutch colonialism did not do the same for Indonesia. In Indonesia, and arguably for the United States, to maintain the cohesion of the nation, the nation-state has had to rely far more on the fictions of religious-ideological unanimity and of extra-national Others.

---

[64] Witness the 2001 re-affirmation of the insertion of "One Nation Under God" in the pledge of allegiance, itself composed and promoted by a member of the Knights of Columbus at the height of the "Red Scare" of the 1950s to assert that atheism, and thus communism, was "un-American."

RELOCATING RECIPROCITY: POLITICS AND THE TRANSFORMATION OF THAI FUNERALS

Thamora Fishel

INTRODUCTION: FIELDWORK IN BLACK AND WHITE

The intersection of religion and politics in Thailand has generally been studied as a question of either political legitimation or state control of religious institutions. The issue of whether everyday ritual practice has political repercussions has been left largely unexamined, particularly in relation to local electoral politics. During my research on provincial politics between 1995 and 1998, I planned to examine how Buddhist practice articulated with politics, but I did not expect that my most frequent visits to temples (*wat*) would be to attend funerals in the company of politicians on the campaign trail. Black and white soon became my standard fieldwork attire, as I attended more wakes and cremations than I did weddings, ordinations, and new-house merit-making ceremonies combined. Some evenings, especially during province-wide campaigns, I went to as many as three or four wakes consecutively, in some cases after having already attended a cremation with the same politician earlier in the afternoon. Not only were funerals given high priority on the campaign trail, but it seemed that my friends and neighbors had an endless series of funerals to attend. The more my circle of acquaintances increased and my relationships with local politicians and other informants developed, the more I was drawn into social networks that encompassed both the living and the dead.

These experiences and observations raise a number of questions: Why do politicians in Thailand place so much emphasis on attending funerals? What makes funerals such a focal point of both religious practice and politics? This paper seeks to explain why campaigning at funerals is an accepted—even expected—part of the contemporary Thai political scene. I approach this question from two perspectives. First, I explore the underlying logic of reciprocity at funerals, showing how patronage relations and Buddhist notions of merit converge in particularly potent ways. Then I analyze the roles that politicians play at funerals in light of historical, spatial shifts in funerary practices, shifts that seem to go hand in hand with the appearance of a provincial middle class in Thailand. These two threads of analysis, taken together, shed light on the contradictions and competing moral discourses of Thai politics. The rationalization of provincial Thai funerals and their relocation to temple halls and crematoriums sacralizes death rituals even as it incorporates them into an emergent public sphere. Funerals show how Buddhist understanding of power based on religious merit and virtue also shape Thai conceptions of democracy, modernity, and what it means to be middle class.

THAI FUNERALS AND THE CONCEPT OF MERIT

In order to explore these questions, I should first sketch out the basic components of a Thai funeral.[1] The word *"ngan sop"* (funeral) combines under one heading two sets of events, the wake and the cremation. In central Thailand, after a person dies, a wake is arranged immediately for three, five, or seven evenings. The number of nights depends on the resources of the family and the social status and age of the deceased. If the deceased is an important monk or community leader, the wake may extend as long as fifteen days.[2] In Thai, a wake is usually referred to as *suat sop,* in reference to the chanting of Buddhist scripture (in Pali) by monks during the ceremony. The ceremony begins like all Buddhist rituals, with the monks and then the laity worshiping the Buddha. The *chaophap* (or "host"), either a family member or a sponsoring guest such as a politician, kneels before the Buddha image to light the candles and incense and then bows, forehead to the ground, three times. Then he or she lights a single stick of incense in front of the coffin, where a picture of the deceased is displayed. During the ritual, the laity chants set phrases to invite the monks to chant and to dedicate merit and pray for the deceased. Midway through the ceremony there is a break, during which refreshments are served to all the guests. Another chapter of scriptures might be recited, and then offerings are made to the monks, followed by more praying and a ritual of pouring water—*kruat nam*—to transfer the merit from the ceremony to the dead person.

Later in the week, or up to a year or more after this ceremony, the final phase of the funeral, the cremation (*phao sop*), is scheduled for an auspicious day. In order to include as many people as possible, cremations generally take place on weekends. On the morning of the cremation, monks are feasted to make merit for the dead person. A large crowd assembles in the afternoon for a service of chanting, a sermon, and offerings to the monks—especially the presentation of robes to individual monks in front of the coffin, recalling Buddha's injunction to use rags and shrouds as robes. A whole series of important guests are called forward to perform this ritual, often including at least one politician, if not several. Then, usually at four o'clock, the

---

[1] Several handbooks on how to stage the proper rituals surrounding death and the religious meaning of funerals were available at bookstores for a primarily middle-class clientele. Sathiankoset approaches the topic from a historical perspective, focusing on folkways. Thiranantho and Phrathamma Kosachan discuss death and explain the rituals surrounding death from a religious perspective. Phrathamma Kosachan (Panya Nanthaphikkhu), *Than dai arai mua pai ngansop* (What do you get when you go to a funeral?) (Krungthep: Samnakphim Duangkaew, nd.). Sathiankoset, *Kantai: prapheni kiawkap chiwit khong Sathiankoset* (Death: life rituals of Sathiankoset) (Krungthep: Samnakphim Sayam, 1996). Thiranantho, ed., *Kantai lae phithi kanthambun* (Death and ceremonies to make merit for the dead) (Krungthep: Samnakphim Duangkaew, nd.).

[2] For instance, in 1968 the wake for a man who had been the mayor and a member of parliament lasted fifteen nights.

sound of rockets or guns being fired alerts everyone in earshot that a cremation fire has been lit. The crowd surges forward, palms together, holding *dokmai chan*, a flower-shaped piece of corn husk or paper, tied together with a piece of incense and a small candle, which are used to participate in lighting the cremation fire.[3]

As my description suggests, the concept of merit *(bun)* is central to understanding Thai Buddhist practice in general, and Thai funeral rituals in particular. Merit is also a key to analyzing how funerals become important to Thai politicians in search of support. In Lucien Hanks's classic essay, "Merit and Power in the Thai Social Order," he describes how the accumulation or loss of merit is used by Thais to explain the social hierarchy and individual mobility and effectiveness within it. Highly meritorious acts, such as giving alms or ordaining as a monk, will increase an individual's store of merit with positive benefits in this life or the next. Hanks lays out the distinction Thais make between effectiveness, which is enduring and derives from merit or virtue, and instrumental power, which comes from special knowledge, experience, or luck, but is short-lived in the absence of merit.[4] In the pursuit of political office and the prestige and material benefits that accompany it, making merit *(thambun* or *bamphenkuson)* is more than just a matter of presenting a public image of one's self as a moral person. Similarly, funerals provide politicians with far more than an opportunity to be visible to a large gathering of people. Politicians go to funerals both to make merit and build or maintain patronage relationships; both of these goals rest on notions of exchange and reciprocity.

GIFT-GIVING AT FUNERALS: SYMMETRICAL AND ASYMMETRICAL EXCHANGE

Funerals in Thailand are all about making merit; and merit, I argue, is deeply embedded in other circuits of reciprocity that politicians must tap into if they are to be successful. Many of my friends described going to funerals in order to make merit on behalf of the deceased, an act of generosity that in turn generates merit for the person attending the funeral. The ritual itself consists of repeated acts of merit-making. Listening to the monks chant and intoning the lay responses in Pali generates merit. The flower wreathes *(phuang rit)* brought to a wake or the envelopes of cash handed to the family at the cremation bring merit to the donor. Merit is put into circulation through the offerings presented to the monks on behalf of the deceased in the form of flowers and incense, beautifully arranged trays of daily necessities, and robes. During the water pouring ritual *(kruat nam)*, merit is explicitly transferred to the dead. The final phase of a cremation ceremony gives everyone present an opportunity to make merit by "offering" *(thawai) dokmai chan* which are placed in the crematorium to help ignite the funeral pyre.

Buddhism as it is practiced in Thailand can be seen as a series of exchanges. Giving alms to monks—that is, feeding them—is the prototypical act of merit-making. Like funerals, most religious ceremonies involve multiple moments of giving, receiving, and transferring. In addition to food, monks are given robes, items for daily use, flowers, and so on. The gift-giving that epitomizes making merit is an

---

[3] *Dokmai chan* literally means "sandalwood flower" because fragrant flowers carved out of sandalwood were originally used by the rich to help ignite the funeral pyre; sandalwood has since grown too expensive to be used for this purpose.

[4] Lucien M. Hanks, Jr., "Merit and Power in the Thai Social Order," *American Anthropologist* 64,6 (1962): 1247-61.

exchange in which the return may be deferred until another lifetime (or one may win the lottery tomorrow), but one that operates nonetheless in the idiom of accumulation and expenditure. Through such exchanges, merit-making provides codes for proper behavior and the justification for existing social hierarchies, while holding out the possibility for individual advancement. In the same way that patronage relations are predicated on the flow of gifts and cash in primarily one direction, the relationship between the laity and the Buddhist *sangha* (monkhood) is the other main area in Thai society where gifts are given without the expectation of a direct return. As Tambiah has pointed out, the Buddhist *sangha* exemplifies non-reciprocity because alms and gifts are only received by monks and never given in return. Nevertheless, most of my informants focused on a return, that is, the merit they received by virtue of their gift-giving, thereby resituating this ritualized non-reciprocity back in the matrix of exchange.[5] The merit that an individual accumulates for this life or the next does not come from the *sangha*, per se, but it is perceived as something one gets by giving. In an odd way, the calculus of exchange discernable in religious behavior resembles the asymmetrical exchanges between patrons and clients. By acting as a patron of Buddhism, one accumulates merit rather than the indebtedness of other people. And, like the vagaries of patronage relations between humans, merit cannot be quantified.

Just as merit-making is conceived of in terms of accumulation and expenditure, the gift-giving that takes place at funerals also operates as a series of short and long-term exchanges between host and guest, linking the social and moral economies. The hanging wreaths and money brought by guests are carefully recorded in notebooks so that the host family may reciprocate at a later date. Depending on their relationship to the deceased, for some people, particularly women and members of poorer families, funerals entail social obligations involving exchanges of one's labor, in the form of cooking, arranging offerings for monks, setting up chairs, and cleaning up. After the final night of a wake, the paper flowers that were mounted on hanging wreaths made from towels and blankets are dismantled and distributed among close kin and friends who helped prepare the food and beverages each night. Even the refreshments at the wake or the small mementos such as coins, tiger balm, or amulets distributed at the conclusion of a cremation could be interpreted as compensation given in return for each person's participation. Most of these exchanges reinforce horizontal relationships based on an even balance of reciprocity.[6]

---

[5] Stanley J. Tambiah, *Buddhism and the Spirit Cults of North-east Thailand* (Cambridge: Cambridge University Press, 1970), p. 68. Strenski elaborates on this point in a discussion of the domestication of the *sangha*. In particular, he applies Lévi-Strauss's concept of restricted and generalized exchange to Theravada Buddhist ritual gift-giving. Ivan Strenski, "On Generalized Exchange and the Domestication of the *Sangha*," *Man* 18 (1983): 463-77. Claude Lévi-Strauss, *The Elementary Structures of Kinship* (Boston: Beacon Press, 1969).

[6] Although I initially felt uncomfortable attending funerals, I also began to sense that being present at funerals—particularly when I went on my own to funerals in and around the municipality where I had the most contacts—made me more a part of the community than any other activity I engaged in. People often seemed surprised and impressed to see me, especially the men and women who had extensive networks and contacts to maintain and, as a result, attended many funerals. The moment of recognition and acknowledgment of my presence seemed to be coupled with a startled reflective response, as though seeing me was like seeing a shadow or hearing an echo of themselves. As an observer at campaign rallies, at city council meetings, or when I sought people out for interviews and assistance, I could still easily be placed outside the network of local social relations that mattered. When the newspaper editor, or the dean of the provincial teachers' college, or the mother of an MP from the province saw

In fact, certain aspects of the interaction between laity and the *sangha* take on the character of symmetrical exchanges as well. A set cash gift for each participating monk is commonly expected when monks provide ritual services. Monks who are invited to come chant for a particular ritual, be it a funeral or a house-blessing or an elderly person's birthday, are given envelopes of cash in addition to the other gifts presented during the course of the ceremony. The cash offered on such occasions is meant to be kept at the disposal of each individual monk, and he may take his savings with him when he leaves the monkhood. Although only a few irreverent Thais would think of these gifts as payments for services, and fewer would express this thought out loud, lay people admit that they feel obliged to provide cash and they do have certain set expectations of the monks who agree to perform these ritual roles.[7]

Amid these asymmetrical and symmetrical exchanges, between laity and *sangha* as well as hosts and guests, politicians add a further layer of complexity. In addition to attending funerals with greater frequency than the average person, politicians also enter into exchanges at funerals, but they do so in a way that forces the flow of cash and gifts in primarily one direction. Often the envelope of cash a politician gives to the family is ten or even twenty times greater than the standard individual contribution. (In Charoenthani in the late 1990s, while most people gave about 100 *baht*—approximately US$4—politicians tended to give as much as one or two thousand baht—US$40–80.) In this case, like an employer or an organization to which the deceased belonged, the politician is publicly recognized as a "host" of that night's wake and asked to perform a ritual role, such as lighting candles before the Buddha, presenting offerings to the monks, or performing the water-pouring ceremony near the end. Politicians also tend to give exceptionally large hanging wreaths that prominently display their name, current title (if they hold office), and—if the funeral takes place during a campaign—their ballot number. Several campaign headquarters I spent time in had their own in-house wreath-making operations because they needed a constant supply of wreathes to send to as many wakes as possible, even when the politician could not attend. Rather than expecting the family of the deceased to reciprocate during ceremonies held by the politician's family, politicians apparently operate on the assumption that the indebtedness generated during funerals tends to work as political capital that they hope will translate into votes. Like the asymmetrical exchanges of merit-making, the indebtedness and sense of obligation generated by this kind of patronage is hard to

---

me at funerals, it was as though they saw me doing what they were doing. I was not simply another one of the many people clad in black or white, my hands together in a *wai* with the *dokmai chan* held between my palms. My appearance meant I was actively building meaningful ties. Over time, as I made friends, I internalized the ethos of exchange obligations connected to funerals. In many ways, nothing made me feel more at home than being able to take an envelope with 100 *baht* to the cremation of a friend's grandfather, or to have a *phuang rit* made with my name spelled in Thai, painted by hand onto the black poster board, and to carry this with me to the wake of a friend's niece.

[7] Morris discusses a similar dynamic in the exchanges between spirits, spirit mediums and their clients: "The money that clients and mediums offer to the spirits . . . is not referred to . . . as *ngeun* (money) or *baht*, but as *suai* or tribute. In this it attempts to escape the general economy and becomes a gift." Furthermore, mediums flatly denied that clients paid them for their services, but then Morris describes in detail the "public secret" of invitations, which are an "implicit demand for offerings." Rosalind C. Morris, *In the Place of Origins: Modernity and Its Mediums in Northern Thailand* (Durham, NC: Duke University Press, 2000), p. 169.

measure or keep track of; it is not possible to quantify the merit or the votes that are generated by attending X number of funerals. Nonetheless, politicians take the risk, since simply having a large supply of cash with which to buy votes cannot guarantee an electoral victory. For politicians without an extensive base of support, attending funerals is an attractive method to try to build new ties, and even established politicians feel compelled to meet the expectation that they will be generous and active participants in the funerals of their supporters. Politicians frequently arranged or even rearranged their schedules around funerals, especially if there was a personal tie. For instance, when the niece of a neighborhood vote canvasser (*hua khanaen*) died in a tragic motorcycle accident, I overheard conversations about which night of the wake the mayor and the member of parliament would attend; no one questioned whether they would attend or not.

CAMPAIGNING AT FUNERALS

Not every politician focuses on funerals with the same degree of intensity, or in the same style, but all do participate in some capacity. Furthermore, the multi-dimensionality of exchanges associated with funerals provides politicians with multiple motivations and opportunities to insinuate themselves in religious ceremonies surrounding death. I first became aware of the political significance of funerals while following individual candidates on the campaign trail for provincial council. Two candidates in particular, M. L. Ratsami and a man who was called "Phi Dam," attended funerals constantly. Despite the fact that most people in Charoenthani were accustomed to seeing politicians at funerals, these two candidates drew comments from local observers. A journalist I knew said, "Phi Dam has a really strong base in the countryside because he attends funerals without fail, and not just during campaign time either." Several times the two candidates overlapped in their attendance at the same funeral, and I had the opportunity to watch their very different ways of campaigning at such events.

During the provincial council campaign in the Muang district in November 1995, I spent most of my days and evenings on the campaign trail with M. L. Ratsami. Rarely did a day pass in which we did not attend a funeral. Her entourage rode in a white van with campaign posters in all the windows, and arriving late at a wake, having been to two others in quick succession, we would climb out and prepare to enter the temple. M. L. Ratsami would adjust the black scarf that neatly framed her pressed white campaign jacket, an ideal accessory for a funeral . . . except for the bright red Thai numeral ten stitched to the back. The president of the district housewives' association, who traveled with our entourage, always wore an enormous gold pendant that flashed against the thick black lace of her blouse as she chatted with one of the hosts who had come to the entrance. After handing the host a cash-filled envelope with the candidate's name typed on it, she introduced the candidate, beckoned to me, and we proceeded to the seats of honor—usually a vinyl sofa—in the front of the hall. The women who had been sitting next to me in the back of the van brought up the rear, distributing a stack of palm-size leaflets with pictures of the candidate and her number on one side and a photo of the Princess Mother on the back as a lucky memento.

This scene was repeated over and over on the campaign trail with M. L. Ratsami. During her run for Parliament, she used the same tactic, but covered more territory. She targeted poorer families, often rural villagers without close relatives in bureaucratic positions—who thus had no access to the funeral assistance provided by some government agencies—and arranged to be a primary sponsor by covering the major expenses (usually a few thousand *baht*) for an evening of chanting and offerings for the invited monks. Arrangements were often made through the connections of her associates and campaign workers from the district-level housewives' associations, but in a number of cases families seeking financial support would call and extend an invitation. After a long night of traveling from wake to wake, one of M. L. Ratsami's campaign staff quipped to me, "If you're poor, you might as well die during an election, then your family won't have to worry about finding a sponsor for the funeral."

Even if we only stayed for a brief portion of the wake, generally half an hour at the most, out of a two to three hour event, M. L. Ratsami gracefully and expertly carried out her ritual duties as a sponsor. At the first stop, she would begin the ceremony by lighting candles and incense in front of the coffin and on the altar with the Buddha by performing three careful, almost exaggerated prostrations to the holy image. Arriving late to another wake, she would light incense for the dead person before being called up to present offerings to the monks, or to pour water transferring merit to the dead. Her make-up was perfect, her posture correct, and except in the van between stops, she tried to exude a benevolent radiance appropriate to a patron of her stature. As she was a politician new to the province, funerals were one of the primary ways M. L. Ratsami could try to establish patronage relations. As a woman, her options for building a patronage network were somewhat constrained, but funerals were the perfect opportunity to cultivate a sense of indebtedness and foreground her regal charisma through ritual performances. Although only distantly related to the royal family, she could lay claim to the lowest ranked royal title, *mom luang*, and she highlighted this connection as much as possible.

For the reasons I have sketched out above, M. L. Ratsami's campaign strategy concentrated on funerals more than did the strategies of most of her competitors, male or female. Although all of the candidates attended funerals regularly, few were as relentless as M. L. Ratsami. Phi Dam was the other provincial council candidate who focused on funerals, but he did so alone, without the large entourage that trailed M. L. Ratsami from event to event. A friend of Phi Dam's explained that Phi Dam had built relationships with local families over the course of years, and his low-key approach to funerals signaled to villagers that he was a steady presence who could be counted on. He tended to eschew the highly formal role of ritual officiant and guest of honor, preferring instead to talk with members of the family and groups of men around the margins, gathering information, expressing his concern and interest in local affairs, and strategizing with supporters. Several times while I was accompanying M. L. Ratsami's entourage, we crossed paths with Phi Dam at a funeral, and I almost missed seeing him on a few of those occasions because he was standing outside talking with a small clump of men in low tones. His approach to campaigning at funerals fits in with the general pattern of male campaign styles in Charoenthani, a style that emphasizes a down-to-earth, behind-the scenes mode of networking and building support. He too helped out the hosts financially, and he made merit by his very presence at funerals. As a man, perhaps, he did not need the formal, ritualized avenues of merit-making in which M. L. Ratsami excelled. Apart from M. L. Ratsami, Phi Dam was the only provincial council candidate elected in the Muang district who did not belong to the team led by the son of a long-time member of parliament (M. L. Ratsami came in first, and Phi Dam came in third). As an independent candidate, Phi Dam needed to shore up his base of support, and like M. L. Ratsami, he did this by devotedly attending funerals. In the parliamentary elections in 2001, Phi Dam managed to translate this support into a seat in parliament under the redistricting required by the 1998 constitution.

Although Phi Dam and M. L. Ratsami had rather different, gendered styles of campaigning at funerals, they were both tapping into the merit and social power generated through processes of exchange. Given the heightened connection between death, karma, and merit, it should come as no surprise that politicians were eager to participate in the funerary gift-giving which sets both merit and reciprocal obligations in motion. Thus when politicians campaign at funerals, even to the extent of advertising their ballot number on a funeral wreath or on a jacket worn to the event, they are generally not perceived as opportunists crassly pursuing political power in a sacred or "private" setting; that is how we might see it from an American vantage point. Instead, the participation of politicians at funerals fits into people's social and moral expectations, both because funerals are among the most public and widely attended merit-making rituals, and because most Thais cynically expect politicians to be constantly promoting themselves.[8]

In Thai politics there are two moral discourses of power that politicians draw upon to promote themselves, and they are evaluated according to these potentially contradictory notions of power. Ideas of potency arising from Buddhist merit and hierarchical interpersonal relationships based on exchange coexist with a conception of power that emphasizes rationality, progress, and the horizontal ties believed to characterize democracy. Funerals manifest the dynamic interplay between these moral evaluations of power and strategies for how to accumulate it. The preceding analysis of merit-making seems to locate funerals squarely in the realm of the first kind of power, where merit and patronage meet and giving translates into power. However, the centrality of merit-making at funerals allows for an alternative interpretation. Because merit-making stands for both reciprocity and non-reciprocity, it bridges the gap between the two moral frameworks. For those who long to be free from the burdens of reciprocity—the constant demands of exchange that so many of my middle-class informants complained about—merit-making in this context, as an act of un-self-interested non-reciprocity, fit into a rhetoric of "democracy" and "clean" politics. Regardless of whether one campaigns as woman or a man, as a "democratic" candidate or as someone who speaks proudly of *bunkhun* (kindness), favors, and assistance, funerals offer opportunities to present oneself in a moral light that transcends these two approaches to politics within the emerging provincial middle class.

---

[8] Even vote-buying was not seen as crass or out-of-line by many of the people I spoke to in Charoenthani. In an ironic twist of middle-class ambivalence, I heard one small shopkeeper complain that he had not received his allotment of the vote-buying money that had been distributed in his neighborhood, even though he regularly criticized the increasing importance of vote-buying and money in Thai politics. As long as it was kept out of sight, vote-buying was merely lamentable. However, overtly flouting the law by handing out money in plain view of a polling area generated too much dissonance, as though exposing an open secret.

HISTORICAL TRANSFORMATIONS: FROM HOME AND JUNGLE TO *WAT*

My analysis thus far explains the logic of why politicians want to attend funerals and why it is a socially acceptable practice, but the relationship between beliefs about merit and power does not fully explain why politicians place such emphasis on attending funerals. After all, merit and social reciprocity are central to many other ceremonies and events in the Thai social world. Is it sufficient to note that death has special significance that leads politicians to grant high priority to funerals in their busy schedules? As one provincial councilor explained, "Funerals are very important to the family of the person who has died; a person only has one funeral in this lifetime." But I still wondered why funerals have such political appeal. Did funerals have this same kind of political and religious significance in the past? Historically, royal funerals were the object of great political and religious elaboration, a tradition I saw enacted in a particularly national, mass-mediated form during the funeral rites for the king's mother in 1996. But how had the funerals of common villagers become political as well? Have the political and economic changes in Thai society over the past few decades shaped the participation of politicians in funerals? Has the formation of a provincial middle class altered funerary practices and the political potential of funerals? Have religious shifts and reforms had an effect on the rituals surrounding death? While there are no simple answers to these questions, I conclude this paper with an analysis of the patterns of transformation I observed in provincial Thai funerals, placing these transformations in the context of political decentralization, economic growth, and an increasingly embattled Buddhist establishment.

By the 1990s, the expansion of the Thai economy had led to the emergence of provincial businessmen who were important political players at the national and local level.[9] During my research, this provincial bourgeoisie was selectively adopting the discourse of democracy, pressing for even greater political decentralization and local autonomy. Although the growing momentum for political reform that resulted in the "People's Constitution" of 1998 has been seen as a triumph of the Bangkok middle class, the provincial elite also had a stake in these reforms. At the same time, new Buddhist movements and frequent scandals were threatening to fragment the highly centralized national *sangha* (monkhood).[10] In the decades of rapid growth that started in the 1960s, many ritual practices have also been changing, but these transformations have largely been taken for granted or ignored.[11]

---

[9] Anderson, Ockey, and Pasuk and Baker document and analyze the increasing number of provincial businessmen entering politics. Benedict Anderson, "Murder and Progress in Modern Siam," *New Left Review*, 181 (1990). James Ockey, "Business Leaders, Gangsters, and the Middle Class: Societal Groups and Civilian Rule in Thailand" (PhD dissertation, Cornell University, 1992). Pasuk Phongpaichit and Chris Baker, *Thailand, Economy and Politics* (New York: Oxford University Press, 1995).

[10] Keyes made a similar argument in his address at the 1999 Thai Studies Conference. Charles F. Keyes, "Buddhism Fragmented: Thai Buddhism and Political Order Since the 1970s," presented at the Seventh International Conference on Thai Studies, Amsterdam, 1999.

[11] One exception is Gray's dissertation on *kathin* ceremonies which mark the end of Buddhist Lent. Her study traces the changing role of the monarchy in relation to this ritual and shows how a Bangkok-based bank used the ritual to facilitate its expansion into the provinces. Christine Gray, "Thailand: The Soteriological State in the 1970s" (PhD dissertation, University of Chicago, 1986).

The most visible, tangible change that shapes the standard funeral sequence has been the widespread construction of crematoriums on temple grounds since the 1960s. In central Thailand, increased wealth and access to rich urban donors has meant that by the nineties almost every community had managed to build a crematorium on the grounds of the local *wat*. These crematoriums are identifiable by the tall chimney flu, topped with a small pointed roof that resembles the *prasat* which had adorned the funeral pyres of the wealthy in the past. The chimney sometimes stands alone, but more and more often it rises above a *sala* (hall) that has been built in front of the crematorium to accommodate mourners. Having a crematorium shifts the site of the final funeral ritual away from charnel grounds situated in forest clearings on the periphery of the community, into the bounded, sacred space of a temple.[12] At the same time, wakes that were formerly held in and around the homes of the deceased are increasingly being held at temples as well.[13]

During two years of fieldwork, I attended almost one hundred funeral rituals, but of this number, only two wakes were held at home, and only once did I stand outside as we watched the flames of a log funeral pyre work their way up to engulf the wooden coffin on top.[14] When I attended the wake of the aged neighbor of one of my friends who lived in a rural village, we sat on chairs lined up haphazardly around and underneath the raised wooden house. No special platform was needed

[12] For evocative descriptions of wandering forest monks (*phra thudong*) meditating in charnel grounds outside of rural hamlets, see Kamala Tiyavanich, *Forest Recollections: Wandering Monks in Twentieth-Century Thailand* (Honolulu: University of Hawaii Press, 1997), pp. 96-105. According to O'Connor, when crematoriums were built for early urban centers such as Ayutthaya and Bangkok, they were located outside of the city limits in specially designated *wats*. Richard O'Connor, "Urbanism and Religion: Community, Hierarchy, and Sanctity in Urban Thai Buddhist Temples" (PhD dissertation, Cornell University, 1978), p. 143. In central Thailand this pattern has all but disappeared; Bangkok sprawl has enveloped the temples that were once outside the city limits, and crematoriums have been built on the grounds of temples within the limits of provincial cities and villages. The ethnographic description of a cremation in Bang Chan in the 1950s indicates that, at that time, even in a community close enough to Bangkok to have since been incorporated into the metropolis, while cremations took place on temple grounds, the participants were still using exposed funeral pyres, not a crematorium. See Lauriston Sharp and Lucien M. Hanks, *Bang Chan: Social History of a Rural Community in Thailand* (Ithaca, NY: Cornell University Press, 1978), pp. 164-8.

[13] The most detailed ethnographic descriptions of home-based wakes come from northeastern and northern Thailand. See Tambiah, *Buddhism and the Spirit Cults of North-east Thailand*, p. 68. Also see Charles F. Keyes, "Tug-of-War for Merit: Cremation of a Senior Monk," *Journal of the Siam Society* 63 (1975). Charles F. Keyes and Phra Khru Anusaranasasanakiarti, "Funerary Rites and the Buddhist Meaning of Death: An Interpretative Text from Northern Thailand," *Journal of the Siam Society* 68 (1980). More recent work by Klima seems to suggest that the pattern of wakes in the home persists in these poorer and more remote parts of the country. Alan Klima, *The Funeral Casino: Meditation, Massacre, and Exchange with the Dead in Thailand* (Princeton: Princeton University Press, 2002).

[14] The outdoor cremation I witnessed was, not coincidentally, for an old man who had been a prominent member of the Lao Song (or *tai dam*, "Black Tai") ethnic minority community. In an extended interview with a middle-aged man from a nearby village, I learned that younger members of their community are increasingly assimilating to and borrowing from the Theravada Buddhist practices of the dominant culture. Although the old man's wake had been held in a temple, his cremation in the small clearing a short walk away was performed according to Lao Song traditions, with specially decorated straw and wood structures that would help convey his soul to heaven. A new crematorium had just been built at the nearby temple with funds from a Bangkok donor, and several participants commented that in the future there would not be outdoor cremations anymore.

to elevate the monks; they were upstairs in the house along with the dead body and close relatives, and we could hear them chanting over loudspeakers that had been rented for the occasion. I watched as women scooped hundreds of bowls of coconut ice cream and loaded them on huge metal trays that my friends helped pass out to the participants between rounds of chanting. The increasing rarity of funerals like these, located outside of the space of the *wat*, elicited commentary from the people that I talked to during and after the rituals. They made a point of telling me, "This is how wakes used to be" or "Soon there will be no more outdoor cremations; this is among the last."

When I asked why this shift had occurred, some people explained that it was no longer convenient to hold a wake at home; houses were not as big as they used to be, and besides you would have to go to the *wat* anyway to borrow chairs and dishes for all of the guests. Others said it was because so few people die at home anymore. "Now it is easier to get to the hospital and more people go there when they are sick. If a person does not die at home, then the corpse must be taken to the *wat*."[15] Both of these rather functional explanations point to significant changes in the spatial and institutional organization of Thai society. Cement houses built on the ground with individual rooms to accommodate members of the nuclear family are rapidly replacing wooden houses built on stilts with wide open spaces shared by a fluid configuration of family members and relatives. There has also been a boom in building both hospitals and *wats*. For example, in Charoenthani, in addition to the existing state-run hospital, two new hospitals were built with investments from private shareholders during the course of my research. Construction projects were also evident at any number of *wat*, including many in more rural parts of the province, evidence, some said, of competition for monastic rank. Despite these broad changes, the home continues to be the focal point of weddings and an array of merit-making ceremonies for birthdays, death anniversaries, and, of course, new houses. Members of the expanding provincial bourgeoisie readily spend their newly acquired wealth on all of these ritual events. So why are funerals the only formerly home-based ritual or rite of passage that has been institutionalized in communal Buddhist space? And does holding funerals in *wats* have any connection to the ubiquitous presence of politicians? In the sections that follow, I draw on the perspectives of the laity, the *sangha*, and local politicians in order to offer some speculative answers to these questions, and to show how these issues are linked to increasingly widespread middle-class ideals and preferences.

FUNERARY DISTINCTIONS: COMPETING FOR STATUS AND MERIT

The lay perspective on the shift in funeral location appears to rest on notions of propriety and status often associated with the middle class, as well as on an ever-expanding competitive desire for merit. Holding funerals at the *wat* must seem like an appropriate, even rational, way to increase merit-making opportunities for yourself and the person who has died, while keeping the disturbing, disruptive

---

[15] According to research by Keyes and Terwiel from the late 1960s, if a person died away from home, the corpse would not be brought back home, but rather, taken directly to the temple. The nationwide increase in mobility and migration, as well as the proliferation of hospitals, has certainly changed the pattern of where people die. Keyes, "Funerary Rites," and B. J. Terwiel, *Monks and Magic: An Analysis of Religious Ceremonies in Central Thailand* (Bangkok: White Lotus, 1994 [1974]).

elements of death at bay.[16] When questioned concerning the shift from outdoor funeral pyres to temple crematoriums, no one I talked to seemed to think that the change required an explanation. They would shrug off my questions, saying at most, "It's easier" or "It's cleaner." When I pressed the issue, a woman in her thirties finally said, "When you cremate someone outdoors it can be obscene or disgusting [*uchatta*]; you might see something you shouldn't see. Sometimes the corpse sits up or you see the skeleton through the fire." In contrast, temple cremations and wakes are orderly, and they separate people from potentially risky exposure to shocking sights or spirits. A municipal school teacher told me, "When the body is at the temple there is less need for family and friends to stay up all night gambling to keep the corpse company—and besides it's not quite proper to gamble at the temple." Similarly, participants at temple cremations are insulated from confronting the scarier aspects of death; they help light the cremation pyre symbolically, rather than actually, placing their *dokmai chan* on a tray, or at most putting it through a small metal door, into the crematorium, from which only a bright flame is visible. Being in a *wat* as opposed to at home or in a clearing in the jungle also heightens the Buddhist elements of the ritual, and by extension the association with merit.[17]

Another way to look at the changes in Thai funerals is to see them as reflective of a tendency for people both in villages and provincial cities to emulate higher-status models from outside their own communities. Thus, amid the ongoing process of urbanization in provincial centers, holding funerals at temples has become the standard to aim for, even in rural villages. Nonetheless, rural notions of displaying high status do not entirely coincide with the patterns favored by the provincial middle class. For instance, I attended one cremation in an outlying rural district with a member of the provincial council. On the grounds of the temple, an elaborate spired structure representing Mount Meru (called a *maen* according to Thai pronunciation) held the urn containing the remains of an elderly woman. The choice of this family was striking, since the use of a *maen* of this type is generally restricted to royalty, except in this province, because of its history as the home of traditional *maen* artisans. While wealthy rural villagers often imitated traditional royal-style funerals, complete with entertainment for their guests in the form of classical

---

[16] For analyses that treat similar transformations in attitudes towards death and dying in the West, see Phillipe Ariés, "The Reversal of Death: Changes in Attitudes Toward Death in Western Societies," in *Death in America*, ed. D. Stannard (Philadelphia: University of Pennsylvania Press, 1974). Walter Benjamin, "The Storyteller," in *Illuminations*, ed. Hannah Arendt (New York: Shocken Books, 1968). And Geoffrey Gorer, "The Pornography of Death," in *Death, Grief, and Mourning in Contemporary Britain* (London: Cresset Press, 1965).

[17] In their study of the formation of a provincial middle class in England, Davidoff and Hall note that middle-class women were "beginning to be considered too delicate to bear the public rituals of death" because of their inability to control their emotions, which the women themselves came to feel was shameful. Davidoff and Hall also stress the significance of membership in a religious community as a route to social honor. Religion "gave both men and women a sense of identity and community which provided social and economic benefits and gave individuals the strength to assert demands, offering new identities in public and private worlds." Leonore Davidoff and Catherine Hall, *Family Fortunes: Men and Women of the English Middle Class, 1780-1850* (Chicago: University of Chicago Press, 1987), p. 408 and p. 103. Gunn also mentions funerals, which he describes as public rituals marked by conspicuous display and respectability in British city life between 1850 and 1914. Simon Gunn, "The Public Sphere, Modernity, and Consumption: New Perspectives on the History of the English Middle Class," in *Gender, Civic Culture and Consumerism: Middle Class Identity in Britain, 1800-1940*, ed. A. Kidd and D. Nicholls (New York: Manchester University Press, 1999), p. 19.

dancers, music,[18] folk opera, a movie, or even fireworks, most provincial urban dwellers, including those who could easily afford to rent a *maen* or hire performers, tended to follow the pattern of more sedate, Bangkok middle-class styles of funerals instead. In the city, funerals were briefer affairs, involving in-and-out visits by mourners, held at temples that specialized in dispatching the dead. Sometimes a contingent of members from a local association such as the Lions Club would attend a funeral as a group, but even so, the crowds were not as large as those I saw at country funerals, a tendency that reflected people's busy schedules and the greater tenuousness of social ties in urban areas. In the municipality of Charoenthani, it was considered up-to-date (*than samai*), and therefore a mark of higher status, to serve small packaged cookies and instant coffee at a wake, despite the muttered complaints I heard from some hungry guests, who said, "In the countryside you'd get a real bowl of noodles, not these tiny things."

Funerals mark social status, both through the differences between funerals and through the incorporation of status distinctions within the ceremony itself, such as those distinctions reflected in seating arrangements and who is called upon to present offerings. The social status of the deceased and his or her family shapes funerals in terms of which temple is chosen for the funeral, the number and status of the monks participating, the presence of powerful and important individuals (including politicians), the style and abundance of hanging towel wreaths (*phuang rit*), fresh flower arrangements and other decorations, and the kinds of mementos handed out to departing guests. At one end of the spectrum, the most important guest might be a city councilor, a sub-district chief, or the superintendent of schools. The area around the coffin would probably be decorated with plastic flowers and blinking lights, and tiger balm would be given to guests after they had put paper *dokmai chan* into the flames. However, at the funeral of a prosperous, well-known member of the community, past and current members of parliament might attend, along with the dean of the local college, a provincial vice-governor, the editor of the local newspaper, and a number of municipal and provincial councilors. Fresh flowers would adorn the coffin, hundreds upon hundreds of *phuang rit* would hang from the temple walls, and guests would use cleverly fashioned cornhusk *dokmai chan* to light the cremation fire. They even might receive a glossy cremation volume, chronicling highlights in the life of the deceased. Instead of a mere dozen monks, hundreds of monks, as well as high-ranking abbots, would be invited to chant, and in some cases, a contingent of *mae chi* (lay nuns) would also be called upon.

The fact that funerals reveal many different gradations of social status and varying capacities to use wealth to generate merit is nothing new in Thai society. What has changed, however, is the introduction of orderly, time-efficient, urban middle-class norms as a model for high-status provincial funerals. The middle class may not imitate the most elaborate elements of royal funerals, but they still eagerly latch on to signs showing connection to royal charisma and power. If the library collections of cremation volumes in Charoenthani are any indication, the past few decades have seen a dramatic increase in the frequency with which members of the provincial middle class have hosted royally sponsored cremations (*phraratchathan phloeng sop*). At this special type of cremation, ranking government officials who

---

[18] Deborah Wong writes specifically about the role of "foreign" Mon music at urban Thai funerals. Deborah Wong, "Mon Music for Thai Deaths: Ethnicity and Status in Thai Urban Funerals," *Asian Folklore Studies* 57 (1998): 99-130.

attend must wear full dress uniform with black arm-bands, and the flame used to ignite the funeral pyre is carried in a glass lamp from the palace in Bangkok. High-ranking members of the bureaucracy can petition for royal sponsorship for the cremation of family members, and even provincial businessmen and women who have been active philanthropists and generously supported royal foundations and projects are often given royal awards and made eligible for royally sponsored funerals as well. When members of the provincial bourgeoisie tap into royal charisma in this way, they heighten their status and demonstrate a large store of merit by mounting such a display of *barami* (transcendent virtue). In many cases, the staging of a royally sponsored cremation is a way for members of the middle class to assert their self-reliance and independence from local patrons. At the royally sponsored cremation I attended for an old woman whose children had become successful bureaucrats, some posted locally and some working in Bangkok, the family insisted that they would not accept gifts of cash, not to mention the assistance of local politicians or other influential people. Their refusal to become indebted is emblematic of the more widespread, but not always acted upon, desire to escape the burdens and obligations of exchange.

INSTITUTIONALIZING FUNERALS: RELIGION, POLITICS, AND THE PUBLIC ARENA

Relocating wakes and cremations to the sacred, public space of the *wat* does not merely reflect the symbolics of status and the spread of middle-class sensibilities; it also serves the interests of religious and political functionaries. Monks and politicians both stand to benefit from the spatial and organizational transformations of Thai funerals. For the Buddhist, *sangha* funerals offer a logical opportunity for expanded religious involvement and practice, especially as other regular holy days diminish in importance and popularity. Just as new, middle-class Buddhist movements such as Thammakai, and practices such as spirit mediumship, have come under scrutiny for the ways in which they commodify religious practice,[19] the widespread practice of holding funerals in *wats* and its financial implications did not

---

[19] These movements have not made big inroads among the provincial middle class in Charoenthani, except perhaps among people who have spent time in Bangkok, especially attending college. Several articles deal specifically with the middle class and new Buddhist movements, including: Peter A. Jackson, *Buddhism, Legitimation, and Conflict: The Political Functions of Urban Thai Buddhism* (Singapore: Institute of Southeast Asian Studies, 1989). Peter A. Jackson, "The Enchanting Spirit of Thai Capitalism: The Cult of Luang Phor Khoon and the Postmodernization of Thai Buddhism," *South East Asia Research* 7,1 (1999): 5-60. Charles F. Keyes, "Buddhism Fragmented," presented at the Seventh International Conference on Thai Studies, Amsterdam, 1999. Suwanna Satha-Anand, "Religious Movements in Contemporary Thailand: Buddhist Struggles for Modern Relevance," *Asian Survey* 30,4 (1990): 395-408. J. L. Taylor, "New Buddhist Movements in Thailand: An 'Individualistic Revolution', Reform and Political Dissonance," *Journal of Southeast Asian Studies* 21 (1990): 135-54. Edwin Zehner, "Reform Symbolism of a Thai Middle-Class Sect: The Growth and Appeal of the Thammakai Movement," *Journal of Southeast Asian Studies* 21,2 (1990): 402-26. For recent work on mediumship, see Morris, *In the Place of Origins*; Pattana Kitiarsa, "'You May Not Believe, But Never Offend the Spirits': Spirit Medium Cult Discourses and the Postmodernization of Thai Religion" (PhD dissertation, University of Washington, 1999); Erick White, "Thai Professional Spirit Mediums and the Search for Religious Legitimacy," paper presented at the Seventh International Conference on Thai Studies, Amsterdam, 1999.

escape the notice of a few of my informants.[20] They explained that the current arrangement is more convenient and lucrative from the perspective of the *wat*: the temple gets a monetary donation for the use of the space; individuals monks do not have to travel as frequently or as far; and they are assured a relatively steady income from the gifts of cash given when they chant.

The rationalization and institutionalization of funerals also makes these ceremonies more accessible to politicians. Deaths are recorded and tabulated by the bureaucracy; for members of any household registered in a municipality, deaths must be reported to municipal officials within twenty-four hours. With increasing contestation for elected positions, local politicians need more ways to build support, and unlike home-based ceremonies, funerals held in a *wat* are easier to schedule and to find. The routinization of the location and times of wakes and cremations makes them part of a regular community rhythm. The conventions are so predictable that public figures such as politicians readily incorporate them into their weekly schedules, and anthropologists are expected to know without being told the appropriate time to arrive for a cremation.[21]

Poor families who arrange such ceremonies are also even more likely to appreciate financial assistance, as the cost of a funeral increases when it is held in the *wat*. Although the majority of funerals that I attended were hosted by families that were too poor and rural to lay claim to middle-classness, even these funerals had been shaped by patterns of religious specialization and commoditization. While members of the provincial middle class organized funerals that expressed values such as rationality, order, and cleanliness, and some even used funerals as an opportunity to demonstrate their economic independence, those with fewer resources struggled to keep up with increasing costs and changing expectations. Politicians readily step into the role of patron by helping out with funeral costs, but they can just as easily play the role of high-status guest, lending luster and honor to the event and making merit along with other guests.

Because wakes were once held at home, and cremations were held outdoors in jungle clearings, holding funerals in temples brings them into a domain that is simultaneously public and sacred. The intensified significance of merit at funerals gives politicians the opportunity to tap into circuits of patronage and reciprocity without leaving "public" space. In the case of candidates who cast themselves as "clean," "democratic," and "non-corrupt," and hold public speeches and rallies as a

---

[20] In Thai, a special religious vocabulary negates and thereby draws attention to the potential for commoditizing religious practice and objects. For example, *nimon,* rather than the common term *choen,* is used to refer to "inviting" monks to chant. One would never refer to "hiring" monks in Thai, a slip that might be easier to make in English. Similarly, it would sound strange to say you are going to "buy" (*seu*) an amulet, when the proper term is "rent" (*chao*), a word that avoids the negative connotations of buying and selling religious objects.

[21] In conducting fieldwork, one often learns most about commonly held assumptions from one's mistakes and *faux pas*. In this case, I almost missed the cremation of the niece of a close friend because I misunderstood the reference to four o'clock. I thought that 4:00 was when I should arrive, when in fact that was the time when the last *dokmai chan* would be thrown into the blaze and the door to the incinerator shut. Part of my confusion stemmed from the fact that 4:00 PM was the time listed on the schedules of the politicians I usually accompanied to funerals. It did not occur to me that the time listed was the ritually significant one, but not the time when one should aim to arrive. It turns out I could have spent all day observing different types of merit-making, but without explicit instruction, I foolishly merged my own notions of being properly "on time" with the times listed on campaign schedules.

sign of their critique of personalistic patronage politics, the public and religious aspects of funerals held in *wat* means that they can tap into reciprocity even as they disavow it.

Funerals hold political significance because of the multiple and simultaneous meanings these ceremonies can encompass. Politicians who attend funerals have complex motivations, and their constituents read the participation of politicians on many different levels. Studying Thai politics and funerals in this light shows that religion and politics in Thailand cannot be reduced to assertions that Buddhism is used for political legitimation and, by extension, that the state seeks to control the Buddhist hierarchy. As an institution, the *sangha* is certainly invested in the strong identification between Buddhist rituals and death, but the state has few stakes in controlling this aspect of Buddhism. Instead, it is local politicians who use the polyvalent meanings of contemporary funerals to negotiate a path to political success through two competing moral frameworks of power.

IMMATERIAL CULTURE: "IDOLATRY" IN THE LOWLAND PHILIPPINES[1]

Fenella Cannell

"If ever there was a place where the schoolmaster's art has been thrown sharply into contrast with education in the true meaning, it is here in the Philippine Islands under the Spanish government. For the Spanish occupants of the islands, whether civil or ecclesiastical, never sought to draw out what there is in the native, but to put that into him which, like the embalming fluid in a corpse, would preserve him from corruption, indeed, but would never make him master either of knowledge or of himself."[2]

INTRODUCTION

In this paper, I want to make two interlinked suggestions. Firstly, I shall argue for a reinterpretation of the material on the early American period in the Philippines, placing *religious* ideas at the heart of an understanding of colonial policy. Secondly, and particularly because both idolatry and the image of a sort of imperfectly realized commodity fetish are central to this analysis, I shall consider the relationship between my argument and William Pietz's intelligent and influential account of the difference between these concepts.

[1] The historical research on which this chapter is based was funded by a Small Research Grant from the British Academy, whose support is gratefully acknowledged. The research was largely conducted at Cornell University, and I would like to thank the Cornell archivists and librarians, and colleagues at Cornell's Southeast Asia Program and Anthropology Department. Some additional research was conducted at Ann Arbor, Michigan, where an earlier version of this chapter was presented, at the invitation of the International Institute, and of Webb Keane. The more general project on Christianity and anthropology referred to at the beginning of this piece has been substantially advanced during research supported by an Economic and Social Research Council grant, number R000239016. For helpful comments on this piece at various stages, I would like to thank Mukalika Banerjee, Ken George, Eva-Lotta Hedman, Deborah Homsher, Simon Jarvis, Webb Keane, Smita Lahiri, Danilyn Rutherford, Harvey Whitehouse, and Andrew Willford.

[2] Report of the educational inspector for the Cebu area, quoted in *Tales of American Teachers in the Philippines,* ed. Geronima T. Pecson and Mary Racelis Hollnsteiner (Manila: Carmelo and Bauermann, 1959), p. 123.

One context for these suggestions is a wider project, on which I have written and am in the process of writing elsewhere, that Christianity functions in several ways as the 'repressed' of anthropology, and of social science generally. That is, that while anthropology founded its professional identity on a claim to secularism, Judeo-Christian theological ideas in fact continue to shape its theoretical preconceptions. It is the reluctance to confront this possibility which partly explains anthropology's general tardiness in producing ethnographies of the various Christian parts of the world which do full justice to their particularities, or which make the fact of their Christianity analytically central.[3]

This is not the place in which to elaborate further on these more general arguments. However, this brief indication may serve to orient the central material of the present paper. In looking at public policy and colonial discourse in the American Philippines, I shall be seeking to demonstrate how pervasive was the influence of what one might call a "naturalized Protestantism" in the creation of categories through which Americans—even Americans of diverse political and religious backgrounds—viewed the Filipino people. Yet even the very best recent accounts of Philippine public life of this period either fail to focus on this religious language in colonialism, or treat it as a matter relevant only to missionary history narrowly defined.

The picture that emerges from the Philippine evidence, I shall argue, has a further claim on our attention because it does not fit easily with the approaches to Christian colonialisms using the work of William Pietz on the fetish, which have become widely popular in anthropological accounts. In fact, as we shall see, the misfit between Pietz's fetish and the Philippine "idol" may suggest an inherent limitation in Pietz's arguments.[4]

In order to develop these points, however, it is necessary to supply some brief historical background.

From invasion in 1897 until Philippine independence in 1946, the Americans had to justify their acquisition both in the Islands and to the large anti-imperialist faction at home. This was done primarily through a defining project, that of providing English-language American-style education throughout the Philippines. In theory, this education was to be universal, at least to the end of primary level, and free, but in fact it was never truly either. Nonetheless both the idea and the flawed reality of the great educational experiment have dominated Filipino and American perceptions of the colonial relationship ever since.

---

[3] For a fuller development of these themes, and qualifications of these general statements, see Fenella Cannell, "Introduction: The Anthropology of Christianity," in *The Anthropology of Christianity* ed. Fenella Cannell (Duke University Press, forthcoming). For key writings by other anthropologists with related critiques, see Marshall Sahlins, "The Sadness of Sweetness: The Native Anthropology of Western Cosmology," *Current Anthropology* 37,3 (1996): 395-428; and Talal Asad, *Genealogies of Religion; Discipline and Reasons of Power in Christianity and Islam* (Baltimore and London: Johns Hopkins University Press, 1993); and by a theologian, see John Milbank, *Theology and Social Theory: Beyond Secular Reason* (Oxford: Blackwells, 1990).

[4] For some of Pietz's fascinating and scholarly essays, see William Pietz, "The problem of the fetish, I," *Res* 9 (Spring 1985): 5-17; "The problem of the fetish, II: The origin of the fetish," *Res* 13 (Spring 1987): 23-45, "The problem of the fetish, IIIa: Bosman's Guinea and the enlightenment theory of fetishism" *Res* 16 (Autumn 1988): 104-123; and "The spirit of civilization: blood sacrifice and monetary debt," *Res* 28 (Autumn 1995): 23-38. For a range of essays exploring Pietz's ideas, see ed. Patricia Spyer, ed., *Border Fetishisms: Material Objects in Unstable Spaces* (New York and London: Routledge, 1998).

Although unusually ambitious and democratic in its claims, the American educational project was not dissimilar to those of many European colonial regimes, in setting out to re-create its subjects as citizens of the modern world. Glenn Anthony May's book, *Social Engineering in the Philippines*,[5] provides a clear account of the rapid shifts in curriculum which were determined by changes in leadership in the Bureau of Education. Under the intelligent, liberal David Barrows, policy was genuinely idealistic, premised on creating a society of literate, civic-minded, and independent Philippine small-holders. Under Director Frank L. Crone, however, policy forged a tighter link between education and colonial production, while the phrase "industrial education" took on a literal and somewhat ominous meaning. This model, then the *dernier cri* of fashionable theory, valued the shaping of children through the discipline of manual work, at least as highly as the acquisition of any academic skills,[6] especially when the products of this work could be sold for a profit through the educational institution.

May's work has recently been placed in a new context by Paul Kramer.[7] Kramer provides an outstanding account of the ways in which the rationale of the unfolding educational policy was driven by its relationship with the emerging discipline of ethnology, as it had been coopted to serve the new colonial administration. What Kramer calls the "pragmatic empire" was to be based on information about local peoples and conditions. The government's information agents included (initially) the occupying military and (later) school teachers, but above all ethnologists, drafted from the United States, from universities, and from the ethnological museums such as the Smithsonian, the Field Museum of Chicago, and the American Museum of Natural History, which were primarily concerned with the collection of "primitive" artifacts.

The connection between education and ethnology was in part institutional; many key figures in the Philippines were, like David Barrows, trained in both fields. When the Bureau of non-Christian Tribes, the center of the ethnological enterprise, fell out of favor with the new and more hard-nosed administration of 1909, much of its work was shunted into the Bureau of Education. The ideological connections were, however, even more fundamental. Kramer demonstrates that American policy was shaped by the adoption of a variant of Morgan's thesis of the evolution of societies, usually referred to as "progressivism."[8] This theory espouses the idea of the reality of "races," and claims that some are at preferential stages of development, while others lag behind. It differs from pessimistic popular Social Darwinism, however, in arguing that exposure to favorable examples can cause more "retarded" peoples to develop and "progress."[9]

---

[5] Glenn Anthony May, *Social Engineering in the Philippines: The Aims, Execution and Impact of American Colonial Policy, 1900-1913* (Westport, CT: Greenwood Press, 1980).

[6] Proponents of industrial education continued to require basic numeracy, literacy, and spoken English, but mainly because these were thought to be necessary for business efficiency.

[7] Paul A. Kramer, "The Pragmatic Empire: US Anthropology and Colonial Politics in the Occupied Philippines, 1898-1916" (PhD dissertation, Princeton University, 1998).

[8] Kramer, "Pragmatic Empire," p. 38.

[9] This at least is the more liberal version of the theory, and that which was most often publicly avowed, although as Kramer shows, a number of leading figures took a more negative approach and argued that certain Filipino "races" were advancing slowly or not at all.

American colonial education then became the arena in which the drama of Filipino "progress" would be played out. This theory proved sufficiently elastic to contain most of the warring variants of educational syllabus and policy through the period 1899–1935 and beyond.[10]

American educational and colonial policy at this period is usually explained in terms of political constraints and motivations. Kramer has shown the part played by the government's adoption of the modern "science" of ethnological knowledge. However, I shall argue that *religious* ideas, in the form of the American Protestant thought of the period, were equally important, and that both policy and "science" relied at a deeper level on Protestant notions of the nature of human interiority, intentionality, and meaning, and of the proper relations between soul, body, and inanimate matter. These ideas were so implicated in "secular" policy making that it becomes redundant to make a distinction between the two.

IMMATERIAL CULTURE

When I first arrived in Bicol, Southern Luzon, in 1988, it was still commonplace to assume that the lowland Philippines had little to offer anthropologists or anyone else interested in "culture." Accounting for and contesting this perception became the organizing theme of the dissertation and monograph which I eventually wrote on my Bicol fieldwork. I argued there and elsewhere[11] that the misperception of the lowlands as "without culture" resulted from the particular definition of "culture" that emerged from the American colonial period, and was perpetuated by social science both within the Philippines and outside it. This view privileged ideas of "culture" as large-scale ritual and/or the deliberate maintenance of unchanging social practices through time. In so doing, it declined to examine the places where much that is most significant in lowland social life is situated, in the subtleties of talk about shifting relationships between persons, spirits, and deities.[12]

In particular, the legacy of American colonialism was to associate the highlands with the notion of "tradition," and the lowlands with the notion of "imitation" or "mimicry." Lowlanders were portrayed as lacking autonomous traditions of their

[10] My own reading of the Bureau of Education's reports through to 1930 shows considerable continuities in language and ideology coupled with frequent but superficial changes in curriculum and educational theory. My field research in Bicol primary and high schools suggests certain powerful continuities in actual classroom practice, often determined by a severely inadequate provision of resources, despite the awareness and best efforts of local school teachers. There are also notable continuities in the content of many commonly used textbooks. See also Niels Mulder "Philippine textbooks and the national self-image," *Philippine Studies* 38 (1990): 84-102. To my knowledge, however, there is at present no historical study of policy changes post-1916 which matches Kramer's analysis in its depth, and such observations are therefore provisional.

[11] Fenella Cannell, "Catholicism, Spirit Mediumship, and the Ideal of Beauty in Bicolano Community, Philippines" (PhD dissertation, University of London, 1991); Fenella Cannell, "The Imitation of Christ in Bicol," *Journal of the Royal Anthropological Institute (N.S.)* I (1995): 377-94; Fenella Cannell, "The Power of Appearances: Beauty, Mimicry, and Transformation in Bicol," in *Discrepant Histories: Translocal Essays on Filipino Cultures*, ed. Vicente L. Rafael (Philadelphia, PA: Temple University Press, and Manila: Anvil Publishing, 1995), pp. 223-258; Fenella Cannell, *Power and Intimacy in the Christian Philippines* (Cambridge: Cambridge University Press, 1999; and Quezon City: Ateneo de Manila University Press, 2000).

[12] See especially Cannell, *Power and Intimacy*, pp. 1, 29, 182, 203, 216, 223, 226, 251.

own, and as mechanically repeating those of others, especially those of their colonizers.

This claim in fact predates the American occupation, and was anticipated by nineteenth-century European travelers and commentators in the islands.[13] The Spanish traveler Guerra, witnessing a *commedia* (Spanish-language folk-theater) in Bicol in 1856, complained that:

> The actors walked on, chattering their parts, which not one of them understood, and moving their arms up and down . . . Their countenances were entirely devoid of expression and they spoke like automatons.[14]

Nor were complaints confined to Americans; the English traveler Mrs. Campell Dauncey was equally bored and depressed by Filipino provincial entertainments and, although often poking acerbic fun at the American colonial enterprise, was often inclined to agree that: "There is nothing in these Filipinos you see."[15]

Nevertheless, it was the Americans who gave impetus and permanence to the idea of lowland cultural vacuity. Under the Bureau (later Division) of Non-Christian Tribes, ethnographers, sometimes accompanied by their adventurous wives, began the work of recording data on the upland peoples and collecting their material culture.

In the highlands, "custom," "culture," and "tradition" are some of the primary categories through which local life is evoked. In these wild areas of the Northern Cordillera among the head-hunting "tribes," anthropologist's wife Mabel Cook Cole felt she had almost attained her dream; "to live unhampered by the rules of modern society,"[16] and instead become part of "the story of the ancestors . . . whose customs must be followed always."[17]

By contrast, in the plains, Cole was as enervated as she was invigorated in the highlands, chafed at her temporary role as school teacher, and longed for the "wild country."[18] She was far from alone in preferring upland society. In the lowlands, as other lady writers of the period tell us, one might be very kindly received, but:

---

[13] I argue that in fact there *is* something 'real' to be perceived here—that is, that lowland culture places rather little value on ideas of unchangingness compared to other cultures, and positively values so-called imitation, giving it a very different significance from that assigned it in the West. My aim here is to explore the other side of the equation—what factors were at work in the creation of the American illusion in particular.

[14] Guerra, quoted in Feodor Jagor, *Travels in the Philippines* (Reisen in der Philippinnen) (Manila: Filipiniana Book Guild, 1965), p. 75. The Spanish edition was published as *Viajes por Filipinas, traducios del aleman por S. Vidal Y Soler* (Madrid: Imprenta de Arbau y C.a. Impresores de Camara de S.M., 1875).

[15] Mrs. Campbell Dauncey, *An Englishwoman in the Philippines* (London: Murray, 1906), pp. 57, 78.

[16] Mabel Cook Cole, *Savage Gentlemen* (New York: D. Van Norstrand Company, Inc. ,1929), p. 3.

[17] Ibid., p. 36.

[18] Ibid., p.148. See, for example, the writings of Albert Jenk's wife on the couple's sojourn with the Bontoc, Maud Huntley Jenks, *Death Stalks the Philippine Wilds: Letters of Maud Huntley Jenks, Selected and Edited by Carmen Nelson Richards, Forward by Albert Ernest Jenks* (Minneapolis, MN: Land Press, 1951)

"Civilization and the civilized life are a bit slow . . . and the wild tribes and Moors are certainly more picturesque than the Europeanized overclad natives of Manila."[19]

As Renato Rosaldo has commented in a different context, "full citizenship and culture appear to be inversely related . . . Full citizens lack culture, and those most culturally endowed lack full citizenship . . . In the Philippines, 'cultural minorities' have culture, and lowlanders do not."[20] Mabel Cole and her husband were never in any doubt that with the Tinguian they were in the presence of a "culture"; although American anthropology at this period was still deeply divided over the question of racial evolution versus cultural relativism,[21] the *de facto* identification of a "primitive culture" was something on which there would probably have been wide agreement. A "culture" meant a small-scale society whose individual and collective actions were directed by rules, but rules based on principles not considered "rational" in modern society, especially by non-monotheistic religions, kinship regulations, or (as with the ancestor-worshipping Tinguian) the two combined. Such cultures persisted through time by the inheritance and transmission of these rules and the sanctions that accompanied them.

According to the theory of racial "progression," primitive cultures would change when brought into contact with modern influences, allowing the capacities of their populations to develop and adapt. By this same logic, lowlanders should have figured simply as the formerly "primitive" people who had ceded their "culture" to the Spanish and had been advancing and developing since the 1600s.

In practice, however, American commentators and their successors have tended to write as though highland Filipino groups were not simply at an earlier stage of development than their lowland counterparts, but were actually possessed of a different interior moral quality. Highland groups were seen as the bearers of a certain form of *authenticity* evidenced by their adherence to their own forms of social rules, and by their reluctance to alter them. Stereotypically, they were seen as honest; as ruthless enemies, therefore, but true friends once won over to the American side; lowlanders were characterized as slippery, evasive, and lacking in individuality, autonomy, and vitality.[22] Lowlanders were reportedly persons of little or no authenticity, as evidenced by their permeability to change, and by their willingness to abandon their own social rules and to imitate those of others. Inducing "progress" in others was not in fact sufficient; what was required was a demonstration that such transformative acts were genuine, involving the sacrifice of a profound commitment to one model of social life, and its replacement by an equally profound commitment to the new one being offered.

Rosaldo is certainly correct that lowland Filipino societies were never really accorded the status of "cultures" by the Americans. It is true that there was an initial attempt, in the 1903 Philippine Census, to classify *all* Filipinos as "tribes," dividing

---

[19] Edith Moses, *Unofficial Letters of an Official's Wife* (New York: D. Appleton, 1908), p. 147.

[20] Renato Rosaldo, *Culture and Truth: The Remaking of Social Analysis* (Boston: Beacon Press, 1989), pp. 198-9.

[21] See Aldona Jonaitis, *From the Land of the Totem Poles: The Northwest Coast Indian Art Collection at the American Museum of Natural History* (New York: The Museum; Seattle: University of Washington Press, 1988).

[22] Stereotypically lowlanders are servants, uplanders are heroes, enemies, friends, primitives. See also, Vicente L. Rafael, *White Love and Other Events in Filipino History* (Durham and London: Duke University Press, 2000), pp. 52ff.

them into the "Christian" and the "non-Christian,"[23] but although there were occasional references to "Christian tribes" in later public documents, the label never gained much currency or much grip on the collective imagination.

On the other hand, and especially in the first decades of colonial rule, Americans were equally reluctant to think of the lowlands as either a "nation" or a "civilization." Lip-service was occasionally paid to the notion that some kind of "cultured" state (but not "culture" itself) had obtained in Spanish times, but these courtesies were never translated into a real recognition of the attainments of the Philippines prior to the arrival of the Americans, or to its inhabitants' claims to be citizens in Rosaldo's sense. The reasons for this were politically over-determined. Both the brutalities of the American occupation, and the anti-imperialist debate at home, raised doubts that needed to be appeased. Neither the civil nor the military arm of the Philippines administration was eager to consider seriously the claims of the defeated Philippine government that it had administered an independent nation-state equal to its conqueror, or Philippine arguments in favor of the right to self-rule. Thus when Dean C. Worcester, Secretary of the Interior from 1901-03,[24] mused in his review of the first thirteen years of American rule, "Was independence promised? . . . Did we destroy a republic?" he was emboldened to answer himself with a resounding "no," confident that most of his readership would agree.[25]

The Filipino lowland elite (*ilustrados*) who had led the revolution were generally Spanish-trained and Spanish speaking. It was therefore convenient to the occupying American regime to belittle the culture they had acquired, and this and the wish to contrast the acts of the former colonizer unfavorably with their own certainly reinforced the widespread and profound anti-Hispanicism that marks American writing of this period. Although some were more violent in the denunciations than others,[26] even liberal commentators such as James Le Roy (secretary to Taft) were not entirely free of these attitudes, which also extended to other formerly Spanish American dominions.[27]

Such political considerations, however, do not provide a complete explanation of American hostility to things Spanish. It was equally generated out of the essentially Protestant logic of American social thinking itself. It is to this religiously determined aspect of American-Filipino relations that I shall now turn.

---

[23] Rafael, *White Love*, p.25.

[24] And subsequently head of the Bureau of Non-Christian Tribes, entrepreneur, and publicist of racial-pessimist theories.

[25] Dean C. Worcester, *The Philippines Past and Present*, vol. 1 (London: Mills and Boon Limited. 1914), pp. 19-66.

[26] Kramer notes the hostile split between the remaining military forces and the incoming civilian administration in the early 1900s; two clubs were formed as a result in Manila. That patronized by the civilians under Taft encouraged association with (educated, elite) Filipinos, admitted them to their clubs, and pursued a policy of "*delicadeza*" aimed to win over the *ilustrados* to American rule. The military club refused admittance to Filipinos and deplored all association with them. See Kramer, "Pragmatic Empire," p.97.

[27] James Alfred Le Roy, *The Americans in the Philippines: A History of the Conquest and First Years of Occupation, with an Introductory Account of the Spanish Rule* (Boston, New York: Houghton Mifflin Company, 1914). On similar phenomena in other spheres of American dominion, including Puerto Rico, the Dominican Republic, and Cuba, see Julian Go, "Chains of Empire, Projects of State: Political Education and US Colonial Rule in Puerto Rico and the Philippines," *Comparative Studies in Society and History* 42,2, (2000): 333-62.

During the era in question, the status of the lowland Philippines became a kind of categorical lacuna within American discourse. The "pragmatic empire" may consciously have demanded that societies should adapt to their environments, but "adaptability" was only valued in individuals or social groups understood to be capable also of refusing to adapt. The failure to recognize the lowlands as either "culture" or "civilization" would eventually short-circuit the colonial project of transformation, since it was never clear what the lowlanders "were" before they were turned by the Americans into "something else." As we shall now see, the intense distaste the Americans felt for the lowlanders' presumed mutability was something to which they gave the provisional name of "idolatry"—although whether lowlanders were even proper idolaters was a matter for doubt.

IDOLATRIES

The colonial endeavor was nominally committed to freedom of religion. Nonetheless, it was very comfortable with the considerable Protestant missionary effort that rapidly began to be directed at the islands.[28] Indeed, both the civil authorities and the missionary churches were often inclined to speak as though the "Christianization" of the Philippines was a task to be achieved from scratch.[29] As Mrs. Campbell Dauncey put it:

> It occurs to me you may imagine we have savages here when I speak of missionaries, but that is not the case . . . for these good people are here—oh such a lot of them!—to convert the Filipinos from Roman Catholicism.[30]

As Kenton Clymer's informative study has shown, American Protestant missionaries were divided; some claimed outright that the Philippines was a "heathen country," that Roman Catholics "worship idols," and the religion "consisted 'of adoration of wooden and stone images.'"[31] Others, in Clymer's view the majority, gave Catholicism some credit for the introduction of Christian teaching,[32] while continuing to feel a grave suspicion of the religion based on the belief that it made no connection "between religion and moral behavior"[33] and the conviction that Catholic priests in the provinces were both corrupt and implacably

---

[28] Kenton J. Clymer in *Protestant Missionaries in the Philippines 1898-1916: An Inquiry into the American Colonial Mentality* (Urbana, IL: University of the Illinois Press, 1986), pp. 3-13, gives the following list, in chronological order, of arrival in the Philippines: YMCA and army chaplains, American (and British) Foreign Bible Societies, Methodists, Presbyterians, Episcopalians, Baptists, United Brethren in Christ, Disciples of Christ, and Seventh Day Adventists. Of these, the Methodists were the largest mission, claiming 45,000 members by 1916.

[29] See also the notorious "little brown brother" speech made by President William McKinley, quoted in David Steinberg, *The Philippines, A Singular and Plural Place* (Boulder, CO: Westview Press, 1982), p. 43.

[30] Campbell Dauncey, *Englishwoman in the Philippines*, pp. 107-08. She continues on that page: "This is really a work of supererogation, for . . . this religion with its mysteries and pomp, appeals to them and suits their dispositions . . . "

[31] Adventist missionary, Herbert Damon, quoted in Clymer, *Philippine Missionaries*, p. 95.

[32] Clymer, *Protestant Missionaries*, p. 96.

[33] Ibid., p. 189.

hostile to the new arrivals. In addition, even those most sympathetic to Catholicism admitted that it "verged uncomfortably close to polytheism" and that the central teaching of monotheism was "'fogged' by the 'dingy and gaudy'" images of saints whose presence was more real to Filipinos than the persons they were made to represent.'"[34] Indeed, given the multiplicity of examples he presents, Clymer seems if anything slightly to understate the missionary association between Catholics and idolatry.

Protestant missionaries largely shared the culture of the colonial civil service. They were certainly familiar with the "scientific" theories of racial progression which Kramer has outlined, and applied them to the Philippine situation, blaming the Spanish for having provided an unfavorable environment for Filipino development.[35] They also associated closely with administrators and school teachers, generally having a high opinion of the government leaders, especially those who, like David Barrows (a Congregationalist), were observant Christians.[36] Neither Kramer nor Clymer, however, points out that the opposite was also true; whether members of the Philippines administration, and other Americans in the islands, happened to be regular churchgoers or not, their thinking was deeply shaped by its participation in a distinctively Protestant culture.

Arguments about "idolatry" could indeed divide the American institution itself, as the interesting case of the Episcopalians shows.[37] Even Governor Cameron W. Forbes, an intimate friend of the head of the Episcopalian church, was shocked on attending a service conducted by this friend, "to see the mummery indulged in by Bishop Brent,"[38] while lower-ranking Americans with High-Church leanings, or school teachers who were actually Roman Catholic, were immediately suspect.

More pervasively implicit was the effect which American assumptions concerning Catholic idolatry had on the perception and understanding of lowland society. Both sympathetic and hostile accounts of even of the most public and formal aspects of Catholic ritual were surprisingly unfocused. Even the observant Maud Huntley Jenks, after the most painstaking discussions of Ifugao religious practices, grants us only the vaguest and most perfunctory account of church ceremonial as she passes through the lowlands:[39]

> Today has been a feast day here—some kind of church day . . . A rather impressive sight was the altar with its images and lighted candles . . . I feel as if I have had a peep back into the Middle Ages today. It's all as it used to be then—fiesta days, religious processions, and a religious life of form! . . . it makes

---

[34] Baptist missionary Forshee, quoted in ibid., p. 95.

[35] Ibid., pp. 65 and 87.

[36] Ibid., p. 185.

[37] Ibid., pp. 105-7, and James J. Halsema, *Bishop Brent's Baguio School: The First 75 Years* (Baguio: Brent School, 1988).

[38] Quoted in Clymer, *Protestant Missionaries*, p. 107.

[39] Accounts of lowland spirit mediumship and shamanism, moreover, were non-existent, except where these featured as part of the continuing resistance to the American occupation. School teachers and civilian visitors seem never to have noticed the rich variety of healing activity that characterizes Philippine neighborhoods in all parts of the country.

my wonderful University classes on medieval European history . . . in Madison, Wisconsin, live again as in my student days.[40]

Many other authors, unable to tell whether any of the numerous processions were solemn or celebratory in character, agreed with Jenks's reference to Medievalism. "The scene" of one Ilokano fiesta mass, according to the teacher William Freer, another sympathetic witness of lowland life, "recalled the middle ages,"[41] for the endless carrying about of the saints' images and the frequent, spasmodic ringing of bells and playing of music conveyed nothing but a senseless "confusion and discord" to the American ear.

Not everyone found this time-travel impressive. Sterner characters like Edwin A. Schell, a lecturer from a religious college in Buffalo, New York, commented that one of the few failures of American policy in the islands was the continued absence in 1913 of "the tall, white angel of the Protestant Sabbath."[42] In any case, the idea that the religious activity of the lowlands was just a kind of arbitrary mock-Medieval milling-about seems to have inclined most writers to give only the most fragmentary accounts of it.

The notion that lowland religion was, because Catholic, idolatrous, seemed at one level too obvious to require explicit statement. Authors who mentioned public worship at all, mentioned the saints that featured in all Filipino processions. "Every town in the Philippines, no matter how poor, has a number of images,"[43] some of which seemed quite striking. "The Jaro church," as one informant from Iloilo tells us,

has a wax figure of the Savior and this figure is dressed for various festivals in various ways: sometimes in evening dress, with white shirt, diamond stud, rings on the fingers, patent leather shoes and a derby hat. . . According to the Spanish calendar in my possession, there is a festival for every day of the year.[44]

Observation of the eccentric costume of the saint could lead easily into a more direct attack on the "vanity" of his worshippers, who, like the image, appeared to have an unsuitable taste for fancy headgear. "I never knew" the author continues:

" . . . that there could be so many kinds of derby as I saw on the heads of these natives. It was said that a ship-load of them was brought over once, and they so charmed the male population that from that time on they all aspired to own a derby, no matter how ancient its appearance. . . And no matter if they did not have a shirt for their back."[45]

---

[40] Jenks, *Death Stalks the Philippine Wilds*, p. 147.

[41] William Bowed Freer, *The Philippine Experiences of an American Teacher: A Narrative of Work and Travel in the Philippine Islands* (New York: C. Scribner's Sons, 1906), p. 77.

[42] Edwin A. Schell, *In Ports Afar* (New York and Cincinnati: The Abingdon Press, 1914), p. 186.

[43] Freer, *Philippine Experiences*, p. 94.

[44] Emily Bronson Conger, *An Ohio Woman in the Philippines, Giving Personal Experiences and Descriptions including Incidents of Honolulu, Ports in Japan and China* (Akron, Ohio: R.H. Leighton, 1904). p. 111.

[45] Ibid., pp. 112-3.

This picture is contrasted with the devotions of the writer, a Mrs. Emily Bronson Conger, styling herself "an Ohio woman in the Philippines." Forced to wash her own laundry if she wants anything to come out a "pure white," she bends over the tub with a revolver within easy reach in case any of the natives should turn treacherous, and sings while tears roll down her face:

> Am I a soldier of the Cross?
> A follower of the Lamb?
> And shall I fear to own His cause
> Or blush to speak His name?[46]

Such trials no doubt led to Mrs. Conger's reflection on the beatings rumored to be administered to Filipinos by Spanish friars; "It may be that these people *need* to be terrorized by the priests."[47]

Mrs. Conger's unfriendly tone is admittedly at one extreme in American writing. She came to Panay in 1898 to keep house for her son, Scout, the head of a battalion of American troops engaged to massacre as many of the surrounding Filipino "insurrectionaries" as possible. Yet she is not alone in linking a contempt for the forms of Filipino religion to a fear of Filipino insurrection. The notion that all saint-worship was at least "confusion," if not downright deception and self-deception, served commentators well in finding ways to suggest that Filipino revolutionary patriotism was a form of fraud.

Freer recounts how at Pagsanjan in 1902:

> . . . the *insurrectos* had been going from hamlet to hamlet, surreptitiously exhibiting religious images for the purpose of raising money to carry on the insurrection. . . A life-size wooden statue with a dark face, attired in rich ecclesiastical robes, was placed in the corner of a room not too well lighted, and the people were invited to visit what was described as a miraculous image of the Savior . . . [a man seated in the next room made oracular statements in Tagalog] . . . and people were enjoined to work for the Americans, but give the money thus earned to the cause.[48]

What Freer called the "credulity" of the "medieval" natives, which would lead them to believe either in false gods or in false governments, is here neatly joined to the idea that their leaders are manipulative. Idolatrous religions produce idolatrous politics full of leaders who set themselves up as false gods; and religion that permits of "confusion" between the real and the false in this way is also a religion of concealment which hides a treacherous heart.

It was this logic which determined that the Filipino forces holding out against the Americans should always be referred to as "bandits" or, in two terms taken over from the Spanish insults for the politically resistant, as "insurrectionaries" (*insurrectos*) or *ladrones*. The army of President Aguinaldo was thus reduced at a stroke to the status of robber outlaws. In fact, it could be argued that it was *only* when lowland religion could be tied to a resurgent political threat that it actually

---

[46] Ibid., p. 159.

[47] Ibid., p. 113. My emphasis.

[48] Freer, *Philippine Experiences*, pp. 10-11.

came into sharp focus at all for the Americans. Lowland healers using indigenous methods, for example, who were both extremely numerous and making use of a rich and subtle indigenous repertoire of religious and medical practice, merited almost no mention whatsoever in these annals. "Filipino swindler poses as the true savior," sneered one headline of the Manila Times of 1904.[49] Perhaps behind the disgust there was also a certain element of relief. At moments like this, one could feel that one had temporarily solved the problem of the "confusion" which looking at lowland society brought about. There was "something to these Filipinos" after all, and even if that "something" turned out to be treachery, one had looked it in the face, and—by dismissing it as deceitful idolatry—one could tell oneself one had stared it down.

For much of the time, however, the nature of the lowland Philippines and its religion remained opaque to American observers. Writers on lowland life could not help responding with both fascination and some horror to the Filipino treatment of the dead. In particular what caught their attention were the funerals of young children of families wealthy enough to bury them with some ceremony. "My feelings were shocked," says Freer, "upon observing that at some funerals the liveliest airs were played: upon one occasion, a funeral procession wended its way to the cemetery to the music of a popular song of which the burden is 'There'll be a hot time in the old town tonight.'"[50]

The "Ohio woman" describes, "a catafalque . . . [containing a child's body dressed in finery] covered with blue satin and trimmed with riffles of satin and lace . . . and long blue satin ribbons whose ends were held by several little girls decked out as brides"[51] as a typical assemblage.

Neither of these observers realized that the funerals of small children in the Philippines are supposed to be conducted with apparent happiness, whatever the feelings of the bereaved, since their souls are considered too young to have sinned.[52] What they were concerned with, I would argue, although they did not articulate it in this way, was a similarity they perceived between the treatment of the corpses decked out and carried through the streets, and the treatment of the saints who were carried in procession. The Americans continued to find something unaccountable about the lowland Filipinos. Not only did they worship idols, but they themselves often appeared to the American imagination as something less than fully alive and human.

With their apparent "parroting" and mimicry, and their "confusion" about real meaning, lowlanders figured either as mechanical automata—a kind of doll, as a saint may be thought of as a kind of doll—or even as uncannily animated corpses. While we might consider these images an effect of American repression of the

---

[49] *Manila Times*, April 29, 1904, p.1.

[50] Freer, *Philippine Experiences*, p. 94.

[51] Conger, *Ohio Woman*, p. 145.

[52] My experience in Bicol was that dead children were certainly said to be "little angels" (*angellitos*), and modifications were made in funerals. For instance, blue coffins were used; the funerary band was asked to play cheerful music, etc. However, this was regarded by most people as a duty imposed by the church and had no impact on the profound grief people felt and expressed over infant deaths (see Cannell, *Spirit Mediums*, pp. 227ff, and Cannell, *Power and intimacy*, p. 191). Such "angel funerals" seem to be found in many parts of the Iberian Catholic world. See Nancy Schepper-Hughes, *Death without Weeping: The Violence of Everyday Life in Brazil* (Berkeley, Los Angeles, and Oxford: University of California Press, 1992), pp. 271, 383, 416-23, 429-30, for a contrasting case.

recognition of the independent life of the lowlands, the Americans did not see it that way. In their view, the preceding Spanish regime had reduced its Filipino subjects to this zombie-like state, and it was now up to the Americans to put the life back into them.

"WHAT THERE IS IN THE NATIVE"

American government documents often discussed Philippine bodies in striking terms. The image of physical degeneracy, stuntedness, or deficiency, like the image of the body as living corpse, was often used to discredit lowland Filipinos. Take, for example, this characterization of the Revolutionary leader Aguinaldo, by the American journalist Halstead in 1898:

> The door from the study opened and a very slender and short young man entered with a preoccupied look that quickly became curious. An attendant said in a low voice, "General Aguinaldo." He was unexpectedly small—could weigh but little over 100 pounds—dressed in pure white, and his modesty of bearing would have become a maiden. The first feeling was a sort of faint compassion that one with such small physical resources should have to bear the weighty responsibilities resting upon him. . . " [53]

If we set aside the implications of effeminacy in this extract, it is fairly typical in its assumption that the relative "backwardness" of the Filipino lowlanders, their inferiority to Americans, would be evident in their bodies. It can thus be classed with, for example, the much-discussed sanitary campaigns against cholera in Manila as an effect of the popular racial theories of the day which we have already encountered.[54] Not only cholera, however, but plague, leprosy, and smallpox were to the forefront of the American mind, and victims of these diseases were regarded as essential sights which the official government visitor should take in.[55]

One might also view in this light the obsessive interest in the physical development of Filipino pupils that characterizes the literature of the Bureau of Education between 1900 and at least 1930. Against images of puny leaders and epidemic-ridden peasantries were to be placed the pictures of what American policy could accomplish through instruction in better nutrition, and through training the Filipino in sports, athletics, and (a little later in the century) the correct kind of playground games to develop the body. A typical headline of an entry in the annual

---

[53] Murat Halstead, *The Story of the Philippines. Natural Riches, Industrial Resources . . . Events of the War in the West with Spain, and the Conquest of Cuba and Puerto Rico* (Chicago: Our Possessions Publishing Co., 1898) p. 54.

[54] Reynaldo Ileto, "Cholera and the Origins of the American Sanitary Regime," in Rafael, ed., *Discrepant Histories*, pp. 51-82; and Warwick Anderson, "'Where every prospect pleases and only man is vile': Laboratory Medicine as Colonial Discourse," in Rafael, ed., *Discrepant Histories*, pp. 83-112.

[55] Many writers even made the highly dubious claim that lowland Filipinos were so accustomed to smallpox that they were somehow indifferent to its symptoms and to the high child mortality it caused, e.g. Conger, *Ohio Woman*, p. 145.

report of the Director of Education for 1913 ran: "What basketball is doing for the girls in Zambales."[56]

Baseball teams had been a theme from the moment of colonization. From 1911 onwards, photographs of athletics competition winners in sports kit also adorned official reports. The government announced its intention to change the bodies of Filipino children through the enormous efforts made to encourage people to eat corn rather than rice. Thousands of schoolchildren were invited to take part in Corn Festivals all over the country, with their parents. In Dumaguete in 1912:

> There were six different dishes of corn prepared and sold, and probably four thousand ate of one or more of these prepared dishes. What a side show the corn-germinating box was, and how the thousands looked at the selected seed-ears! . . . A swarm of boys, some of them dressed as fat, husky clowns, wore placards "I eat corn," others, dressed as lean clowns, wore other placards, "I eat rice" . . . Rice is the Oriental food . . . But corn and corn pone, and corn cakes, like science and the English language, and the Christian faith belong to the Occidental civilization. It is suggestive of fat swine, thick beefsteaks, butter and cheese, and the introduction of corn to the Philippine Islands is naturalization, revolution and revelation.[57]

Actually, of course, corn is generally regarded as a poverty food and as far less sustaining than rice. Most Filipinos find fresh dairy produce indigestible. The passage is more indicative of passionate attachment to a threatened mode of American agricultural life, than of solutions to Filipino rural development.[58] Obviously, one could present this material in terms of familiar (over-familiar) tropes of colonial discourses of embodiment. What interests me about it, however, is something slightly different; that is, that one finds equally strongly implied here a relationship between the body and the *soul*. Take, for example, the comment of a local Protestant missionary on the value of including universal manual labor in Philippine industrial education; these "manly" exertions, he believed, were designed: " . . . to help men possessed of bodies, to create those outward conditions which will best enable them to use their bodies as instruments of the enlarged mind and soul which are the earliest gift of Christian conversion."[59]

The body, in other words, was one special part of the outward material world, and with it, formed the arena of action for the Christian soul. In popular thought, the body could also be read as an outward sign of the state of the interior man, as in this missionary account of a clerical meeting:

---

[56] Quoted in Pecson and Racelis, eds., *American Teachers*, p. 191.

[57] Schell, *Ports Afar*, p. 177.

[58] John Thorn with Matt Lewis Thorn, *Serious Pig: An American Book in Search of his Roots* (New York: North Point Press, 2000). It is interesting to note that although highland populations were obviously also vulnerable to infectious diseases (and government reports documented their ailments), contemporary writing tended to stress a counter-stereotype of the highland body as muscular, fit, and admirably masculine. Only lowlanders were portrayed as physically enfeebled.

[59] Clymer, *Protestant Missionaries*, p. 84. No reference is given for the speaker, but it may be David Husband.

They typified the whole wide-world difference between American Protestantism and Spanish Romanism . . . the missionary with his high forehead, frank blue eyes, clear-cut features, whose every line and expression betokened temperate living and high thinking, and the Bishop—well, there was a noticeable difference."[60]

Thus, the teaching of sport was not merely an effort towards physical improvement of a so-called backward race, but also an attempt to awaken the soul to action:

The boy who has even for a season or two experienced the stirring discipline of public censure and public applause in hard athletic battles, has learned lessons which will remain with him longer than any maxim learned from books . . . [the force of athletics is] actively revolutionary, and with it come new standards, new ideals of conduct, and what is more important, new ideals of character . . . "[61]

Sport would, it was believed, develop "discipline" in persons previously lacking in it, but it would also develop that internal force of personality that was thought to have "atrophied" to such an abysmal extent under the Spaniards, or even not to be present at all; baseball was, in a sense, the American cure not just for smallpox, but for idolatry.

One sees a similar logic at work in the American obsession with retraining Filipino voices. American dismay at Spanish teaching methods is a set-piece of schoolteachers' writing. A Babel of sound is always described as characterizing the Spanish-style classroom, punctuated by the thwack of the master's stick disciplining some unfortunate child for a minor error in recitation. Pupils were set only rote-learning tasks, mostly derived from religious literature, and each pupil repeated his lessons out loud in the classroom without any regard to what his neighbors were trying to learn.[62]

The new teachers thus saw a double task for themselves. Firstly, they had to replace this "confusion" of noise with, in particular, the well modulated and tuneful group singing of "My Old Kentucky Home" or "America the Beautiful."[63] Secondly, the teacher had to extirpate—sometimes with great difficulty—the habits of reading aloud, rote learning, and anxious repetitive mimicry in his or her pupils, and substitute for them the habits of reading individually and silently, "with understanding," and speaking with comprehension, expression, and meaning.

The suppression of what was usually called "the rhetorical voice" in Filipino children speaking English, and its replacement by a voice which signaled just that cultivated interiority, that link between inward reflection and outward action, which the Americans were so anxious to create in their colonial subjects, was a theme that persisted in annual education reports well into the Commonwealth period. Indeed, I would argue that it was an instance of the drive to establish what Webb Keane has

---

[60] Brown, "Report of a Visitation," quoted in Clymer, *Protestant Missionaries,* p. 73.

[61] Bureau of Education, *1921* (Manila: Bureau of Printing, 1921), p. 31.

[62] Freer, *Philippine Experiences,* pp. 112 ff.; Pecson and Racelis, *American Teachers,* p. 91.

[63] There is more to be said about the recasting of Filipino singing techniques, but no space to tell that story here.

referred to as "sincerity" in Filipinos.[64] As Rafael and others have pointed out, the relationship between words and thoughts is one which is central to all Christian theology,[65] since all Christian thinking is in some ways logocentric. Words on the page, text, are not meant to have an existence prior to words that issue from and reflect the mind and soul of the speaker. In its beginnings, the world is a thought spoken by God himself. The Catholic church has wrestled from its origins with the problem of establishing the relationship between actions and interior states, and between declarations of belief and true states of belief.[66] However, in many forms of Protestantism this issue becomes focused on the individual in a particular way, perhaps because the Christian person is now outside the regulatory structure of Catholic confession. Bauman and others have shown us how, in the case of the Quakers, for instance, religious practice becomes centered on interrogating the self about the origins of what one is prompted to say, and rejecting those impulses which do not come from the Spirit; hence the Quaker injunction, "Let your words be few."[67]

Behind the problem of establishing sincerity, according to Protestant thought, lies yet another problem. In order to be an origin of sincere speech, the self (or soul) must hold itself in some ways discrete. A person cannot be sincere if the boundary between that self and another self is constantly blurred, for in that case, who is it that we hear speaking? Even (and especially) a Christian's openness to being overshadowed by the Holy Spirit carries with it the obligation to resist other forms of blurring of the self. Many of these, within both Catholic and Protestant thinking, have been called possession.

In the Philippines, imitation does not have the sense of mere derivativeness and passivity generally given to it in the West; instead, it encompasses a series of ways of relating to power, through which the weaker party can share in the experiences and identity of the stronger. Imitation can often be a religious act as well as a political one, and devotional practices that center on identifying oneself with Christ or other holy figures are common.[68] Saints are a central focus for this kind of religious imitation.

For the American observer, however, Filipino "imitativeness" meant something very different. On the one hand, adaptability to the new regime, and the willingness to learn, was to be encouraged and should have been understood as a sign of the possibility of racial "progress." On the other hand, this "quickness" suggested a readiness to capitulate and to surrender the boundaries of the self, which produced a profound unease in the mind accustomed to Protestant ideas of personal authenticity.

---

[64] Webb Keane, "Sincerity, Modernity and the Protestants," unpublished manuscript dated 2001.

[65] Vicente L. Rafael, *Contracting Colonialism: Translation and Christian Conversion in Tagalog Society under Early Spanish Rule* (Ithaca, NY: Cornell University Press, 1988. Esp. preface and chapters 2 and 3.

[66] This is, indeed, the issue which the early Inquisition was established to address. See e.g. Pierre Schmidt *The Holy Greyhound: Guinefort, Healer of Children since the Thirteenth Century* (Cambridge: Cambridge University Press, 1983); and Emmanuel Le Roy Ladurie, *Montaillou: Cathars and Catholics in a French Village, 1294-1324* (London: Scholars Press, 1978).

[67] Richard Bauman, *Let Your Words Be Few: The Symbolism of Speaking and Silence among Seventeenth-Century Quaker.* (Cambridge: Cambridge University Press, 1983).

[68] Cannell, *Power and Intimacy*, pp. 180-81.

Ironically, the American educational program itself relied on precisely these disturbing imitative abilities. The colonial authorities had a large number of schools to staff, and very few native American teachers. As much as possible, they needed to retain the existing Filipino teachers from the Spanish regime. But since the new regime despised Spanish teaching methods, the Filipino teachers needed to be re-trained. Above all, they needed to cease teaching in Spanish, and to become competent purveyors of the new English-language syllabus.

Chronically short of funds, the Bureau of Education decided to allow for this transformation the period of one month. American inspectors attended schools to train and supervise the transition, and it is difficult to say who was made more anxious by the process; but it was probably the Filipino teachers, who were in danger of losing their jobs if they failed to make the grade. One American inspector, commenting on the "astonishingly good" results obtained in just a few weeks, stubs his toe, as it were, on a realization of the contradictions involved:

> This [success] results from their [lowland Filipinos'] ability to imitate closely the methods which they have seen used by their instructors. Where the young and inexperienced American would partially fail by reason of his independence and originality, the little-schooled Filipino succeeds by virtue of his faithful imitation of the ways of others, so that his ability in this respect works to the advantage of the Philippine primary schools . . . "[69]

In other words, whether the lowland Filipinos did what their new colonial government asked them to or not, they could never entirely satisfy this new master. The logic of American Protestant thought and its lack of comprehension of local meanings endlessly revived the idea that Filipinos were lacking in sincerity, in authenticity, in the kind of interiority which it compulsively sought. However much the colonial institutions produced changes in Filipino life which could be read as evidence of lowland racial progress, doubts still remained. The highland "savages" could be fitted neatly into the colonial game of "before" and "after, but the lowlanders presented the Americans with endless difficulties. The label "idolatry" was an attempt to identify what the Americans felt was wrong with the lowlanders, but even this label was not self-explanatory, and contained layers of meaning, at the core of which was the notion of a person lacking Protestant authenticity.

Important though the dominance of racial ethnology is in explaining the early American period, therefore, it does not capture everything about it. The educational experiment actually worked according to a logic approximating that of Christian conversion. The idea of transformation through "progress" could not function without a conviction of interior transformation; colonials were in very much the same kind of position of constant uncertainty as missionaries faced with the problem of deciding whether the newly baptized have truly been converted in their hearts.[70]

Moreover, the language of idolatry goes beyond a mere game of defamatory similes—fraudulent gods equal fraudulent Filipinos. One can in fact say that there was an implicit *economy* of idolatry at work here. If an idol is wood or stone to which

[69] Freer, *Philippine Experiences,* p. 112.

[70] Rafael, *Contracting Colonialism*; John N. Schumacher, S. J., *Readings in Philippine Church History* (Quezon City: Ateneo de Manila University Press, 1987), pp. 73-4.

is attributed inappropriately, almost obscenely, the qualities of the animate, then the correlate appears to be that the human beings who worship it become thereby *less* than fully alive. They come to be seen as dolls, or automata, or even (as in the quotation which heads this article) to be described as their own carefully preserved and displayed corpses.[71] And as we shall see, this economy of idolatry also placed lowland objects within particular kinds of relations.

THE IDOL VANISHES

Given this almost obsessive preoccupation with lowland "idolatry," one might have expected Americans to pay close attention to the actual saints' images which were the focus of their disapproval. In fact, as with the accounts of lowland religious practice in general, one gains only the vaguest impression of these images, and in many contexts they were ignored altogether.

This is the more striking when one considers the actual significance of saint's images in lowland life, about which I have written at length elsewhere.[72] Filipino saints are vivid presences, who also occupy in some parts of the islands an intimate and important place in family life, as they do in Bicol. Sharing in the devotion of a saint is one way in which kinship links can be either maintained or evaded over time. In these and other ways, saints seem one of the only categories of objects in Bicol which could be considered close to what Annette Weiner called "inalienable possessions."[73] In other ways, as I have hinted above, Bicol culture does not primarily constitute itself through ideas of unchangingness or through the transmission over time of objects of "cosmological" significance, and in some ways therefore poses problems for Weiner's kind of thesis.

Now, objects that captured the key religious and kinship values of a social group were precisely the one crucial category of things which Philippine ethnologists were eagerly seeking in upland "cultures." So eager were anthropologists to acquire religious artifacts, in fact, that at times they even resorted to stealing them.[74] Yet objects which had a parallel significance in lowland societies were systematically disregarded.

American colonial writing includes almost no descriptions of lowland arts and artifacts; one can find (as I mentioned earlier) a range of derogatory references to lowland theater and performance, but little or nothing on clothing, jewelry, books, or religious objects, although many distinctive, high-quality items were being produced at this time for the Filipino elite. Philippine houses are occasionally mentioned, but generally in the context of remarks about the difficulties of running a colonial household.[75] Nothing is said about the structure, arrangement, internal logic, and decoration of Filipino houses, or the significance of their various rooms. The richness

---

[71] It is usual for Filipinos to display the deceased in open coffins for some nights at the wake prior to the funeral. Because of the difficulties of preserving bodies in tropical conditions, commercial embalming is now standard even for the poor. In the past, and still today for the very poor, deodorant herbs may be used: in this case, the wake is necessarily shorter.

[72] Cannell, *Power and Intimacy*; Cannell, "The Imitation of Christ."

[73] Annette B. Weiner, *Inalienable Possessions: The Paradox of Keeping-while-giving* (Berkeley, Los Angeles, Oxford: University of California Press, 1992).

[74] Jenks, *Death Stalks the Philippine Wilds.*

[75] See Rafael, *White Love,* for discussions of colonial domestic discourse.

of associations which a wealthy Filipino mansion of this period might have had for its elite inhabitants[76] or the complex ways in which various parts of even the humblest village home were associated with cooking, childbirth, death, and the entry and exit of spirits during mediumship rituals passed entirely unnoticed.

The attitude with which the selection of lowland objects for the various World's Fairs and Expositions of the period was approached is also instructive. The hastily assembled collection for the Pan-American Exposition of 1900 leant heavily on war trophies from the still-continuing hostilities.[77] The 1904 St. Louis Exposition, whose intellectually ambitious but ill-fated exhibits were assembled by the ethnologist Albert Jenks, included a greater variety of lowland objects, in part because of the display of a Luzon and a Visayan "village," as well as the real attention-getters, the "Igorrotte" villages. Little is mentioned about the lowland villages, except that they consisted of *nipa* buildings within a palisade, and obviously the press was not much interested in their contents and details.[78] Small household altars are found in every Catholic lowland home and should have featured in the Visayan houses, but if lowland saints did find their way to St. Louis, no one appears to have spared them a glance or a mention.

The other great Exposition of the period, the 1915 Panama-Pacific Exposition, was organized not by anthropologists such as Jenks, but by the then Director of Education, Frank L. Crone, who was driven by the determination to show that his new industrial education policy produced objects that could be sold on an international market. The main exhibition building devoted to the Philippines was therefore intended as a public salesroom for vast quantities of hats, lace, embroidery, mats, textiles, hardwood furniture and "artistic things like . . . lampshades," made of Capiz shell.[79] Although some of these objects were made by adults, the heart of the Philippine School's exhibit was in effect a range of goods produced by compulsory child labor for the profit of the colonial government.[80] The exhibition space itself was

---

[76] Fernando Nakpil Zialcita and Martin I.Timio Jr., *Philippine Ancestral House s(1810-1930)* (Quezon City: GCF Books, 1980).

[77] It also featured agricultural tools and an array of skulls meant to demonstrate Filipino physical types. Kramer, *Pragmatic Empire*, p. 80

[78] The list of objects offered for sale to American museums at the end of the Exposition included "pictures and statuary, articles of gold, silver, ivory, shell, brass, bronze and bone, silks, pineapple and hemp fiber cloth, mantillas, lace and embroidery, beadwork and fine sample of wood carving from Bilabid prison." *St. Louis Post-Dispatch*, November 2, 1904, p. 5, quoted in Kramer, *Pragmatic Empire*, p. 138. Of this list, the mantillas, pineapple, and hemp cloth were almost certainly from the lowlands, and probably also some of the shell and gold objects. "Pictures and statuary" is more difficult to interpret. These could be highland artifacts of the kind which were eagerly identified as religious exotica and which were sought after by museums as totems of culture. It might mean secular elite art. Or it might imply that one or two of the religious images which are placed on household altars by every Catholic lowland family had found their way into the furnishings of the Visayan exhibit "village"; at any event, if so they went undiscussed and unappreciated.

[79] Frank Morton Todd, *The Story of the Exposition, being the official history of the international celebration held at San Francisco in 1915 to commemorate the discovery of the Pacific Ocean and the construction of the Panama Canal*, vol. 4 (New York and London: G. P. Putnam's sons, 1921), p. 378.

[80] Besides the schools products, there were brass boxes from Mindanao and a range of objects which one might think of as the beginning of the mass production of highland tribal souvenirs; "crooked knives, bolos, savage-looking head axes, spears and shields," (Todd, *Story*

also for sale; made of narra hardwood planks and shell panels, the Philippines Building was designed to demonstrate the properties of native building materials to potential constructors and investors.

Philippine objects did feature in some of the other buildings of the Exposition. The Palace of Education contained a celebration of the American schools policy and a range of schools-produced goods which was largely a recapitulation of the Philippines Building Exhibit.[81] There was a large array of Philippine agricultural products in the Foreign Farming exhibit,[82] and the famous Fine Arts Gallery included, among its 11,403 exhibits, thirty-six items from the Philippine islands, which we learn were "paintings and drawings, distinguished for the proofs they gave of the recent assimilation of European art."[83]

Nowhere, however, were there any objects which would have been recognized by Philippine lowlanders as items of beauty and value which Filipinos produced for themselves. And there were certainly no exhibits including lowland religious art of any kind, and apparently no examples of Philippine saints' images.[84]

The Philippines at the Exposition was, therefore, restrictively represented as and by its commodities, and no indicator of alternative economies of value was allowed ingress. Judged by obvious criteria, the display was a success. Yet the literature that accompanied the exhibition, and other documents from this period produced by the Bureau of Education, argued an ineradicable anxiety about these objects.

For Frank L. Crone, as for the vast majority of American colonial commentators, there was little point in viewing lowland goods as potential trophies or collectibles. While highland deities and weapons might be bought by those who wished to own a piece of highland "culture," lowland objects could not appeal in this way because, as we have seen, the lowlands were not really considered to have a culture at all. An alternative approach to lowland products was therefore required.

Crone was astute enough to have realized that profit from Philippine industrial education would not be maximized by aiming at totally mechanized mass production. Instead, he aimed to catch the mood of a buying public that already preferred the "hand-made" to the machine-made, at least in items of personal apparel.[85] He therefore intended to present Philippine goods as *artisanal*, as representing time-consuming hand labor and craft authenticity, both of which could be sold for a premium. At the same time, the goods were in fact to be marketed in bulk. Crone therefore ferociously discouraged existing individual or local variations

---

of the Exposition, vol. 4, p. 378), all of which items Crone planned to have mass produced. Kramer, *Pragmatic Empire,* esp. 230 ff.)

[81] Todd, *Story of the Exposition,* vol. 4, p. 39 . Explanations of American successes in improving sanitation and reducing infant mortality were included in the exhibit on public hygiene. Todd, *Story of the Exposition,* vol. 4, pp. 59-60.

[82] Ibid., p. 283. Samples of Philippine maps and printing presses were featured in the exhibit on Liberal Arts in Other Lands. Ibid., pp. 111-14)

[83] Ibid., p. 30.

[84] Philippine work was as conspicuous for the exhibits in which it did *not* appear as for those in which it did. Clearly, vernacular folk arts were not totally unappreciated by the Exposition audience; the exhibit on Wares of Foreign Lands included embroidered Balkan peasant costumes, and elaborately carved Indian furniture. Ibid., pp. 145-49. The Arts and Crafts Exhibit was an enormous display of applied arts such as jewelry, many of them submitted by the craftspeople themselves, but it was almost exclusively of American work. Ibid., p. 149).

[85] Kramer, *Pragmatic Empire,* pp. 203 ff.

in the product. What he wanted was not hats which people in lowlands crafts villages might actually make and wear, but hats with a Philippine flavor for American citizens.

This is a common situation in international commoditization. Crone however was caught in a dilemma. Looking at lowland products, he could in truth see nothing that he could identify—and sell—as that Philippine flavor, because to him all marks of local variation and intentionality in manufacture were simply meaningless twitches. He wanted to commodify lowland "culture," yet he and most of his compatriots did not really believe that lowland culture existed.[86]

Department of Education literature at this period is therefore marked by a tone of suppressed anxiety and irritation. Noting the "thousand articles made by the pupils in their prescribed school work,"[87] the pamphlet accompanying the Philippine exhibition on education comments, "There has been in the past no design or color or form of manufacture that has been to the country unique."[88] Thus Philippine products have easily been mistaken for goods from elsewhere; they have not had a distinctive profile; their hold on the world market has been a tenuous one. "Evidently," this source continues, "something must be done to bring the Philippines into its own: there must be introduced into the commercial market something distinctively Philippine in makeup and design."[89]

There must be an urgent "search for suitable motifs" by the branches of the government, who will forthwith distribute them for copying to Filipino schoolchildren. *"There must be found something Philippine"*[90]—but Filipino school children, trained in conformity to American education, are to be provided with this salable authenticity by the American colonial government

We have come full circle to the bored white ladies' infuriated cry: "There is nothing about these Filipinos, you see." Even the commodities of the educational miracle seem always to be withholding that essential element of authenticity, of difference. The lowland idol had been made to vanish from the image of the Philippine lowlands that America exported internationally, because from the American point of view it did not signify a "culture," and in that sense, it was not even a "real" idol at all. The notion of lowland "idolatry" in the sense of the collapse of distinctiveness, however, persisted even into the realm of commoditization.

---

[86] Or, in the alternative language available, lowland "civilization." See for example, Todd, *Story of the Exposition,* vol. 4, p. 376. "There was a civilization in the islands long before the Spanish War, and the human material was there with which to work; quick , adaptable, responsive.' This comment accompanied the token exhibition of Filipiniana (antique books) in the Philippine Building. Todd also compares the Building to a 'Philippine mansion' although in fact it is a hybridized affair more reminiscent of public school architecture. But the idea of civilization, like the idea of primitive culture, implies the idea of continuity and tradition, which the lowlands were thought to lack. The flip side of the Morgan thesis on social adaptation—to be too adaptable is not a good thing. To be adaptable is very American; but so is to be aware of your 'roots', and to hold onto to your 'identity'.

[87] Manila, Bureau of Printing (No author), *The Philippine Islands, Their Industrial and Commercial Possibilities, the Country and the People,* 16 vols., vol. 1, *The Philippine Public Schools at the Panama-Pacific Industrial Exposition; The Exhibit in the Palace of Education; Organization and Administration of the Philippine Public Schools; Facts and Figures on the Islands and their Schools* (Manila: Bureau of Printing, c. 1915).

[88] Ibid., p. 100.

[89] Ibid., p. 11

[90] My emphasis.

Perhaps for this reason, one finds photographic images of these failed lowland commodities endlessly repeated in government publications of this period; pages and pages of headless hats, necklace lace collars, handless handkerchiefs, disembodied frocks and other articles, accompanied by fervently enumerative prose—"In the 1914 Exhibition, the Bureau exhibited over 51,000 articles valued at nearly P99,000 housed in its own building erected by students of the Philippine school of arts and trades."[91]—breathes one annual report of education. One is left with the impression that these unsatisfactory articles had come to stand in the mind of the colonial bureaucrats for the limbs and identities of the unsatisfactory persons who produced them, and for the failure of either to demonstrate the required transformation from "culture" to modernity.

THE IDOL IN THE FETISH

Let me turn, at this point, to the link between lowland "idolatry" and the idea of the fetish, or more specifically, to William Pietz's influential essays on the fetish. The fetish has been given multiple contradictory meanings, but Pietz refuses to be bogged down, instead electing a radically historical approach which defines the truth of the term as the sum of its uses over time.[92] Stressing that the idea of the fetish spawned social actions and not merely phantasms, Pietz is nonetheless fastidious in drawing our attention to its historical development *as* an idea.

For Pietz, however, the "fetish" has a crucial period of development, when it becomes dominant and is used in unprecedented ways. This is the period of the encounter between West African societies and European mercantile capitalists—originally, the Portuguese, from whose language the word itself is most immediately derived.[93] In the eyes of Portuguese traders, and later Dutch, British, French, and other European colonialists, the "fetish" becomes a synoptic label for African cultures viewed as a bizarre and ultimately sinister inversion of European (i.e. capitalist) notions of value. While for "economic man" all action is governed by rational self-interest within the systematic application of the rules of monetary exchange, Africans were seen as swayed by utterly arbitrary and impulsive attributions of value to objects which simply happened across their path—a stick, a stone, or some other small thing which could be carried on the body as a form of amulet. Moreover, these "fetish" objects, imaginatively imbued with power, were not imbued with the power of anything which Europeans could recognize as a god or spirit; rather they were "irreducibly material"[94]—matter to which a power was assigned as such. So threatening an inversion did this seem that eventually Europeans came to elide the practices they named "fetishism" with war against whites and human sacrifice.[95]

The kernel of Pietz's idea appears to be this: the "fetish" is a field of phenomena and social actions, produced by radical misrecognition of incompatible ideas of value between two widely different cultures. It therefore occurs at the "border" or boundary between these cultures, specifically in the exploitative conditions of proto-

---

[91] Bureau of Education, *Annual Report, . . . 1914.* p. 87.

[92] Pietz, "The problem of the fetish, II," p. 23.

[93] Ibid., p. 31.

[94] Pietz, "The problem of the fetish, I," p. 7.

[95] Pietz, "The spirit of civilization."

colonial and colonial trade. As Pietz says, the fetish has never existed as a reality within a single culture, but is an intercultural artifact.[96]

The decisiveness with which Pietz has made the distinction between the evolution of the fetish understood in this way, and related ideas frequently confused with it, including the idea of the idol, has been extremely fruitful. Yet in pursuit of this clarity, Pietz sometimes appears to overstate his own case. He provides, for example, early in the argument, a very interesting account of the category of "idolatry" in Augustine. For Pietz, this serves to stress the distinction between idol and fetish by establishing the importance of the idea of the worship of (images of) false gods as the basis of idolatry. Yet he is too interested in the detail of the account not to tell us that there is also in Augustine, as in all later writers, a secondary meaning of idolatry: that is, a meaning of the erroneous worship of the image *as material thing* and not just as the proxy of a non-existent deity. In fact, these two meanings are ambiguously elided in Augustine and remain so throughout much of the patristic writing on the topic,[97] and they produce, as Pietz notes, an associated tradition of a disdain for the material in both theological and popular usage.[98]

Similarly, Pietz provides a very interesting account of the elusive category of the *fetissio* in Portuguese medieval Catholicism as the "made thing" to which sorcery and other superstitious practices are attached. He notes that the treatment of these objects in the legal literature is ambiguous,[99] but seems progressively to become generalized from artifacts to the whole practice of witchcraft. But it seems likely that the ambiguity he tries to resolve is actually inherent in the category itself, and corresponds to Augustine's failure to designate precisely the difference between the worship of the wrong god and the "superstitious" attribution of powers to the material form itself. In other words, it could be argued, the popular mind, unlike the minds of elite theologians, did not distinguish very forcefully between the "matter" and "spirit" in the idol.[100]

While Pietz insists that the essence of the idol is that it is an image, while the essence of the fetish is its irreducible materiality, "superstitious" practices of course involve all sorts of other, less obviously image-like objects, such as prayers, amulets, charms, pieces of bead and ribbon, etc. One might therefore be forgiven at least a little jolt of surprise when Pietz asserts roundly at the close of this very interesting account that the transposition of the idea of the *fetissio* to the West African context had "almost nothing to do with" medieval Catholic meanings and practices,[101] and that the idea of the "fetish" has displaced that of the "idol".

Pietz himself comments on the fact that contemporary commentators who are the key formulators of the term "fetish" themselves often used it almost interchangeably with the term "idol."[102] This is supposedly accounted for by the fact

---

[96] Pietz, "The problem of the fetish, I," p. 11.

[97] Pietz, "The problem of the fetish, II," p. 27ff.

[98] This of course all derives even more fundamentally from the claim in most mainstream Christianities (but not in all Christianities) that matter and spirit are absolutely separate, and that God is a God of spirit and not matter, who also transcends matter. On this, see also Cannell "Introduction."

[99] Pietz, "The problem of the fetish, II" p. 33

[100] Ibid., p. 36.

[101] Ibid., pp. 35-6.

[102] Ibid., p. 37.

that these writers were reaching for a familiar language to describe the unfamiliar, which may well be so; yet the fact that they did so seems worthy of a little more notice. More particularly since, at least according to Pietz's sources, objects worn as "fetishes" were explicitly compared to "gods" by some of their African users.[103]

My reading of Pietz's own evidence, then, suggests that he may have insisted too much on the almost total lack of continuity between the language of the idol and the language of the fetish in his African colonial material. This leads one inevitably to wonder why. In answer I can only propose that, for all his careful and subtle attention to the changing nuances of Christian definitions, Pietz's own argument is finally (as indeed, he says himself) a "materialist" one, and so privileges the development of capitalism over other engines of historical change. Given the key moment in colonial mercantile capitalism with which he is concerned in his analysis of Brosnan's book on Guinea, he has perhaps tilted the balance of his analysis slightly too far in favor of emphasizing a break with the past corresponding to the magnitude of these global developments.

Pietz's argument may indeed hold for many parts of the world, and may well provoke fruitful directions for the further understanding of what is, in fact, novel about the idea of the fetish at this period. But the problem with a discussion as successful as Pietz's is that it may produce a tendency to think of all intercultural colonial encounters in terms of the category of the fetish as he defines it, and/or to concentrate scholarship on instances which might feasibly replicate some of the conditions of the encounter Pietz describes.

However, if we take our cue instead from Pietz's insistence on *historical specificity*, it is in fact impossible to discount the idea of the idol when discussing the Philippines. For it is in this language, rather than in the language of the fetish, that this rethinking of "value" occurs. The Philippines was already familiar with both Western colonialists and Christianity at the time of its contact with the Americans; the term "fetishism" had acquired three hundred years' more history since the first encounters Pietz describes, and had already been inherited by Marx, who used it as an analogy to describe capitalism's misrecognition of its *own* value system.

Why was the lowland Philippines construed so overwhelmingly in the language of idolatry? In my previous, and directly ethnographic, writing on the area, I have given one kind of answer to this question. The "mimicry" which European and American observers saw, and which so dismayed them, had a very different

---

[103] Here we reach a difficult point; Pietz in this essay is not purporting to give an ethnography of indigenous West African ideas, but a history of European usages developed in the contact. Yet at this stage, one feels that some reading of the ethnography is almost necessary. No doubt behind the misrepresentations of the reporter, whatever practices these West African people were engaged in were products of a very different economy than that of Christian Europe. Yet since the worship of "irreducible materiality" as such existed (if I follow Pietz correctly) largely in the minds of the Europeans rather than the minds of the West Africans, one would very much like to know more about the experiences and intentions of the "fetish" wearers themselves (other than the practice of communicating with or hiding the meanings of these objects from Europeans, that is). What if any relationship between object and power was actually supposed by the users and wearers of these artifacts? Did it bear any resemblances to the focus on the split between matter and spirit so crucial to Western Christian thinking, or was it as radically different, albeit in other ways, as some Europeans feared and imagined? Obviously the historical experience of many of these West African people is not recoverable, yet reading of some contemporary ethnography might be thought provoking. As it is, we are left with only the question hanging in the air.[103]

meaning for the people who practiced it, a meaning that centered around participating in the nature and therefore the power of the thing imitated, and not on a demeaning notion of derivativeness.[104] In this paper, however, I have been attempting to look more closely at the other kind of answer which can be given—that which emphasizes what "idolatry" meant to those who deployed the label.

Beyond its convenience as an insult in an anti-Hispanic period, the term was clearly polyvalent. At one level, to call the lowland Filipinos idolaters was, like calling them "tribes," an attempt to assimilate them to the model of primitive cultures which was being more successfully applied in the highlands. But we have seen that this attempt failed; the Americans could never fully envisage the lowlands as a culture of any kind; indeed, one could argue from this point of view that they thought the lowlanders not quite "idolatrous" enough.

At another level, however, the language of idolatry persisted because it summoned up precisely those associations of confusion and *lack* of clear definition which most troubled the American interpretation of lowland society. Idols were false deities; their worshippers were those who could not tell the real from the false and who had become infected with the properties of what they worshipped. Idols were imitations of god; idolaters were those whose souls had become reduced to nothing but imitation. Idols were things masquerading as persons;[105] idolaters were persons who had degenerated so that they were lacking in genuine life and had become like a corpse—body as matter without spirit—or an inanimate object. Idolaters, above all, were those who did not exert themselves in purposive action, but allowed themselves to succumb to meaningless and almost obsessive repetitive behavior, thus (from the Protestant point of view) threatening the whole economy of proper relations between man as conscious actor and the world on which he acts.

Behind this again, perhaps, is the work that the category of idol has performed in Christian thought in general. Pietz points to the lack of clarity between the definition of idolatry as the worship of false gods and as the worship of material forms, but his argument assumes that the prior definition is the dominant one. My view would be that it is precisely the persistent ambiguity between these two aspects of idolatry which makes it as powerful a category for understanding and misunderstanding in the early twentieth century as it had been in the fourteenth.

"Industrial education" in the Philippines was undertaken with the specific objective of producing international commodities, but I have argued that these commodities were never entirely satisfactory to the American regime. Something about them remained troubling, and in attempt to solve that trouble, the Bureau of Education took to a relentless repetition of photographs and images of the objects concerned, as if insistence in itself would make them convincing. The parade of Philippine hats and other items thus took on a quasi-animated quality, which accords well with one commonly used definition of the term "fetishization."

The absent term which these objects appeared to suggest, however, was not, as in Pietz's West African examples, the attraction of an "irreducible materiality" standing for a simple inversion of capitalist rationality; it was the missing "authenticity" of the lowlands, the characteristic which made them "idolatrous." If this was a fetish, it was a fetish of idolatry, an idol in a fetish. And if, as Pietz claims,

---

[104] Cannell, *Power and Intimacy*, pp. 224 ff.

[105] Persons in the sense of both body-substitute, and the claim to be inhabited by a more-than-human spirit.

one of the dominant ways in which capitalism has reflected on non-capitalist systems of value has been through the fetish, then we could equally argue[106] that one of the dominant ways in which capitalism has reflected on its own *Christian* inheritance has continued to be through the figure of the idol.[107]

Finally, if anthropologists have been somewhat reluctant to dwell on the ways in which idolatry and other Christian concepts define the colonial encounter, we should continue to recall that this is not accidental. Christian thinking has a legacy in social science thinking itself, and it may be that, like the American educationalists, in looking at Christian subjects we see something which reminds us, disconcertingly, of ourselves.

---

[106] See also Simon Jarvis, "'Old Idolatry': Rethinking Ideology and Materialism," in *Between the Pysche and the Polis,* ed. Michael Rossington and Anne Whitehead (Aldershot: Ashgate Press, 2000).

[107] See Cannell, *Anthropology of Christianity.*

PICTURING ACEH:
VIOLENCE, RELIGION, AND
A PAINTER'S TALE[1]

Kenneth M. George

The Acehnese have long been pictured as a thoroughly Islamic society, a people whose fervent attachment to *dar-al-Islam* ("the abode of Islam") has earned their Sumatran homeland the name *Serambi Mekkah*, "Mecca's Verandah." For a time between 1945 and 1953, or—by another reckoning—from 1945 through 1976, the Acehnese also proved to be fervent Indonesian nationalists, playing a key role in the formation of the Republic of Indonesia. The discourses of a transcendent religion and a transcendent nation have been powerfully compelling forces in Acehnese public life, yet they could not put a check to the spread of grievance and fear or to the culture of violence and martial law that have possessed Aceh for the past fifteen years. Indonesia's calculated civic interventions—renaming the province *Nanggroe Aceh Darussalam* ("The State of Aceh: The Abode of Peace") in 2001 and instituting *syari'ah* law in Aceh in 2002—have been ineffective in soothing social wounds and bridging the troubled gap between identifications: Acehnese, Indonesian.

That gap has become visible in Indonesia's own visual culture, especially that precinct we might call "Islamic art" because of the way its practitioners conjure an Islamic aesthetic heritage and future. It is made visible in the embrace and

[1] I wish to thank the Aga Khan Trust for Culture, the Social Science Research Council, and the Wenner-Gren Foundation for their support as I pursued the field research that led to this paper. A fellowship from the John Simon Guggenheim Foundation and one from the Vilas Associates Fellowship Program at the University of Wisconsin-Madison gave me time to write it. I thank as well my three institutional sponsors in Indonesia: Yayasan Festival Istiqlal (The Istiqlal Festival Foundation); FSRD-ITB(Fakultas Seni Rupa dan Desain di Institut Teknologi Bandung, the Department of Fine Arts and Design at the Bandung Institute of Technology); and LIPI (Lembaga Ilmu Pengetahuan Indonesia, the Indonesian Institute of Science). My deepest, warmest, and most abundant thanks of course go to A. D. Pirous, Erna Garnasih Pirous, and their family for their years of patience, interest, conversation, and hospitality. It was a pleasure to give this paper in seminars at the Department of Anthropology at Cornell University, and at the Center for Southeast Asian Studies, Northern Illinois University. I thank my hosts and colleagues in these venues for their critical response. Last, and not least, Andrew Willford and James Siegel deserve special mention for their discerning comments and criticisms about this work. I am grateful for their encouragement and interest.

repudiation of images, and in the ratios of abstraction and figuration seen in painting. It can be found in the split between words and images and sometimes in their virtual fusion. Its history is a history of art and violence, and is told in a painter's tale.

THE ART AND ART HISTORY OF THE LEAST WELL-MANNERED

Consider first a passage taken from Snouck Hurgronje's classic ethnographic work, *The Acehnese*.[2] Brought to Aceh to assist the Dutch in their program of pacification and rule near the close of the nineteenth century, Snouck was charged with the task of assembling a political and cultural report on Sumatra's northernmost sultanate. Snouck considered the Acehnese to be "among the least well-mannered" people in the Dutch East Indies,[3] and he had this to say about their art and art history:

> On the whole we gain the impression that the artistic sense of the Acehnese is but little developed, except in the manufacture of silk fabrics, in which much taste is displayed in both coloring and in pattern. During the period of the prosperity of port-kings, constant intercourse with strangers, and the desire of those of high rank to rival other peoples in show and splendor, may have led to the temporary importation of some degree of art, but this quickly disappeared with the political degeneration which supervened. The foreign civilization which has exercised the most lasting influence on the Acehnese, namely that of Islam, is but little favourable to the awakening or development of the artistic sense.[4]

Snouck's picture of Acehnese art is consistent with the dismissive and antagonistic views expressed in his work as a whole. But the passage is worth a few moments' reflection. In it, we see Snouck drawing a line between the indigenous and the alien: most Acehnese art—Snouck hardly wants to call it that—is imported, he says, and it is the stranger—most likely the Muslim stranger—who has brought it to Aceh. It is brought at a time of prosperity and global reach, and it serves the vanities and rivalries of the elite. Its moment is the sixteenth and seventeenth centuries. The subsequent era of "political degeneration" puts it into eclipse. Though Snouck looked upon the Acehnese largely as failed Muslims,[5] he suggests here that Islam—an alien civilizing force—had little capacity to stir artistic expression. He reserves his admiration for the taste shown in local silk fabrics—their color, their pattern. Their makers are invisible and unnamed, however. He does not say so here, but these silks are usually the fabrications of women, and so the passage surreptitiously conjoins the indigenous with the hands and eyes, the looms and dyes, of Aceh's mothers, daughters, sisters, and wives. Acehnese men, by implication, are

---

[2] C. Snouck Hurgronje, *The Acehnese*, translated by A. W. S. O'Sullivan, 2 vols. (Leiden: E. J. Brill, 1906).

[3] Ibid., vol. I, p. 119.

[4] Ibid., vol. II, p. 65.

[5] See James T. Siegel, *Shadow and Sound: The Historical Thought of a Sumatran People* (Chicago: University of Chicago Press, 1979), p. 14.

artless and visibly so. Their metalwork, jewelry, and carving don't seem to count for much.[6]

Artlessness perhaps was next to boorishness for the ethnographer. What fascinates me about the passage is how closely Snouck ties the historical trajectory of Acehnese art to politics, religion, and gender. Art's absence—its not being seen—relates directly to political decline, the influence of Islam, and the marginality or eclipse of women with respect to public cultural expression. At the same time, art's absence relates directly to Snouck's ethnographic vision. His report is empty of any Acehnese claims with respect to local visual culture, and he surely had a biased view regarding what counted as "art." I also wince at his remarks on Islam, which merely repeat commonly held ideas about the way Islam is indifferent or hostile to artistic work.[7] Treating Islam as a predominantly "artless" faith is but yet another political gesture aimed at subordinating and debasing this religion vis-à-vis the Christian West and its aesthetic or visual traditions.

Yet it is not only discursive violence that haunts Snouck's account. His ethnographic report was prepared while the Dutch sought complete occupation of Aceh in the longest war of the colonial era (1873-1914). His observations followed upon atrocities and acquiescence, and it is hard to imagine how the art of the vanquished would have been as eye-catching as the unacknowledged spectacle of death and dislocation that claimed nearly an eighth of Aceh's inhabitants.[8] "No plunder here," the ethnography could be reporting. In Snouck's eyes, the vanquished were hardly an exalted people, and in most respects were already dispossessed of cultural splendor. That lack of splendor, that absence of art, foretold political and cultural defeat before the disciplined energies and vision of the Dutch.

But perhaps the art and art history of "the least well-mannered" was not so meager as this report suggests, even in the face of colonial violence. Consider the work of images evoked in language: although certain visual arts may have languished in Aceh, a distinct and religiously impassioned imagery endured in the *Hikayat Prang Sabil*—the *Chronicles of the Holy War*. Written by *ulama* and sung by Acehnese men, the *Hikayat Prang Sabil* were versions of an epic poem that recounted the stories of the Acehnese who martyred themselves in the forty-year struggle against the infidel Dutch.[9] Visions of paradise are central to these poems and inducement to young men who assembled at the *pesantren* (Muslim boarding school) and *meunasah* (a kind of dormitory and meeting hall) to martyr themselves. Paradise is radiant with gold and opal and pearls, redolent with perfume, incense, and oil of roses, and traversed by rivers of honey and paths of diamond dust. Nymphs of astonishing and incomparable beauty attend to the pleasure and desires of the martyred. (Women stand problematically with respect to the rewards of martyrdom, which the *Hikayat* pictures as a masculine pursuit.) Paradise, of course, can only be

---

[6] Acehnese men were also prominent in several genres of dance. I thank A. D. Pirous for this observation and his reminder about the role of men in carving, jewelry, and metalwork.

[7] Muslim religious authorities, it is true, have not always looked upon the arts with favor. To presume an intrinsic or widespread antipathy toward art among them is a mistake, however, and dismisses prospects for a cultural and historical understanding of art production and reception in the Islamic world.

[8] See Anthony Reid, *The Contest for North Sumatra: Atjeh, the Netherlands, and Britain, 1858-1898* (London: Oxford University Press, 1969); Siegel, *Shadow and Sound*.

[9] For an introduction to the cultural politics of reading the *Hikayat Prang Sabil*, see Siegel, *Shadow and Sound*, pp. 229-265.

seen after death and—according to the *Hikayat*—in reward for the violence of one's martyrdom. Violent, masculine self-sacrifice of this sort initiates a gift exchange with Allah and acts as a bridge leading over the gulf between word and image. The *Hikayat Prang Sabil*—regarded as a sort of image-text—promises (men, seldom women) a sort of visuality more immediate and present than that which can be evoked by the imagistic and image-making words that must suffice in this worldly existence.

The image-text of the *Hikayat Prang Sabil* is thus a different fabric (cf., the etymology of "text"), but an Acehnese fabric nonetheless, and one Snouck does not see or grasp as visual art. Nor could he, unless Snouck held decidedly un-Western ideas about the relationship of word and image. Unlike the striking silk fabrics that caught Snouck's eye, the *Hikayat Prang Sabil* circulated in secret recitation and manuscript form, and led some of those who heard or read it to slay infidel Europeans in what the Dutch would come to call acts of *Atjehmoord*—"Acehnese murder."[10] Violence threatened to spill forth from such recitations, and so they earned violent suppression from Dutch authorities. Silks were permitted to remain in the open in a pacified colonial public, while a regime-menacing image-text was withdrawn to the margins of colonial surveillance. Acehnese visual culture in the early years of the twentieth century was thus subject to the violent dialectics at work between colonizer and colonized. I have selected Snouck Hurgronje as its principal historian, but now turn to someone else as a figure of that history's future.

Abdul Djalil Pirous
Photograph courtesy of Yayasan Serambi Pirous.

---

[10] The Acehnese had a different term for the incidents: *poh kaphe*, "killing the infidel."

ACEHNESE FIGURES

Although he was destined to become one of Indonesia's leading painters, my friend Abdul Djalil Pirous was not "born Indonesian." Rather, he was born in 1932 in the coastal town of Meulaboh, Aceh, as a colonial subject of the Dutch East Indies. In local reckoning, things got off to an auspicious start. Pirous was born at noon on Friday, March 11 of that year. The Friday noon hour is of course the time set aside for the weekly convocation known as *shalat Jum'at*, a time when Muslims gather together to make their obligatory midday prayers at the mosque or prayer-room and to listen to sermons. His father, Mouna Piroes Noor Muhammad (1871-1946), asked the religious teacher who boarded with the family, Fakih Nurdin, to name his infant son. And so young Pirous came into the world bearing the name Abdul Djalil Saifuddin (meaning, "son of"–"the sublime"–"the sword of the faith"). Mouna Piroes Noor Muhammad was the descendant of a Gujarati-Sumatran trading family and was given the nickname "Piroes" because of the unusual turquoise (*pirus*) birthmark on his left arm. Many thought the birthmark a sign of spiritual significance and potency, one that set Mouna Piroes Noor Muhammad apart from others. Indeed, he was the head of the town's *Asia Muka* (South Asian) community, and had built a *madrasah* (religious school) and *surau* (prayer room). Djalil—as his son was called—was thus blessed, born during an auspicious moment of communal *shalat* (prayer) and *dzikir* (remembrance), and in time taking the name derived from the potent bluish birthmark on his father's arm.

Djalil's mother, Hamidah, (1892–1957), was Acehnese, though it isn't clear that one would have used in those years an ethnic term like that about people or art from Aceh. Hamidah was from Meulaboh and did not trace descent beyond her natal town. She was no less pious than her outsider husband, but unlike him, Hamidah was drawn toward religious practices associated with the mystical Islamic *tarekat*—for example, reciting the twenty exalted qualities of God or the ninety-nine "beautiful names" of God (*asma Tuhan*). And unlike Mouna Piroes Noor Muhammad, who frowned on art as something that conflicted with Islam, Hamidah seems to have pursued her faith in part through artistic endeavors. When speaking to curators, art journalists, critics, and scholars, Pirous generally points to his mother Hamidah as a driving force and inspiration in his becoming an artist. As he put it, "My mother was truly an artist. My father didn't have a drop of artistic blood, but my mother had it strong." Hamidah was an adept in several of the Islamic arts. She was especially skilled in Qur'anic recitation and in storytelling, and made a practice of writing down Acehnese and Malay-language stories and poems in Arabic script. She also excelled at sewing the gold-embroidered velvets, felts, and silks used for ceremonial occasions like weddings and circumcisions. Among these are the *kasab* (see Figure 1), the geometric patterns from which Pirous would later appropriate as icons of his ethnic roots. Making a *kasab* could take a year or two of labor, sometimes more, and Hamidah was assisted by her children in preparing patterns, stretching fabric, and so on. It often fell to Djalil to mix inks and prepare varnishes, and to this day Pirous can detail every step and technique used in preparing the *kasab*. Pirous's enchanted reverence for the artistry his mother brought to stories and fabric found its most explicit expression in a 1982 serigraph (see Figure 2) called "Sura Isra II: Homage to Mother" (*Sura Isra II: Penghormatan buat Ibunda*). It features brightly colored vertical borders patterned directly after Acehnese ceremonial curtains called *tabir*; an image of the winged *bouraq*, the Prophet Muhammad's legendary mount; and a two-dimensional reproduction of a red and gold *kasab* made by Hamidah herself, inscribed with the Qur'anic verse revealed at Mecca and traditionally associated with the Prophet's night journey and ascension to Heaven on the *bouraq* (*QS 17 Bani-Isra'il*: 1).

Figure 1: A *kasab* designed and embroidered by Hamidah in 1941.
Courtesy of A. D. Pirous.

Figure 2: *Sura Isra II: Homage to Mother*, A. D. Pirous, 1982.
80 x 54 cm, serigraph. Courtesy of the artist.

At first glance, it might seem that Pirous's recollections more or less recapitulate the views of Snouck Hurgronje from a century before regarding Acehnese art. Pirous's father appears a bit foreign and artless, and that artlessness coincides with a conventional Muslim piety that looks unfavorably upon the arts. His mother's artfulness, in contrast, finds expression in fabric, the Acehnese material that Snouck prized for exceptional workings of color and pattern. But I want to suggest that Pirous's homage to Hamidah does not accord so fully or simply with his recollections about his artistic roots, or with Snouck's art historical views. Let us examine that silkscreened image, "Sura Isra II," again, this time in juxtaposition with the *kasab* of Hamidah's original manufacture. The serigraph erases the gold arabesque that Hamidah embroidered into the *kasab*'s central diamond of blue and replaces it with Qur'anic calligraphy. This gesture, in my view, does two things—it defaces and replaces the visual center of an originary, remembered, and revered object. It substitutes writing for the arabesque image, and at the same time turns writing into image—writing not just to be read, but writing at which one will contemplatively look.

Not reading but looking at the single Qur'anic verse in "Surat Isra II," I note the way it is placed on a diamond of blue that recedes from the eye, giving the illusion of disclosed depth behind the advancing reds of the *kasab*-square. The writing is thus made to float. Even so, the floating image of Qur'anic verse is complicated by a square pane of white and dark blue at the center of the *kasab*-shaped field, a pane that formally recuperates the arabesque square at the heart of Hamidah's embroidery. The orthographic form of "Allah" resides as an icon of divinity at the top of the blue diamond, just beneath the mathematical center of the serigraph as a whole.

The image is that of revealed writing. What that writing signifies—when read—is the initial line of the Qur'an's story of the Prophet's night journey. It is paired with the iconic image of the *bouraq*, taken from Hamidah's oral versions of Muslim legend. The serigraph thus pictorially renders Qur'anic scripture and religious legend as linked dimensions of Aceh's Islamic visual culture. I would argue, too, that this pairing potentially draws upon the contrast of father and mother, or masculine-feminine, as well. That is, broadly held ideas about Acehnese men and their association with Qur'anic verse and *akal*, or rationality, conjoin in the serigraph with ideas about Acehnese women and their association with the sensuousness of color, pattern, and narrative (though we should keep in mind that Hamidah and many other Acehnese women did write and recite Qur'anic verse). "Sura Isra II: Homage to Mother" thus captures some of the contending oppositions in Acehnese visual culture, and potentially refigures them through the use of writing as image.

At this point, I have gotten ahead of myself in the story I wish to tell. What will suffice for now is appreciation of the way Pirous's work may be drawn into tensions between, and hybridizations of, word and image. That work did not just take place in paintings and serigraphs, but even in one of the most personal signs of subjectivity and identity, the writing of his name in national orthography. In the mid-1950s as he was just starting formal art training at the Bandung Institute of Technology, Indonesian orthography was officially revised so that "oe" would be rendered as "u." The artist did not like the "look" of "Pirus." To suit his graphic tastes, he wrote his name as "Pirous." Had the nation not intervened, he might still be signing himself as "Piroes." Had the nation not intervened, he might be picturing Aceh rather differently than he does today, and not as an Indonesian citizen.

NATIONALISM FROM ABOVE, ISLAMIC ART FROM AFAR

Pirous was fifteen when he started to think of himself as Indonesian. It was 1945. Aceh's part in an Indonesian identity and an Indonesian national community was not easily imagined into being at the time. Pirous remembers back:

> What did independence truly mean? The only thing we knew was that we had been ruled by the Dutch, ruled by the Japanese, and that we now wanted to have our own government . . . One day a plane suddenly appeared overhead dropping leaflets and I picked one up and there was the text of the declaration . . . "Our independence" and so forth. "So that the people live as one" and so on. I didn't understand what it really meant. . . .[11]

Dropping a people's identity papers on them from the sky may not be a particularly efficacious speech act (and makes us realize that J. L. Austin's discussion of felicity conditions in *How to Do Things with Words* does not take readers to the political heart and horizons of "Says who?").[12] But like they say, it's a start. At age sixteen, Pirous joined the Indonesian Student Army and put his art skills to work making handbills and leaflets for the nationalist campaign. So commenced his affiliation with the nation. It was through art, revolutionary violence, and *Bahasa Indonesia* that Pirous began to shape and understand himself as an Indonesian citizen.

A decade later, Pirous was in Bandung, West Java, pursuing formal art training with Dutch cubist Ries Mulder and absorbing the latest lessons on modernism and abstraction emanating from New York. By now, he was deeply drawn into the social and cultural energies of an urban postcolonial world, and into its tensions and debates as well. Throughout this time, Indonesian nationalism provided Pirous and his colleagues with the most crucial terms for personal allegiance, for forms of collective solidarity, for reckoning cultural pasts, and for working toward cultural and political futures. Just as crucially, nationalism also established the principal terms for mediating the artist's place in a global art world.

Not long ago while browsing in Pirous's library in Bandung, I came across a 1957 paperback copy of Henri Pirenne's *Mohammed and Charlemagne*. The bastard page is inscribed in ink and in Pirous's hand. It reads, "States are as men, they grow out of the character of men—Plato." On the title page that follows, Pirous has placed his signature in brown pencil and beneath that the date "4/58." The inscription reads as aphorism and lesson to the artist himself, for who else other than Pirous would likely peruse this very volume, kept in his private library? I perhaps read too much into the passage, but to me its rings of a mystifying cultural nationalism as it traces the roots of the nation-state back to the ethical conduct and thought of those individuals who are its citizens. It certainly requires of us a romantic and heroic idea of the citizen if we are to give it our assent.

But such thinking was no doubt common among the artists of the early postcolonial period. Writing about another postcolonial nation—India—Geeta Kapur

---

[11] Interview with the author, March 22, 1994.

[12] J. L. Austin, *How to Do Things with Words* (Cambridge: Harvard University Press, 1962).

has portrayed the early postcolonial artist-citizen as a figure formed by two very modern and contraposed modes of political and aesthetic will: To aspire not only to a unique and innovative artistic subjectivity, but also to an identity as a representative of a people and a nation.[13] Holding those contradictory strains together was a faith in a unified and bounded cultural location—a nation—and an "idealized notion of the artist immersed in an undivided community."[14] The heroic stature of the artist, the unitary nation, and their links to the modern are normative constructs now undergoing acute interrogation. Such interrogations notwithstanding, the pull between pursuing an autonomous and unique subjectivity and serving as a representative of a people and a nation has been the principal (if normative) tension for most Indonesian artists and art critics in the post-independence period (1945–present). In short, searching for a distinctive national identity has been as crucial to locating postcolonial aesthetic projects as it has been to asserting political autonomy. To be modern, the "imagined community" aspiring to nationhood needed modern artists whose work would be emblematic of the nation.[15] At the same time, achieving a modern artistic subjectivity, and securing a place in an international art world, demanded that an artist claim a national identity and location. Being subject to a nation, then, meant acknowledging a set of imagined political and social differences that when refracted through the discourses and techniques of art production would yield a recognizable "Indonesian" art.

Those same differences and discourses would have obscured "Acehnese art" or "Acehnese visual culture" as distinct modalities and precincts of expression, and would have rendered them as "Indonesian." Pirous, for example, showed no interest in Acehnese aesthetic traditions at this time. Nor did he claim to be making, or understand himself to be making, Acehnese art. The idea of "Aceh" or "Acehnese-ness" did not mediate his relationship to the Indonesian nation-state, the wider world, or his art. Neither did "Islam." To the contrary, he thought of himself in rather universalist and humanist terms as an Indonesian who made "modern art." That stance was not without its problems and dangers in the late Sukarno years, when Socialist Realism and its romantic politics of visuality were in their heyday. Pirous's rejection of realism and his decision to opt instead for the elite, universalist, and bourgeois language of the abstract was interpreted by many as a rejection of the *rakyat*—"the people"—and their socialist national identity. Pirous's circumstances changed abruptly and favorably following the anti-leftist massacres of 1965 and 1966 that ushered in the Suharto era. Abstraction was no longer in danger of attracting public rebuke and ridicule, and for a time, was the preeminent form of Indonesian painting. Pirous felt secure, and the three years following mass violence reveal the daring and romantic reinventions of an artist who is convinced that abstraction affords a direct and privileged inscription of one's unique painterly subjectivity.

Pirous's immersion in abstract modernism during the 1950s and 60s in some ways produced a rupture in his artistic life. The arts of his Acehnese homeland and personal past were not recognizable to him as art, but, at best, as the sort of craft or tradition from which the modernist wants to escape. What beckoned him away from

---

[13] Geeta Kapur, "Dismantling the Norm," in *Traditions/Tensions: Contemporary Art in Asia*, ed. Apinan Poshyananda (New York: Asia Society, 1996), pp. 60-69.

[14] Ibid., p. 60

[15] I borrow the term from Benedict R. O'G. Anderson, *Imagined Communities: Reflections on the Origin and Spread of Nationalism*, rev. ed. (London: Verso, 1991).

this art was a glimpse of a globalizing art world, the horizons of which were largely inscribed by Euro-American institutions and ideologies. Oblivious at the time to the Orientalist hierarchies within Euro-American discourse that would dismiss Indonesian modern art as "derivative" and "inauthentic," Pirous pursued an unconstrained subjectivity, even while mimicking—in ways charted for us by Albert Memmi, Ashis Nandy, and Homi Bhabha[16]—the emergent trends of the Euro-American avant garde.

His attitude changed significantly in the winter of 1969-70 while Pirous was on an art fellowship in the United States. The painful and growing realization that Indonesia did not count for much in the galleries and museums of the West provoked a period of search and reflection that would end in an embrace of Islamic aesthetics. Visiting the New York Metropolitan Museum of Art, he experienced what he has described in published interviews as a moment of intimate self-recognition. Looking at the Museum's standing collection of Islamic art—ceramic fragments, manuscripts, calligraphy, miniatures—he saw "Aceh." From Pirous's vantage point at that moment, Acehnese art looked neither ethnic nor primitive, but civilizational and museum-class, a local Indonesian expression of something global in scale. Once-familiar possibilities of expression, long ignored during his training in modernism, returned to enthrall him. They reoriented his eye and his imagination, and suggested a way to express a self-conscious Indonesian-ness in his art.

ACEHNESE ISLAMIC ART IN AUTHORITARIAN TIMES

That moment of self-recognition in New York City posed a problem for Pirous: What made an object or a set of practices "Islamic," "art," and "Indonesian?" What made them "Acehnese"? What made them "modern"? Exploring these terms and coming up with solutions was not free and open-ended work, especially in the nascent and arrested art public of Suharto's Indonesia. It is true that ideas and ideologies of nation, ethnicity, religion, modernity, and art are never settled matters; they are continually up for grabs. They shift and intermingle and become subject to political maneuver in the most open of publics. Suharto's authoritarian regime, however, placed severe constraints on artistic expression in an attempt to purge it—and the public sphere in general—of political critique and threatening oppositional discourses. To mention just one especially relevant example, Suharto personally intervened to prevent the 1991 Istiqlal Festival from being promoted as a celebration of "Islamic Art in Indonesia" (*Seni Islami di Indonesia*). Suspicious of any gesture that would place faith before nation, he insisted instead that the event be billed as a festival of "Indonesian Art Inspired by the Spirit of Islam" (*Seni Indonesia yang Bernafaskan Islam*).

How Pirous has rethought and repositioned his art over the course of five decades is the subject of the broader work I have under way. Here, I want to dwell on the picture of Aceh that we get from his artwork. I need to emphasize that from 1945 until 1970, the prevailing discourses of Indonesian nationalism and aesthetic modernism more or less trumped his Acehnese heritage and estranged him from it politically and artistically. Whatever else it might be, however else it may be

---

[16] Albert Memmi, *The Colonizer and the Colonized*, expanded edition (Boston: Beacon Press, 1991 [1957]); Ashis Nandy, *Exiled at Home* (New Delhi: Oxford University Press, 1998); Homi Bhabha, *The Location of Culture* (New York: Routledge, 1994).

conjured, Aceh was for a time a sign of dislocation for the artist, the social, political, and cultural home he had left behind. Pirous's rediscovery of "Aceh" was more than a postcolonial artist's sincere but self-mystifying and nostalgic search for lost roots. His effort to recuperate an Acehnese-ness in his art was a calculated way to assert a distinctive religious and national identity within Indonesia, the West, and the Islamic world. Pursued during a time of authoritarian rule, this project lacked overt oppositional or critical expression and resulted in a largely acclamatory art. Following the regime's collapse in 1998 and revelations of state-sponsored atrocities in Aceh, Pirous took direct steps to depict the tragedies of state and separatist violence. That effort, on the one hand, included a re-embrace of human figuration, something that Pirous had largely abandoned after 1970. On the other hand, it also involved a reworking of the word-image emblematics that he had articulated in his thirty-year exploration of Qur'anic themes and Qur'anic calligraphy. These changes, I want to argue, are materials through which we may discern a split, or a gap, in Pirous's political and aesthetic subjectivity.

It is important to see that Pirous required not only a national Indonesian identity, but also a working notion of Islamic art, as the legitimating framework for recuperating his Acehnese-ness. That is, his painterly and graphic exploration of "Aceh" was intended to show Acehnese culture as an example of a transnational and multicultural Islamic civilization. In this respect, Pirous, the postcolonial artist, is not that different from Snouck Hurgronje, the colonial ethnographer: both see Acehnese art as Islamic in character. But whereas Snouck saw little in Islam to favor "the awakening or development of the artistic sense," Pirous sees in it an enormously productive aesthetics. His years of formal art training, of course, left him unacquainted with Islamic art. For the fifteen-year period between 1955 and 1970, Pirous gave little thought to Islamic art, neither missing it nor paying any attention to it. To have done so would have served him poorly, given the polemics of nationalism and modernism to which he was subject. Following his return from New York, he had to sort out for himself what Islamic art could or should be.

I do not have the space here to rehearse all the challenges Pirous faced in sorting out possible answers to this question. The fact is that Islamic art at this historical moment has become so thoroughly diversified, pluralized, and contestatory, so frequently recruited for struggles against Western cultural imperialism, and so often demonized as a sin by Islamist regimes, that it was, and is, misleading to think of Islamic aesthetics as a settled matter in a world of such varied nationalisms, transnationalisms, and traveling cultures. That said, Pirous adapted into his abstract modernist work two gestures or features—one ending in an absence, the other in a presence—commonly associated with Islamic visual culture: the abandonment of human figuration, and the celebration of calligraphy. The strategy of fusing calligraphy—Islam's most privileged and sacred art form—with abstraction happened to coincide with Pirous's first experiments with high-viscosity etching techniques in printmaking, and his initial explorations with acrylics and modeling paste in painting. A tension resulted: the discipline and self-surrender associated with the precincts of calligraphy and Islam met the impulse and self-assertion associated with abstract modernism.

Unsurprisingly, discipline and self-assertion achieve different ratios in his earliest paintings, done between 1971 and 1974. These paintings featured deformations of Arabic or Arabic-like characters worked up in modeling paste and acrylics. All bore titles that referred to inscribed objects of considerable antiquity—plaques, pillars, tombstones, manuscripts—or to textual genres or styles of writing. A good example is "White Writing" (*Tulisan Putih*, 1974; see Figure 3) in which characters are deformed beyond legibility, a style that Pirous today calls "expressive calligraphy" (*kaligrafi ekspressif*). Differences between legible and illegible Arabic may have been lost on Western or non-Muslim viewers, who generally are unable to read Arabic and can only see such writing as image. For many Indonesians, however, "White Writing" was a disturbing deformation of sacred orthography, and indeed the painting drew criticism from Muslim clerics. By 1975, Pirous moved closer to what we might call a "Qur'anic aesthetic." For his calligraphic works of 1975 and after, Qur'anic verses enjoy special focus; orthographic clarity, wholeness, immutability, and an emphasis on moral reflection and vision usually prevail over self-expression. Untethered self-expression gives way to a contemplative and harmonious abstract iconography aimed at illuminating Qur'anic passages that appear in the paintings. "And God the Utmost" (*Dan Dia Yang Maha Segala*, 1978) is a good example (see Figure 4). This is a small canvas done in acrylics, modeling paste, and gold leaf. Symmetries and triangular forms surround a turquoise (*pirus*) field, in which is inscribed the 189th verse of QS 3 Al-'Imran, which reads: "For God's is the kingdom of the heavens and earth, and God's is the power over all things." "The Night Journey" (*Perjalanan Malam*, 1976) is another example, this one quoting several verses from the QS 17 Bani-Isra'il (1, 12-14, 16, 35-37), the same *sura* that would appear so prominently in "Homage to Mother" six years later. Here the iconography and symmetries of weathered plates or tablets evoke the material culture of Aceh, where the earliest Islamic inscriptions appear on segmented tombstones called *nisan*.

It was 1981 before Pirous produced a work of art that made explicit reference to "Aceh" in its title or in its iconographies. The occasion was the Twelfth National *Musabaqah Tilwatil Qur'an* (Qur'anic reading competition) or *MTQ*, held in June 1981 in the city of Banda Aceh, for which Pirous served as one of the organizers. His most demanding task for the *MTQ* was staging a massive display of calligraphy rendered with electric lights for ceremonies attended by President Suharto. But his efforts also included organizing and curating an innovative exhibit of calligraphic paintings, prints, photographs, and carving.[17] It was here that Pirous exhibited three stunning paintings and a silkscreened homage to Aceh—the first of his works to make visual reference to Aceh. All three paintings measured one by one-and-a-half meters, and were prepared with canvas, panels, etched copper, and acrylics. The three paintings together constituted a series, *The Wall of Aceh I, II, and III* (*Dinding Aceh I, II, and III*, 1981). The first work consists of six etched plates bearing twenty-three of God's beautiful names, and borders patterned after Acehnese fabric design. The second features a large copper plate shaped and etched in the fashion of an Acehnese *nisan*, or tombstone; on it is etched QS 96 Al-'Alaq, verses 1-15, generally regarded as the first *sura* revealed to the Prophet Muhammad, and thus holding special place for Muslims of any background. Two vertical curtain-like panels frame the copper etching. The last painting includes QS 114 An-Nas, the recitation of which is considered a talisman for warding off evil.[18]

---

[17] The exhibit and the accompanying competition in Qur'anic calligraphy were so successful that they became part of the standard program at subsequent *MTQ* competitions.

[18] Pirous no longer has complete documentation about "The Wall of Aceh III." I have yet to see the painting or a reproduction of it.

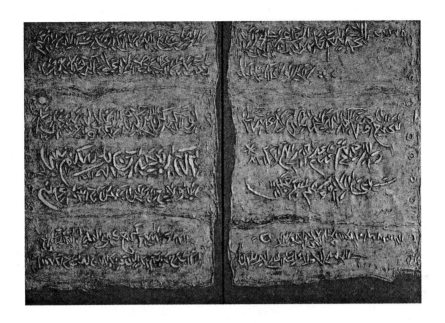

Figure 3: *White Writing,* A. D. Pirous, 1972.
100 x 180 cm, marble paste, acrylic on canvas. Courtesy of the artist.

Figure 4: *And God the Utmost,* A. D. Pirous, 1978.
30 x 30 cm, marble paste, gold, acrylic on canvas. Courtesy of the artist.

The serigraph, meanwhile, is called "Prayer XII/Homage to Tanöh Abée" (*Doa XII/Penghormatan Kepada Tanöh Abée*, 1981; see Figure 5), the site of a famous Muslim library and *pesantren* founded by the revered historical figure, Teungku Tanöh Abée. The library is the pride of Aceh and holds hundreds of religious and historical manuscripts dating back to the seventeenth century. Calligraphy abounds in this silkscreen print: some from the Qur'an; some from fragments of Acehnese and Malay manuscripts; and even some in the form of seals, such as the one in the lower left that bears the painter's name. The print in its entirety presents a landscape of sorts, with sky, clouds, sunlight, hills and mountains, sea, and earth—perhaps suggesting that Aceh is "grounded" in Muslim manuscript culture. Above and below are recognizable Qur'anic passages—"God's is the power over all things" (a fragment of *QS 3 Al-Imran*: 29), and *QS 5 Al-Ma'idah*, verse 74: "Why do they not turn to God and ask His forgiveness? God is forgiving and kind." The text fragments forming hills and mountains in the center of the print are in Arabic and in Jawi, that is, in Malay and Acehnese written in Arabic orthography (the dominant form of writing in Aceh until the twentieth century).

Figure 5: *Prayer XII/Homage to Tanöh Abée*, A. D. Pirous, 1981.
84 x 56 cm, serigraph. Courtesy of the artist.

The politics behind this exhibit need comment and prefigure opportunities and crises to come. As early as 1953, many Acehnese had grown disenchanted with the erosion of their political autonomy and Indonesia's failure to become an Islamic nation-state. A rebellion led by Daud Beureuèh began that year and continued until 1961, when an agreement was reached with Jakarta. Fifteen years later, in reaction to what its leaders perceived as Javanese neo-colonialism in the guise of the nation-state, GAM—the Movement for a Free Aceh (*Gerakan Acheh Merdeka*)—launched another separatist rebellion. This one has persisted until today. Staging the national Qur'anic recitation contest in Banda Aceh in June of 1981 was not a coincidence. It has to be seen as an effort on the part of the central government to use religious and cultural events as a means of quelling separatist sentiment and power. In particular, the festival served as a vehicle for the government to coopt and neutralize Islam and the local *ulama*, drawing the religious leadership away from separatist leanings and into the national fold.[19]

Pirous has never acknowledged or admitted to me that he was recruited for political goals such as these, or that his Indonesian nationalist outlook and identity might represent the sort of political subjectivity the central government would like to instill in all Acehnese.[20] The opportunity to exhibit in Aceh was no doubt an inducement to making the works he did, when he did. In fact, the artist is, in my experience, shrewd enough to have knowingly used the central government to advance his own aesthetic project. The point I wish to make here is that Pirous's exploration of Islamic, Acehnese, and Indonesian art could not be worked out in the precincts of aesthetics alone. It required, first, a nationalist political imagination as described by Geeta Kapur, noted above, and second, a public venue in which to exhibit. The project unfolded in a politically circumstanced art world in which the authoritarian nation-state figured as a powerful patron and censor.[21] Pirous's art would never have appeared in an Acehnese exhibit hall had the Suharto regime construed any separatist sentiment in its iconographies and visual representations.

The Qur'anic passages in the works shown in Banda Aceh are familiar to most Muslims, and are to be read, of course. At the same time, the inscriptions are to be taken in whole, as part of the work's visual totality. They are simultaneously word and image, and in ways that challenge ideologies of pictorial and linguistic signs in the non-Muslim West.[22] One of the passages, however, betrays a political stance unforeseen and unremarked upon by the festival's government sponsors. It is the one situated at the foot of "Prayer XII/Homage to Tanöh Abée": "Why do they not turn to God and ask His forgiveness? God is forgiving and kind." I asked Pirous

---

[19] Cf., Tim Kell, *The Roots of Acehnese Rebellion, 1989-1992* (Ithaca: Cornell Modern Indonesia Project, 1995); James T. Siegel, *The Rope of God*, new edition (Ann Arbor: University of Michigan Press, 2000), pp. 336-339.

[20] After reading the penultimate draft of this paper, Pirous remarked that organizers in Aceh were eager to have a turn at hosting the 1981 MTQ so that Aceh could outshine other provinces in running the competition. It is important not to discount the civic and religious prestige that comes with outdoing rivals in "show and splendor" (to use Snouck's phrase) as a "local" motivation for holding the event in Aceh. Nonetheless, Pirous went on to acknowledge that, "At the same time, the national MTQ succeeded in erasing political wounds such as the one Aceh made in opposing Jakarta since 1953, or—in the case of the 1983 MTQ in Padang—the one in West Sumatra that came as a result of the PRRI [Pemerintah Revolusioner Republik Indonesia, the Revolutionary Government of the Indonesian Republic, 1958-1961] revolt." Personal email communication with the author, November 6, 2003.

[21] See Kenneth M. George, "Designs on Indonesia's Muslim Communities," *Journal of Asian Studies* 57, 3 (1998):693-713; and "Some Things that Have Happened to *The Sun After September 1965*: Politics and the Interpretation of an Indonesian Painting," *Comparative Studies in Society and History* 39, 4 (1997): 599-634.

[22] For a superb discussion on ideologies of the image, see: W. J. T. Mitchell, *Iconology: Image, Text, Ideology* (Chicago: University of Chicago Press, 1986); and W. J. T. Mitchell, *Picture Theory* (Chicago: University of Chicago Press, 1994).

about this passage, whose tone seems so curious in a work meant to pay homage to his homeland:

> The passage from *Sura* 5 was for all Indonesians. The shock of modernization in Indonesia's development began to include several kinds of secular deviations and distractions, ones that were increasingly colliding with the faith. But the passage was also intended especially for the people of Aceh, whose character was being ruined . . . because of modern urban values. The direction of society and economy, ala Jakarta, was increasingly . . . in collision with local tradition and faith. [The] passage from *Sura* 5 is a reprimand, an admonition.[23]

Here is a critique, one conjured from the oppositional space of Islam. Both Indonesian and Acehnese Muslims appear out of touch with their religious roots and teachings, and Pirous is urging them to return to a more pious, observant way of life. Yet the threat to Islam, to Aceh, and to the nation as a whole, according to the artist, stems from Jakarta, a complaint not unfamiliar to supporters of GAM.

LATE AUTHORITARIAN OCCUPATIONS

Throughout the 1980's, the Suharto regime recognized that the oppositional potential of Islam was too threatening to be left unpoliced and unchecked. By 1985, the central government successfully pressured Islamic political parties and organizations into adopting *Pancasila*, the state ideology, as the basis of their activities. Having choked the political aspirations of Islamic groups, the regime quickly began to establish itself as the central patron for Islamic values and culture. Suharto went on the *haj* (pilgrimage to Mecca), state funds were dispensed for Islamic schools and *da'wah* (missionary and religious outreach), and highly placed bureaucrats formed ICMI, the Indonesian Association of Muslim Intellectuals (Ikatan Cendekiawan Muslim Indonesia). In Aceh, the central government had succeeded in putting into place a leadership that owed allegiance to Jakarta. When the separatist movement reemerged in the late 1980s with increased spark, Indonesia unleashed a deadly program of counterinsurgency and military terror.[24]

Pirous never again exhibited in Aceh, but continued to explore what he calls the "visual language" of Aceh. In some respects, this exploration resulted in a visual meta-language—an art about art—especially in the way modernist and Islamic visual idioms are used to depict the visual language of Aceh. Overall, this project led to an iconographic "folklorization" and "essentialization" of Acehnese aesthetics. In Pirous's version of Acehnese aesthetics, authenticity resides in old textual materials written in Arabic orthography and in the artful objects he associates with his mother, Hamidah: *tabir*-curtains, *kasab*-embroidery, and *tilampandak*-patterns. This very selection of materials renders Acehnese art as anonymous and shared; empty of difference, debate, and contradiction; and expressive of Islamic aesthetic principles.

---

[23] Interview with the author, March 13, 2001.

[24] See Kell, *The Roots of Acehnese Rebellion*; Geoffrey Robinson, "*Rawan* is as *Rawan* Does: The Origins of Disorder in New Order Aceh," in *Violence and the State in Suharto's Indonesia*, ed. Benedict R. O'G. Anderson (Ithaca: Cornell Southeast Asia Program Publications, 2001), pp. 213-242; Siegel, *A New Criminal Type in Jakarta*.

A heterodox and hybrid Aceh, perhaps best personified by Pirous's Gujarati-Sumatran father, is left artless and out of the picture.

Pirous put this sort of approach to work in organizing the national Istiqlal Festivals of 1991 and 1995 for government sponsors.[25] By showcasing regional arts that would reveal the spirit and cultural impact of Islam throughout Indonesia, Pirous and his colleagues made a bold moral and civic claim on the cultural heritage and future of the nation-state: the nation had its roots in an Islamic multiculturalism, or *tamadun*, and in this owed more to Aceh, Sumatra, and other Melayu regions than to the Hindu-Buddhist traditions of Java and Bali. This claim, and the visual logic used to support it, are most clear in Pirous's immense collaborative and public artwork, the "Al-Qur'an Mushaf Istiqlal—The National Independence Illuminated Qur'an." Completed in 1995 during the opening ceremonies of the second Istiqlal Festival, and in celebration of Indonesia's fiftieth year of independence, the "Al-Qur'an Mushaf Istiqlal" was an icon of the country's national Muslim *ummat*, or community, viewed as "united and peaceful in its ethnic plurality."[26] Carving Indonesia into over forty Muslim culture regions, Pirous and his team of graphic artists and computer-assisted-design specialists borrowed freely from the country's folk arts and came up with border illuminations representing each cultural area. Aceh was divided into several regions and had designs on roughly eighty pages of the finished text, including the prologue, *al-Fatihah*, and the closing of the Qur'an, *Sura* 114.

In the end, the *mushaf* project is a form of acclamatory art, both for the nation and for Islam. Its appeal to constituent folk aesthetic and manuscript traditions in conjuring a multicultural nationalism and a multicultural Islam, it seems to me, leans heavily on a Herderian notion of culture. As both Seyla Benhabib and Terence Turner have pointed out, the epistemic premises behind such appeals give a faulty and reductionist picture of cultural life: The emblematic iconographies to which they have given rise presume a congruence, homogeneity, conformity, and force that seldom obtain in social life.[27] They also pose a trap for political and artistic subjectivity, especially when the image of a unified polity is brought into question by asymmetries of power and violence.

PICTURING THE ACEHNESE TRAGEDY

The fall of Suharto in May 1998 was followed soon after by public disclosure of state-sponsored atrocities in Aceh. It is ironic that Pirous was born in the waning years of the *Prang Sabil* and *Atjehmoord*, only to live to see a different war in his homeland, this time between Indonesian compatriots. For someone of such creativity, good will, and national pride, this tragedy is very hard to bear. He expressed his anguish and anger most clearly in a public speech he delivered in

---

[25] See George, "Designs on Indonesia's Muslim Communities."

[26] Machmud Buchari, *Al-Qur'an Mushaf Istiqlal Indonesia* (Jakarta: Yayasan Festival Istiqlal, 1994), p. 6.

[27] Seyla Benhabib, *The Claims of Culture: Equality and Diversity in the Global Era* (Princeton: Princeton University Press, 2002), pp. 3-4; Terence Turner, "Anthropology and Multiculturalism: What is Anthropology that Multiculturalists Should be Mindful of It," *Cultural Anthropology* 8, 4 (1993): 411-429.

Bandung in August of that year, around the time state military operations were temporarily suspended in Aceh:

> With every day it is increasingly clear that the dead did no wrong, did not get a proper burial, and were killed without reason. And now it is in the open. This didn't happen just in Aceh, but throughout Indonesia, it happened everywhere.[28]

Earlier that day, he showed me the first of the paintings he would make having to do with the atrocities in Aceh (see Figure 6). It is called, "Once There Was a Holy War in Aceh: Homage to the Intrepid Hero Teuku Oemar, 1854-1899" (*Suatu Waktu Ada Prang Sabil di Aceh: Penghormatan Kepada Pahlawan yang Gagah Berani Teuku Oemar, 1854-1899*). There as the visual focus of this lurid painting was the figure of Teuku Oemar, a martyr from the Dutch-Acehnese War. His figure is surrounded by excerpts from the *Hikayat Prang Sabil* and other related poems. The raised red Arabic characters about him are Acehnese and quote the "Oath of the Holy War" (*Sumpah Prang Sabil*). The oath reads: "Rather than die in the home of your wife, better to be slain by the infidel's weapon. Rather than die on a pillow, better to be sprawled as a martyr in the front lines." Pirous appeared to shudder when he finished reading it to me in Indonesian.[29]

Figure 6: *Once There was a Holy War in Aceh: Homage to the Intrepid Hero Teuku Oemar, 1854-1899*, A. D. Pirous, 1998.
145 x 150 cm, mixed media on canvas. Courtesy of the artist.

---

[28] Excerpt from a talk on art and oppression delivered at an evening ceremony in memory of Dharsono, Bandung, August 22, 1998.

[29] For an anecdote about how an Acehnese *ulama* would shiver upon hearing anything about the *prang sabil*, see C. Snouck Hurgronje, "Eene onbezonnen vraag," in *Verspreide Geschriften van C. Snouck Hurgronje*, vol. IV (Bonn and Leipzig: Kurt Schroeder, 1924), Part One, p. 1. This passage is also quoted and translated in Siegel, *The Rope of God*, p. 81.

Pirous had abandoned human figuration years before, during his early embrace of Islamic aesthetics. When I pressed him about his willingness to include figurative elements in this painting, he explained:

> In an atmosphere like this, themes in art tell stories of turmoil. . . . Because of that, figurative forms that are realistic rather than abstract have become important. They are a very common language for telling stories. . . . I look at the army, I look at the people in GAM. They can't think, they can only see. Because of that, a picture is worth a thousand words.[30]

In his reply, Pirous is depicting his painting as narrative—it tells stories. The character of the violence that needs to be narrated is such that it demands "realism" in figurative form. Vision is key to the agents of violence, just as it is to the artist who looks at them from afar. Seeing is understanding, and the realistic figure is regarded as a transparent window on a violent world. What figures do we see in this work? There is a likeness of Teuku Oemar bearing a weapon, splatters and gashes of red that we may see as blood, the oath in written form and in the color of blood, and fragments of the *Hikayat Prang Sabil*, written in Arabic orthography but unreadable to those who do not know Acehnese (Pirous himself has difficulty reading the fragments and does not understand them).[31] Unlike the Qur'anic passages often found in his paintings, the *hikayat* passages here are cut and placed on the work's surface in a way that would thwart a "grammatical" reading of the *hikayat* narrative.

An ideology in which figurative images are said to have special purchase on reality is recruited for a portrayal of recurrent violence. Here figuration plays a part in a visual allegory in which the violence of present-day Aceh is understood through historical reference to the Acehnese anticolonial *jihad* of the late nineteenth and early twentieth centuries. The painting summons the Indonesian national hero, Teuku Oemar, from the dead and reclaims him as Acehnese, as the honored figure of local resistance to all colonialism, be it Dutch or Indonesian.[32] Icons from Hamidah's Aceh are absent in this work. Instead, we see icons from a culture of violence that Pirous has long left out of his artwork. Another absence: missing, too, is Qur'anic calligraphy, the very image of Islam. Calligraphy remains, but in place of Qur'anic verse, we have the Acehnese Oath of the Holy War. The exhortative verse of the Qur'an is regarded as Truth by Muslims, and would call upon the reader to submit to Allah, something we saw in "Prayer XII/Homage to Tanöh Abée." In "Once There Was a Holy War in Aceh," by contrast, the Oath of the Holy War calls upon readers to resist, but the religiosity of that call is largely left out of the picture. Islam does not figure strongly here, and indeed, the painting does not conform easily with any aesthetic that Pirous has deemed "Islamic."

---

[30] Interview with the author, March 15, 2001.

[31] That is, Pirous is not well versed in how to apply phonemic values in Acehnese to Arabic orthography.

[32] Compare this local reclamation of Teuku Oemar from national precincts to the Kodinese reclamation of their hero, Wono Kaka, from Jakarta. See Janet Hoskins, "The Headhunter as Hero: Local Traditions and Their Reinterpretation in National History," *American Ethnologist* 14, 4 (1987): 605-622.

For Pirous, it seems, the visual culture of violence in Aceh cannot or should not be rendered "Islamic." That violence is the very antithesis of the peace and harmony he has sought in his faith. He does not want the current conflict to become a *jihad*, he tells me, for holy wars are never quenched by amplified violence. Other paintings in what he has come to call his *Acehnese Series* seem more anguished than the homage to the fallen hero, Teuku Oemar. In them we see the human figure brought back as an anonymous ghost or corpse. Take for example, "A Face Buried with No Name" (*Wajah Terkubur Tanpa Name,* 2000). Or "They Who are Buried Without Names" (*Mereka yang Terkubur Tanpa Nama,* 2001; see Figure 7). Or "The Heads II: They No Longer Know What to Dream" (*Kepala-Kepala II: Mereka Sudah Tak Tahu Bermimpi Apa,* 1999). These are paintings that lead one to grieve and grow angry, or so Pirous would have it. Yet identification with the murdered threatens to turn into vows for vengeance. The Chronicle of the Holy War has to be kept bound and sealed as in "The Restraining of the Chronicle of the Holy War II" (*Pemasungan Kitab Prang Sabil II,* 1999; see Figure 8). Paradise does not await those seeking vengeance. This is not a holy war. It is the nation splitting apart, unhealed by common faith.

Pirous's paintings make visible his troubled national self and remind us that an individual does not have a singular and univocal political self, but a hybrid one constituted through conflicting narratives and images of affiliation, allegiance, and betrayal.[33] As James Siegel has remarked, there was for the longest time "no contradiction between being Acehnese and being Indonesian."[34] But the "and" in "being Acehnese *and* being Indonesian" is now a conjunction far more fraught and uncertain than it has been in the past. The fracture, I should insist, takes place in distinct locations, not in some abstract conceptual realm. For the time being, Pirous has located himself rather squarely in the space of the Indonesian nation-state, and so the culture of violence in Aceh is seen and depicted by him from the precincts of Indonesian visual culture. One reason for saying so is that Pirous has not exhibited his *Acehnese Series* beyond Bandung and Jakarta. In fact, the *Acehnese Series* was placed in the gallery hall that served as entry to Pirous's recent career retrospective show in Jakarta's Galeri Nasional. Although these works some day may be seen by separatist Acehnese in Aceh, Pirous has made sure that they have come to the attention of Indonesia's gallery-going elite. In exhibiting and talking about this series as he has, Pirous seems intent on displaying his outrage and anguish before an Indonesian art public, rather than before an Acehnese one, where such display might incite violence.

There is one more abstract image I want to discuss, one that I will place in counterpoint to the *Acehnese Series*. Begun in October 1999 as a sketch entitled "Has That Light Already Shone Down from Above?" (*Telah Turunkah Cahaya Itu?*), it eventually made its way into paint and onto canvas in early 2002 as "A People's Fate is in Their Own Hands" (*Nasib Suatu Kaum Terletak di Tangannya Sendiri;* see Figure 9). It features two Qur'anic passages. The first is from *QS 13 Al-Ra'd*: 11, "Verily God does not change the state of a people till they change themselves. When God intends misfortune for a people no one can avert it, and no savior will they have

---

[33] Cf., Begoña Aretxaga, "Before the Law: The Narrative of the Unconscious in Basque Political Violence," unpublished ms. presented at the workshop on the "The Poetics of Violence," School of American Research, Santa Fe, May 2002; Benhabib, *The Claims of Culture,* pp. 15-16; Kirin Narayan, "How Native is a Native Anthropologist?" *American Anthropologist* 95 (1993): 671-686.

[34] Siegel, *The Rope of God,* p. 366.

Figure 7: *They Who are Buried without Names*, A. D. Pirous, 2001.
122 x 122 cm, marble paste, sand, acrylic on canvas. Courtesy of the artist.

Figure 8: Detail from *The Restraining of the Chronicle of the Holy War, II*,
A. D. Pirous, 1999.
72 x 77 cm, mixed media on canvas. Courtesy of the artist.
Photograph by the author, 2002.

apart from Him." The second is from *QS 2 Al-Baqarah* : 153, "O you who believe seek courage in fortitude and prayer, for God is with those who are patient and persevere." The title of the image in its life as a sketch invites us to see the steeply pitched diagonal of color that splits the surface of the painting as a shaft of light. That same gesture formally separates the two Qur'anic verses. Pirous has been a bit of a wag about this painting, in that he has refrained from clearing up its ambiguous politics. I frankly saw the painting as a potential incitement to Acehnese separatist sentiment—"take matters into your own hands and persevere"—and told him so. "Well, you see what you want to see," he replied. A few short weeks later, this painting was taken to Jakarta for inclusion in Pirous's retrospective show and displayed apart from the *Acehnese Series* on walls and panels displaying his abstract calligraphic work. I wasn't surprised by the move, for it seems to me that the painting's Quranic passages and its title (see Figure 10) show a kinship with the nationalist inscription Pirous placed on the bastard page of *Mohammed and Charlemagne* forty-four years earlier. Both regard a people's outward state—especially that manifest in a polity—as a product of their spiritual character and interior virtue. "Who are your people?" I once asked Pirous. He rejoined without a moment's pause, "Why the Indonesian people!"[35]

Figure 9. *A People's Fate is in Their Own Hands*, A. D. Pirous, 2002.
140 x 190 cm, marble paste, gold, acrylic on canvas.
Courtesy of the artist. Photograph by the author, 2002.

---

[35] Interview with the author, March 13, 2001.

Figure 10. In his own hand(s). Putting the title and signature
on the reverse of the canvas.
Photograph by the author, 2002.

CONCLUSION

Picturing Aceh as tragedy, I want to suggest, requires a vantage point and a visual culture *outside* of a location marked or claimed as "Aceh." Picturing Aceh as outrage places us *within* its suffering and wounds. Pirous's artistic recuperation of Aceh until 1998 served the transcendent discourses of nationalism, Islam, and abstraction. As state-sponsored atrocities came into public view—and with traumatic effects for Indonesian visual culture—Pirous suffered a betrayal. The goodness of the nation-state was never guaranteed by the character of its artist-citizens, or by their piety and faith. Pirous is not trying to make the Acehnese see what they already see too well. His appeal is Indonesian. He is trying to make Indonesians see, recognize, and acknowledge their nation-state's self-wounding and self-negating culture of violence, even at the risk of inciting separatist hostilities should his images make their way to Aceh.

Pirous's Acehnese series makes visible the ghosts and secret recitations of the colonial era and allows them to haunt the present. Teuku Oemar and the *Hikayat Prang Sabil* are pried loose from national history, summoned onto his canvasses, and turned back against the contemporary nation-state. What is it about resurrecting the Acehnese past and exhuming the nameless dead from Aceh's mass graves that calls for "realism?" What gives the conventions of realism special purchase on suffering and pain? The visual language Pirous once contrived for things Acehnese, grounded as it was in an exceedingly formalist visual philology, offered no images for that pain. In that sense, it was well suited to the political quiescence of the New Order.

The return of realism announces a politics and a visuality that Pirous left unformulated in his earlier explorations of Islamic aesthetics. But I should caution against pitting that realism against the transcendentalism of his abstract work in too sharp a fashion. We need to bear in mind that Pirous has long been a Qur'anic realist, in that his Qur'anic paintings demand orthographic precision in making visible a divine and immutable text. So long as the Qur'an is in this world in a way no less real than the deaths of the innocent in Aceh, it is impossible for the politics of word and image, of orthographic and human figures, to remain a strictly iconological issue. For Indonesians in particular, the ideological struggles over word and image will make visible the problem of citizenship, its tragedies, and its sometimes violent effects.

CONTRIBUTORS

Andrew J. Abalahin earned his PhD in History from Cornell University in 2003, submitting a dissertation entitled "Prostitution Policy and the Project of Modernity: A Comparative Study of Colonial Indonesia and the Philippines, 1850-1940" (nominated for the Lauriston Sharp Prize). He is currently Postdoctoral Fellow in Southeast Asian Studies at the Weatherhead East Asian Institute, Columbia University. His present research interests focus on the influence of different religions on state-formation processes around the Celebes Sea.

Suzanne Brenner is Associate Professor in the Department of Anthropology at the University of California, San Diego. Her recent research has focused on women's involvement in the Islamic movement in Indonesia. She is the author of *The Domestication of Desire: Women, Wealth, and Modernity in Java* (Princeton, 1998), which won the 2000 Harry J. Benda Prize in Southeast Asian Studies from the Association for Asian Studies.

Fenella Cannell is Lecturer in Anthropology at the London School of Economics and has held visiting posts at IRSEA, Michigan, Ann Arbor, and the Southeast Asia Program at Cornell. She has worked on the Philippines since 1988, and her book, *Power and Intimacy in the Christian Philippines*, won the Harry J. Benda Prize for Southeast Asian Studies in 2001. Her most recent work focuses on the relationship between Christianity and anthropology, and on American Mormonism—the subjects of the Malinowski Lecture for 2004. An edited collection, *The Anthropology of Christianity*, is forthcoming with Duke University Press.

Thamora Fishel is Assistant Professor of Anthropology at California State University, Long Beach. Her research focuses on gender, reciprocity, and the cultural construction of power in provincial Thailand.

Kenneth M. George is Professor and Chair of the Department of Anthropology at the University of Wisconsin, Madison, and will assume the editorship of the *Journal of Asian Studies* in 2005. Ken's first book, *Showing Signs of Violence* (1996), won the 1998 Harry J. Benda Prize in Southeast Asian Studies. His ongoing collaboration with Indonesian painter A. D. Pirous is the subject of two books, *A. D. Pirous: Vision, Faith, and a Journey in Indonesian Art, 1955-2002* (2002), co-authored with Mamannoor, and *Seni Sebagai Kerja Budaya* (2004), a collection of essays.

Smita Lahiri received her PhD in Sociocultural Anthropology from Cornell University in 2002 and is now Assistant Professor of Anthropology at Harvard University. She is currently working on a book on popular religion and the Filipino nation.

Erick White is an Instructor in Antioch University's Buddhist Studies Program. He is currently completing his dissertation, tentatively titled "Sociality, Charisma, and Syncretism: The Subculture of Professional Spirit Mediums in Contemporary Thailand."

Andrew C. Willford is Assistant Professor of Anthropology and Asian Studies at Cornell University. His research on Tamil Hindu religious revivalism and ethnic politics in Malaysia has been the subject of several articles and of a new book entitled, *Cage of Freedom: The Vicissitudes of Malaysian Tamil Identity*. He was Visiting Fulbright Professor at the University of Malaya, Kuala Lumpur, in 2003-4.

SOUTHEAST ASIA PROGRAM PUBLICATIONS
Cornell University

Studies on Southeast Asia

Number 39 *The Indonesian Supreme Court: A Study of Institutional Collapse,* Sebastiaan Pompe. 2005. 494 pp. ISBN 0-877277-38-9 (pb).

Number 38 *Spirited Politics: Religion and Public Life in Contemporary Southeast Asia,* ed. Andrew C. Willford and Kenneth M. George. 2005. 210 pp. ISBN 0-87727-737-0.

Number 37 *Sumatran Sultanate and Colonial State: Jambi and the Rise of Dutch Imperialism, 1830-1907,* Elsbeth Locher-Scholten, trans. Beverley Jackson. 2004. 332 pp. ISBN 0-87727-736-2.

Number 36 *Southeast Asia over Three Generations: Essays Presented to Benedict R. O'G. Anderson,* ed. James T. Siegel and Audrey R. Kahin. 2003. 398 pp. ISBN 0-87727-735-4.

Number 35 *Nationalism and Revolution in Indonesia,* George McTurnan Kahin, intro. Benedict R. O'G. Anderson (reprinted from 1952 edition, Cornell University Press, with permission). 2003. 530 pp. ISBN 0-87727-734-6.

Number 34 *Golddiggers, Farmers, and Traders in the "Chinese Districts" of West Kalimantan, Indonesia,* Mary Somers Heidhues. 2003. 316 pp. ISBN 0-87727-733-8.

Number 33 *Opusculum de Sectis apud Sinenses et Tunkinenses (A Small Treatise on the Sects among the Chinese and Tonkinese): A Study of Religion in China and North Vietnam in the Eighteenth Century,* Father Adriano de St. Thecla, trans. Olga Dror, with Mariya Berezovska. 2002. 363 pp. ISBN 0-87727-732-X.

Number 32 *Fear and Sanctuary: Burmese Refugees in Thailand,* Hazel J. Lang. 2002. 204 pp. ISBN 0-87727-731-1.

Number 31 *Modern Dreams: An Inquiry into Power, Cultural Production, and the Cityscape in Contemporary Urban Penang, Malaysia,* Beng-Lan Goh. 2002. 225 pp. ISBN 0-87727-730-3.

Number 30 *Violence and the State in Suharto's Indonesia,* ed. Benedict R. O'G. Anderson. 2001. Second printing, 2002. 247 pp. ISBN 0-87727-729-X.

Number 29 *Studies in Southeast Asian Art: Essays in Honor of Stanley J. O'Connor,* ed. Nora A. Taylor. 2000. 243 pp. Illustrations. ISBN 0-87727-728-1.

Number 28 *The Hadrami Awakening: Community and Identity in the Netherlands East Indies, 1900-1942,* Natalie Mobini-Kesheh. 1999. 174 pp. ISBN 0-87727-727-3.

Number 27 *Tales from Djakarta: Caricatures of Circumstances and their Human Beings,* Pramoedya Ananta Toer. 1999. 145 pp. ISBN 0-87727-726-5.

Number 26 *History, Culture, and Region in Southeast Asian Perspectives,* rev. ed., O. W. Wolters. 1999. Second printing, 2004. 275 pp. ISBN 0-87727-725-7.

Number 25 *Figures of Criminality in Indonesia, the Philippines, and Colonial Vietnam,* ed. Vicente L. Rafael. 1999. 259 pp. ISBN 0-87727-724-9.

Number 24 *Paths to Conflagration: Fifty Years of Diplomacy and Warfare in Laos, Thailand, and Vietnam, 1778-1828,* Mayoury Ngaosyvathn and Pheuiphanh Ngaosyvathn. 1998. 268 pp. ISBN 0-87727-723-0.

Number 23 *Nguyễn Cochinchina: Southern Vietnam in the Seventeenth and Eighteenth Centuries*, Li Tana. 1998. Second printing, 2002. 194 pp. ISBN 0-87727-722-2.

Number 22 *Young Heroes: The Indonesian Family in Politics*, Saya S. Shiraishi. 1997. 183 pp. ISBN 0-87727-721-4.

Number 21 *Interpreting Development: Capitalism, Democracy, and the Middle Class in Thailand*, John Girling. 1996. 95 pp. ISBN 0-87727-720-6.

Number 20 *Making Indonesia*, ed. Daniel S. Lev, Ruth McVey. 1996. 201 pp. ISBN 0-87727-719-2.

Number 19 *Essays into Vietnamese Pasts*, ed. K. W. Taylor, John K. Whitmore. 1995. 288 pp. ISBN 0-87727-718-4.

Number 18 *In the Land of Lady White Blood: Southern Thailand and the Meaning of History*, Lorraine M. Gesick. 1995. 106 pp. ISBN 0-87727-717-6.

Number 17 *The Vernacular Press and the Emergence of Modern Indonesian Consciousness*, Ahmat Adam. 1995. 220 pp. ISBN 0-87727-716-8.

Number 16 *The Nan Chronicle*, trans., ed. David K. Wyatt. 1994. 158 pp. ISBN 0-87727-715-X.

Number 15 *Selective Judicial Competence: The Cirebon-Priangan Legal Administration, 1680–1792*, Mason C. Hoadley. 1994. 185 pp. ISBN 0-87727-714-1.

Number 14 *Sjahrir: Politics and Exile in Indonesia*, Rudolf Mrázek. 1994. 536 pp. ISBN 0-87727-713-3.

Number 13 *Fair Land Sarawak: Some Recollections of an Expatriate Officer*, Alastair Morrison. 1993. 196 pp. ISBN 0-87727-712-5.

Number 12 *Fields from the Sea: Chinese Junk Trade with Siam during the Late Eighteenth and Early Nineteenth Centuries*, Jennifer Cushman. 1993. 206 pp. ISBN 0-87727-711-7.

Number 11 *Money, Markets, and Trade in Early Southeast Asia: The Development of Indigenous Monetary Systems to AD 1400*, Robert S. Wicks. 1992. 2nd printing 1996. 354 pp., 78 tables, illus., maps. ISBN 0-87727-710-9.

Number 10 *Tai Ahoms and the Stars: Three Ritual Texts to Ward Off Danger*, trans., ed. B. J. Terwiel, Ranoo Wichasin. 1992. 170 pp. ISBN 0-87727-709-5.

Number 9 *Southeast Asian Capitalists*, ed. Ruth McVey. 1992. 2nd printing 1993. 220 pp. ISBN 0-87727-708-7.

Number 8 *The Politics of Colonial Exploitation: Java, the Dutch, and the Cultivation System*, Cornelis Fasseur, ed. R. E. Elson, trans. R. E. Elson, Ary Kraal. 1992. 2nd printing 1994. 266 pp. ISBN 0-87727-707-9.

Number 7 *A Malay Frontier: Unity and Duality in a Sumatran Kingdom*, Jane Drakard. 1990. 2nd printing 2003. 215 pp. ISBN 0-87727-706-0.

Number 6 *Trends in Khmer Art*, Jean Boisselier, ed. Natasha Eilenberg, trans. Natasha Eilenberg, Melvin Elliott. 1989. 124 pp., 24 plates. ISBN 0-87727-705-2.

Number 5 *Southeast Asian Ephemeris: Solar and Planetary Positions, A.D. 638–2000*, J. C. Eade. 1989. 175 pp. ISBN 0-87727-704-4.

Number 3 *Thai Radical Discourse: The Real Face of Thai Feudalism Today*, Craig J. Reynolds. 1987. 2nd printing 1994. 186 pp. ISBN 0-87727-702-8.

Number 1   *The Symbolism of the Stupa*, Adrian Snodgrass. 1985. Revised with index, 1988. 3rd printing 1998. 469 pp. ISBN 0-87727-700-1.

SEAP Series

Number 22   *The Industry of Marrying Europeans*, Vũ Trọng Phụng, trans. Thúy Tranviet. 2006. 66 pp. ISBN 0-877271-40-2 (pb).

Number 21   *Securing a Place: Small-Scale Artisans in Modern Indonesia*, Elizabeth Morrell. 2005. 220 pp. ISBN 0-877271-39-9.

Number 20   *Southern Vietnam under the Reign of Minh M¬ng (1820-1841): Central Policies and Local Response*, Choi Byung Wook. 2004. 226pp. ISBN 0-0-877271-40-2.

Number 19   *Gender, Household, State: [Ái Mîi in ViŸt Nam*, ed. Jayne Werner and Danièle Bélanger. 2002. 151 pp. ISBN 0-87727-137-2.

Number 18   *Culture and Power in Traditional Siamese Government*, Neil A. Englehart. 2001. 130 pp. ISBN 0-87727-135-6.

Number 17   *Gangsters, Democracy, and the State*, ed. Carl A. Trocki. 1998. Second printing, 2002. 94 pp. ISBN 0-87727-134-8.

Number 16   *Cutting across the Lands: An Annotated Bibliography on Natural Resource Management and Community Development in Indonesia, the Philippines, and Malaysia*, ed. Eveline Ferretti. 1997. 329 pp. ISBN 0-87727-133-X.

Number 15   *The Revolution Falters: The Left in Philippine Politics after 1986*, ed. Patricio N. Abinales. 1996. Second printing, 2002. 182 pp. ISBN 0-87727-132-1.

Number 14   *Being Kammu: My Village, My Life*, Damrong Tayanin. 1994. 138 pp., 22 tables, illus., maps. ISBN 0-87727-130-5.

Number 13   *The American War in Vietnam*, ed. Jayne Werner, David Hunt. 1993. 132 pp. ISBN 0-87727-131-3.

Number 12   *The Voice of Young Burma*, Aye Kyaw. 1993. 92 pp. ISBN 0-87727-129-1.

Number 11   *The Political Legacy of Aung San*, ed. Josef Silverstein. Revised edition 1993. 169 pp. ISBN 0-87727-128-3.

Number 10   *Studies on Vietnamese Language and Literature: A Preliminary Bibliography*, Nguyen Dinh Tham. 1992. 227 pp. ISBN 0-87727-127-5.

Number 8   *From PKI to the Comintern, 1924–1941: The Apprenticeship of the Malayan Communist Party*, Cheah Boon Kheng. 1992. 147 pp. ISBN 0-87727-125-9.

Number 7   *Intellectual Property and US Relations with Indonesia, Malaysia, Singapore, and Thailand*, Elisabeth Uphoff. 1991. 67 pp. ISBN 0-87727-124-0.

Number 6   *The Rise and Fall of the Communist Party of Burma (CPB)*, Bertil Lintner. 1990. 124 pp. 26 illus., 14 maps. ISBN 0-87727-123-2.

Number 5   *Japanese Relations with Vietnam: 1951–1987*, Masaya Shiraishi. 1990. 174 pp. ISBN 0-87727-122-4.

Number 3   *Postwar Vietnam: Dilemmas in Socialist Development*, ed. Christine White, David Marr. 1988. 2nd printing 1993. 260 pp. ISBN 0-87727-120-8.

Number 2   *The Dobama Movement in Burma (1930–1938)*, Khin Yi. 1988. 160 pp. ISBN 0-87727-118-6.

Cornell Modern Indonesia Project Publications

Number 75 *A Tour of Duty: Changing Patterns of Military Politics in Indonesia in the 1990s*. Douglas Kammen and Siddharth Chandra. 1999. 99 pp. ISBN 0-87763-049-6.

Number 74 *The Roots of Acehnese Rebellion 1989–1992*, Tim Kell. 1995. 103 pp. ISBN 0-87763-040-2.

Number 73 *"White Book" on the 1992 General Election in Indonesia*, trans. Dwight King. 1994. 72 pp. ISBN 0-87763-039-9.

Number 72 *Popular Indonesian Literature of the Qur'an*, Howard M. Federspiel. 1994. 170 pp. ISBN 0-87763-038-0.

Number 71 *A Javanese Memoir of Sumatra, 1945–1946: Love and Hatred in the Liberation War*, Takao Fusayama. 1993. 150 pp. ISBN 0-87763-037-2.

Number 70 *East Kalimantan: The Decline of a Commercial Aristocracy*, Burhan Magenda. 1991. 120 pp. ISBN 0-87763-036-4.

Number 69 *The Road to Madiun: The Indonesian Communist Uprising of 1948*, Elizabeth Ann Swift. 1989. 120 pp. ISBN 0-87763-035-6.

Number 68 *Intellectuals and Nationalism in Indonesia: A Study of the Following Recruited by Sutan Sjahrir in Occupation Jakarta*, J. D. Legge. 1988. 159 pp. ISBN 0-87763-034-8.

Number 67 *Indonesia Free: A Biography of Mohammad Hatta*, Mavis Rose. 1987. 252 pp. ISBN 0-87763-033-X.

Number 66 *Prisoners at Kota Cane*, Leon Salim, trans. Audrey Kahin. 1986. 112 pp. ISBN 0-87763-032-1.

Number 65 *The Kenpeitai in Java and Sumatra*, trans. Barbara G. Shimer, Guy Hobbs, intro. Theodore Friend. 1986. 80 pp. ISBN 0-87763-031-3.

Number 64 *Suharto and His Generals: Indonesia's Military Politics, 1975–1983*, David Jenkins. 1984. 4th printing 1997. 300 pp. ISBN 0-87763-030-5.

Number 62 *Interpreting Indonesian Politics: Thirteen Contributions to the Debate, 1964–1981*, ed. Benedict Anderson, Audrey Kahin, intro. Daniel S. Lev. 1982. 3rd printing 1991. 172 pp. ISBN 0-87763-028-3.

Number 60 *The Minangkabau Response to Dutch Colonial Rule in the Nineteenth Century*, Elizabeth E. Graves. 1981. 157 pp. ISBN 0-87763-000-3.

Number 59 *Breaking the Chains of Oppression of the Indonesian People: Defense Statement at His Trial on Charges of Insulting the Head of State, Bandung, June 7–10, 1979*, Heri Akhmadi. 1981. 201 pp. ISBN 0-87763-001-1.

Number 57 *Permesta: Half a Rebellion*, Barbara S. Harvey. 1977. 174 pp. ISBN 0-87763-003-8.

Number 55 *Report from Banaran: The Story of the Experiences of a Soldier during the War of Independence*, Maj. Gen. T. B. Simatupang. 1972. 186 pp. ISBN 0-87763-005-4.

Number 52 *A Preliminary Analysis of the October 1 1965, Coup in Indonesia (Prepared in January 1966)*, Benedict R. Anderson, Ruth T. McVey, assist. Frederick P. Bunnell. 1971. 3rd printing 1990. 174 pp. ISBN 0-87763-008-9.

Number 51   *The Putera Reports: Problems in Indonesian-Japanese War-Time Cooperation*, Mohammad Hatta, trans., intro. William H. Frederick. 1971. 114 pp. ISBN 0-87763-009-7.

Number 50   *Schools and Politics: The Kaum Muda Movement in West Sumatra (1927–1933)*, Taufik Abdullah. 1971. 257 pp. ISBN 0-87763-010-0.

Number 49   *The Foundation of the Partai Muslimin Indonesia*, K. E. Ward. 1970. 75 pp. ISBN 0-87763-011-9.

Number 48   *Nationalism, Islam and Marxism*, Soekarno, intro. Ruth T. McVey. 1970. 2nd printing 1984. 62 pp. ISBN 0-87763-012-7.

Number 43   *State and Statecraft in Old Java: A Study of the Later Mataram Period, 16th to 19th Century*, Soemarsaid Moertono. Revised edition 1981. 180 pp. ISBN 0-87763-017-8.

Number 39   Preliminary Checklist of Indonesian Imprints (1945-1949), John M. Echols. 186 pp. ISBN 0-87763-025-9.

Number 37   *Mythology and the Tolerance of the Javanese*, Benedict R. O'G. Anderson. 2nd edition, 1996. Reprinted 2004. 104 pp., 65 illus. ISBN 0-87763-041-0.

Number 25   *The Communist Uprisings of 1926–1927 in Indonesia: Key Documents*, ed., intro. Harry J. Benda, Ruth T. McVey. 1960. 2nd printing 1969. 177 pp. ISBN 0-87763-024-0.

Number 7   *The Soviet View of the Indonesian Revolution*, Ruth T. McVey. 1957. 3rd printing 1969. 90 pp. ISBN 0-87763-018-6.

Number 6   *The Indonesian Elections of 1955*, Herbert Feith. 1957. 2nd printing 1971. 91 pp. ISBN 0-87763-020-8.

Translation Series

Volume 4   *Approaching Suharto's Indonesia from the Margins*, ed. Takashi Shiraishi. 1994. 153 pp. ISBN 0-87727-403-7.

Volume 3   *The Japanese in Colonial Southeast Asia*, ed. Saya Shiraishi, Takashi Shiraishi. 1993. 172 pp. ISBN 0-87727-402-9.

Volume 2   *Indochina in the 1940s and 1950s*, ed. Takashi Shiraishi, Motoo Furuta. 1992. 196 pp. ISBN 0-87727-401-0.

Volume 1   *Reading Southeast Asia*, ed. Takashi Shiraishi. 1990. 188 pp. ISBN 0-87727-400-2.

Language Texts

INDONESIAN

Beginning Indonesian through Self-Instruction, John U. Wolff, Dédé Oetomo, Daniel Fietkiewicz. 3rd revised edition 1992. Vol. 1. 115 pp. ISBN 0-87727-529-7. Vol. 2. 434 pp. ISBN 0-87727-530-0. Vol. 3. 473 pp. ISBN 0-87727-531-9.

Indonesian Readings, John U. Wolff. 1978. 4th printing 1992. 480 pp. ISBN 0-87727-517-3

Indonesian Conversations, John U. Wolff. 1978. 3rd printing 1991. 297 pp. ISBN 0-87727-516-5

Formal Indonesian, John U. Wolff. 2nd revised edition 1986. 446 pp. ISBN 0-87727-515-7

TAGALOG

Pilipino through Self-Instruction, John U. Wolff, Maria Theresa C. Centeno, Der-Hwa V. Rau. 1991. Vol. 1. 342 pp. ISBN 0-87727—525-4. Vol. 2., revised 2005, 378 pp. ISBN 0-87727-526-2. Vol 3., revised 2005, 431 pp. ISBN 0-87727-527-0. Vol. 4. 306 pp. ISBN 0-87727-528-9.

THAI

A. U. A. Language Center Thai Course, J. Marvin Brown. Originally published by the American University Alumni Association Language Center, 1974. Reissued by Cornell Southeast Asia Program, 1991, 1992. Book 1. 267 pp. ISBN 0-87727-506-8. Book 2. 288 pp. ISBN 0-87727-507-6. Book 3. 247 pp. ISBN 0-87727-508-4.

A. U. A. Language Center Thai Course, Reading and Writing Text (mostly reading), 1979. Reissued 1997. 164 pp. ISBN 0-87727-511-4.

A. U. A. Language Center Thai Course, Reading and Writing Workbook (mostly writing), 1979. Reissued 1997. 99 pp. ISBN 0-87727-512-2.

KHMER

Cambodian System of Writing and Beginning Reader, Franklin E. Huffman. Originally published by Yale University Press, 1970. Reissued by Cornell Southeast Asia Program, 4th printing 2002. 365 pp. ISBN 0-300-01314-0.

Modern Spoken Cambodian, Franklin E. Huffman, assist. Charan Promchan, Chhom-Rak Thong Lambert. Originally published by Yale University Press, 1970. Reissued by Cornell Southeast Asia Program, 3rd printing 1991. 451 pp. ISBN 0-300-01316-7.

Intermediate Cambodian Reader, ed. Franklin E. Huffman, assist. Im Proum. Originally published by Yale University Press, 1972. Reissued by Cornell Southeast Asia Program, 1988. 499 pp. ISBN 0-300-01552-6.

Cambodian Literary Reader and Glossary, Franklin E. Huffman, Im Proum. Originally published by Yale University Press, 1977. Reissued by Cornell Southeast Asia Program, 1988. 494 pp. ISBN 0-300-02069-4.

HMONG

White Hmong-English Dictionary, Ernest E. Heimbach. 1969. 8th printing, 2002. 523 pp. ISBN 0-87727-075-9.

VIETNAMESE

Intermediate Spoken Vietnamese, Franklin E. Huffman, Tran Trong Hai. 1980. 3rd printing 1994. ISBN 0-87727-500-9.

* * *

Southeast Asian Studies: Reorientations. Craig J. Reynolds and Ruth McVey. Frank H. Golay Lectures 2 & 3. 70 pp. ISBN 0-87727-301-4.

Javanese Literature in Surakarta Manuscripts, Nancy K. Florida. Vol. 1, *Introduction and Manuscripts of the Karaton Surakarta.* 1993. 410 pp. Frontispiece, illustrations. Hard cover, ISBN 0-87727-602-1, Paperback, ISBN 0-87727-603-X. Vol. 2, *Manuscripts of the Mangkunagaran Palace.* 2000. 576 pp. Frontispiece, illustrations. Paperback, ISBN 0-87727-604-8.

Sbek Thom: Khmer Shadow Theater. Pech Tum Kravel, trans. Sos Kem, ed. Thavro Phim, Sos Kem, Martin Hatch. 1996. 363 pp., 153 photographs. ISBN 0-87727-620-X.

In the Mirror: Literature and Politics in Siam in the American Era, ed. Benedict R. O'G. Anderson, trans. Benedict R. O'G. Anderson, Ruchira Mendiones. 1985. 2nd printing 1991. 303 pp. Paperback. ISBN 974-210-380-1.

To order, please contact:

Cornell University
Southeast Asia Program Publications
95 Brown Road
Box 1004
Ithaca NY 14850

Online: http://www.einaudi.cornell.edu/southeastasia/publications/
Tel: 1-877-865-2432 (Toll free – U.S.)
Fax: (607) 255-7534

E-mail: SEAP-Pubs@cornell.edu
Orders must be prepaid by check or credit card (VISA, MasterCard, Discover).